❀   TWO MEN AND MUSIC   ❀

TWO MEN AND MUSIC

Nationalism

in the

Making of an Indian

Classical Tradition

Janaki Bakhle

OXFORD
UNIVERSITY PRESS

2005

Oxford University Press, Inc., publishes works that further
Oxford University's objective of excellence
in research, scholarship, and education.

Oxford   New York
Auckland   Cape Town   Dar es Salaam   Hong Kong   Karachi
Kuala Lumpur   Madrid   Melbourne   Mexico City   Nairobi
New Delhi   Shanghai   Taipei   Toronto

With offices in
Argentina   Austria   Brazil   Chile   Czech Republic   France   Greece
Guatemala   Hungary   Italy   Japan   Poland   Portugal   Singapore
South Korea   Switzerland   Thailand   Turkey   Ukraine   Vietnam

Published by Oxford University Press, Inc.
198 Madison Avenue, New York, New York 10016

www.oup.com

Oxford is a registered trademark of Oxford University Press

Library of Congress Cataloging-in-Publication Data
Bakhle, Janaki.
Two men and music : nationalism in the making of an Indian classical tradition / Janaki Bakhle.
p. cm.
Includes bibliographical references.
ISBN-13 978-0-19-516610-1; 978-0-19-516611-8 (pbk.)
ISBN 0-19-516610-8; 0-19-516611-6 (pbk.)
1. Music—Social aspects—India.   2. Bhatkhande, Vishnu Narayan, 1860-1936.   3. Paluskar,
Vishnu Degamber, 1872–1931.   I. Title.
ML338 .B23 2005
780′.954—dc22   2004020776

1 3 5 7 9 8 6 4 2
Printed in the United States of America
on acid-free paper

For Nick

❀ PREFACE ❀

Growing up as a teenager in Bombay and Pune, I attended a number of music recitals, formal and informal, in people's houses and in auditoriums. It was not unusual to hear from my uncle, Prabhakar Jathar, himself a music critic and musician, that Kumar Gandharva's student, to give one example, was giving a *baithak* in a common friend's living room. The audience would often consist of no more than twenty people, and we sat on the floor and listened to music that was recorded without the benefit of a professional studio. The tapes of the evening's performance would subsequently circulate in an informal economy among the cognoscenti. In addition to these informal, quickly put together *baithaks*, there were also the formal performances held in places like the National Center for the Performing Arts or the auditorium of the Dadar Matunga Music Circle. Both types of performances were part of the everyday life of music in modern India.

For middle-class women in Maharashtra, attending one of these performances was the logical extension of having augmented one's college education with music and dance instruction. Small schools, often named after the instructor (Gokhale Music School, for instance), dotted the urban landscape. Classes (music in particular) were often conducted in rooms no larger than

250 square feet. Often, in a very small room five students sat on the floor in a close circle, each one propping up her *tanpura*, facing the instructor. When the lesson for the day ended, the space of musical instruction reverted back to a domestic apartment occupied by the instructor and his family. Yet for all its informality, music and dance were somewhat like finishing school, because a great many middle-class women in Bombay could still imagine the possibility of an arranged marriage, even if many contested it in practice. Music and dance were important markers of modern refinement that aided one's chances in the marriage circuit. But it had not always been so, nor could either the performance or pedagogy of music be easily categorized as deriving from colonial influence or said to be strictly traditional, irrespective of what the term connotes.

Music, then and now, occupies a space—public, cultural, national, gendered—that is not easy to categorize in the singular. Even though music was taught in an instructor's tiny apartment, the ambience was somewhat formal, and the instruction was certainly systematic. Schools might not have conformed to the conventional notion of an institution, but they nonetheless administered exams that were nationally recognized and conferred degrees, even if the exam itself took place in a space similar to that of the school. From these spaces and with this instruction, many talented students went on to further their training with famous musicians.

The native informant's account presented here is the salutary one, but the genesis of this book, a book of history, comes from the underbelly of the learning and experience of North Indian classical music. In Bombay and Pune (and no doubt in other cities as well) it was fairly commonplace for people to voice their appreciation of Muslim *ustads* and simultaneously make nasty, often abusive and prejudicial comments about the Muslim population in general. Within the world of music, this form of prejudice was particularly peculiar since there was near unanimous agreement that the *ustads* were extraordinarily gifted but Islam and Muslim fanaticism were equally invariably invoked as the reason for the decline in music. My project began with trying to understand how and why it was, and indeed if it was the case, that in a region that had spawned organizations as virulent as the Rashtriya Swayamsevak Sangh (RSS) and the Shiv Sena, there was in the case (and performative space) of music a temporary suspension of prejudice. Furthermore, I wondered if this temporary suspension of prejudice could be attributed to some feature inherent to the music itself.

As soon as I began conducting research, these initial questions took on much larger dimensions, and some of them changed altogether. While there was a clear regional dimension to my inquiry, the issues were relevant far beyond Maharashtra. While Marathi chauvinism saw an inevitable and logical passing of the musical baton, en masse if you will, from Muslims in the late nineteenth century to Maharashtrians in the twentieth, there seemed a much more robust and interesting history at work. While prejudice no doubt animated the endeavors of some of the key players in music's history, prejudice alone did not answer other questions in particular those that related to the survival of the *gharana*s. Lastly, it was not at all clear that there was indeed a suspension of prejudice. The reverse appeared to be much more the case, namely, that prejudice was itself deeply implicated in the history of music. For all these reasons, the history told in this book is a history of Indian classical music that does not in any way claim the status of "the history of music." It has been my attempt to turn the story of music complicated, a task made enormously interesting and productive because of the generosity of a number of people and institutions.

My book began as a dissertation, and I would like to thank the members of my doctoral committee, Ayesha Jalal, Carol Gluck, Partha Chatterjee, Valentine Daniel, and Anders Stephanson, for their support and encouragement of this project. I am grateful for the care with which they read every single chapter and for their insightful comments. I conducted research in India funded by a dissertation research grant awarded by the American Institute of Indian Studies. I am grateful to Dr. Mehendiratta and Purnima Mehta for all their help during my research year. In Bombay, I had many conversations with Dr. Sharatchandra Gokhale, who gave generously of his knowledge. Dr. Gokhale passed away soon after my return to the States. I will always regret not being able to show him my book: he would have chuckled with wicked delight. I would also like to thank Ramdas Bhatkal, Ashok Ranade, Nana Bodas, Pandit Athavale, Pandit Dinkar Kaikini, and Balwantrao Joshi, to whom I owe a special debt for offering me the resources of the Gandharva Mahavidyalaya in Meraj and Vashi. I would like to thank Shaila Datar, the Abbasaheb Muzumdar Foundation, and the Bharat Gayan Samaj in Pune. In Lucknow, I would like to thank Rai Swareshwar Bali for his generosity and help and the staff of the Bhatkhande Sangeet Vidyapith for their help in locating documents. I owe a special thanks to the librarian and the staff of Indumati Palace in Baroda for their generosity. I also owe a debt of gratitude to Dr. and Mrs. Chitale for their extraordinary hospitality and generosity. Members of my extended family with whom I stayed made conducting research in six cities in one year a much less daunting prospect than it could have been. In particular, I would like to thank Kuki, Da, and M in Delhi, and Atti and Anna in Pune for their hospitality and warmth. Hema atti, who has always been one of my champions, ploughed her way through my introduction only to plead with me to write more lucidly. I hope she will like the final version. I am grateful to the staff of the following institutions where research for this project was conducted: Maharashtra State Archives, Bombay; NCPA Library, Bombay; Mumbai Marathi Grantha Sangrahalaya; Bombay University Library; Asiatic Society Library, Bombay; and the Oriental and India Office Collection, London. Thanks to the department of history at Columbia University, I was able to augment my research year with an additional grant for research in London, after my research year in India.

Gyan Prakash not only read my manuscript and gave me detailed suggestions for revision including the need to write a new chapter on performers, which I have done; he has also been consistently encouraging and supportive, both of this project and the one I am about to begin. Barbara Metcalf's careful reading, intellectual generosity, and personal warmth have bolstered my confidence in more ways than I can mention. Michael Fisher gave me early feedback on the dissertation and suggestions for making it comparative. Peter Manuel and James Kippen gave me tough reads, saving me from a number of musicological and ethnomusicological errors and giving me very useful citations and critical suggestions. Partho Datta read the manuscript for Permanent Black and gave me the benefit of his own extraordinary knowledge of Hindustani music. Milind Wakankar read new versions of the same last chapter on more than a few occasions and gave me spectacularly insightful theoretical comments and suggestions. I have not been able to do justice to his comments, because I need a few years to mull over what he said. Rukun Advani was enthusiastic about this project right from the beginning and has stayed so even when I have tried his patience. In addition, I am deeply grateful to him for securing for me an early and wonderful review from the late Sheila Dhar which boosted my confidence at a crucial point when I felt nervous writing about music as an outsider to the profession. I am also grateful to a number of individuals and institutions for inviting me to deliver versions of what would subsequently become chapters 3, 4, and 6 of this book at conferences and seminars. In particular, I would like to express my gratitude to

Christian Novetzke at the University of Pennsylvania, Dipesh Chakrabarty at the University of Chicago, Barbara Metcalf at the University of Michigan, and the Subaltern Studies Collective for inviting me to present my work at their seminars.

Over and above everyone else, this book owes its argument to my adviser, Partha Chatterjee. My debt to him is too large to easily express. Partha is not only my adviser, he is a close friend and mentor, the first reader of my dissertation chapters, and de facto member of my family. He is also quite simply the most erudite and generous senior scholar that I have ever known. Not only has he read this project in dissertation form and forced me to defend my arguments (no easy task when he is the interlocutor), he has also reread every chapter as I revised it. Without expressly doing so, he has pushed me to conceptualize this project in complicated ways, not to reduce it to either a currently fashionable argument or to ignore the weight of an earlier history. Partha's intellectual influence is all over this book.

Gyan Pandey, to whom I owe an enormous debt as well for a tough, critical, reading of the manuscript, insisted, along with Partha Chatterjee, that there was much more to the development of music in the nineteenth century than could be reduced to a "Hindu/Muslim" question. Gyan has been consistent in pushing me to recognize that there was, as he put it, "lots more going on," and I have taken his and Partha's advice seriously. I hope both of them will see their influence in this final version.

Anupama Rao, my colleague, comrade, interlocutor, critic, and close friend across the street, dropped everything in the midst of her own frantic schedule to read fragments, parts of chapters, whole chapters, even musings hastily put down on paper, and has been a tremendous source of support and laughter throughout this project. Keya Ganguly has been a fellow traveler (*raah bani khud manzil*), intellectual interlocutor, and closest of friends through life and career changes and the many years of feeling home is neither here nor there even as it has simultaneously been **both** here and there. Even more important, she has been a laughing buddy across the years and in places as varied as Sahar airport (the suitcase and the spoon), the Pensione Suisse in Rome (Bengali from Cameroon and jail), and the road to Pittsburgh (the ruffians). Saloni Mathur's extraordinary friendship, laughter, and martinis have seen me through not only the transition from editor to graduate student to assistant professor but also through the tough times during my pregnancy and Ishan's early troubles. Neni Panourgia, who could be a star chef in her own right, has been a comrade in cooking, second mother to my son, and best of friends. Jenny Davidson, my friend and colleague at Columbia University, volunteered to proofread chapters for me in the midst of submitting her own manuscript for publication. Not only did she pick up many mistakes I missed, she also forced me to hunker down and proofread when I wanted to procrastinate. I hope in the years to come I can show my gratitude to her with many visits to BLT Fish.

For their sanity and humor sustaining friendship over the years and for their encouragement in a number of ways, I would like to especially thank Aamir Mufti, Arvind Rajagopal, Lila Abu-Lughod, Tim Mitchell, Mira Nair, Mahmood Mamdani, Lisa Mitchell, Dard Neuman, Stathis Gourgouris (and Galaxeidi!), Karen Seeley, Brinkley Messick, Elizabeth Kolsky, Gil Anidjar, Joseph Massad, Hamid Dabashi, Frances Pritchett, Judy Walsh, Indira Peterson, Susham Bedi, Martha Howell, Alice Kessler-Harris, and Elliott Gorn.

My mother-in-law, Annabelle Dirks, one of my major champions, has over the years given me her unflagging support and help. My brother-in-law, Christopher Dirks, took on the task of formatting first my dissertation and then this book and also asked me a question to which I don't have an answer—"What's with you and commas?" The compliment I received from the production department at Oxford about this being one of the better-organized manuscripts they'd seen belongs properly to Chris.

I could not have chosen a better editor to work with than Dedi Felman at Oxford University Press. I thank her for her quick and insightful readings of individual chapters and her encouragement to stay away from jargon. Even more than that, I am deeply grateful to her for bearing with all my anxieties and neuroses as a first-time author, and for being consistently thoughtful and accommodating, in particular at times when I must have frustrated her enormously. Likewise, Linda Donnelly responded to every query of mine within minutes, with unfailing good humor and encouragement. My book is what it is because of the care and patience of Oxford's production staff. I am grateful to Jim Cohen for his assistance with the nitty-gritty matters of publishing that I should have remembered from my own years in the business, but seem to have repressed—in particular, things like the vital importance of the author questionnaire and the need to return a manuscript on time. I am grateful, as well, to Rob Fellman for taking time out of his busy schedule to go over my manuscript a second time.

Three graduate students at Columbia University saved me enormous time during the most hectic period of the semester. Saira Hamidi's help with the glossary of terms and Natalja Czarnecki's extraordinary help in hunting down page numbers for citations, as well as Yogesh Chandrani's extremely valuable help with the index, are greatly appreciated.

Finally, I would like to thank my parents and my brother. Without their belief in me and their unconditional love and help, I could neither have conducted research nor written this book. In many ways, this is my mother's book. She got a bachelor's degree with Sanskrit honors, studied classical music as a young woman, had a brief professional life as a musician; and I would like to think that in another time, this is the kind of book she might have written. My father, whom I have aggravated for many years now, is my rock of strength. Over the past twenty years there have been many events and moments that I could not have seen through without his decisiveness and clarity. My brother, whom too I have driven crazy with my intemperateness, never once lost his own temper with me and has been a continuous source of strength and support.

In the years in which I conducted research, wrote my dissertation, and revised it for publication, my son, Ishan, was born, almost died, had head surgery when he was eight months old, and emerged from his early years of trauma to take his place in the world as a happy, energetic little boy who has forged a deep bond with his sister, Sandhya. Their relationship is a constant reminder to me that tough beginnings can yield wonderful connections.

Lastly I would like to express my gratitude and debt to Nicholas Dirks. The dissertation on which this book is based was written in one year in our home in Southfield, Massachusetts. He not only ordered me to write at least four pages every single day, he also read everything I wrote and gave me ruthless criticism combined with quiet encouragement. When I began revising the manuscript for publication, he read everything yet again, sometimes two and three times over. Every idea in this book has been discussed with him, at the crack of dawn, right before falling asleep, and at no point did he ever say he'd heard more than enough about two men and music. Furthermore, even as I was outraged at the time, I am deeply grateful that on more than one occasion he returned a fifty-page chapter to me with the pithy sentence "Radically rewrite pages 3–48," on the back and asked me, "What is your theory of the comma?" Most of all, I thank him for April 18, 1994. It is not often that an academic talk changes one's life, but this one did. This book marks a decade of togetherness, and I dedicate it to him in the hopes of several more.

CONTENTS

❀ TWO MEN AND MUSIC ❀

INTRODUCTION

India was colonized by the British for close to two hundred years. Virtually no aspect of Indian society remained untouched through the course of that long occupation, which began in the middle of the eighteenth and ended in the middle of the twentieth century. Modern Indian law, education, medicine, literature, and art all bear in varying shades of intensity the touch (or stigma) of colonial influence. The one (and perhaps only) art form said to have successfully resisted colonial influence during the nineteenth century was Indian classical music, both North Indian (Hindustani) and South Indian (Carnatic).

In nineteenth-century British colonial India, music was performed mainly in courts of princely states as *tappa, thumri, hori, dhrupad, dhamar,* and *khayal,* to name just a few performative/poetic compositional forms. A century later, the same music was still performed, but with a major difference. It was now seen as simultaneously classical and national. This trajectory calls forth no surprise, since it is by now a truism to assert that classicism invariably accompanies the processes of modernity and nationalism. But there is something both noteworthy and surprising about music that plays a critical role in the development of Indian cultural nationalism. Music's practitioners were not automatically treated as the rightful authors of its future, but had to battle for their right to determine the nature of music's modernity with nationalists, who were determined to leave them out of the conversation.

This book focuses on music's history in the Deccan region of western India. By the last two decades of the nineteenth century, music, however and wherever performed, had been disciplined, cleansed, and regulated. In Marathi folk theater, music was a central part of theatrical forms such as *lavani, bhaand, tamasha,* and *bahuroopi* which ranged in content from the raucous and bawdy to the devotional. With the emergence of the proscenium stage, earlier theatrical forms were replaced with Marathi adaptations of classical Sanskrit plays such as Kalidasa's *Shakuntala* and Shakespeare's *Othello, Hamlet,* and the like. In 1870, a Bombay philanthropist named K. N. Kabraji founded one of the earliest music appreciation societies in western India, the Parsi Gayan Uttejak Mandali. Kabraji inveighed against the low-class prostitutes who had co-opted music and urged middle-class married women to learn music so their husbands did not have to leave their homes at night in search of musical entertainment. In the more modern princely courts like Baroda, which provided the main employment opportunity for peripatetic musicians, rules governing all aspects of musicians' lives, from their performance to their clothing, were already well in place. In 1899, a rule book called the *Kalavant Khatyache Niyam* (Rules of the Department of Entertainment) was published, placing musicians in categories and requiring them to check in with the superintendent every day and have the content of their performances preapproved.

Music went from being an unmarked practice in the eighteenth century to being marked as classical music in the twentieth. From performing for small audiences in princely courts, musicians moved into the larger cultural public sphere to give ticketed-entry performances in modern auditoriums. Music's content, which ranged from raucous and ribald to devotional, was rewritten into respectable fare. Music was viewed as one type of entertainment among many others in princely courts, but by the twentieth century, it had become a high art form that occupied pride of place in the national imagination. While its upper-level pedagogy remained dominated by hereditary musicians, it became possible even for respectable middle-class Hindu housewives to imagine themselves as performers. Last but not least, a modern history was authored for music. The authors of this history aimed to restore to music its ancient origins and address colonial denigrations of it as native caterwauling.

Despite these changes to music's larger cultural context, the precise nature and character of the early musical public sphere were still undetermined: it was not identified with a particular ideology, religious group, or ethnic identity. Music was yet to be fully classicized. This last transformation happened only when two men—Vishnu Narayan Bhatkhande and Vishnu Digambar Paluskar—stepped into the fray in the late nineteenth century to give Indian classical music, as we understand and recognize it today, its distinct shape, form, and identity. Largely because of their efforts, there is a vast network of small training schools that allows for the dissemination of a base-level knowledge about music within the middle class, which helps to keep music "traditional" and national. A whole generation of courtesans (*baijis*) has been replaced by upper-caste women performers. Lastly, in response to a musicological challenge, hereditary musicians refashioned themselves and their pedagogy to accommodate a new set of demands, making music much more democratic than it had been. Bhatkhande and Paluskar are treated in this book as the key orchestrators of music's modernization. Although these two men are at the center of this history, they will not be seen here as heroic figures who changed the world of Hindustani music on their own; instead, I will use their lifework to highlight the larger sociopolitical effects of music's transformation.

These numerous linked histories, with Bhatkhande and Paluskar as exemplary figures representing the complexity of music's transformation, affected one group in particular: the hereditary *khayal* musicians. Etymologically, *khayal* is claimed in histories and biographies as deriving both from the Sanskrit *khelapad* (the lighter counterpart to the more serious and austere *dhruvapad*), as well as from Persian textual sources. Musically, *khayal* is a melodic and ornamentally lyrical compositional form, played or sung in two parts (the first *sthayi*, and the second *antara*) in a long (*bada khayal*) and short version (*chota khayal*), to the accompaniment of the drone (*tanpura*), the *sarangi* (a stringed instrument similar to the violin) or, in the twentieth century, the harmonium, an instrument similar to the accordion.[1] Although other compositional forms such as *dhrupad* and *thumri* are still performed and sung in contemporary India, *khayal*, more than any other type of music, came to occupy the status of the exemplary and representative form of North Indian classical music.

Dominant in North India, *khayal* had been introduced to central and Western India in the late nineteenth century by visiting musicians.[2] Before it became "classical," *khayal* was performed and taught in the nineteenth century mostly by hereditary musician families known as *gharana*s, which operated as semi-professional guilds in which successful maestros handed down musical learning to their sons, nephews, grandsons, and grandnephews, and, on occasion, to a talented male apprentice from outside the family.[3] Both *gharana*s and *khayal* found hospitable ground in Maharashtra and were key vehicles in the modernization of music (unlike in Bengal, for instance, where social reformers from Ram Mohun Roy to Rabindranath Tagore wrote songs based on *dhrupad*).[4] Most major practitioners of *khayal* were Sunni Muslim men. This is not to say that the music itself was Muslim, or that non-Muslims did not perform it, or that religion was the primary social marker of either the families or the musicians. But it is to say that the performance and pedagogy of *khayal* was dominated by *gharana*s, at least for a time. The entrenchment within the *gharana* system was unique to *khayal* musicians, in marked contrast to the situation of other hereditary musicians who were experts in forms such as *hori* or *dhrupad*.

The history of *khayal*'s rise to prominence in the twentieth century is significant for several reasons. Unlike older forms of art that were transformed into systematic fields of inquiry by the forces of nationalism, such as sculpture or painting, *khayal*'s practitioners were alive and well in the late nineteenth century, and many of them would resist the changes music's modernizers had in mind. For their part, these modernizers would see *gharana* musicians as performers of an already existing music, but not as its authors. They would, furthermore, attempt to write a musicological, theoretical, and religious nationalism over the bodies, practices, and histories of music's practitioners. Inevitably, this desire on the part of music's modernizers to classicize *khayal* would run afoul of *gharana* musicians, for whom it was simply their family music.

Gharana maestros (*ustad*s) had erratic, self-protective, and sometimes capricious pedagogical habits. They also tended to be secretive about their art, tradition, and history. As a result, music's modernizers held them responsible for impeding music's progress. This interaction produced its share of hostility, and *gharana* musicians had to accommodate themselves to a new notion of pedagogy and performance without rendering themselves obsolete. Any history of music's nineteenth-century transformation must address the dialogue and confrontation between *gharana* musicians, on the one side, and nationalism—along with its attendant colonial forms of discipline—on the other. I will do so here, but I must add at the outset that this is only the most obvious part of the larger story I plan to tell. There is much more to the story of modern music than can be reduced to a simple transformation from Muslim to Hindu music or, for that matter, a confrontation between the two.

Bhatkhande and Paluskar occupy center stage in this book precisely because they enable the telling of a capacious and critical history that situates music as a part of and participant in a historical transformation that throws larger questions into relief: questions about nationalism, secularism, and modern religiosity in the public sphere, and about gendered respectability and progressive histories. Additionally, Bhatkhande's and Paluskar's contributions to music's transformation were part of a much larger national project that was born out of a colonial situation. The changes around music may not have affected the formal properties of the music, but they were nonetheless significant and long lasting. And these changes, many of them rendered through music's deep engagement with nationalism in both its secular and religious forms, have fundamentally transformed the very Indian cultural sphere in which music has often been held to take pride of place.

Cultural nationalists, some of whom were themselves musicians, worked hard to reclaim the space of music for the nation. In the hands of bhakti nationalists like Paluskar, so named here because his claims were on behalf of a sacralized bhakti (devotionalism) rather than Vedic textual Brahminism, music was envisioned as the instrument of Hindu proselytizing, with *bhajans* (devotional music) supplanting all other forms. For secular musicologists like Bhatkhande, music was the hope for a new modern, national, and academic art that would stay away from religion. What both sets of nationalists had in common was the sense that music itself was on the verge of extinction, either because it had lapsed into degeneracy or because it had failed to become adequately modern.

Both men worried about the imminent disappearance of music. Its recovery hinged on what Indian music lacked—namely, a connected history, a systematic and orderly pedagogy, and respectability. For music to possess such a history, it needed an archive. However, the archive of music was not easily accessible. Sanskrit texts offered little that was useful in understanding contemporary music. This once again brought musicians (the only people who had historical knowledge of music) and new historians into conflict with each other. The archive in the possession of the musicians was not textual but based on family memory. *Gharana* musicians, many of whom were poor and uneducated, came under attack not only for their so-called unsystematic pedagogy, but also for holding hostage, through their secrecy, music's national future. In effect, *ustad*s and *gharana*s came under attack for their putative refusal to accept the forces of the modern. Under the weight of this pressure, some *ustad*s and *gharana*s adjusted to the changing milieu, and some of them did not. For those who did accommodate themselves to new political and social forces, the adjustments were difficult.

Bhatkhande and Paluskar set the parameters within which *gharana* musicians made adjustments. They contested the manner in which music was disciplined by musicologists and turned devotional by bhakti nationalists. The two men are national icons in modern India for their efforts, but they have received little critical attention. Both men were Marathi Brahmins. One wrote in the elite language of rational and secular musicology (Bhatkhande), and the other in the populist rhetoric of bhakti nationalism (Paluskar). The two men were not friends but antagonists, representing two distinct ideological conceptualizations of music and two different understandings of nationalism. Bhatkhande tried to classify, categorize, and classicize music, whereas Paluskar worked to cleanse and sacralize it. Both men attempted to bypass the authorial role played by the *ustad*s, and together they both posed a serious challenge to *gharana* musicians. The legacies of these two men, as well as of the older *gharana* musicians, have survived to the present day in small schools of music that use elementary musicology to train students and expand the horizons of musical understanding well beyond courts and performers; in the hold that bhakti nationalism continues to have on larger institutions of music pedagogy through the sacralization of the space of performance; and in the fact that modern *ustad*s continue to train the extraordinary students who go on to perform on the national stage.

The years during which music underwent these changes coincided with the period of colonial rule. While this is not a book about the colonial construction of music, it would not be accurate to claim that colonialism had nothing to do with the development of classical music. There are histories of music that trace a gradual evolution of music from lowbrow to highbrow and from feudal to modern. Other accounts write of music in terms of a steady decline from ancient times to the present. Still others view music as possessing an unbroken history from ancient times to the present, with a few periods (such as the later Mughal period) marking a dark epoch or a period of neglect. Indian classical music's fundamentally modern character is infrequently remarked, and colonialism, in many of these accounts, is either absent as a force or plays only an altruistic, benign, and distant role.[5] However, I argue here that colonialism marked the ideological and epistemological beginnings of music's transformation. Both Bhatkhande and Paluskar, in different ways, engaged colonial challenges. Paradoxically, Bhatkhande's textual obsessions, despite their elitism, were ultimately more secular and less colonially derivative than Paluskar's antitextual advocacy of true and pure music.

In order to understand the colonial role in music's modern history, we will take a brief look at the article "On the Musical Modes of the Hindus," drafted in 1784 by Sir William Jones, the most important colonial and Orientalist scholar to write about Indian music. Jones had been in India for only a year when he took on the task of composing a treatise on Indian music. At the time, he did not know Sanskrit well, nor is it apparent that he was wellschooled in Western classical music. When Jones wrote about music, he did so using Indo-Persian musicological literature that relied on transliterated versions of Sanskritic musicological terms. He described the development of all Indian knowledge (divine and human) including music as emanating from the Vedas. In his article, he described the seven pitches of the Indian scale, the semitones ascribed to each one, and the different ragas, which he translated as "modes" that "properly signif[ied] a passion or affection of the mind."[6] He wrote that "every branch of knowledge in this country has been embellished by poetic fables; and the inventive talents of the Greeks never suggested a more charming allegory than the lovely families of the six Ragas,"[7] noting in the concluding passages of his essay that "had the Indian empire continued in full energy for the last two thousand years, religion would, no doubt, have given permanence to systems of music invented, as the Hindus believe, by their Gods, and adapted to mystical poetry."[8] All that was left of music in India was its theory as it was preserved in Sanskrit books, and "the practice of it seems almost wholly lost," Jones remarked, citing as his authority not musicians but "Pandits and Rajas."[9] The history of "Hindoo" music was also, for Jones, the history of theory, not performance. This was a claim Bhatkhande would pick up and turn on its head.

Jones's primary interest was not music but rather the ethnological Mosaic account that begins the book of Genesis in the Old Testament. In his line of argument, Sanskrit literature offered the Western world some of its most sought-after details about the beginnings of primitive monotheism as well as about the natural truths told to the patriarchs of the Bible, which were in turn handed down by Noah to his progeny. He treated Genesis as if it were a secular narrative and ancient Sanskrit sources as linguistic proofs of the links between the three foundational nations deriving from each of Noah's sons, one of whom was the originator of the Hindu nation.[10] Hindu musical modes were not at all analogous to the more complex modern European modes but better suited for comparison with "those of the Roman Church, where some valuable remnants of old *Grecian* music are preserved in the sweet, majestic, simple and affecting strains of the plain Song."[11] For his treatise, Jones used Sanskrit texts such as Damodara's *Sangitdarpan*, Ahobal Pandit's *Sangit Parijat*, and Somanatha's *Ragavibodha*. He was interested not in modern music, Eastern or Western, but in the survival unscathed into the modern period of ancient forms. The history of "Hindu" music could be put to instrumental use in helping Orientalists recover their own true history of music, in particular the history of the seven Grecian modes. Furthermore, in identifying the music of India as that which belonged to a "Hindu nation," Jones was not making a claim for modern Hindu nationalism but designating a group of people from Biblical times.

Jones's article on Hindu musical modes went through several revisions and was finally published in the third volume of the publication of the Royal Asiatic Society, *Asiatick Researches*. It was first reprinted in 1799 and reprinted four additional times by 1807. It was republished on numerous occasions in books and compilations put together by late nineteenth-century travelogue writers such as Ethel Rosenthal and influential musicologists like Sir Raja Sourindro Mohun Tagore. The article was cited in virtually every English article on Indian music. Indian writers used it to document that no less a figure than the great Orientalist Sir William Jones had discerned the beauty and scientific antiquity of Indian music, thereby lending weight to the claim that Jones was the rare European that truly appreciated and loved India. As a result, Jones was never challenged on any of his historical presumptions or his conclusions about music and religion. As the leading Oriental scholar of his time, he was frequently cited—but not critically examined—in the subsequent literature on music.

Jones was followed by a succession of other colonial authors who augmented his theory by producing, over the course of the nineteenth century, a canonic understanding of what Indian music needed in order to become genuinely classical. According to these writers, music needed three things: nation, notation, and religion. These colonial authors invariably assumed the presence of all three in the Western context as evidence of aesthetic and organizational superiority. Notation, they argued, would remove inconsistency and enable music to be read off the page, as was the case with Western classical music. However, Indian music was predicated on the very opposite of faithful duplicability, and as a result, notation did not make the inroads it was expected to make. Similarly, Jones's theory about the natural inextricability between the music and the religion of the nation of "Hindoos" suffered when subjected to serious scrutiny. How then might one make sense of colonial writings on Indian music?

In the course of conducting his own research into the origins and history of North Indian music, Bhatkhande had read most colonial writings on music, from Jones to the writings of colonial officials in the twentieth century. A little over a century after Jones had written his seminal and influential article, Bhatkhande found the Vedas irrelevant to the performance of music. In his attempt to write the connected history that he believed music needed, Bhatkhande forced ancient and medieval texts into a conversation with contemporary performance, only to have it end in an impasse. There was no evident dialogue, let alone correspondence, between contemporary music (*prachaarit sangit*) and the various Sanskrit treatises (*shastra*). At one level, Bhatkhande's findings concurred with Jones's claim that ancient Hindu music remained only as a theory in treatises. Unlike Jones, however, Bhatkhande was less interested in the history of ancient music than in writing a historical account of contemporary music. Paluskar, by contrast, would stand on firm colonial epistemological grounds when he ignored the lack of fit between text and performance, assumed that India's true music had always been ancient and scientific, and focused his attention on music's new role as gendered and devotional.

The owl of Minerva, Hegel famously observed, flies only at dusk. The distance of a century reveals some of the contradictions, failures, and Pyrrhic successes of the national project. Paluskar's bhakti nationalism "Hinduized" music and sacralized its pedagogy, but it also created the conditions under which women, albeit middle-class ones, could enter a public cultural sphere without the fear of social disapproval. Yet even as middle-class women moved slowly into a new public cultural space, they replaced an entire generation of women courtesan performers, known pejoratively as *baijis*, whose voices have mostly been lost under the weight of what E. P. Thompson once called the "enormous condescension of posterity."[12] For all that the arrogant project of Bhatkhande's typology erased the individual contributions of hereditary musicians, it also offered a vision of genuinely egalitarian music education for all Indians. Hereditary musicians, for their part, resisted musicology and Hinduization, but their self-fashioning fell short of accommodating women performers as part of music's future. Women performers were able to use bhakti nationalism as a way to declare their own professional status, but regardless of their musical talent or prowess, *ustad*s never conceded their own status or title to them. There was a term for female *ustad*s, *ustani*, but it was (and is) never applied to women performers.

For all these reasons, a history of music can neither be written in a straight line nor be rendered as a triumphant account. It can, however, still be written as a critical history, with the acknowledgment that any account of successful transformation needs to be tempered by the equal recognition of visions that did not take hold as well as by hidden and incomplete successes. In writing what might be called a "yes, but" critical history of music, I ask and answer some uncomfortable questions about the long-term social and political effects of its transformations and examine the political role played by music as a modernizing instrument.

In order to begin this book chronologically, the first chapter looks at the world of princely states, memorialized in many biographies as the halcyon and bygone days of true connoisseurship and benevolent patronage. I have taken the princely state of Baroda as my exemplary case for several reasons. Baroda was a modern and thoroughly modernized princely state run by an efficient prime minister, and was ruled in the late nineteenth and twentieth centuries by Sayajirao Gaekwad, known as a liberal patron of the arts. In 1916, Baroda played host to Bhatkhande's first All India Music Conference, and Sayajirao Gaekwad solicited both Bhatkhande's and Paluskar's advice about the music curricula of the state's schools. The story told in this book begins with Baroda, stays connected to it through the other chapters, and ends with the account of a father-daughter musician duo: Abdul Karim Khan, who began his career in Baroda's court, and Hirabai Barodekar, who exemplified the move of women into the professional performing space of music.

In the first chapter, I ask questions about the daily lives of court-appointed musicians, looking at their daily routines and what was expected of them. If one puts aside both nostalgia and romance, it becomes clear that a regime of colonial discipline had long been in place in princely states like Baroda. Not only was music systematized by the end of the nineteenth century, musicians were treated less as artists who adorned the court and more as salaried employees of the department of entertainment. Lastly, the ideal of the connoisseur maharaja appears symptomatic of musicians' anxieties and desires rather than a statement of the real.

The second chapter moves out into the larger world of the emerging cultural public sphere without relinquishing its connection to princely states. Princely state rulers were part of a patronage network for peripatetic folk theater as well as acting as donors to music appreciation societies and sponsors of grand events such as the All India Music Conferences. Through these activities, one sees the coming into being of a new cultural public sphere produced by literary activity (the response by native writers to colonial writings on the degeneracy of Indian music) as well as by the founding of fledgling education and music appreciation societies and music theater.

From the historical stage set by the first two chapters, I move directly to the centerpiece of this book: a chapter each on Bhatkhande and Paluskar. These are the longest chapters in the book, and I address in detail the biographies of the two men, as well as their aspirations, accomplishments, and ideological understandings of music's past and future. Toward the close of both men's lives, the nation's classical music had begun to take shape. Following the format set by the annual sessions of the Indian National Congress, both men convened annual music conferences. In the fifth chapter, I examine the debates and discussions at these national music conferences and the two institutions of musical learning set up by Bhatkhande and Paluskar.

The penultimate chapter is the riskiest one in this book. Unlike the preceding five chapters, it is not based on primary-source research. In a book of history, it stands out as unconventional, but the story I tell would be incomplete without it. This chapter is my attempt as a historian to read critically a few central biographies of two musicians in order to address the question of how musicians responded to the changes around them. Had musicians just accepted these changes? Had they resisted them? Were they indifferent to the efforts of musicologists? Could they simply ignore Paluskar and dismiss Bhatkhande? Rather than viewing musicians as artists who lived in their own worlds, transcending the hubbub of everyday political activity, I view them as actors in the world who negotiated the forces of the modern in order to ensure the survival of their musical traditions.

Insofar as I seek to make a contribution to cultural history, there are three interesting comparative frames of reference to consider. The first is internal to the domain of Indian cultural history. While there is a national academy for music in postcolonial, independent India, the Sangeet Natak Akademi, as well as colleges that teach music in various cities, top-level performers do not typically emerge from their ranks. *Gharana ustads,* though diminished in number compared to the end of the nineteenth century, still train the high-level performers. Inasmuch as the histories of nationalism and colonialism are constitutively important for music's transformation, Indian classical music remains one of the few forms of national art that was never completely disciplined by the juggernaut of colonial or nationalist modernity. By not focusing on the music itself, and broadening the category to include social, institutional, and political histories, it becomes possible to write about both continuity and rupture, colonial discipline, and nationalist control without losing sight of the musicians or music's role as a key participant in the gendered transformation of the cultural public sphere.

The second comparative frame of reference has to do with the type of classical music that acquired dominance in India. Compared to other Asian countries such as Korea, China, or Japan, where Western classical music planted deep roots, very few such roots were set down in India. A small fraction of the male urban and English-educated population listened to Western classical music and learned how to appreciate it; they even encouraged their wives to study a little bit of it. Instead, what emerged as classical music in the twentieth century was native to the subcontinent. This music has stayed at the center of the classical arts in India, never challenged in any significant way by music from outside. The fundamental form of the music—both its grammar and its aesthetic logic—did not so much actively resist colonial influence as stay indifferently impervious to it.

Chords did not replace *tan*s (melismatic arrangements), symphonies did not replace ragas (the fundamental unit of composition), melodic compositions did not succumb to the so-called superiority of contrapuntal harmony, and notated music entered the domain only as an early pedagogical tool. Opera houses were built in colonial cities such as Calcutta and Bombay, but as a musical form, opera put down even fewer roots than did orchestral, instrumental Western classical music. Western orchestration did become part of modern ceremonial activities, and it moved into film music even as it was played by ersatz marching bands. However, the modern middle class in the twentieth century did not send its children to learn Bach, Beethoven, and Mozart, let alone Verdi or Puccini. Additionally, middle-class children were sent, not to national academies, but to small, local, domestically operated schools where they learned the intricacies of raga and tala (meter). Was there something intrinsic to Indian music that made this possible? This is an unavoidable question, and yet, addressed historically without recourse either to essentialist or ontological categories, it may seem ultimately unanswerable.

Third, how does the history of classical music in India compare to the transformation of Western classical music? There is a large body of literature that traces the trajectory of music from being the source of entertainment in royal courts to the emblematic classical music of Western Europe.[13] In the process, Western classical music became secularized and its links with organized religion became increasingly attenuated. The story I tell in this book cannot be the same. First, Indian classical music emerged in a period of colonial modernity, and as I show in this book, colonialism cannot be ignored as a constitutive influence. Second, a separation between the secular and the religious is difficult to make in the case of Indian music. Pedagogical spaces, where the teaching of music in everyday life takes place, were sacralized, whereas others, such as the performance stage upon which an *ustad* sang, were not. One might further suggest, using Talal Asad's incisive analysis of the Christian entailments of modern Western secularism, that notwithstanding the self-conscious distinctions between secular and religious music (as in the case of Bach's cantatas, for instance), all Western classical music could be viewed as fundamentally religious.[14] Stuart Isacoff's work on the history of just, equal, and mean-tone temperament in Western classical music offers plentiful evidence to show how every suggestion about tuning was viewed as an attack on nature, divinity, and Grecian antiquity.[15] Clearly, notions of the divine and the sacred were important for the development of Western classical music. Even so, if there is an affinity at all between Western and Indian classical music, it resides not in a common history or historical trajectory, but in a shared resistance to the unlocking of the sealed hermeneutic that characterizes both discourses.

Ethnomusicologists have infused the study of comparative musical systems with a vitality drawn largely from contemporary music and musicians, and they have been critical of the dominant paradigms in the field that have invariably derived from the history of Western classical music. Ethnomusicological scholars of South Asia have been especially skillful in portraying the intimate world of performers and the complex protocols governing both the musical systems of South Asia and their lived social worlds.[16] And yet, in privileging a live present over a theoretical past, an organic lived reality of performance over the theoretically austere aesthetic of classical form, critical history becomes somewhat secondary. For the most part, neither colonialism nor modernity has been systematically examined as a transformative or constitutive force in the creation of musical tradition and music's growing historiographical corpus. History, within an ethnomusicological domain, often appears as either background information, a theoretical gesture, or predominantly local, remaining relatively unconnected to larger historical events. Because ethnomusicological understanding has been structurally founded on a relationship between interlocutor and ethnographer, a relationship made even more difficult by the fact that the ethnographer's interlocutor is often his or her music teacher (guru), to whom a great deal of respect is afforded, this is to a large extent inevitable. What can sometimes result, however, is insufficiently critical attention to the histories that musicians and their hagiographers tell. Additionally, since narrations of such histories and ethnographies are in the contemporary milieu constructed under the rubric of attending to the subaltern, the absence of either historical time or a hermeneutics of suspicion can also be naturalized as the progressive language of an antielitist scholarly endeavor. As a result, there has sometimes been a tendency within much early ethnomusicological writing to participate in a romanticization of the figure of the musician.

At the same time, the field of Indian music is itself marked by particular difficulties. Sources are hard to find, and those that are potentially available are virtually inaccessible, since documents are jealously guarded and rarely relinquished to an archive or a library. Indeed, ethnomusicologists make up the one group that has worked assiduously to rectify this state of affairs, depositing their field notes in a recently created archive (the Archives and Research Center for Ethnomusicology [ARCE]).[17] For this book, what is relevant is the paucity of sources and information about eighteenth- and nineteenth-century musical practices, pedagogy, and history. Even as ethnomusicologists are willing to share their notes and experiences, musicians remain secretive and suspicious, not merely of other musicians, but of scholars even when they are not musicians. Hindustani classical music does not possess a systematic historical archive, so each scholar makes his or her own archive, the details of which, such as the location of sources and specific dates, are not easily accessible. There is no systematic ordering of annual reports, conference proceedings, letters, private collections, or papers in a state archive. Archives of large princely states have large collections of documents, but it is not uncommon to find sheaves of material that for lack of funding are still uncatalogued and in considerable disrepair.

When one turns to published works on music, other problems arise. In general, modern Indian historians have left the subject alone. Critics, journalists, and music scholars have written most of the books on music's history. This has produced a peculiar corpus that includes adulatory biographies, journalistic anecdotes, and historical accounts that usually take the form of a chronicle, either of a great musician or of India's great and ancient musical heritage. These writings, while useful and relevant to any historical account, pose their own difficulties, since some of them frequently omit the conventions and protocols of modern history writing, such as an emphasis on verifiable dates, primary sources, detailed footnotes, and complete citations. Critique is reserved for little things, such as a particular performance or the behavior of a particular musician at an event. There are, of course, exceptions, such as the treatise editions put out by the Indira Gandhi Center or the writings of Dr. Sharatchandra Gokhale and Dr. Ashok Ranade, combining both musical knowledge and an "objective" view of musicians.[18] By and large, however, there is a large collection of published works about music in which India's "history" is constantly invoked, but it is not a historical corpus in the conventional, disciplinary sense of the term.

Nonetheless, this corpus, all its limitations notwithstanding, is a key part of the music's archive, requiring a different understanding of research than might be expected from a more conventionally documented field. The body of literature with which this book engages includes not only primary sources such as administrative records of the princely states, letters, colonial documents, books, pedagogical guides, notated compositions, memoranda, and the like, but also selections in Marathi, Hindi, and Gujarati from the large body of hagiographical, biographical, and journalistic literature. The eclectic mix makes it possible to cross-reference and check dates, with the caveat that often the best one can offer is an approximation.

In this book, I identify musicians deliberately and knowingly as Hindu or Muslim. However, I do not mean to suggest that religion was the sole or even primary self-identification, or that there was always in place a fixity of religious identity. Nor do I mean to suggest that musical practices themselves were religiously defined. However, they were named as Hindu or Muslim first by colonial writers and later by nationalists with consequences that have lasted into the present. It would be appropriate but cumbersome (for the reader) to put scare quotes around the various terms I use to signal my recognition of their unstable, contingent, fluid, and fundamentally historical nature. Instead, I will state the limits of the use to which I put them here in the introduction.

Throughout this book, when I use the term *bourgeoisie*, I will refer to an urban and elite population that was Brahminized if not Brahmin, and largely Hindu. I use the term *Indian classical music* in this book, but will refer only to North Indian classical music. Lakshmi Subramanian and Amanda Weidman have both written on Carnatic music and the national project.[19] This book is in conversation with their work but stakes out a different terrain of inquiry. This book builds, as well, on the insights offered by Gerry Farrell on Orientalism and recording and the roles of nationalist and reformist discourses in music.[20] By *colonial discipline*, I mean a range of activities that include systematization, order, discipline, surveillance, and notation. I have also made frequent use of the term *secular*. I cannot claim that Bhatkhande and Paluskar were drawing from a fully elaborated ideology or state policy about the equal treatment of religious constituencies. Nor do I mean to suggest that either figure deviated from a set of secular convictions that might have been readily available in the context of colonial modernity. I am aware of the critiques of secularism made by such critics as Ashis Nandy and Trilokinath Madan, who have argued that modern Indian secularism has failed to accommodate the tolerant, syncretic, and yet fundamentally religious character of Indian culture. I am also aware that the colonial state, as Partha Chatterjee and others have pointed out, was so concerned to legitimate itself through its putative protection of an autonomous religious domain that it produced many of the problems the postcolonial state confronts. On the one hand, I have no alternative but to emphasize the contradictions that became inherent when secularism was itself implicated in the promises of modernity. On the other hand, I wish to retain the possibility of an alternative vision of modernity in which the *ideal* of secularism could have been realized without relinquishing historicist critique.[21]

In a continuation of his longstanding conversation with Benedict Anderson, Partha Chatterjee has recently argued that homogeneous time—the time of Capital—is not the determining characteristic of modernity. Instead, he argues, heterogeneous time, in which the mass of the population in the non-Western world accommodated competing conceptions of time, such as linear time and circular time, is the modal time of modernity.[22] What I take from him is the clarity of his conviction that the coexistence of simultaneous time(s) is decidedly modern, and that to posit it instead as the romantic alternative time of the premodern is to maintain the privilege of a fictive dominance of homogeneous time against which other times can be seen only as oppositional. Chatterjee argues against the romance of the "premodern" at the same time that he insists that postcolonial criticism can function effectively only if it privileges neither "global cosmopolitanism" nor "ethnic chauvinism." Where music is concerned, I use his conceptions to argue that Indian classical music is neither the result of colonial mimesis nor the remnant of an ancient musical form that survived into the modern period. Given the contradictory and contingent space that music occupies, the hope of this book is that once historicized, music's modern accomplishments can be properly appreciated, and its modern failures adequately considered.23

Two final points: first, I have conceived of this book visually as a wheel with several spokes, all of which are necessary to keep it in motion. The wheel at the center is Indian classical music. The spokes are all historical vectors, each with its own starting point, such that the chapter on princely states begins with the history of Baroda but ends with its implications for classical music. Likewise, the chapter on the public cultural sphere begins with the founding of different organizations whose histories feed what will become national classical music's audience. Each chapter has a discrete beginning, in other words, but a linked end. Second, I tell the story of modern music from the perspective of a historian, not of a classicist or Indologist, a musicologist, or an ethnomusicologist. In the pages to follow, there are no technical analyses of sheet music, no ethnographic interviews with musicians, no attempts to write a comprehensive history of music from ancient times to the present using classical treatises written in Sanskrit. I turn now to the first chapter on the princely state of Baroda, its ruler, and the lives of court musicians.

⊛ ONE ⊛

THE PRINCE AND THE MUSICIAN

Native States, Bureaucracy,

and Colonial Influence

The Prince

In 1896, a man named Sayajirao Gaekwad ordered his staff to have makeshift beds for his wife and himself made out of silver while their permanent beds, made out of gold, were being repaired.[1] He had the money to order a hundred such beds if he so desired. He was the ruler of a wealthy princely state, Baroda, and the eighth-richest man in the world in the early years of the twentieth century.[2] As a Baroda ruler, moreover, he was merely carrying on an established practice of spending vast sums of money on jewelry and precious metals. A previous ruler, Khanderrao Gaekwad, had cannons cast out of gold and silver and carpets woven from pearls. He diverted money (thirty-six lakhs of rupees) earmarked to provide the residents of the capital city with clear drinking water to build a palace for his bride and added eccentricity to extravagance by conducting pigeon marriages with solemnity and ostentatious pomp.

Sayajirao, gold and silver beds notwithstanding, was a different kind of ruler. By the end of his reign, he would be known for his progressiveness and enlightenment, unlike the rulers of numerous other princely states, who typically pursued lives of playboy pleasures without responsibility. Sayajirao, by contradistinction, was a champion of women's education and a patron of the arts. He had claimed that the era of "rubbishy princely states" was fast coming to an end. Despite the confident quality of this declaration, princely states were alive, well, and wealthy in the nineteenth and early twentieth centuries, and their courts were often the main source of employment for musicians and other entertainers.

When Sayajirao came to the throne, Baroda was well on its way to becoming the model princely state, modernized along colonial lines. All aspects of courtly life had been standardized, regulated, and turned bureaucratically efficient, including the lives of musicians. One of these was Maula Baksh Ghisse Khan (1833–96). A wrestler turned musician, Maula Baksh had served three consecutive Baroda rulers—Khanderrao Gaekwad (reigned 1857–70), Malharrao Gaekwad (reigned 1870–75), and Sayajirao Gaekwad (reigned 1881–1939). Most importantly for my story, he dreamed up and implemented a possible future for music that was extraordinary for its time, and he did so within the bureaucratic and modernized feudalism that characterized Sayajirao's court.

Sayajirao Gaekwad and Maula Baksh Ghisse Khan, the prince and the musician, reveal a great deal about both India's nineteenth-century "feudal" regimes and their significance in the history of the colonial cultural sphere. Both men are revered in Baroda—Sayajirao for the benevolence of his rule and Maula Baksh for his pioneering work in music education. They are also connected by music. Fatesingrao Gaekwad, Sayajirao's great-grandson, claimed that the ruling princes of India had saved classical music from disappearing.[3] This is not quite the case. Maula Baksh and Sayajirao's lives show us the various contradictions of a princely court (and, by extension, a princely state) that was modern, colonial, and feudal at the same time, and in which musicians had little independence and the ruler had little interest in music. Yet, precisely within the contradictory mix of a colonial princely state, Maula Baksh envisioned a future for music that could be modern, nonsectarian, and still Indian. The music bore recognizable signs of colonial modernity, involving written notation, systematization, institutionalization, codification, and the use of pedagogical textbooks, yet it did not require making exclusionary choices between modern and traditional, classical and folk, or Hindu and Muslim.

Baroda today is the major city of the western Indian state of Gujarat. In the late seventeenth century, what is now Gujarat was a province held by the Mughal emperor. In 1664, the legendary Maratha king, Shivaji, led the first of several raids into Gujarat, then Mughal territory, to forcefully collect revenue. Shivaji died in 1680, and in the early years of the eighteenth century, his successors the Bhonsles were increasingly controlled by their Brahmin prime ministers (the *peshwa*). The *peshwa* exercised a great deal of authority, something that irked the three powerful Maratha families, who struck out on their own as quasi-independent ruler chieftains—the Holkars, Shindes, and Gaekwads.[4]

Sayajirao was a distant cousin of the ruling family of Gaekwads. Until the age of thirteen he was known as Gopalrao, the name his parents gave him at his birth. He had spent his childhood in the village working as a farmhand. He was not in the direct line of succession to the throne of Baroda and might well have stayed in the village, far from the pomp and wealth of the court, had it not been for a series of events concerning Khanderrao Gaekwad (of gold cannon and pearl carpet fame). Khanderrao had aided the British in the 1857 anticolonial rebellion. When he died in 1870, his wife, Maharani Jamnabai, was pregnant. She gave birth to a female child, who, according to colonial law, could not inherit the throne.[5] Even though her infant daughter could not be named heir apparent, Khanderrao's collaboration with the British would be rewarded with a gift to his widow.

Succession to princely state thrones was vital to British colonial interests. The colonial government monitored and frequently manipulated succession through a system of indirect control first employed in the late eighteenth century by the East India Company. Following the Rebellion of 1857 and the assumption of crown rule over territories controlled directly by the East India Company, a colonial Resident oversaw all aspects of the daily functioning of princely states, though the ruler was given a measure of autonomy over his or her subjects. In theory, by bestowing upon a "native" ruler a small amount of independence, the colonial government ensured that British coffers stayed full, the potential of anticolonial insurgency was kept at bay, and the ruler was controlled but content. For the theory to work, it needed a pliant or a puppet ruler. The chances of finding such a ruler were far greater if the colonial Resident could control who succeeded to the throne.

As a token of gratitude for her husband's loyalty to the British during the 1857 revolt, Queen Victoria granted Khanderrao's widow, Jamnabai, the right to adopt an heir for the throne from her husband's extended family after the interim ruler, Malharrao, had been deposed by the British in 1874. She picked Gopalrao, a distant cousin from the Kavlana branch of the family. He was brought to Baroda from his village, renamed Sayajirao Gaekwad III, and put through an intensive program of colonially supervised education. The training was intended to erase his rural illiteracy and lack of refinement and transform him into a member of princely India's ruling elite. Sayajirao took to his training fairly well, but he would disappoint the British later on by not being quite as pliant as they would have preferred. In 1881, however, he seemed the perfect choice, and the British appointed him ruler of Baroda.[6]

In 1881, Baroda was well on its way to becoming the model princely state. A colonially derived bureaucratic order had taken hold in princely states much more effectively than it had in parts of India over which the British ruled directly. The agents of bureaucratic modernization and control in princely courts were the colonial Resident and the chief ministers, known as *dewan*s, by far the most powerful officials of the court. The Resident and the *dewan* were often the de facto rulers of the state.[7] Rulers were rarely free to pick their own *dewan*. The Resident had to be consulted, and without his consent no *dewan* could be appointed. Typically, the Resident made a recommendation that the ruler was not free to refuse. Baroda, since 1875, had been run by its *dewan*, Sir T. Madhav Rao, a learned Brahmin who spoke six languages. He was a favorite of the British, had previous experience in two princely courts (Travancore and Indore), and was a powerful and influential figure.[8] Madhav Rao modernized Baroda's bureaucracy along the lines of a British district.[9] He established a court of justice, created an administrative service, a police force, built hospitals, public works, set up schools, reduced taxes, and balanced the budget. In 1881, at the end of his tenure, he left Baroda financially healthy, with eight million rupees in the treasury and thirteen million in invested funds.[10]

The bureaucratic modernization begun by Madhav Rao encompassed the domain of culture as well, including within its ambit the world of music and musicians. Baroda had over the years amassed a motley collection of entertainers: some were permanent employees, others were informal court retainers. The group of entertainers was collectively known as the *kalavant karkhaana*, or the "warehouse of artists." All court entertainers—mimes, wrestlers, singers, dancers, dramatists, and instrumentalists—were housed, for accounting purposes, within the *karkhaana* which was run by officials known as the *khaangi karbhaari*s (ministers of personnel affairs).

In the early years of Sayajirao's rule, the *karkhaana* was represented to him by its different *khaangi karbhaaris* as a department in disrepair, and in urgent need of reform. Over the next eighteen years, Sayajirao made a series of rulings on individual cases that became the foundation for the publication, in 1899, of a book of rules titled *Kalavant Khatyache Niyam* (hereafter *Niyam*). The *Niyam* put in place a new kind of princely patronage for the twentieth century. Artists were placed in one of three categories, and every detail of their lives was monitored: what they could wear, when they could go on leave, and what they were to perform.[11]

The *Niyam* tells us how artists must have lived their daily lives, the conditions of their employment, and the requirements placed upon them. It also documents the successful enactment of a careful transformation from a hazy and ill-determined period of unsystematic patronage—an earlier, perhaps more "authentic" feudalism—to the centralized, efficient, and streamlined patronage of colonial feudalism. The authors of the *Niyam* had identified, without naming it as such, feudal patronage as the problem in need of attention.[12] However, simple modernization was not the solution. Instead, they advocated a modernized feudalism, empowering senior appointed ministers of the *khaata* to keep a tighter rein on the finances and a closer eye on the entertainers.

The peculiarity of this modern feudalism lies in its combining bureaucratic efficiency with the glamorous trappings of a putative historical privilege. In theory, and according to the rule book, the *khaata* had been retained as a permanent department of the court because its primary function was to provide the ruler with *vishraanti* (tranquil relaxation) and *karmanuk* (distraction) after a day of onerous duties.[13] In practice, from 1886 (five years after he came to the throne) until his death in 1939, Sayajirao got most of his rest and relaxation in Europe, barring a few months every other winter when he returned to India.[14] During these years, he was largely an absentee maharaja, something that was remarked upon by his own family, who recognized that he showed an "exaggerated intolerance towards Baroda's climate and escaped from it at the flimsiest of pretexts."[15] He had little use for an entire warehouse of entertainers—at one point numbering as many as five hundred—and he did most of the administrative work related to the *khaata* by mail. In this revamped feudal order, the *khaata* performed mostly a symbolic function, keeping alive, albeit in new ways, the "traditional" privileges of the ruler.

These twin pillars of feudalistic modernity—bureaucracy and tradition—

were the naturalized outcome of Baroda's checkered history of patronage, narrated in the preface to the actual rules of the *Niyam*. Patronage began with the founding of the *khaata*, for which neither a date nor the precise number of members on its payroll at any given point is available. No systematic expenditure was associated with the comings and goings of entertainers until 1817. Two years later, in 1819, the first male singer was hired as a permanent salaried employee. This act was deemed the founding of the *kalavant karkhaana*, thereby linking patronage to centralized account keeping.[16] Despite this, entertainers were paid out of a number of noncentralized accounts well into the nineteenth century. Baroda's ministers, when writing this account at the end of the nineteenth century, were making a qualitative distinction between a "feudal patronage" defined by nonpermanent employment and unsalaried remuneration and its modern cousin, defined in terms of centralized accounting practices and categorized employment. In fact, by the terms of an internal court reckoning, Baroda had no system of patronage for the first five decades of the nineteenth century.[17]

Over the course of the century, the remuneration for both permanent employees and occasional performers ranged from Rs. 700 at the high end to Rs. 50 at the low end. Most Gaekwad rulers favored women singers and dancers over men, and until the middle of the century, they were paid more than all other entertainers.[18] Unofficial accounts often hint that the various nobles (*sardars*) of the court kept female entertainers as their mistresses, further throwing into question the categorical definition of the term *patronage*. Mime and mimicry shows, wrestling acts, and song and dance troupes were given equal time if not more by the Gaekwads.[19] By 1843, in addition to the twenty-two artists in the permanent employ of the court, various mime artists and a troupe that performed devotional music related to an auspicious festival (*lalitacha tamaasha*) were also part of the roster.[20]

While this variety certainly points to a court that liked different forms of entertainment, it does not suggest an active patronage of "serious" music. Music was never the mainstay of court entertainment, even though the first eight employees of the *karkhaana* were all male singers. Even during the heyday of Baroda patronage, identified in the *Niyam* as the eleven-year period leading up to the year of the Great Rebellion (1857), when the *khaata* boasted an extensive roster of entertainers from varied caste groups, religions, and regions, music as such was not particularly favored.[21] In the years following the rebellion, the fortunes of the *khaata* fluctuated, its numbers shrinking before swelling again.[22] At its best, a repertoire ranging from festive music to mime shows, from Tanjavur dance to North Indian *khayal*, from instrumental music to large theatrical shows, characterized Baroda's courtly entertainment. No qualitative distinction was made between the devotional and the bawdy, no hierarchical ranking ordered artists as less or more classical. No male singer was especially privileged, and in fact, male singers were rather low in the pecking order, far below mimes and theatrical troupes.[23] This would not be particularly significant were it not for the fact that this was the period during which male musicians from *gharana*s had established semiprofessional guilds and had begun to carry the representational burden of "serious" music.[24] Yet male singers, from the beginnings of Gaekwad patronage through its eleven-year period of glory, saw their remuneration diminish steadily.[25] And well into the first two decades of the twentieth century, female singers and dancers earned more than double the amount paid to famous male musicians such as Faiyaz Khan.[26]

That courtly entertainment was not about serious art was recognized by the authors of the *Niyam*, who painted a picture of Baroda's history of patronage as an uneven, but nonetheless steady, decline marked by favoritism to female entertainers and vaudeville (*tamasha*).[27] The pressing concern was that of respectability, said in the *Niyam* to be desirable and urgently required. In the actual rules themselves, respectability was written in as a mandate for the superintendent, who was empowered to monitor all aspects of his artists' lives, from the content of their performances to the cleanliness of their clothes. *Rajashraya,* or princely patronage, would become a set of rules by the end of the nineteenth century. The other issue, linked to the authors' concerns with favoritism and respectability (paying too much to female entertainers), was the need for drastic financial streamlining.[28] Beginning in 1881, Sayajirao's ministers initiated a systematic standardization of the *khaata* and, by 1924, they had decreased its budget (Rs. 30,000) to less than what was spent on it in the year of its founding.[29]

Sayajirao began the process of streamlining by resolving older and unsettled accounts as soon as he came to power. In 1867, Malharrao Gaekwad, the black sheep of the family, had ordered that a female singer, Amba Kotwaleen, be given Rs. 2000 to build herself a house, but it was not clear whether the money was given as a gift or a loan. Sayajirao ruled that the money be considered a gift. It was not a ruling he ever repeated for any other singer or dancer.[30] He adjudicated the first performances by singing and dancing girls and determined whether they should be included in the *khaata*.[31] He granted requests by dancers for additional money for the purchase of jewelry only on the condition that the money be spent on what it had been asked for, and he treated these additional disbursements as loans, deducted in monthly installments from the dancers' salary.[32] All matters, however minor they may have been, were sent to Sayajirao. In the early years of his rule, he maintained strict vigilance over issues as seemingly inconsequential as raising a musician's salary by Rs. 5 per month. He also curtailed the power that officials had exercised in previous eras.[33]

The thoroughness with which all aspects of entertainment were standardized cannot be emphasized enough. In many accounts about the lives of musicians in the late nineteenth and early twentieth centuries, we read about whimsical, connoisseur maharajas who bestow upon the musician knowledgeable attention, while the musician is free to live an otherworldly life in which the cares of the material world are subordinated to the pursuit of true art. Baroda's comprehensive bureaucratic standardization does not conform to such a picture. The maharaja himself was not rule-bound, but even his idiosyncratic preferences were turned into rules. Take the case of drama troupes, for instance, who were the favored entertainers of the court, often performing on successive days.[34] Sayajirao elaborated a personalized schedule of payments. "Let there be two categories of *natak*s [dramas]," he ruled.

> *Natak*s that I liked and were well performed should be placed in the first category. If I saw it in the theater, the troupe should be paid expenses and a *bakshees* of Rs. 300. If they performed at court, they should receive Rs. 400. If the *natak* was mediocre it should be in the second category, and as per the difference written earlier, they should receive Rs. 200 and Rs. 300, respectively. After the performance, ask me which category I would assign to the *natak* and let the *natakkar*s [participants in the *natak*] be apprised of this rule so that there will be no complaints later.[35]

Payments (*bakshees*) remained fairly consistent, even if they were deemed unfair by the troupes.[36] Even Sayajirao's whimsical notions of remuneration were standardized by the court.

Standardization was accompanied by house cleaning. Slots left empty by either absconding musicians or deceased musicians were filled, salaries were scaled down and fixed, and permanence of employment was made conditional upon improvement.[37] In 1888, Pestonjee Dorabjee, one of the *khaangi karbhaaris*, suggested that talent ought perhaps to determine remuneration, recommending the founding of a committee to look into the matter of artistic reform. The committee would pay close attention to the optimal number of artists who should be a part of the *karkhaana*, the kinds of instruments that should be used, how to weed out unproductive musicians, how to maximize the use of artists, and how to raise the standards of the performances.[38] Yet talent did not, in fact, determine salary, and the ceiling for the salaries of male singers hovered around the Rs. 100 mark for the next several decades— for court-appointed and visiting musicians, and for famous and unknown musicians. Talent determined whether or not a musician could secure an appointment, but salaries were pegged to the categories in which the artist was placed upon being hired.

Indeed, categories were all-important, determining not just salaries but also pensions. When Jaysingrao Angre, another *khaangi karbhaari*, asked for a monthly pension of Rs. 15 for an aged *tabla* player, Illahi Baksh, he combined financial shrewdness with a small measure of altruism. Illahi Baksh was old, Angre noted, and had been earning a monthly income of Rs. 30 without performing. A Rs. 15 pension would save the court money—unless, of course, he was replaced by another *tabla* player.[39] Angre also used the occasion to argue in favor of a categorical distinction between wrestlers and male singers (*pehelvaan*s and *gavai*s), on the one hand, and other employees of the court such as washermen or those deputed to wind the clocks. Singers and wrestlers had much in common. They worked harder than the other workers, were more diligent, and ultimately were more restricted in their activities, disallowed as they were by contract from seeking supplemental employment. Moreover, Angre continued, they spent what income they earned in perfecting their entertainment skills. They did not travel outside Baroda, and no one other than the court had permission to hire their services.[40] Consequently, they belonged in a different category for pension purposes.

The caretakers of the *khaata* were concerned to make efficient and full use (*purna upyog*) of existing *kalavant*s, to make better use of *nalayak* (slack) workers, and to save additional money by not paying newcomers the salary old-timers had held.[41] Under the new regime, no financial matters were left hanging. Not only were salaries, pensions, and gifts standardized, all tardiness of payments was prohibited as well.[42] In a number of orders, the *khaangi karbhaari* raised the issue of saving money by not replacing every member of the *khaata* who either left without giving notice or was merely earning money without performing. At the same time, artists were brought under a fairly comprehensive system of supervision.[43]

Where previously musicians received permission to leave Baroda for a few weeks and often did not return for months, or even years, a new monitoring system made such departures, if not impossible, very costly. The new rules stated that absences without explanation would be punished by a cut in salary corresponding to the number of days they had not been present.[44] When musicians resisted the court practice of loaning out their services to wealthy patrons, they were chastised and fined. In July 1890, Krishna Mudholakarin refused an order to sing outside the court, demanding (with what was reported as unseemly hauteur) that someone of her status needed assurance of appropriate remuneration. Pestonjee Dorabjee, the *khaangi karbhaari*, complained that her arrogance reflected badly on the *khaata*, and Sayajirao responded, "I think performers like these should not generally be made to go by order, though, when given, they are bound to go. Krishna Mudholakarin should be punished by a fine of Rs. 5."[45] Neither status nor the age of a performer stood in the way of princely state rulers treating them as possessions or commodities to be traded back and forth.

In 1895, Bibijaan, a singer who impressed Sayajirao, was sent to study with Faiz Mohammed Khan, a senior and widely respected court musician. Musicians often prejudicially viewed women dancers as prostitutes. The royal order to use their artistic talents to train women of ill repute was often viewed by them as the epitome of their degradation by indolent princes. At the same time, Bibijaan was put on notice. "She has to keep her demeanor and clothing in immaculate condition," stated the order, and she would receive Rs. 80 per month as a salary, but "if her singing and dancing did not improve in a year she would be dismissed."[46] Both musician and courtesan were kept in their place by such a ruling.

Bibijaan also had to hire, at her own expense, two *sarangi* players and one *tabla* player, perform as ordered at the Makarpura Palace or anywhere else, and pay for her transportation herself. Biographers often claim that, for their transportation, musicians had motorcars and elephants at their disposal. Balkrishnabua Ichalkaranjikar, court musician at Meraj, remembered having witnessed musicians arriving at princely courts to sing on special occasions in palanquins or on the backs of elephants, a transport usually used only by members of the royal family.[47] When he recalled the incident, in 1919, Balkrishnabua was old and feeble. His tenure as a court musician of Meraj had been punctuated by princely disrespect and indifference. Was his memory accurate, or can one read his late-in-life remembrances symptomatically as expressing a wistful desire for a life that he had not led? In Baroda, at any rate, when Sayajirao moved to his summer palace at Makarpura, entertainers were expected to go there and perform. For their transportation they could use the state bullock carts, and if the ruler was in residence in Baroda proper, their transportation to and from their residence was paid for. But there were restrictions on the subvention. In 1897, a *veena* player, Mangmabai, was fined for having overstepped her bounds by using a *sarkaari gaadi* (state vehicle) instead of using her transportation allowance to make travel arrangements.[48] Abdul Karim Khan, a prodigiously gifted musician who visited Baroda from 1894 through 1889, moved about on horseback.[49] The horses might have been gifts, but they could also have been loans by a patron. On the two occasions when Faiyaz Khan was "lent" to the ruler of Mysore, in 1930 and 1938, he was transported to and from the railway station in a court vehicle.[50] But while in Baroda, he rented a horse-driven carriage and later bought his own car.

By 1899, when the *Niyam* was published, the *khaata* no longer needed to be a part of the *faujdar khaata* (military department), which had been created in 1883 and 1884 and into which all departments that dealt with personnel affairs had been amalgamated. In 1900, the *kalavant karkhaana* was turned over to the independent control of the newly created position of superintendent, who would administer the rules in the *Niyam*. No longer was it the case that a peripatetic musician who happened to be in the area could persuade a colleague to let him perform and thus secure employment. Singers had to apply for a job, fill out forms, and couch the application in precise and binding language. They had to give details about their repertoire of compositional forms, and agree to a quasi-contractual agreement guaranteeing hours of service, no repetition of performances, and cooperation with the rules.[51] Gender distinctions were much in evidence in this new set of rules. Male singers were given a literacy test, questioned about the number of ragas they knew, and tested on their bookish knowledge of music and dance.[52] Female singers had to be able to sing in Marathi, Gujarati, Hindustani (an admixture of Hindi and Urdu), and Brijbhasha.[53] Women were not tested on their practices, while men were tested on their formal textual knowledge.

Once hired, artists were put in categories and told to remember their assigned place. The superintendent of the *khaata* was in the first category. Second after him were those who performed every day, namely the *holaar* and the *gurav vajantri* (the instrumentalist that accompanied the priest at prayer). Musicians, singing and dancing girls, southern dance troupes, mime troupes, *tabla* players, *sarangi* players, and *tambora* players were members of the third category and had to make themselves available as ordered. All artists except the women singers and dancers had to report to duty each morning, whether they were to perform or not.[54] Although this rule caused artists such as Faiyaz Khan (and visiting musicians like Abdul Karim Khan) to express displeasure, it was never rescinded. Faiyaz Khan was a "third-category" member, not required to perform every day, but he had to check in with the superintendent every day and sign his name in the register of record.[55] The rest of the entertainers (*pakhawaj* players, harmonium players, sitar players, *saaz* players, and other instrumentalists) were on call as needed and formed the fourth category.[56]

Additionally, artists were instructed to obey without question (*bin bobhat*) anything and everything the superintendent might order.[57] They could be loaned on occasion to other rulers and they had to comply without complaint (*bin takraar*).[58] The superintendent was empowered with a range of duties, both panoptical and punitive. He monitored the content of all performances for artistic virtuosity and social message. He replaced old and bought new instruments and kept in his possession all the belongings of the entertainers, including the clothes they wore for special performances. An officer of the court checked everything the artists did, from the cleanliness of the clothes they wore to the jewels they bought with their own earnings. The superintendent chose the appropriate entertainer for a specified occasion and monitored all the entertainers, punishing them as needed, levying fines for bad behavior, and granting leave as he saw fit.[59]

No member of the *kalavant khaata* could go on leave without permission, although singers and dancers who wanted to perform at weddings in the village or neighboring towns could do so by applying for leave. Even favored court musicians, such as Faiz Mohammed Khan, were not readily given permission to travel. In 1902, Sayajirao allowed musicians a little more travel flexibility when he was out of town, but only to better their skills.[60] This rule was further relaxed in 1904, when singers and musicians were allowed to seek supplemental income from performances outside the court but within the city of Baroda.[61] Musicians had to apply for leave to visit their native village and family.

As the rituals of the court became increasingly regulated, the *kalavant karkhaana* was summoned to put on public shows. In 1918, the *karkhaana* was placed under the joint supervision of the director of entertainment and the principal of the School of Indian Music, which had been founded in 1886. As addenda to the *Niyam*, Sayajirao's ministers also began a series of smaller rule books—the *Puravani Aine Rajmahal*—related to every one of the auspicious occasions (the Marathi new year, *gudhi padava*) or festive rituals (*halad kunku, vatasavitri,* or *chaitragouri puja*) celebrated by the royal family. The rituals themselves were recognizably Brahminic even though the Gaekwads were not themselves Brahmins. But Sayajirao had ruled in 1896 that all religious rituals of the court had to be performed in accordance with Vedic prescriptions. Consequently, the series of smaller rule books performed two functions. On one level, they simply stipulated in detail what the *kalavant*s were expected to do when the royal family celebrated a festival—where to stand, when to start singing, when to stop, and how to behave. On another level, the *Puravani Aine Rajmahal* naturalized the religious rituals of court as Brahminic, right down to the last details of the correct manner in which members of the royal family should take their ritual cleansing bath for the Marathi new year, *gudhi padava.*[62] Once again, music and the *khaata* itself served instrumental ends—in this case, the augmentation not merely of royalty but of royal religion.[63]

The most famous musician to sing in Baroda's court was Faiyaz Khan. The maharaja of Mysore, who "borrowed" him from Sayajirao for the second time in 1938, bestowed upon Faiyaz Khan the title of *Aftab-e-Mausiki* (the Radiance of Music). Faiyaz Khan's student, Dipali Nag, herself an accomplished musician, wrote a biographical account of her teacher's life. Here I am concerned only with that part of the account that relates to his life in Baroda. Some of what Nag represents as exceptional concessions made for an extraordinary musician by an appreciative Maharaja were, in fact, routine concessions written into the rules of the *khaata* that applied equally to all musicians, famous and unknown alike. Let us take the question of salary. In 1890, a trio of visiting musicians (Ghulam Husein Khan, Kareem Husain Khan, and Ramzan Ali Khan) from Patiala in the north of India performed in Baroda, each receiving Rs. 100.[64] In 1913, over two decades later, Faiyaz Khan, far more famous than the Patiala trio, received the same salary (Rs. 100) upon his appointment as a member of the *khaata*. It was no measure of his fame or talent but an amount halfway along on a salary scale that had been fixed years before he arrived in Baroda.[65] Faiyaz Khan demanded that he be excused from duty during *Mohurrum.* This was granted to him as it was granted to *all* Muslim musicians as a matter of policy.[66] Nag notes that Sayajirao raised Faiyaz Khan's salary by Rs. 5, but he also granted larger increases in salary for much less well-known musicians.[67] Exceptional as he was, Faiyaz Khan's everyday life as a "third category" musician of the *kalavant khaata* was far from that of an independent virtuoso. While he may have received extraordinary gifts of money for performances at other princely courts, within Baroda, as a *sarkaari nokar,* he had to abide by the standard rules and regulations that applied to all *khaata* members. He was required to teach in the school, even when the routine and the schedule irritated him greatly. He was asked to sing at the hospital to alleviate the suffering of the ailing. Outraged by the request, he prevaricated, demurred, balked, and finally compromised by agreeing to sing at a different public venue.[68]

In most of the literature about music, this bureaucratic and distant relationship between prince and musician is given short shrift. Maharajahs are commonly represented as aesthetes and lovers of classical music and generous in their support of musicians. In these narrative accounts, musicians flourished under the protective umbrella of *rajashraya.* They performed for select audiences and had ample time and independence in which to hone their art. Few of these claims hold good for the princely court of Baroda. When Faiyaz Khan first performed in the *darbar,* Sayajirao needed his bandmaster to identify the raga to him and informed the court that he had only a limited time in which to hear the maestro.[69] On one occasion, Faiyaz Khan was ordered to remain unseen by the royal family while they ate their lunch "Western style," and in another instance he was told that his art might be put to practical use as a health benefit in a public park.[70] Some years earlier, Sayajirao had recommended that musicians should emulate the tradition of vocal performances in Western high art music and break their habit of singing while seated. As a recommendation, it was no different from what colonial commentators had advocated a century earlier.[71] According to his great-grandson, Sayajirao made "a conscious effort to understand, to gain a proper appreciation, even to reform" the music he listened to occasionally and deal with "the lack of tidiness and discipline that [were] all but inseparable from Indian music."[72] What we see here is not necessarily a maharaja's aesthetic appreciation of a fine art, but a desire for comprehensive efficiency. Music was not the object of anyone's particular concern, but rather was one part of the overall ensemble of cultural forms that needed bureaucratic and systematic overhaul as part of the larger drive to modernize the state along colonial lines.

I chose Baroda to argue my case for a feudalistic modernity that was unconcerned with music *as* music for several reasons. It is one of a set of wealthy princely states, along with Rampur, Jaipur, Hyderabad, Kolhapur, Indore, and Mysore, that crops up frequently in the informal literature on music. Baroda shares many features with the other states in the group. It had been awarded a twenty-one-gun salute denoting its high status and importance for the British. It was also among the wealthiest of princely states in India. Down to the present day, the heirs to the throne are contesting the division of property and jewels worth millions. Baroda was also exemplary in its colonially influenced modernization. Madhav Rao was a legendary *dewan*, and his efforts can still be seen in the various amenities the city of Baroda has to offer its citizens. But most importantly, Sayajirao Gaekwad was known as a patron of learning and of the arts.[73]

The composite image of Sayajirao that one can put together is that of a ruler who partook of feudal privileges because they augmented the aura of his royalty, even though he spent over eight months of each year in either England or Switzerland. The *karkhaana* itself was reformulated to be a modern department of entertainment, and its *Niyam* shows us the instantiation of modern *rajashraya* as a set of panoptic, standardized, and bureaucratic rules. Only one mention was made of music as *shastriya* (classical) at the very end of the *Niyam*, and this was linked to a plea to reform the *karkhaana*. If classical music was at all "saved" by the princely states, as Sayajirao's great-grandson claimed, it was as a late by-product of the regulatory effort tied to the improvement of the overall appearance of the *karkhaana* and the behavior of its members.

An unwittingly negative description of the comings and goings in Sayajirao's court is offered to us in a biography of Abdul Karim Khan, a musician who visited Baroda. Musicians performed in the homes of court ministers and nobles far more than they ever did in the court proper. In this biographical remembrance of Baroda, Sayajirao is said to have destroyed music. As a result of his infatuation with the West, he is reported to have ushered in an age of fascination with wrestlers and newfangled innovations such as the playing of music in gardens. We even get an accurate, if embittered, depiction of the effect that the *Niyam* had on the life of musicians under the new regime. "What music, what singing? To appear before the Maharajah, all dressed up, keep him happy, nod in agreement all the time, that is our job now."[74] The worst offense against music perpetuated in his court was the use of notation. Take this narration of a conversation between Khadeem Husein Khan, an older musician in Baroda, and the visiting Abdul Karim Khan: "Before you came, Natthan Khan from Agra, Alladiya Khan from Atrauli came here, but our Superintendent brandished notation in front of them and the poor men ran away without singing." This account seems to offer a clear criticism of simple colonial mimicry. Khanderrao Gaekwad, who conducted pigeon marriages and ordered pearl carpets, is resurrected as the model ruler in whose time Khadeem Husein is reported as having heard "singing and instrumental performances such as we don't hear any more, nor will we ever again." While this is clearly a nostalgic rendering of a bygone era, there are perhaps other ways to view this account when placed next to both a materialist history and the productive possibilities of its own critique.

We know from the financial records in Baroda that Khanderrao and Sayajirao had similar tastes in entertainment. Both spent money on drama troupes and dancing girls, not on "true" music. So what function does the narration of Khadeem Husein's nostalgia perform? We get a glimpse of what the author, Balkrishnabua Kapileshwari, biographer of the famous Abdul Karim Khan (whom we shall meet again in chapter 6), perhaps means us to target through the numerous invocations of real musicians who fought hybrid innovations and stayed true to tradition by remaining respectful of age, protocol, ritual, and hierarchy. Even though Abdul Karim is presented to us as the exemplary musician, we know that he ran off with the daughter of his patron and went on to found a school, try his hand at notation, and participate in semiscientific musical experiments. Finally, we also know that the paradox of the modern, colonial, feudal princely court, despite Sayajirao's status as an absent maharaja and no connoisseur of music, lay in the fact that it provided the best of all possible opportunities for musicians, who were in fact treated better overall by Sayajirao than they were by Khanderrao. Even more important, Baroda offered a space within which the hybridity of a Maula Baksh could flourish. Biographical remembrances of Baroda's court occlude both its colonial modernity and its contradictions. In these narrative accounts, nostalgia is deployed solely to criticize the modern character of contemporaneous circumstances combined with a valorization of an unchanging "tradition." That this revered tradition was always located either somewhere else, or in a time "before," only makes clearer the extent to which it was real only in its critical function with respect to the present.

The Musician

The musician who was most vilified for having given in to the maharaja's many idiotic experiments was Maula Baksh Ghisse Khan. Maula Baksh was the superintendent who, in Kapileshwari's account, used notation as an intellectual bludgeon with which to drive away visiting musicians. In his time, Maula Baksh was a powerful figure. He was the head musician (*pramukh*) of the *kalavant karkhaana* and a friend of Baroda's *dewan*, Madhav Rao.[75] He virtually founded a musical dynasty in his own name—distinct from the prevalent *gharana* system—and he was known by colonial and court officials as "Professor Maula Baksh," an unusual title for a musician in his time. He and his male progeny aggressively claimed for music and its practitioners a status that at least in name suggested that they were more than mere *sarkaari nokars* (court servants), even if that was their official designation. After his death, he was valorized by his disciples as "The Late Mowlabux Founder of the Indian Musical Notation."[76]

What is singularly important about Maula Baksh, apart from all this, was his role in creating a cultural sphere in Baroda that extended beyond the boundaries of the actual court. In many cities in British India, a cultural sphere was emerging in the late nineteenth century. It was a small sphere, catering to a growing bourgeoisie that was urban, middle-class, and educated. Newly formed education societies encouraged women to learn music, while music appreciation societies held classes and semipublic performances. These institutions of musical learning and performance made possible the consumption of music as a form of entertainment by an audience different from the ministers and nobles of a princely court. The nature of entertainment was also changing, becoming increasingly more respectable, pious, and restrained. Most striking, colonial understandings of religion and culture had started to enter this sphere, and new distinctions between Hindu and Muslim, as well as between classical and nonclassical, were beginning to take hold in the world of art and music. In the twentieth century, possessive notions of "our" culture and art would move Muslim performers to the sidelines as incidental contributors to an ancient tradition. But in Baroda, at around the same time, Maula Baksh expanded the world of music without recourse to any of these exclusionary categories. As the cultural sphere was being primed to cement distinctions and differences, Maula Baksh was blurring those very same distinctions by setting music's agenda as both folk and classical, North and South Indian, Hindu and Muslim.

We have little firsthand knowledge of Maula Baksh, barring his grandson's memoirs. The accounts that fall in the category of "informal" sources do not follow any of the protocols of academic history writing. Let me pause briefly to say a word about the genre of musical biographies. Most biographies of musicians are written under the banner of truth, usually by an author who had been the musician's student. The purpose of the biography is to put to rest all circulating rumors and falsities. Truth, by the terms of this conceit, inheres in the student's memory. It is neither a critical nor a critically scrutinized memory, and most biographies, although some are far better written than others, follow a pattern. For the most part, they are collections of moral fables that have a thin narrative or historical thread running through them. It is rare to find an argument about a musician and his time. Instead, the musician is figuratively turned into the exemplary man or woman, whose impeccable character shines through every page. His life is depicted as a series of minor epic battles over evil, malice, and the forces of untruth. Tale after tale piles up, punctuated occasionally by the lapidary moral lesson.

These biographies are the bulk of the secondary source literature in music. They are interesting for what they suggest symptomatically both about the genre and about music in particular. Musicians are depicted as childlike. Their brilliance is precocious, not rational, and their naïveté is a marker of their otherworldliness. They are also wedded to family tradition and are deeply spiritual, sometimes devout. If there is attention to history, it is limited to a simple chronological fetishism. Inordinate attention is paid to whether this or that date of a performance is accurate or perhaps off the mark by, say, one year. That said, biographies constitute the archive that music historians have to contend with, and it is not an archive that can be either dismissed (as useless) or celebrated (as exemplary subaltern writing) for having consciously resisted the rationalist and nationalist protocols of history writing. Barring biographies, the available material itself is not very voluminous; a preface here and an introduction there offer the rare date or some other nugget of information. One stumbles across a rare pamphlet, but in the secondary source literature, it, too, is not critically or symptomatically read but seen as indisputable evidence of that which is already known.

While most musicians have been turned into godlike figures, Maula Baksh is unusual in being depicted as a royal sycophant who cravenly followed the ruler's every misbegotten Western idea, such as founding a school or inventing a notational system. This alone makes him an interesting figure for having escaped the beatification most other musicians routinely received from their students. What stands out even more than his vilification, however, was the resentment about his hybridity. Compared to Faiz Mohammed Khan, his rival in Baroda—considered the "true" musician, interested in none of these frivolous and newfangled activities such as notation—Maula Baksh was indeed a man who seemed well adapted to the more colonial feudalism of Sayajirao.

Maula Baksh was born in 1833 in a village in what is now Haryana in the north of India and studied vocal music from Ghasit Khan as well as the *been* (a stringed instrument).[77] Ghasit Khan's brother was Faiz Mohammed Khan, the musician with whom Maula Baksh would maintain a longstanding rivalry in his years at Baroda.[78] His initial choice of career was wrestling, but he moved to music fairly soon. He began his professional life in music by performing in a popular theatrical form called the *lavani*. His first job was at the court of Mysore, where he encountered South Indian (Carnatic) music for the first time. In Mysore, he came to appreciate that South Indian music's practitioners did not see themselves as simple mimics repeating by rote what they had heard other singers or players perform. They believed that South Indian music had a long, traditional, and classical history. All Maula Baksh's biographers, formal and informal, agree that through the knowledge of music he acquired in South India, he recognized himself anew as an artist, not just an entertainer. Wishing to know more about South Indian music's history, he left Mysore and proceeded south to Tanjore, where he met a famous musician, Subramaniam Aiyar, who taught him both Sanskrit and the compositions of Tyagaraja and Dikshitar, two of the great eighteenth-century composers of Carnatic music.[79] Following these lessons, he returned to Mysore a little before 1863.[80]

Given his newly acquired prowess, Maula Baksh was once again employed in Mysore, but he left in a year, got married, and, in the course of his musical tours, arrived in Baroda somewhere between 1863 and 1870.[81] In 1870, in association with a close friend, Ramchandra Viswanath Kale, Maula Baksh founded one of India's earliest music magazines, *Gayan-abdi-Setu*.[82] The magazine was short-lived but foundational for its time. Consisting of six pages, it contained information about singing and playing. No copies of this magazine have survived, and information about it is anecdotal. The name of the magazine offers a clue about the personality of its founder: it means a "bridge across the ocean of music." The bridge, however, collapsed rather quickly. The first issue was published in April 1870 with an annual subscription cost of Rs. 3. Two months later, in June, the price was raised to Rs. 4 to accommodate rising costs, and by August the magazine was defunct. But the daring of the enterprise itself established Maula Baksh as a pioneer.

Soon thereafter, Maula Baksh left Baroda for Hyderabad at the request of Sir Salar Jung, prime minister to the Nizam. He returned to Baroda but was suspected by courtiers of collaborating with the British to overthrow the ruler. Suspicion fell upon him because of his friendship with the colonial Resident, from whom he apparently learned about Western staff notation.[83] He left Baroda again to travel and, in 1875, was a guest of Calcutta's wealthy *zamindar*, musician and patron Raja Jyotindramohun Tagore, who invited him to teach music to his grandson. Pleased with his grandson's progress, Tagore commended Maula Baksh to the viceroy, Lord Northbrook, following which Maula Baksh began to be known as "professor of music."[84] He also traveled to Jaipur and Hyderabad and returned to Baroda for the last and final time during Sayajirao's reign (1881–1939). During Sayajirao's reign he was made head of the *kalavant khaata* and began to implement his institutional ambitions for music by founding a school.

Maula Baksh founded his school of Indian music on February 1, 1886. It was recorded as an "interesting and novel institution on this side of the Bombay Presidency," and as "an experimental measure" designed to supplement general education "with a view to teach[ing] the science and art of music as an accomplishment to students of the 5th and higher Vernacular Standards."[85] Maula Baksh's credentials were endorsed as well. "Professor Maulabux [*sic*], the *well-known scientific native musician*, was placed in charge of this school, and the necessary musical instruments and other articles were supplied." Presumably, Maula Baksh's desire to use notation to teach music was what had earned him the appellation of "scientific." In this he was not alone. Experiments with notating Indian music along Western lines were also being performed in other parts of India.[86] What set him apart from other modernizers was his integrative approach to North Indian music.

The first raga that all students had to learn was *Shankarabharanam*, a South Indian raga. He also used a typology for ragas that he had learned in Tanjore, anticipating what later modernizers, including Bhatkhande, would do. He added his own notation system based on the European model to these two borrowings from South India. Given his personal training in both North and South Indian music, itself exceptional, Maula Baksh clearly wanted to retain all facets of his training in the new school. He was not a professionally trained Carnatic singer, but a singer of the North Indian compositional form called *Dhrupad*, and he trained his students mostly in North Indian musical compositions. However, because his school was based on the "Karnataki style of music," he began with a South Indian raga.[87] Famous singers such as Abdul Karim Khan, who visited Baroda during Maula Baksh's tenure, ridiculed his integrative use of South Indian ragas to teach North Indian music and dismissed his attempts at notation as an attempt to curry royal favor.[88]

Founding a school based on the North Indian style of music would have been important, no doubt, but to found a school teaching North Indian music using South Indian ragas was for its time quite unusual. A combination of circumstantial factors aided his efforts. Most Gaekwad rulers favored music and dance from Tanjore, which was not only a center for South Indian cultural activity, but one that had been ruled by the Marathas in the eighteenth century. Marathi was still spoken in the court through the late nineteenth century. Both Sayajirao's first wife (she died in 1884; he remarried in 1885) and Madhav Rao (also a friend of Maula Baksh) were natives of Tanjore and were well disposed to its cultural activities. Consequently, Maula Baksh's desire to teach North Indian music using what he had learned in his travels in South India received royal support such as he might not have received in another court. Finally, his own training, eclectic and well rounded, provided the individual expertise required to implement an integrative curriculum. All these factors notwithstanding, it is to his credit that he imagined, with Baroda providing the ideal historical conditions, a school based on Hindustani music that used Carnatic techniques of learning. The nonconformist nature of his approach did not discourage the seventy candidates who applied at the school's opening. Thirty of these were picked for admission, and the exam held to ascertain their merit revealed enough talent to designate the school as a permanent institution with an annual cost to the state of Rs. 1200.[89]

In the following year, two more classes were added for the Gujarati and Marathi Girls' School, raising the total number of admitted students to fifty-two.[90] The school was open to both sexes, but classes for the boys were held in the evenings so as not to compromise their other studies. A student of the school, Pandit Brijlal, remembered that "in the same preliminary education school we got musical instruction free of charge, in the evening from 6 pm until 7 pm, from the school of the famous musician Professor Maula Baksh

. . . In this school my musical education continued for six years."[91] For all that Maula Baksh was seen by his detractors as aping the West by favoring notation and institutional learning, his rival in the Baroda court, Faiz Mohammed Khan, considered the "truer" of the two musicians, did the same. Within the year, Faiz Mohammed Khan founded his own school "on the Hindustani, or Upper India, style." In the years to follow, both the "hybrid" and the "true" musicians, Maula Baksh and Faiz Mohammed Khan, battled over the field of musical education.[92]

Both men competed for resources and funds for their schools. In 1887, G. S. Sardesai, newly hired as Sayajirao's secretary, remembered the differences between both men in his dealings with them.[93] Sardesai later went on to become a well-known historian of Marathi history, and his letters offer us a rare firsthand account of Maula Baksh's personality and demeanor.[94] Within a year of his arrival in Baroda, Sardesai wrote, "two of Baroda's musicians, the first one's name was Maula Baksh and the second was Faiz Mohammed Khan," came to meet him.[95] "Both were Musalman [Muslim]. I could not understand their language very well. Both were *sarkari nokar*s [court employees] and wished to present their complaints to the Maharaj. Both had music schools and needed funds, space and had come to tell the Maharaja about their difficulties . . . I deduced their intentions to be that Maula Baksh wanted the *jaltarang* established in the school whereas Faiz Mohammed wanted the sitar." The requests for the schools left less of an impression on Sardesai than did the difference in attitude between the two men.

Sardesai gave them both the once-over: "Very quickly I also understood the differences in their personalities. The differences between them in both physique and behavior were not such as to be easily concealed." We are fortunate that Sardesai's letter included a description of the musicians. "Maula Baksh was well-built, forceful looking, obdurate, dressed in very colorful and ornamented clothing, a colorful *pheta* (headgear similar to a turban) on his head, and robust, twirled mustaches," and Sardesai added, "this was not just his appearance but also his demeanor." He noted, with humor, that Maula Baksh did not appear to welcome his mediation. "He said to me that he did not want to tell me—a young boy such as me—his request. He said, let me meet the Maharaja, I'll tell him what I want myself." The conflicts between the two musicians resounded through Baroda for the next several years. Because of his position as Sayajirao's secretary, Sardesai was able to procure an audience for both musicians with the maharaja on one of his rare appearances in Baroda, something he had to arrange since neither musician had direct access to him. Sayajirao did not so much settle the matter as defer it; he ordered them both to put their requests in writing and agreed to give them his due consideration. "Maula Baksh was one to push his opinions on everyone and make his influence felt," noted Sardesai in closing. As Sayajirao's secretary, he was not impressed by the confidence of a mere *sarkari nokar*, but perhaps because of his pushy personality, Maula Baksh was able to make his presence known despite whatever irritation he might have caused, especially in the spread of musical education in the state.

Both schools were initially successful and, in 1888, Sayajirao authorized the opening of another music school in Patan some miles outside Baroda.[96] A few years later, in 1891, yet another school was founded in Navsari. Six years after the founding of the first school, there were four music schools for boys and two music classes for girls, using both Marathi and Gujarati.[97] Of the four music schools, two were within the city, in Raopura and Dandia Bazar, and two outside, in Patan and Navsari. Maula Baksh ran the school in Raopura and Faiz Mohammed Khan ran his own in Dandia Bazar. In 1893, an additional section on Tanjore dance was added to the repertoire of music classes but enthusiasm for broadening the curriculum was perhaps premature and the dance class was cancelled in the following year. The music schools had done enormously well from the date of their founding and could afford to experiment with the curriculum, meaning that the loss of the Tanjore dance class was not a major event. In 1893, the schools registered 353 boys and 108 girls as students. The numbers had risen tenfold in less than a decade following the founding of the first school.[98]

While both Maula Baksh and Faiz Mohammed Khan ran their own schools, Maula Baksh's agenda was much larger than that of his rival, which may explain his school's survival well past its initial success. In 1887, one year after his school was up and running, he embarked on a publication project. He put forth his idea for notating Indian music along European lines and received support to supervise the printing of "a set of books on oriental music on the western system of notation."[99] He authored the first of these books in Gujarati using his full title: Professor Maula Baksh Ghisse Khan. Beginning in 1888, Maula Baksh and his sons published eighteen short books on music education, including in them not just Marathi compositions, Gujarati *Garbas*, and Urdu *Gazals* but also notated compositions of English songs such as "Home Sweet Home," "Gaily the Troubadour," and "God Save the Maharajah," set to the music of, predictably, "God Save the Queen."[100] In 1891, he supervised the translation of *Sangit Parijat*—a seventeenth-century treatise on music theory—which was undertaken by the Gaekwad Oriental Series, founded to excavate and publish old manuscripts. In addition, he supervised the editing and translation of eight additional works on "original music," which is to say works in Sanskrit. These translations moved ahead quickly. By 1893, the translation of *Sangit Parijat* was completed and the translation of *Sangit Ratnakara* (a thirteenth-century Sanskrit text) was deemed close to completion.[101]

In 1895, the schools of the two musicians were compared in the annual report. Both had started promisingly, but Faiz Mohammed Khan's school was not doing so well as that of Maula Baksh.[102] The number of students who had appeared for and passed the annual examination was used as the yardstick to determine the relative merits of each school. In Maula Baksh's school, ninety-four students had appeared for the examination and seventy-six of them passed. Such was not the case with Faiz Mohammed Khan's school.[103] More than half the students taking the examinations had failed.[104] The school had gotten off to a good start, even sending thirty-one of its young women students to perform in Sayajirao's new palace in 1890, but five years later it was foundering compared to Maula Baksh's school.[105] In all fairness, however, it must be mentioned that all examinations were conducted with, as the report put it, the "aid of Professor Maulabax," and given the rivalry between the two singers, perhaps Faiz Mohammed Khan's students had to work against a built-in handicap. At any rate, his school was shut down shortly thereafter, leaving the field of music education in the state of Baroda solely in the hands of Maula Baksh and his sons.

Maula Baksh had established himself as an exceptional institution builder by 1893, which is why perhaps Sayajirao Gaekwad paid for Maula Baksh's second son, Alauddin Khan, to study music in England. Alauddin Khan did his father proud. He returned a doctor of music, having passed the "highest examinations on music in England."[106] A few months before his father's death, in February 1896, Maula Baksh's other son, Murtaza Mustapha Pathan, known as "Dadumiya," sang before the court and was appointed to the *kalavant khaata*.[107] Dadumiya was appointed Maula Baksh's assistant in the central school of music, which put him in the prime slot to eventually take over his father's position.

Maula Baksh died on July 10, 1896. He received an official obituary in the annual report of the Vernacular Educational Department, which noted that "the science of native music, at all events in this part of India, has suffered an irreparable loss in the lamented death of Maula Baksha [*sic*]."[108] But his two sons and grandson kept his legacy alive. Murtaza Khan was made the head teacher of the Baroda Music School in 1896, and Alauddin Khan, upon his return from England in 1897, was appointed bandmaster and superintendent of all three music schools. Maula Baksh's grandson, Inayat Khan, began his musical career by performing in Baroda's *darbar* in August 1895, for which he received a Rs. 5 scholarship.[109] From such a small start, Inayat Khan went on to become a famous musician and prominent Sufi leader in the early twentieth century.

Both of Maula Baksh's sons maintained the spirit of innovation fostered by their father. In 1895, the year before he died, what had begun as a class designed to teach girls to sing to the accompaniment of musical instruments had blossomed into the founding of a girls' orchestra. The orchestra, once founded, performed with great success at opening ceremonies, public exhibitions, and important state ceremonials.[110] By 1898, the schools were routinely teaching vocal music to the accompaniment of instruments, the boys were taught the fiddle, sitar, harmonium, and *tabla*, and occasional scholarships were given to deserving students. In 1904, pupils from the music schools were reported as having opened classes in "Bombay and other parts of India and through them the music and notation of Mowla Baksh [*sic*] have acquired a wide celebrity," and by 1905, diplomas and certificates in music were awarded for proficiency in the various instruments taught in the schools.[111]

It was not just his sons who carried on Maula Baksh's project. Shivram Sadashiv Manohar, one of Maula Baksh's pupils, founded "The Bombay Moulabux Music School," also known in Marathi as "Mumbai Gayan Vadan Shala," in 1902.[112] He published a short pamphlet called *Swaraprastaar*, in which he declared that notated knowledge of the seven pitches and their various permutations and combinations was essential and basic to music learning. Like his teacher, he, too, wrote in praise of Carnatic music and musicians, stating that "those singers and players do what they do with full knowledge but our singers and players, even if they work harder than those musicians can not find a pitch or tell one what they are doing. This is because they don't even know the seven pitches."[113] In 1904, there were eighty students in the school, and yearly anniversaries were celebrated with fanfare and orchestral performances.[114] A few years later, Manohar wrote and published a relatively large, 120-page book called *Sangit Shikshak* (*The Music Teacher*). He laid out basic information about singing, dancing, and the playing of instruments, a range of compositions, information about the *tabla*, sitar, and harmonium, and an annotated glossary of common terms used in music.

While his other students followed in the general direction of Maula Baksh's forged path for music, his son, Alauddin Khan, took the spirit of innovation in musical instruction to new heights. He was superintendent for eleven years, during which time he put his training in Western music to good use. In 1908, students displayed the variety of musical training available in the three schools, as evidenced by the number of examination subjects. Students took exams in Indian instruments such as the *dilruba*, *jal tarang*, and sitar, but also in Western instruments such as piano, euphonium, piccolo, coronet, and tenor trombone. A few students even sat for exams in the theory of music and baritone singing.[115] This was a school Maula Baksh had founded to teach Hindustani music according to the Carnatic style. In the two decades following, it had done much more than had been claimed as its mandate.

By the end of the first decade of the twentieth century, the Baroda school was well enough established to be subjected to outside examiners. Sayajirao invited Pandit Paluskar, the principal of the Gandharva Mahavidyalaya in Bombay, and Pandit Bhatkhande, the well-known music theorist and historian, to evaluate the curriculum.[116] In the early decades of the twentieth century, other musicians would try to elevate the status of music by linking it to religious devotion or constructing a typology and notation for North Indian music based on both Carnatic music and European staff notation. Maula Baksh had anticipated both these projects in Baroda but had implemented them without making music religious or affiliating it solely with Brahminic ideology, as his successors in Bombay and Pune were to do. In the early years of the twentieth century, Pandit Paluskar would sound the clarion call for musicians to consider themselves on par with royalty by virtue of being classical artists. In Baroda, through an understanding of the politics of simple naming, Maula Baksh would anticipate that call by titling himself "Professor" and inculcating in his sons, students, and grandson the same pride in their musical profession. Long before musical instruction for women became commonplace, Maula Baksh's schools were registering strikingly large numbers of women students. In 1908, there were 473 girls who were studying music in the schools. Of them, 320 took exams and 294 passed them.[117] As an index of the success of the endeavor, the numbers speak volumes. Music's better-known modernizers could not claim such success in educating women until several decades into the twentieth century.

Such then is the paradox of princely patronage and the contradictory history of the prince and the musician in the court of Baroda. Sayajirao Gaekwad, a politically liberal and progressive ruler, cared little for music and, in the process of modernizing his court, infused it with newfangled colonial inventions. The situation for musicians was not, on an absolute scale, entirely optimal, but relatively better than it was in other courts. Within this court, Maula Baksh, consummate musician, integrative theorist, founder of institutions, first editor of a music magazine and head of a dynasty, thrived as the *pramukh* of the *kalavant khaata*, where the rules for other artists were restrictive and infantilizing. Reviled by other musicians for his hybridity and integrative approach to music, he turned his knowledge to an inclusive understanding of music without resorting to the kinds of hierarchies that later became naturalized in music. It was a knowledge that he could have acquired only under the conditions of colonial modernity, but his vision for Indian music was not colonial. Before a Hindu-dominated nationalism made such imaginings difficult, Maula Baksh envisioned a music that was nonsectarian, multilingual, and religiously inclusive. He also encompassed within the larger domain of music what later codifiers would separate into Hindu texts and Muslim practices.

Music histories refer to him briefly, if at all, as an early pioneer for having founded a school and invented a system of notation. Although Sharatchandra Gokhale, a senior Marathi scholar of music, had written of Maula Baksh as a *payacha dagad* (foundation stone) of music's modernization, such characterizations are rare.[118] For the most part, Maula Baksh is represented in Marathi biographies of musicians who visited the court of Baroda, such as Alladiya Khan, as megalomaniacal, diabolical, and treacherous, having prevented other talented musicians from securing permanent positions in Baroda. In a recent memoir, his perfidiousness is claimed to have "disrupt[ed] the unwritten code of conduct" in the world of music.[119] This is perhaps true, and my attempt here has been not to whitewash Maula Baksh but to remark on an early instance of border crossing—geographical, musical, religious—that appears the major hallmark of Maula Baksh's contribution to the world of music.

Historicizing Nostalgia

In March 1916, twenty years after Maula Baksh's death, the first All India Music Conference was held in Baroda. Pandit Bhatkhande, one of the outside examiners of Maula Baksh's school, was its chief organizer and Sayajirao was the royal patron. At the opening ceremony, girls and boys from Maula Baksh's schools sang the glories of Sayajirao Gaekwad and his wife, Maharani Chimnabai. They sang compositions in raga *bahar* and *bhairavi* to the accompaniment of an orchestra.

Three years later, Pandit Paluskar, the other outside examiner of Maula Baksh's school, hosted his own music conference in Bombay and invited his old teacher, Balkrishnabua Ichalkaranjikar (1849–1926), to give the presiding address. Balkrishnabua had been a court musician in first Meraj and then Ichalkaranji (hence his last name), and he reminisced about the bygone days of the splendor of royal patronage. Those were different days, he claimed, when music affected true devotees such as the maharaja of Gwalior, Jayajirao, who "stood on the streets in the pouring rain for hours on end," rendered immobile by the beauty of Baba Dixit's singing.[120] For Balkrishnabua, the days of princely patronage were halcyon and gone forever, replaced by modern schools and notational systems. But how had the combination of institutions and colonial modernity changed music, other than in the ways imagined by Maula Baksh?

By the first two decades of the twentieth century, music had taken its place in the cultural sphere, primarily because of the institutionalization of musical pedagogy and, in part, because of the changes underway in domains related to music. Music drama, one of the chief performing venues for musicians in the region, had become increasingly Sanskritic when not Shakespearean. Puranic mythology and upper-caste ritual forms of worship had become naturalized as part of musical education. Musicians themselves, many of whom were Muslim, were seen as talented savants who were holding an emerging nation's heritage hostage by their secretiveness and intransigence. Women were increasingly being recruited to use music as a proselytizing tool, beginning with their children at home. A new understanding of "Hindu religion" was taking hold in the cultural sphere. Strict separations were emerging between North and South Indian music, and *dhrupad, dhamar,* and *khayal* were classified as "classical," leaving *lavani* and *tamasha* to fall by the wayside as lowbrow and inappropriate for respectable audiences. All these factors combined to produce a very different future for music than had been imagined and implemented by Maula Baksh in princely Baroda. Yet when Balkrishnabua remembered the best days of princely patronage, he was not speaking about Maula Baksh's integrative and inclusive vision of music, he was speaking of the days when Jayajirao of Gwalior stood in the rain to listen to a musician.

The point here is not to focus ungenerously on an old and feeble musician for not recognizing the modernity of a princely court, but to remark critically on what would become the script for nostalgia for *rajashraya* despite massive evidence to the contrary about musicians and maharajas.[121] Nostalgia is not the only problem here. Close to a century later, scholars writing on music are unwilling to acknowledge that there was anything at all modern, let alone colonial, about princely states, preferring to accept them as the authentic remnants of Indian royalty. In doing so, they simply repeat what Balkrishnabua said eighty years ago. In this perception, they are joined by those anthropologists and ethnomusicologists who also deny colonial influence, positing instead a romantic and exotic princely India as the living spirit of an ancient tradition.[122] A new group of historians accepts the evidence of colonialism but sees princely states as exemplars of prenationalist resistance.[123] They attempt to replace not only a colonial perception of princely rulers as primarily upstart brigands with too much money, but also a critical nationalist perception of rulers as colonial toadies. Baroda was colonial, modern, and feudal all at the same time. Attention to these constitutive contradictions explains how and why Maula Baksh could envision a school for North Indian music based on his musical education in South India and still conjure up a musical curriculum that could include the teaching of the violin, training in baritone singing, the piano, and clarinet.

Maula Baksh's legacy in Baroda is unmistakable. The fledgling school of music he founded in 1886 celebrated its seventieth anniversary as the College of Indian Music, Dance, and Dramatics in 1956. In the souvenir publication, Maula Baksh is acknowledged for having founded the school and invented a notation system. Yet the violence of modern historiographic writing on music is revealed in the very pieces that claim to do him justice. Inasmuch as he is acknowledged as a pioneer, he is virtually unrecognized for his integration of North Indian and South Indian music. While he is recognized for having invented a notational system, he is not applauded for having encouraged women to learn music. While he is celebrated for having done so much for "our" music, he is not credited with having put forth a nonsectarian under-standing of what that music could be. Those who retain and enshrine his memory do so solely in terms of his notational and institutional contribution. Had his musical hybridity been as celebrated on its own merit, or as much as his institutional contribution, it might have preempted the modern history of music this book will go on to tell. This is a history in which the cementing of hard and fast distinctions between religions, regions, and languages became naturalized in late-twentieth-century national classical music. But before they could do so, music had to move out of princely courts and into the larger public sphere. How it did so is the subject of the next chapter.

❋ TWO ❋

MUSIC ENTERS THE PUBLIC SPHERE

Colonial Writing, Marathi Theater,

and Music Appreciation Societies

In this chapter, music moves out of the secluded world of princely states into a larger public domain. In order to get a sense of this domain, let us recall from the previous chapter the Baroda musician Abdul Karim Khan, who sang at the court for four years. Abdul Karim Khan was a *gharana ustad* who performed in princely courts before moving to Bombay where he set up a school for music, among other things. We shall meet Abdul Karim in some detail in the last chapter and follow his career as a famous musician. In this chapter, the focus is not on Abdul Karim's career but on the creation of a public cultural sphere, one in which his daughter, Hirabai Barodekar, made a name for herself in music.

Hirabai was one of the first women to act and sing on the Marathi stage, to record devotional music, and to give classical music performances. She was also a happily married woman with children. What was the nature of a public cultural sphere in which the female child of a nineteenth-century Muslim court musician could imagine for herself a career in music that was both respectable and recognized as such? Who and what were the agents in creating a public space women could enter? In the nineteenth century, women musicians were known as *baijis*—a euphemism for women of ill repute.

When Hirabai began her career, she too had to battle the perception of women musicians as disreputable. By the middle of her career, she was known in musical circles by her family nickname, and she gave her last performance as a respected national artist. This could have happened only if the "woman question" had become central to the making of the public cultural sphere.

The gendered public cultural sphere Hirabai entered in the 1920s was not a unitary public sphere, in the Habermasian sense, brought into existence by literary activity or conventional political discussions. Instead, it was simultaneously literary, aural, visual, and dramatic. In the making of this multifaceted cultural sphere, music was a key participant. This chapter takes as its central problematic the history of music's transformative role in the creation of a gendered, and national, public cultural sphere and, at the same time, the transformation of music itself.

In the coming together of this multidimensional cultural sphere, no single event can be isolated as its inaugural moment. In all likelihood, it came together in bits and pieces in the culmination of several minor histories. The histories do not have obvious connections between them, and often the meeting points are contiguous rather than continuous. This chapter focuses on three seemingly unrelated historical trajectories that together contributed to the early emergence of the cultural public sphere: the colonial sociology of music; early education and music appreciation societies; and the transformation of Marathi folk theater into respectable Marathi music drama (*sangeet natak*) theater.

There are significant ties between these three abovementioned histories. Sir William Jones's influential article on the music of the "Hindoos" inaugurated a colonial sociology of music. Beginning in the late eighteenth century, journals such as the *Indian Antiquary* published ethnographic descriptions of a variety of music, from fishermen's songs to *ustadi* music. The group of writers, here termed colonial commentators, included army officers jotting down their observations and sending them to journals, travelers penning travelogues, and civil servants taking down notes. In general, they assumed there was a unified Hindu community defined by and subservient to religion. Consequently, they began with the premise that to understand Indian music, it was necessary to understand Indian religions. Colonial writers shared Jones's sense that Indian music was "Hindoo"—religious and national—but they did so without any of his appreciation of the civilizational complexity of Hinduism (or Islam) or his antiquarian and historicist conception of the idea of the "nation." Furthermore, unlike Jones, these commentators focused their attention on the many deficiencies of Indian music. In expanding and building on Jones's work, three modern concepts—nation, notation, and religion—emerged as the sine qua non of music.

Colonial writers saw these three concepts—nation, notation, and religion—as central to Indian music, in relation not merely to its definitional criteria but also to what Indian music needed in order to become classical. The introduction of these criticisms into public discourse generated an almost immediate response from native writers, many of whom were members of newly founded music appreciation societies. They took seriously the colonial charge that music needed to be religious, notated, and national, publishing a number of notated compositions and pedagogical texts. Their objective was to demonstrate publicly that notation was easy to incorporate within an ancient system of music that had always been both religious and scientific. Insofar as this was colonial mimicry, notated texts also paved the way for facilitating a base-level knowledge of music that would be further disseminated in sophisticated ways by late-nineteenth-century musicians and lay music scholars through their own publications.

An important by-product of this flurry of activity was that women, even though in the nineteenth century they were far from being viewed as respectable performers, could begin to learn music at home using notated pedagogical guides; by the mid- and late twentieth century, women could even envision the possibility of a career in music. There were, of course, limits to who could entertain these dreams and how they could live them. Even though reformers thought of "woman" as both the goal and the instrument of music's reform, the beneficiaries of their efforts to change music's perception, pedagogy, and performance were upper-caste, middle-class women—not all women, by any means. Furthermore, even middle-class women could only go so far and no further. Theater remained dominated by men well into the third decade of the twentieth century, and women musicians were only just beginning to be considered respectable performers. What is clear, however, is that notions of gendered respectability were central to the creation of a public cultural domain.

The public art form that underwent changes particularly relevant to women was Marathi music theater (*sangeet natak*). In the eighteenth and nineteenth centuries, princely courts such as Baroda were hospitable to traveling troupes offering an eclectic fare. Toward the end of the century, the troupes metamorphosed into theater companies that enlarged the audience for music at the same time that they offered new opportunities for performers who wanted to break free of an earlier mold. Performances by these new companies moved out of informal and spontaneous small-town and village settings to fixed buildings and halls in urban cities and were advertised through pamphlets. Not merely large princely states such as Baroda but even smaller states like Meraj, Sangli, and Ichalkaranjikar had immediate connections to Marathi music theater. It was in the small princely state of Meraj that the famous Marathi singer/actor Bal Gandharva launched his career by singing in the title role of Shakuntala. As Kathryn Hansen has pointed out, Bal Gandharva—a man playing a woman's role—played his part so well that middle-class women imitated his speech patterns, the manner in which he draped his sari, how he wore flowers in his hair, and even his walk.[1] Musicians such as Abdul Karim Khan looked askance at such cross-dressing, but his daughter, like many other middle-class Marathi women, was entranced by Bal Gandharva. Hirabai not only mimicked Bal Gandharva's singing, she also found theater vastly appealing. It offered the opportunity for fame and the potential for financial independence along with the chance to perform in public.

After examining the links between the three histories narrated in this chapter, it will be clear that colonial sociology had a much more direct connection to the publications of music appreciation societies than to the development of Marathi *sangeet natak*. However, in late-nineteenth-century cities like Pune, theater companies translating Shakespeare's *Hamlet* into Marathi solicited the opinions and approval of high-ranking colonial army officers, some of whom wrote about music and were occasional patrons of the theater. Music directors of the early Marathi stage were hired as teachers by music appreciation societies to teach small classes of young men. Military personnel were also connected to the key patrons of the new *sangeet natak*, namely princely state rulers and their *dewan*s as well as urban industrialists. Both Bhatkhande and Paluskar, the subjects of the next two chapters, had dealings with music appreciation societies and music theater, and both were keenly aware of colonial (mis)perceptions of music. Colonial sociology, music appreciation societies, and *sangeet natak* had more links among them than are readily apparent. To tease out these connections, this chapter begins with an examination of colonial writings on music.

Colonial Writings, Notation, and Native Responses

It is possible to divide early-nineteenth-century writing about music into two basic categories: anthropological and Orientalist. Archaeologists discovered temple sculptures depicting musicians and instruments and ethnologists cataloged the different "songs" and "airs" sung by fishermen, washerwomen, oarsmen, and other laborers in different parts of the country. Articles on music were published in journals such as *Indian Antiquary* and *Asiatick Researches* (the journal of the Royal Asiatic Society, the first issue of which was published in 1788). Lay travelers noted their descriptions of performances and musicians in their journeys across India, which were published as anthropological observations about the peculiar culture of Indian music.[2] While these de facto colonial anthropologists focused on performance, costume, and the timbre of voice, Orientalist scholarship, in keeping with Jones, was uninterested in performance. The classicizing impulse in Orientalist scholarship linked highbrow intellectual music to esoteric Hinduism, philology, etymology, and music theory.

After Jones, commentators on music were not all learned scholars of language and philology, but also included military officers who had some interest in music. Lt. Col. Robert Kyd, for instance, penned his observations on Indian music while serving as a member of the Bengal Army. He sent his notes to Sir William Jones in the hope that they might be published in *Asiatick Researches*. It was also not uncommon for army officers to accept employment as bandmasters of princely state armies. One of the many functions of the British army in India was to demonstrate the order and precision of the colonial state through secular processions such as parades. The army marched on festive occasions, such as the coronation of a new king in England, and on mournful occasions, such as the death of a duke. It also came out in full regalia, complete with a marching band, for all events staged by the colonial government that required ceremonial pomp. In princely India, too, rulers used their armies, often led by retired British army officers, to mimic British military pomp and show.[3] Military bands were sometimes the sole source of musical entertainment for stationed military personnel. In the 1850s, for example, officers of the East India Company's navy held their soirees at the Bombay Club to the musical accompaniment of a military band. Additionally, military officers, as representatives of colonial rule in India, were invited to events at music appreciation societies and the theater, as we shall see in later sections. Some of these military officers—whether they worked for the Company or a princely state—were the first de facto ethnomusicologists of India. That their writings were taken seriously is evident in the care with which Kyd's notes are cataloged and kept in the manuscripts collection of the British Library under the title "Indian Music." Army ethnographers such as Kyd did not necessarily appreciate Indian music by the standards of a Western high art tradition but accepted that it was treated as such by its practitioners and listeners. They described the performance of music as an exotic ritual and translated unfamiliar pitches into terms recognizable to an audience schooled in Western high art music. They also wrote in a language that was recognizably Christian in tone, judgment, and sentiment.

N. Augustus Willard, a captain in the British Army who commanded the forces of the Nawab of Banda, wrote an influential tract on music, *A Treatise on the Music of India,* first published in 1793. An important as well as representative writer, his work was cited by later, native writers as exemplary for its appreciation of Indian music. Similar to other authors writing in the same period, his account of Indian music was anthropological. He described the varieties of music sung and performed, debated with other European writers about minutiae, and listed many of the fables that accompanied the performance of ragas such as *Deepak,* which the best musicians refused to sing for fear of setting their surroundings and themselves ablaze. Willard's account was marked by his ethnographic interest in music, but it also carried with it a passionate missionary tone.

Willard had none of Jones's love for India, nor did he share his respect for paganism, Greek or otherwise. "The invention of all arts and sciences . . . has always been attributed by heathen nations to beings of superior order, of celestial origin, to demigods," he wrote, in contradistinction to Sir William Jones, who understood the "celestial origins" as the voices of the Brahmins.[4] Like Jones, he too viewed Hindus as constituting a nation, but he had none of Jones's admiration for its antiquity. Yet it was neither this nation named India, nor the religious community identified as Hindu, that bore the brunt of his most damning observations. Those were reserved for the Muslims. "The Hindus, although an idolatrous, were never so luxurious and vicious a nation as their conquerors, the Muhammadans; most of the vices existing in this country having been introduced after the conquest." This was just for starters.

Willard's account was deeply concerned with behavioral and psychological issues related to religion. Drunkenness was the subject of most Indian songs, he claimed, misreading the metaphorical significance of "intoxication" as the result of an encounter with divinity, common to both bhakti (devotion) and Sufism, but hardly unknown even within heterodox Christian practices of worship. On the subject of alcohol, Hindus, according to Willard, were slightly better off than the Muslims because they, albeit of a lower order, had a religious escape hatch from the ill effects of libation. "The fear of the loss of caste, in the want of sound religion and refined morality, acted as a very wholesome check against promiscuous and unguarded indulgence of passion, except amongst the very lowest classes of society and outcastes." Not so in the case of Islam. Muslim monarchs and nobles aspired to excessive consumption of alcohol as a goal. "They know no medium," claimed Willard; "it was, and now is, drunk by such as make use of it to excess. They never dilute their liquor with water and, in times of their prosperity, it was contrived to be so pure and strong that it could not be drunk, in which case roast meat was a constant companion to liquor, in which they dipped the bits of roast, as we do in sauce."[5] Willard's judgments on both Hindu heathenism and Muslim machismo suggest an ideology weighted less in favor of ethnographic accuracy and more in Christian moral outrage.

Music in India was tied to a weak sense of social responsibility, he wrote, as evidenced by polygamy, child marriages, and the position of women. Willard saw a sociological connection between lyrics that conveyed a woman's desire for reconciliation with her beloved, the heartbreak of betrayal, or the hours spent waiting for the anticipated arrival of a lover, as literal if slightly poetic depictions of a generalized indifference in which Indian men held their women. A different religion had caused such a state of affairs, and the advent of Muslim rule had brought about "the decline of all arts and sciences purely Hindu, for the Muhammadans were no great patrons to learning, and the more bigoted of them were not only great iconoclasts but discouragers of the learning of the country. The progress of the theory of music once arrested, its decline was speedy," he concluded. Willard combined the seemingly irreconcilable tropes of Muslim essentialism and Muslim licentiousness into a singular cause to which could be attributed both the lassitude he associated with Hindu heathenism and the destruction of music. It is also evident that there was a hierarchy of evil in his account. While Hinduism was heathen and idolatrous, it did not pose a threat of the same magnitude as Islam.

Willard's treatise on music was one of the sources most cited by late-nineteenth-century Indian writers, along with the writings of Sir William Jones. However, they were rarely quoted in detail. Furthermore, even when the odd comment made by one of them about the lyricism or beauty of an "air" or movement was quoted, none of their historical, ideological, or religious passages was ever brought to light, let alone subjected to critical scrutiny. Like Jones, Willard was referred to simply as an early European who wrote on Indian music. This simple fact was held sufficient to demonstrate, or even prove, that discerning Europeans deemed Indian music a subject worth paying attention to, but the precise nature of the attention so bestowed was rarely considered. If Willard began the crusading process for music in the 1830s, Lieutenant C. R. Day of the Oxfordshire Light Infantry, stationed in Pune at the end of the nineteenth century, brought it to a somber and quiet close in his book, the South Indian equivalent to Willard's treatise on North Indian music. Day wrote more gently but just as firmly in his belief that for Indian music to take its place alongside other national music it had to be brought within a European fold, defined yet again in moral terms as excluding undue passion, flourish, grimace, and embellishment.

The publication of Day's manuscript was neither simple nor straightforward. The tortuous route that his manuscript had to traverse before it saw the light of day had to do with the question of his credentials. When he first submitted his manuscript to an English publisher, Thacker Spink and Co., it was rejected. The author of the letter, dated June 1886, was polite, appreciative, but unambiguous. "It is quite out of the question to undertake the production of [the manuscript] in India," he wrote, claiming that such a work was commercially unsustainable. Day was advised to seek a special publisher who focused on music publications or request the government of India and the secretary of state to commit to the purchase of a certain number of copies, which would help to defray the cost of publication.[6] In such a manner, the colonial government in Bombay was brought directly into the matter of publishing one of the three most influential works on Indian music written in English.

Day took his publisher's advice and wrote to C. S. Bayly, undersecretary to the government of India in Poona. He justified his request for financial aid with the claim that while there had been an increased interest in music, there had been correspondingly few useful books published on the subject of music: "With the exception of some works by the Rajah S. M. Tagore, and those of Sir William Jones and Captain Willard, there exist as far as I am aware no books which give anything but a cursory account of the national music of this country."[7] Day claimed that his manuscript would fill the need for a detailed work on Indian music, but the undersecretary of the Home Department was unconvinced. He forwarded the entire matter to the secretary of the government of India, requesting the governor to opine on the matter "generally and especially as to whether Lieutenant Day's qualifications are such as to render it probable that he will produce a thoroughly good work on Indian music."[8] The governor's office asked for the opinion of the Military Department. The commander in chief referred it to the adjutant general. From the adjutant general's office in Poona, a report was filed in September 1886.

The officer commanding the infantry division of which Day was a member reported simply that he was "unable to say whether Lieutenant C. R. Day [had] special qualifications for producing a good work on Indian music," although he was willing to acknowledge Day's knowledge of music in general. He also noted that Day had been assisted by various notables, such as the ruler of Mysore, the musicologist S. M. Tagore, and the secretary of the Madras branch of the Poona Gayan Samaj (PGS). This report was forwarded in September 1866 to a Mr. Chatfield, the director of public instruction, who suggested, coming full circle, that the "Government should place the ms in the hands of some gentleman learned in music for opinion."[9] The government concurred with Mr. Chatfield's opinion and forwarded Day's manuscript to two men: M. M. Kunte of the Poona Gayan Samaj and K. N. Kabraji of the Gayan Uttejak Mandali (GUM). The colonial government, the army, music appreciation societies, and maharajas were all now implicated in the publication of the book.

Between 1886 and 1891, when the book was finally published, the Education Department claimed that it was a "very valuable contribution to Indian musical literature," but because "music is unfortunately not included in our 'Education'" decided not to forward copies of the book to the director of public instruction, recommending instead that a copy be sent to each of four libraries in the city of Bombay, one to the Poona Gayan Samaj, and perhaps an additional one to Mr. Kabraji.[10] The fracas over publishing and Day's credentials notwithstanding, the book soon attained pride of place in the colonial lexicon of musical works, buttressed by the support of the GUM and the PGS.

Day's *The Music and Musical Instruments of South India and the Deccan* was more detailed than previous books, hand-illustrated, and beautifully designed. In thirteen chapters, Day laid out the details of Indian music: its history, geographical specificity, and theory along with musicological explications of ragas and talas. At the outset, he identified how music in India was frequently misperceived: "Almost every traveler in India comes away with the idea that the music of the country consists of mere noise and nasal drawling of the most repulsive kind, often accompanied by contortions and gestures of the most ludicrous description."[11] This was not the impression he wished Europeans to maintain. Day's appreciation of music resembled Jones's more closely than it did Willard's, though Day quoted profusely from Willard as well as Jones. India possessed "music of great intrinsic beauty," wrote Day, and if Europeans would only leave their prejudices behind, they would soon learn to appreciate its wonders. Like Jones, he declared that all Indian music was ancient Hindu religious music derived from the Vedic chant, which Day regarded as bearing the same relationship to Hindus as the plainsong did to Christians.[12] Day asserted as well that "the earlier music of the Sanskrit period bears a close resemblance, as far as we can judge, to that of the ancient Greeks, going far to prove that music has been derived from the same Aryan source." Jones had stopped short of such an assertion, claiming that no real knowledge about ancient Greek music was available. Without Jones's scholarly reticence to make assertions without philological demonstrations, however, Day was more confident. Talented Muslim musicians were few and far between. Although he accepted that Maula Baksh of Baroda was one of them, he added that "Mahomedan music, taken as a whole, has little to recommend itself even at the present day."[13] Yet what was "Mahomedan music"? None of these three foundational authors defined or in any other way described what they believed constituted "Mahomedan music." Hindu music originated from the Vedas; this was assumed. But was it the case that Mohammedan music had originated from the Quran? Could it have been the music sung and played by Muslim musicians? This was never considered Muslim music. Or perhaps it was a subsection of Indian music that had developed during the Mughal period? No author described it adequately, nor could they have, even as they were clear in their dismissal of it.[14]

Day also wrote that although Indian melodies were beautiful, they were rarely well sung. In an illustrative passage that demonstrates how much early writing on music scorned the actual practices of musicians, Day wrote that singers of the ordinary type often entirely ruin the effect of the music; for native singers appear to have an idea that the highest form of their art consists in introducing as much grace as possible, whether it adds to the beauty of their songs or not; in fact, they try to disguise the real melody as much as possible by embellishments of their own, and so, in nine cases out of ten, it is quite impossible to follow either the air [raga] or the words of a song, since the singer is only anxious to exhibit what he fondly imagines to be his skill.[15]

But skill—individual and improvisational—was the defining characteristic of the music Day was listening to. Yet he argued that "native singers rarely practice, for they think that practice, to even a moderate extent, ruins their voices" and wrote further that the voices of the musicians "are almost always weak and deficient in volume—one result doubtless of their system of training, by which a full clear tone is made to give way to incessant small inflections." Women singers fared no better in this tribunal. "Girls, too, are taught singing when much too young, so that their voices either break or become harsh and shrill." And finally, the performance of music was simply unacceptable. "A singer rarely stands while he sings," wrote Day, "and instead of using his proper range of voice, he prefers a most unnatural falsetto, which he can rarely control." However, this accusation is immediately countered by the assertion that "there *are* singers in India whose voices are wonderfully sweet, and when they sing their own songs in their simple form, no hearer can doubt that, like other national music, that of India possesses a charm peculiarly its own." Jones's early understanding of the Vedic chant as the essence and embodiment of pure Indian music returns to center stage through Day's ethnomusicological survey a century later.

Day's beliefs about Indian music emerge in full relief when we identify the contradictions in his positions. First, Indian music had a training regimen that involved no practice but was nonetheless systematically producing deficient voices, both male and female. Second, Indian music was being sullied through its performance, seen in this case as modern contamination by superstition and ignorance. Third, musicians, by insisting on improvisation and embellishment, were camouflaging true melodies to the point of indecipherability. Day's standards for evaluation were so rigidly European that it was unlikely that any performance of Indian music would have satisfied him. For this music to have met with his approval, it would have needed to be performed without melismatic graces, without improvisation, and without complexity by standing, not seated, musicians. In other words, it would have had to be something other than Indian music. In retrospect, the colonial government's hesitation about Day's credentials appears quite reasonable.

Nevertheless, Day was one of the more influential of the many English writers who followed in Jones's footsteps because he wrote a history in which the ideal of music bore no relationship other than a negative one to the actual performers and their performances. Day enacted in his own writing precisely what he enjoined other Europeans to eschew. He imagined Indian music in European classical terms, divorced it from performance, and misread it as authored not by a composer, as in a European high art tradition, but by the performer. Such a misreading gets to the heart of early English writings on music. Faced with the absence of the composer as author, writers such as Willard and Day took upon themselves the task of attributing authorship either to Sanskrit texts or to themselves as the new scribes.

While both Willard and Day referred in reverential terms to Sir William Jones, what most distinguished the two military men from him was the recognizably Christian tone of their writings. Conceptual descriptions that have embedded within them Christian missionary passion, such as "heathen" or "idolatry," are absent from Jones's prose, whereas they punctuate the writings of Willard and to a lesser extent Day. Jones expressed no desire to turn "Hindoo" music European either by notation or by denuding it of passion, as suggested by Day, and his prose lacks the vituperation of a fictive Muslim propinquity to alcohol, for instance, as voiced by Willard. Perhaps one can see, in retrospect, why a scholar such as Sharatchandra Gokhale, who was aware of Jones's condemnation of Mughal translators, nonetheless believed that no European writer about India could ever measure up to him.

These three authors—Jones, Willard, and Day—exemplify much of the English writing on music in the eighteenth and nineteenth centuries. Musicological passages, asides about the potential beauty of Indian music, and statements about Indian music's antiquity are sometimes quoted by other writers. On occasion, their mistakes are gently pointed out as the misperceptions of otherwise discerning connoisseurs. Rarely if ever are their historical passages quoted and examined. If I have cited only nontechnical, nonmusicological, quasi-historical, and editorial passages, it is because the musicological details themselves do not reveal the full-blown Western and Christian ideologies that suffused these writings. These were the key books that later modernizers used to construct a comprehensive theory of Indian music. V. N. Bhatkhande, the leading scholar of music, took Day's book with him when he embarked on his four tours of the country, searching for the true history of India's music. He cited Jones, Day, and Willard in his theoretical texts. The conception of Indian music as Hindu, which began with Jones and was reiterated in new ways by Day and Willard, would take on a rather different life in an emerging period of Indian nationalism. What had begun as a Biblical quest for Jones in the late eighteenth century had come to a close with a Pyrrhic victory for Christian proselytizing writers such as Day by the end of the nineteenth century. Indeed, as was often the case even with missionary activity in India, one of its unintended consequences was that it fostered an evangelical Hinduism. Missionary activity may not have persuaded caste Hindus of the need to convert to Christianity, but it frequently brought about the implementation of Christian organization within a newly conceived evangelical Hinduism. Likewise, while Indian music did not turn itself Christian, as Day had advocated, it did embark on a bhakti-influenced devotional path. And insofar as music came together with devotion in the nineteenth century, it was increasingly combined in urban centers with the movement for women's education in general and musical education in particular. What linked women's education with their musical education was the ability to read—and play or sing—notated music.

Educational Reform and Music Appreciation Societies: 1848–1900

Women stood at the center of musical reform in educational reform associations and music appreciation societies. These associations advocated a particular and circumscribed education for women on the assumption that Western-educated Indian women might then take on the responsibility for achieving the ideal of companionate marriage. Musical education was one of the key components of this overall female education, since it could be used to link women with both purity and antiquity, on the one hand, and nationalism, on the other. An early institution that offered this kind of secular education to both the Marathi and the Gujarati community was the Students Scientific and Literary Society (SLSS).[16] It was founded in June 1848 by four men, Dadabhai Naoroji, Naoroji Furdunji, Sorabji Shapurji Bengali, and Bhau Daji, all of whom had studied at Elphinstone College, founded in 1834.

The initial intention behind the founding of the society was that it function as a quasi-public debating forum to discuss intellectual issues.[17] The society did not survive as a single cosmopolitan intellectual venue for long, soon splitting along linguistic lines into three separate but linked societies, one each for Gujaratis, Marathis, and Parsis.[18] The inaugural meeting of the Marathi wing was held in September, and the president of the Sabha declared its aims to be the dissemination, in Marathi, of subjects of classical nature.[19] The differences between these three societies notwithstanding, they had in common one cause, namely, women's education. Between 1849 and 1851, the SLSS founded schools for young girls, one each for Marathi, Gujarati, and Parsi students.

In the year that the first of these schools was founded, the population of Bombay was estimated at 566,120, including 296,431 Hindu, 124,155 Muslim, and 114,698 Parsi.[20] Muslims were a larger community in number than the Parsis, but the society's vernacular schools excluded Muslim girls. By 1856, the year before the Great Rebellion, girls were receiving instruction in reading, writing, and arithmetic. Two books of moral songs were used to teach them singing.[21] Long before music was formally acknowledged as a subject for serious study in institutions of formal learning, the SLSS introduced it as part of the curriculum in vernacular schools. It had a role to play. It was to be the instrument that would instill in these young women the appropriate and necessary morals they would need in a new world.

In 1862, the committee of the SLSS perceived a serious want of books on a number of subjects such as drawing, health, domestic medicine, and domestic bookkeeping. It also perceived the need for a "simple Educator on singing especially adapted to the females of this country."[22] A prize of Rs. 200 was offered to anyone who could write a reasonable but small treatise on music. In 1863 Raosaheb Vishwanath Mandlik, industrialist, patron of the Marathi theater, and secretary of the SLSS, mused about the state of music in the society's annual report: "Music has met with a curious treatment in India. On the one hand, it is regarded as sacred and used on the occasion of all social and religious festivals; while on the other, it is considered immoral or at all events unfit for respectable persons of either sex. In this dilemma, the Society has deemed it proper to pursue the middle course, and to this, I trust, it will always adhere." He pointed out that "whilst adopting music as an integral part of its curriculum, [the Society] is careful to give no unnecessary offence to time-honoured customs, which can only be reformed by the silent, but unceasing influence of a higher standard of moral feeling."[23] The SLSS's officers were inaugurating a new voice for music, one that was couched in the language of morality, a language perhaps learned from colonial masters.

Mandlik was in favor of the SLSS paying some attention to the question of music instruction. "Music, purified and improved by a high moral tone, will drive before it many of those vices which unfortunately prey over native Indian society," he wrote, noting that "the high character of the agency employed by this Society in popularizing this essential branch of female education has hitherto maintained its prestige unimpaired." Yet Mandlik was not prepared to make any radical suggestions. Although the SLSS was quite prepared to discharge its responsibility, it was also "content to flow its bark along with the tide instead of incurring the danger of running it aground by unnecessarily sailing too boldly in shallow waters."[24] He was willing to add music to the curriculum and write passages about the need for uplifted morality, but left the larger issue of music's reform to other societies. His interest in adding music to the curriculum had to do with the desire to broaden and modernize women's education along colonial lines, which for him meant the introduction of notation in musical instruction. In order to accomplish this goal, the SLSS needed more than ennobling rhetoric: it required teachers and textbooks.

Mandlik persuaded his friend, Govardhan Vinayak Chatre, and his brother, Nilakanth Vinayak Chatre, to prepare a small treatise on music, titled *Geetlipi*. In 1850, Bhaushastri Ashtaputre had published *Gayan Prakash*, a hand-illustrated history of ragas and *ragini*s. Mandlik, however, wanted to do more. In the preface to *Geetlipi*, he remarked on his original intention: "For many days now I have wished to bring out a book on music based on present knowledge and through which the art of singing and playing could be made easier by notation in Marathi."[25] Mandlik had commissioned the book as a potential text for the Marathi branch of the SLSS vernacular schools. The 1864 publication of *Geetlipi* made it one of the earliest notated Marathi textbooks of music used in curricular instruction in Bombay.

In the introduction, the authors identified the lack of notation as causing the near demise of music in India altogether. "Although numerous singers and instrumentalists have visited our country, they did not have the knowledge of notation and their art died with them," wrote Govardhan Vinayak Chatre. But he was quick to note, "It is not that our people have no knowledge of such matters; we have numerous treatises on music . . . but we do not have the resources we need to teach the art of singing."[26] The perceived problem was instrumental rather than either epistemological or intellectual, and the absence of notation was not a native problem. In *Geetlipi*, Chatre foresaw no problems of inconsistency with what he had written in his introduction, and he used, without modification, Western high art notation—the bass and treble clefs—to translate ragas for easy learning. Halftones were translated into Marathi literally as *ardhaswar*, and altered pitches within the septet were reclassified according to sharps, flats, and double flats. He used the bass and treble clefs to notate not just pitch but meter as well. Chatre died before *Geetlipi* was finished; the manuscript was reviewed and edited by his brother, Nilakanth Vinayak Chatre, and a Mr. Narayan Shastri.

Shastri had been recently appointed to the Marathi school as the music teacher, and in his classes he used *Geetlipi* as the assigned text. His appointment and teaching proved to be a mixed success. It produced "happy results, some of the girls being now able to show real skill in the art." As a teacher, he was seen as "labor[ing] under a mistake in teaching those pupils only who have a naturally pleasing voice and who can join with others in a chorus."[27] Shastri's emphasis on teaching only musically gifted girls went against the philosophy of the SLSS, which was interested not in producing female prodigies or women musicians, but in using music as an instrument of educational reform.

While the SLSS had embraced notation as an instrumental means by which to further the education of women, other associations were less enthusiastic. The Poona Gayan Samaj (PGS, founded in 1874) declared in 1876 that it was not only opposed to notation but proud of Indian music for having resisted it: "The Samaj will be instrumental in preserving our nationality in the sense of our possessing an indigenous art of singing which unlike English music has challenged all attempts at its being reduced to writing."[28] But such an attitude posed another problem. Virtually every English writer on the subject—from Lt. Col. Robert Kyd, who sent Sir William Jones his observations about music in the late eighteenth century, to Lt. Gen. Mark Kerr, stationed in Pune, who urged the secretary of the Poona Gayan Samaj to notate Indian music in the late nineteenth century—saw notation as fundamental to music. Notation consequently became a prominent issue in the debate about Indian music, as it was linked to a native science with an ancient pedigree.[29]

In its early years, the PGS had undertaken the publication of a series of musical treatises in Marathi, the first of which, published in 1878, was

Svarashastra or *The Science of Sound*.[30] In this flagship publication, the author demonstrated that Indian music was scientific (that is, modern) and encompassing of all virtues seen to be present in the extant Western high art music of the time. Not only had Hindu music invented a scientific system of notation, it also possessed its own scientifically derived complex harmonies: "We have in our ancients the means by which to keep our music written. It is neither new nor needs to be searched out. Indeed, it is given in the *Rag Vibodha* [a thirteenth-century Sanskrit treatise on music]."[31]

The assertion of the existence of India's ancient notation system was not, however, the same as showing the applicability of such a system to contemporaneous musical practices. Purshottam Ganesh Gharpure, an early author of a musical textbook and founding editor of the Marathi magazine *Sangeet Mimansak* (1886), went the extra mile in this direction. In his notated treatise on the sitar, *Sataareeche Pahile Pustak* (*Book on Sitar*, no. 1), published by the PGS in 1883, he explained how he had made use of ancient notational systems: "There are signs and symbols that had been long decided by the writers of these ancient Sanskrit texts . . . those that were useful I have retained in exactly the same form but have added some more to make the notation simple and clear."[32] Notation had become a matter of national equivalence and a key to Indian music's recognition in the larger Western world as a classical music.

Notation became the lynchpin for other historical claims as well. In 1887, writing as the representative voice of the PGS, its secretary, Balwant Trimbuck Sahasrabuddhe, stated unambiguously that Hindu music was not modern. In fact, he went on, Hindu music's lack of modernity was its strength. In explication of this claim, Sahasrabuddhe wrote: "If Hindu music had been a growth of modern times, containing all the several charms of different musical systems, it would perhaps have answered the expectations of these connoisseurs." However, he assured his readers that "upon the testimony of works of great antiquity lying around us (some 4,000 to 8,000 years old), we can safely affirm that Hindu music was developed into a system in very ancient times; in times of which we have no genuine records; in times when all other nations of the world were struggling with the elements of existence; in times when Hindu *Rishi*s were enjoying the fruits of civilization, and occupying themselves with the contemplation of the mighty powers of the eternal Brahma."[33] Jones could not have said it better.

Gharpure made much the same point in a short book that he had coauthored with V. M. Herlekar, an educated connoisseur of music who had three years earlier written the first letter to the editor that was published in *Sangeet Mimansak*. The letter was in the form of an essay on music in which Herlekar quoted from diverse sources, including Jones. It ended by commending the work of societies such as the Poona Gayan Samaj. In *Studies in Indian Music* (1889), Gharpure and Herlekar declared their intentions: "The chapter we are going to write is very important in the literature of music. It can safely be called the corner stone. . . . Those who take any interest in the science of music can be safely divided into two classes. One is exclusively for the art, the other is for science and art both. We beg to assert that we belong to the latter class. . . . We speak with pride that our music properly so called has a thoroughly scientific foundation."[34] Note that in this case, Hindu music is described as Indian music. Although the school had been initially reluctant to embark on notation, PGS music teachers Balkoba Natekar and Narayan Daso Banhatti compiled a series of graduated musical texts in Marathi, *Bal Sangit Bodha,* which were used in various PGS classes. Additionally, the PGS published musical treatises relevant to Carnatic music, such as the English *Treatise on Hindu Music* by Mr. Seshagiri Shastri and a series in Telugu for primary musical education by Mr. T. Shringaracharlu, a member of the Madras branch, all of which used notation.

In the first year of the twentieth century, Pandit Paluskar, founder of the Gandharva Mahavidyalaya in Lahore, claimed that "our notation system that has come down from the Samaveda has been lost, so our knowledge is lost. The proof of this is that when I studied English music, I found out that we have not the practice of notating our music." In order to rectify this loss, Paluskar claimed to have "consulted weighty texts and invented a system of notation . . . liked by both English and native people."[35] Notation as a concept served many purposes. It allowed native writers to translate their music into a language that allowed for easy comprehension by Western readers. Notation also enabled music to be disseminated as printed text without the permission of actual performers, and facilitated the transformation—whether fictive or otherwise—of an ancient theory into a modern method, offering further proof of India's innate superiority in the field of classical music, along with complex mathematics and science as they pertained to music theory.

Because early writers tinkered with India's ancient notational system to make it applicable for modern use, they also rushed to notate a variety of Western ditties for elite anglicized consumption at the same time that they notated Indian melodies for Western instruments. In 1883, Pramod Kumar Tagore published *First Thoughts on Indian Music, or Twenty Indian Melodies Composed for the Pianoforte,* an attempt on his part to "compose tunes on Indian themes and to arrange them according to European system of music." In 1889, Priya Nath Roy published *Indian Music in European Notation,* including in his compilation English verses set to Indian airs and Bengali songs in European notation.[36] Rajah S. M. Tagore set English verses to Hindu music in honor of the Prince of Wales, translated a Vedic hymn into English, and set it to Western notation. He even set the English national anthem, "Rule Britannia," to the raga *Hameer Kalyan.*[37]

The question of notation, while important in the last years of the nineteenth century, was both more and less influential than many had feared. Many Indian writers and some musicians readily adopted notation as the means by which to render Indian music more comprehensible and accessible to Western listeners. In so doing, they no doubt bore witness to the extraordinary influence of colonial epistemology. However, while notation served a few instrumental ends, none of them produced "Westernized" Indian music. In fact, notation soon encountered the limits of its transformative power. While notation transformed an oral tradition into a written one, suggesting that it had thereby vanquished the resistance that was mounted by many musicians, not only did it fail to make performances any more somber, as Willard and Day recommended, it also reflected, paradoxically, the ultimate triumph of the musicians. While notation was embraced by many musicians, it was seen by others as a threat to their professional position. In the long run, the fears of the musicians, although understandable, were groundless. Notation never took over the entire system of classical music as English writers believed it needed to do. Even the most enthusiastic Indian supporters of notation saw it in instrumental terms. In the late nineteenth century, Maula Baksh (and Pandit Paluskar in the early twentieth century) used notation to demonstrate that native bands, composed of native instruments, could play music in unison. While there were minor skirmishes over which notation system to use, when it came right down to it, notation worked less at the level of the performer than it did in the creation of a musically educated audience. What was much more central to the formation of the public sphere was the colonial understanding of all music as religious.

There are two principal reasons for this. The first is that the highly acclaimed European ability to read music right off the page simply did not translate into a worthy ideal in the higher echelons of professional music. Notation enabled the beginning music student to understand and memorize the basic rules and parameters and helped in the creation of a musically educated listening public, but that was all. If students chose to move into a professional arena of performance they were evaluated and judged not on their ability to "read music right off the page," but on their improvisational and expositional skills. In the world of professional performance, learning was by rote, by improvisation, and by practice (*riaz*), which Day confidently claimed was absent from the world of most singers. No professional musician needed notated melismas as aids or guides for performances; had they hypothetically ever chosen to use sheets of notated music while performing, they would have been seen, at best, as amateurish, and, at worst, as inadequately prepared or incompetent.

The second reason is that at the professional level, Indian music was (and is) fundamentally a performer- and performance-centered system. Even if the performer was not named as the composer or author per se, the very structure of Indian music privileged the individual artist rather than a real or notional composer. Indeed, Indian classical music, as it is raga-based, allows for every artist who performs a raga to, in effect, author his or her own composition. This means that while all musicians can be considered composers, there is inherent to Indian classical music no conceptual category analogous to that of the single composer in Western classical music whose compositions require notation in order to be faithfully played as they were written. In the absence of a central role played by a composer in Indian classical music, duplication for duplication's sake simply does not have great value. The emphasis on notation could be a feature only of a music dominated by individual composers, whereas Indian music was dominated by individual artists and performers. This was not a feature of the music that was ever recognized as such by colonial writers. Indian music bore (and still bears) a negative relationship to the faithful duplication that notation would have made possible. Put simply, there is a large investment in the absence of duplication and repetition, even as improvisation is not expected to drift too far afield of set rules and parameters. While raga-based music does not have a conventional European narrative, it nonetheless does have a recognizable formal trajectory with a beginning, middle, and end. Yet, if professional performers rendered with exactitude what they had sung/played on a previous occasion, disapprobation would have been heaped on them. Indeed, in some cases, as in Baroda in the late nineteenth century, musicians had to sign a contract stating that they would consciously eschew duplicating their performances.

Finally, notation was useful in preserving and documenting the names and rules of the one hundred different ragas commonly sung or played. But once most ragas had been ordered into groups (called *mel* or *thaat*) and meters had been notated, notation had served its use. Furthermore, even with forms such as *khayal* and *dhrupad,* which are sung in short couplets, minimal notation was required to record them for posterity. This is not to suggest that notation was useless or that it disappeared off the face of Indian music. However, it was not the trumpet call that brought down the walls of Jericho. Notation loosened some of the layers, no doubt, but the edifice of music, epitomized by performers, adjusted to these minor seismic changes. Indeed, the limited use of notation can be seen as not just the limit of colonial mimicry but also the resilience of an alternative modernity on the part of the performers themselves.[38] In the imagination of writers like Willard and Day, notation might have been the key that would have transformed what they saw as a disorganized craft into an organized, disciplined, and professional art, but it never came to pass. The notation of music, its supporters and detractors notwithstanding, did not turn Indian music into a professionalized career option for talented students. But it did do something else. Notated books of music, used as part of women's educational programs, changed the composition of the audience. Notation allowed for a previously impossible access to music that made for a new audience that had some, if only a rudimentary, knowledge of the theoretical basics of music. Musicians had many reasons to worry about notation, but what they eventually had to contend with was not the challenge it posed to them professionally, but rather a new audience that would make demands they could not quite afford to ignore.

Notation may even be said to have facilitated the movement of women into the musical sphere, a path previously denied them by both hereditary *ustad*s and the conservative dictates of patriarchal society. To that end, notation served a useful end, if a different one from what had been imagined for it. In this regard, notation worked in tandem with concerted efforts to link music to general efforts to bring women into education. One of the three splinter societies of the SLSS, the Parsi Dnyan Prasarak Mandali, pioneered the project to link women, music, and education. A key member of the society, Kaikhushroo Naoroji Kabraji, was a man of many talents and contradictory impulses. He was a member of the Bombay Municipal Corporation and a loyal subject of the crown. He supported women's education and was interested in theater, having adapted Persian plays in Gujarati.[39] He was also editor of the Gujarati newspaper *Rast Goftar.* In 1870, he founded the Parsi Gayan Uttejak Mandali.[40]

In the report of the GUM, written not merely to document the workings of the GUM but to highlight the contribution of the Parsi community to social life in Bombay, in particular, and India, in general, Kabraji received a stirring portrayal. Parsi ancestors were described as "gritty Zoroastrian warriors" and "crusaders," of whom Kabraji was the best example. During the tenure of his leadership, he fought to bring music to women at the same time that he encouraged middle-class women to fight to keep their marriages alive by bringing music into their lives. But what music? Not the music of courtesans or even the "mishmash of Narsee Mehta's *bhajans*" (Mehta was a fifteenth-century Gujarati saint), which Maula Baksh had included in his teaching repertoire in Baroda, but a different music, one much more overtly linked to the temple and religious devotion and that would foster modern companionate marriage.

Like other industrialist reformers such as Mandlik, Kabraji viewed music as an acceptable means by which to bring respectable women out of seclusion and more squarely into a battle with the forces that threatened their marriages. Kabraji wanted women to embrace the ideal of companionate marriage, an ideal under threat from the prostitutes and courtesans he perceived as having commandeered the knowledge of music. He was not alone in this perception or in the emphasis on the role of women of ill repute in taking over music. Not only did musicians themselves complain of having to teach their art to prostitutes, even when it was sanctioned by princely rulers such as Sayajirao of Baroda, but even music's early reformers pointed without specificity to the element of debauchery that had pervaded music. British colonial writers had amassed an array of terms to describe music and dance performances, most notably the "nautch," an anglicized form of the Hindustani *naach*, meaning "dance." Kabraji had learned his lessons well, but the women he encouraged to leave their homes and learn music were not those who had unlimited social freedom, but middle-class Parsi women who were kept under as much scrutiny as women from other communities. D. E. Wacha may have had fond memories of the preeminence of the elite "progressive" Parsi community in Bombay's public sphere in the mid-nineteenth century, but as late as 1866, the Gujarati newspaper, *Rast Goftar,* published editorials against women moving about freely in public, opposing any association between them and music. When Kabraji undertook the task of ending women's seclusion by recommending that they learn music—"the prerogative of the condemned class, the concubines, and whores"—he could only invite controversy.[41]

Kabraji was not easily discouraged. He accepted that "the rich [maintained] their sacrilegious practice of bringing the prostitutes home for musical performances, thus spoiling the sanctity of home as also of the divine art," but recommended that if it were possible to encourage "respectable ladies to take to music [that] would be a great service to God and to society."[42] As a member of one of the splinter societies of the SLSS, he believed that music's reform and women's education went hand in hand. The SLSS had instituted music classes in its Marathi vernacular school, and Kabraji attempted the same in Parsi schools. It was not just music but women who were being led into the light of modernity. Both music and women were (re)defined in keeping with their "true" nature, which was depicted as frail, pure, delicate, celestial, and spiritual. And both music and women were turned traditional under the aegis of modernity.

Kabraji urged his readers to turn their houses into the temple of Lord Ahura.[43] He wrote incessantly about the links between music and prostitution and believed that if respectable women could learn music, they could prevent their husbands from leaving them at night for extramarital nocturnal entertainment. Not that Kabraji defended such profligate husbands. In 1866, four years before he founded the GUM, he wrote an editorial in *Rast Goftar* in which he inveighed against "those who love music to the extent of not minding the presence of whores," warning that they "should always remember that music is divine. It is God's gift, a gift He has never denied to a single soul. But, always remember that even crystal-clear water looks turbid in a black vessel. Similarly, music is also threatened in the possession of wrong hands and emits a stink instead of a perfume."[44] In case his stand against men visiting prostitutes was seen as tarring all of Indian music with debauchery, he hastened to clarify his position. "Never make the mistake of assuming that the dancing of whores and Hindustani music are the same," he wrote, adding in a somewhat exculpatory note "that it was a sad turn of events that to listen to music men had no choice but to solicit the company of prostitutes."[45]

In order to take music back from the debauchery of nocturnal entertainment and return it to the "higher" classes, Kabraji appealed to other educational institutions for help. It was not immediately forthcoming, and he again used his pen to solicit support: "Singing is basically a woman's art. It is a woman's duty to become accomplished enough to please her spouse. She is naturally endowed with a melodious voice, and why is there any objection to her using it?" If women were well trained in music, he argued, men would stay at home and not seek out prostitutes for the music to which they sang and danced.[46] Kabraji's efforts to institute curricular reform in Parsi schools did not get off to a flying start, but the new society he founded was quick to get off the ground.

The GUM's first members were all associated in some fashion with music and theater. Dadabhai Thunthi, known as "Dadi Christ," was the owner of the Victoria Natak Mandali; Ferozeshah Rustomjee Baliwala was a poet; Manekshaw Doctor played the *pakhawaj;* Mancherjee Nariyalwala played the sitar; and the list included a social reformer and a barrister.[47] In 1871, the GUM secured the services of a well-known and talented singer, Khan Saheb Imadad Khan, holding its first concert.[48] The performance was in three parts. In the first third of the performance, thirteen different compositional forms including *pada, rang, khayal, tappa, gazal, thumri,* and *dadra* were sung. The second part of the performance was primarily instrumental and concluded with an English song, "Just Before the Battle, Mother," and a reading of "The Trial of Rekurck [*sic*]" from Dickens. In the last third of the performance, the audience was given the opportunity to make requests of the performers. The GUM maintained this format in other concerts held the same year and, at the first annual meeting, the directors of the society decided to continue hosting concerts without throwing them open to the general public.[49]

Three years after the founding of the GUM, Kabraji's repeatedly cited fear that music had been taken over by "whores" had somewhat abated. Kapadia noted that, by 1873, audiences seemed to prefer moral and devotional music to the more licentious compositions they had hitherto chosen. In 1874, the GUM held its first public concert. It was very well received, and the following letter was printed in *Rast Goftar:* "It is a pleasure to acknowledge the recent decision of the Gayan Uttejak Mandali to hold public concerts in Hindustani Music. This *mandali,* consisting of the Parsee gentry, began with a noble purpose to awaken and spread among Parsis a love for music, particularly Hindustani classical music. It therefore offers an intensive training to its members, who eventually display their talents in concerts so far held only for its members; another equally important purpose is to erase the stigma with which music is generally associated. What better way to achieve this than a public performance?"[50]

Although Kabraji wished women to take center stage in modernizing music, they were still not part of either the performance or the audience. Perhaps this was a deliberate tactic on Kabraji's part, since even the small steps taken by him were frowned upon by many observers. Even though the GUM would go on to publish many tracts—little editorial pamphlets and short notated music texts—in newspapers such as *Jaame Jamshed* and *Mumbai Samachar*, it was seen as too quickly and unthinkingly aping the West.[51] However, Kabraji was both undeterred and indefatigable. He worked to expand the reach of the GUM by introducing the concept of "family concerts" and, despite the criticisms leveled against him, he tried to include Western classical music in the *mandali*. On the one hand, his success was measurable—by 1878, he had held eighteen concerts—but on the other, the member tally of the GUM remained relatively small, with only ninety members eight years after the founding of the society. Two years later, in 1880, Kabraji held a concert for children. It was a seemingly innocuous event to host, but it proved to be more than he could handle or ought to have attempted. A journalist named Mansukh wrote disparagingly about the morals espoused by the new GUM, and Kabraji filed a police case against him on the grounds of slander. He brought along a heavyweight lawyer, Sir Pherozeshah Mehta, who presented the printed program sheet of the children's concert to the court, and Kabraji was exonerated of all wrongdoing.[52] Even so, he resigned soon thereafter, bringing to a close a decade of tireless efforts on behalf of music.

The GUM carried on Kabraji's agenda long after his resignation and went on to boast the names of leading progressive Parsi intellectuals and political figures among its members. The GUM continued in existence for many years, adding concerts and classes to its activities. It commissioned portrait memorials for its founders, collected funds for various causes, celebrated Queen Victoria's jubilee, instituted prizes and scholarships for music students, compiled a collection of all the songs performed at the *mandali*, celebrated Parsi, Hindu, and Christian festivals (but not Muslim ones), and published books of poetry by famous Parsis.[53] Between 1871 and 1886, the *mandali* organized thirty-four concerts, of which three were public. Dadabhai Naoroji, the "Great Old Man of Indian Nationalism," the chief architect of the theory of economic nationalism and the first Indian member of the House of Commons in the British Parliament, was not only a member of the GUM but also its chairman for five years from 1885 to 1892. By 1895, the GUM was financially healthy. It had reserve funds in the amount of Rs. 2,500, and by 1897 its membership rose to over one hundred members. However, despite Kabraji's passionate entreaties for the community elders to encourage women to learn music, classes at the GUM solely for women and children would not start until 1912, forty-two years after the founding of the society.

When Kabraji looked back over a quarter of a century of the *mandali*'s activities, he found much to celebrate but also much to condemn. Even though he had begun his career in public entertainment in the theater, he was not in favor of the "stage," complaining that music and theater had become so synonymous that "people are not willing to accept a play, however good, without music. It is only musicals that reign on the stage."[54] He also complained that the GUM had completely lost sight of its original manifesto. "When this Mandali was created, it was with lofty dreams and impressive plans, with the serious study of music as an aim. This aim has been lost altogether. It is now so focused on merriment and partying, rather than purpose, that its name could well be changed to *Khayan* [consumption of food] *Uttejak Mandali*."[55] Yet he was pleased that, because of the GUM, other music clubs had been founded in the city and no stigma attached to music anymore.

When Kapadia, the author of the GUM report, wrote the retrospective, he made much of its eschewing of "religious intolerance." Yet what is apparent is that with a few exceptions, such as V. N. Bhatkhande and his friend, G. S. Chandorkar, the members were Parsi and male. However, following on the heels of the founding of the GUM, other music appreciation societies had sprung up in a number of cities such as Sangli, Dharwar, Kalyan, and Pune. Kabraji warned Hindus who were embarking on their own music appreciation societies to "refrain from the mistakes of the Parsis before them, that is, keep away from card games and other gambling."[56] One society that implicitly took his advice, focusing solely on music, was the Poona Gayan Samaj.

Kabraji's royalism and conservatism was exemplified in the other fountainhead music appreciation society of its time, the Poona Gayan Samaj (PGS), founded in 1874. Its secretary was the energetic Balwant Trimbuck Sahasrabuddhe, who shared Kabraji's temperament and enthusiasm. Sahasrabuddhe was an indefatigable letter writer who dashed off notes to everyone, including the prince of Wales, the governor of Bombay, rulers of princely states, and industrialists. He was thus able to secure the patronage of a number of elite and wealthy people, and the energy and dynamism of the

PGS in the last years of the nineteenth century was a direct reflection of his energy and enterprise. Whereas the GUM was founded mainly to bring music to respectable Parsi women, the PGS began with a much larger agenda and explicitly sought colonial approbation in order to secure a wide audience. This attempt to broaden the sphere of music beyond what had been imagined by the GUM spurred a vigorous discussion published in the English-language newspaper the *Times of India.*

Formal colonial approbation, requiring little other than the occasional token presence of a high-ranking British army officer or civil servant at a musical event, was relatively easy to secure, as such an event at the PGS was relatively small and not likely to garner widespread attention. Sahasrabuddhe, however, must have made a splash with his activities, because two years after the founding of the PGS, a correspondent to the *Times of India,* published in Bombay, wrote strongly against the encroachment of the PGS into the larger public sphere. The article can be read as a statement of Sahasrabuddhe's success. It begins with a deceptively simple statement of fact. "In the year 1874, there was established at Poona an institution called the 'Gayan Samaj.' It was one of the outgrowths of an ambition to revive the ancient Arts and Sciences of India and to restore to the land, under the great seal of time, the glory, and the prestige which have been usurped by the nations of Europe."[57] The article continues in an unpleasant tone. "'Singing,' it seems, 'is one of the original powers of the emotional constitution of the human race.'" Further, "'singing,' as tradition goes, 'allures the denizens of the forest,'" and "'its power to please and amuse cannot therefore fail with human beings.'" The correspondent to the *Times* concludes on a note of polite puzzlement: "In this view has been established the 'Gayan Samaj' for the encouragement of the art of singing including as the objects of its patronage instrumental music and everything in that comprehensive term 'goon.'"[58] The term "gun," meaning virtue/virtuosity/value, is a word common to several modern Indian languages, including Marathi, Hindi, and Bengali, and is difficult if not impossible to transliterate accurately. Why had the society provoked such a negative response? The actual aims of the *samaj*, as stated in annual financial reports, were "To establish schools for regular instruction in music, provide occasional lectures, encourage the revival of the study of singing and popularizing old Sanskrit works, adopt measures to notate music, award prizes for special skills in vocal and instrumental music, hold meetings to discuss additional performances, hold annual concerts as the Samaj's means would permit, and work towards the encouragement of Indian music in general."59

A clue as to why the writer might have been so annoyed with the *samaj*'s activities is offered later in the article. The *samaj*'s energetic founder, Sahasrabuddhe, had approached Lt. Gen. Lord Mark Kerr, commanding officer of the Poona Division of the British Army, to solicit his support. The *Times of India* correspondent praised Kerr for his theoretical knowledge of music (for which no evidence was offered), while reprimanding him for suggesting to the newly founded PGS that it undertake the notation of Indian music. Therein, perhaps, lay the rub. "Bombay, as we all know," claimed the writer, "is chiefly famous for 'music and ladders,' and here by night the sound of tom-tom and the plaintive refrain of 'Tazza-ba-Tazza nazbanaz' is never missing: but we have not yet attained the full blown glory of a 'Gayan Samaj.' So, though we know how miserable we are, we cannot tell, with this terrible example before us, how miserable we may be." In other words, the difficulty of putting up with the sounds of native music was going to be made much worse. Notating music could only mean that it would have increased purchase in the larger world. Consequently, the writer in the *Times* warned his readers that no appointment of a senior British official to the PGS would "reconcile us to a cool perpetuation of these dolorous sounds in black and white." Close to a hundred years after Sir William Jones, European perceptions of music seemed not to have changed at all, and the old debate was once again alive and well: was Indian music simply the wailing of the drunken natives, or an ancient art unknown to ignorant Europeans?

Three months later, a predictable response to the *Times of India* article came in the newspaper *Dnyan Prakash*. The author began by noting that there was nothing so very unusual about the PGS or its stated aims: "It is, we think, the legitimate duty of young India to revive what was once the glory of their country . . . is it a crime, worthy of being made a subject of severe criticism . . . to revive the art and science of India?"60 The *Times*, he noted, had "ever been conciliating and moderate. It has never thrown cold water on sensible endeavours of the natives of this country to do something useful to themselves and their country, and we therefore regard that the performance of the journal originated in caprice which mankind is sometimes heir to." Magnanimity aside, it was difficult to understand the otherwise sensible nature of the newspaper, which had allowed the article to "ru[n] down native music, instrumental and vocal, and reduc[e] it to the level of the disgusting street 'tom tom' and the still more disgusting songs sung by the low caste. . . . The claims of native music, as we understand it, are very high, and those who rank it with street 'tom tom' only betray their own ignorance." Furthermore, he claimed that European gentlemen such as Sir William Jones, Augustus Willard, Sir W. Ousley, and others all had agreed that "Hindu music is based on scientific principle."

Having dispensed this strong rejoinder, the PGS moved full steam ahead. In 1879, two years after this newspaper debate, the PGS opened a boys' school for Indian music with twenty students. The number rose to over one hundred by 1882 and to 150 by 1888, after which it made plans to instruct young girls as well.[61] Early in the PGS's career, Sahasrabuddhe recognized that for the *samaj* to both survive and thrive, it would need the patronage of more than just the wealthy elite of India. He went straight to the top by appealing to England's royal family for their patronage. In August 1882, a deputation from the PGS, made up of two *sirdar*s of the Deccan, Jamshetjee Jijibhoy, fellows of the Bombay University, and eighteen other signatories, wrote to the governor of Bombay, Sir James Fergusson, asking for his help in soliciting the patronage of the prince of Wales and the duke of Edinburgh.[62] In his letter of appeal, Sahasrabuddhe narrated a brief history of the *samaj* and wrote of its larger accomplishments: "The Samaj since its foundation has endeavoured to lay before the community, both Indian and European, the beauties of Indian Music and has succeeded in creating in sympathy with and appreciation of, the science as is practiced in this Country. It has also tended to draw closer . . . the bonds of social friendship, between the two communities."[63] Here Sahasrabuddhe revealed that the communities he wished to unite were not the disparate ones within India but a select Indian community with Europeans in India. With remarkable foresight, Sahasrabuddhe also noted that the great want was that of a musical academy, and he proposed the establishment of such an institute "where the school, a musical library, and Museum of Instruments from different parts of the world may be located and concerts held."[64] Grandiose as his aims were, they no doubt caught the attention of the Governor, whose assistant noted upon receiving the request that "no precedents can be traced either in the General or in the Political Depts [*sic*] recommending any Society for Royal Patronage."[65] The request was forwarded to the Government of India, Foreign Office and, in 1883, the prince of Wales and the duke of Edinburgh consented to become patrons.

The events of 1883 received attention not just from English newspapers but also from the premier Marathi newspaper, the *Kesari*. In reporting the annual program of the PGS, the *Kesari* reported that "this year, the secretary of the Samaj decided to do something new and determined that at least once a year all ragas and *ragini*s should be performed. Morning, noon, evening, and night schedules were somehow put together for four consecutive days and the event was so performed. Raosaheb Balwantrao Sahasrabuddhe was in Madras but the proceedings moved forward without a break and the work of the Samaj is carrying on uninterrupted, despite his absence, for which he should be commended."[66] The patronage of the duke of Edinburgh received mention in the *Kesari* as a gift that could not but "please the well wishers of the Samaj and all loyal subjects of the Raj."[67] Sahasrabuddhe's views on the subject of Indo-European unity were noticed as well: "One particular benefit that society gains from organizations like the Samaj and their efforts is that European and Native peoples draw increasingly closer in affection and understanding."[68] By 1883, the PGS was already a well-recognized organization, hosting a second annual concert in two parts, instrumental and vocal. For the concert, the organizers printed programs and Mahadev Moreshwar Kunte, author of several important works in Marathi, presented a short lecture on Indian music with sets of illustrative plates.[69] The event was attended by notables such as the governor and also by, as noted in the *Kesari*, "a great many important European gentlemen and their madams [wives] . . . and well known Parsis and Natives, which goes without saying." The *Kesari* was both confirming and affirming the PGS's reputation for securing the patronage of the wealthy and elite native Indian population, on the one hand, and colonial dignitaries on the other.

Princes and wealthy *zamindar*s followed suit in lending their support to the PGS.[70] The list of patrons of the *samaj* soon included the maharajas of Travancore, Baroda, Mysore, and Vizianagaram, the Petit family of Bombay (also patrons of the GUM), and Sir Richard Temple and Sir James Fergusson, successive governors of Bombay. In 1886, the *samaj* entertained the duke and duchess of Connaught.[71] The PGS expanded its reach by establishing the Madras branch of the Gayan Samaj with the help of Baroda's *dewan*, Sir T. Madhav Rao, and Sahasrabuddhe appealed to the Maharaja of Travancore to help in securing the services of a teacher who could teach students Carnatic music. Between 1885 and 1886, a branch of the PGS was established in Bombay that, in the following year, celebrated Queen Victoria's ascension to the throne.[72] In 1895, the PGS held an annual awards ceremony presided over by the governor at which Sahasrabuddhe read out the annual report of the *samaj*. The work of the *samaj*, according to the *Kesari*, was going very well.[73]

In 1903, PGS members established a music class at the Pune Training College for men and another for women. In 1904, the *samaj* started music classes in one of Pune's high schools for girls. The Department of Public Instruction soon managed the classes, thereby freeing the PGS from all pedagogical responsibilities. A government music teacher was appointed and the *samaj* ceased to formally impart instruction after 1906, but it was still approached for advice when, in 1909 and 1910, music classes were established in two additional girls' high schools. Even though the *samaj* was not formally involved, the government music teacher was Balkoba Natekar, famous stage actor/singer and a member of the *samaj*; through his appointment, the PGS maintained its influence over music education. The PGS's educational efforts, apart from setting up classes in a number of institutions of learning, were concentrated in the Nutan Marathi Vidyalaya in Pune. In 1905, it had 297 students on its roll. The school was financially supported by a government grant-in-aid as well as by annual subscriptions and donations from wealthy patrons like the Maharaja of Travancore.[74]

There were many links and connections between, on the one hand, actors and directors of music theater, and, on the other, members of music appreciation societies and authors of music treatises. There were also many collaborative exchanges between the PGS and GUM. Kabraji, founder of the GUM, was an active supporter and occasional speaker at the PGS. He offered the services of the GUM's musicians to the PGS, which in turn invited him to be a keynote speaker at one of their events. One of the three non-Parsi members of the GUM was Pandit Bhatkhande, who wrote his authoritative works on Indian music theory and history while enrolled as a member. Bhatkhande also invited Pandit Paluskar, the principal of the Lahore Gandharva Mahavidyalaya, to perform at the GUM, following which Paluskar established the Gandharva Mahavidyalaya in Bombay, where a number of Marathi theater actors received musical instruction. The influential Parsi Petit family became members not just of the GUM but also of the Bombay branch of the PGS. Sardar Abbasaheb Mazumdar, secretary of the PGS, hosted many gatherings at his *wada* (ancestral home) to discuss the inappropriateness of Western notation for Indian music, a theme echoed by Pandit Paluskar when he lectured there.

Obviously, this was a small elite community, made up of upper-class Parsis and Brahmin musicians and musicologists who served on one another's boards and committees. It comes as little surprise that during a time of reform, the community actively supported and encouraged similar activities. What cannot be forgotten, however, is that this was the same period when Muslim musicians made up the majority of performers. Throughout the nineteenth century, the field of music was dominated by Muslim musicians. This is not to say that there were no musicians who were not Muslim, but that there were conspicuously more Muslim musicians than non-Muslim. Why and how this was so is a matter for another study. Throughout the nineteenth century, a familial and quasi-guild system developed, linked to particular families' *gharana*s and their unique performative styles, which came to be seen as a system. Yet, in the new age of reform, Muslims are conspicuous by their absence in these societies as organizers, lecturers, and authors. Here and there a Muslim musician was hired as a teacher at the GUM, and they were still sought after as performers, but while there were many Brahmin students of Muslim teachers, there were virtually no Muslim students of Brahmin teachers. Muslims were also significantly underrepresented in both societies. In 1906 and 1907, only one Muslim was listed as an honorary secretary of both the Bombay and Pune PGS. Why would that be so if the societies, as the author of the GUM report declared, had been formed absent of all religious considerations?

One reason perhaps is that most music teachers in the PGS were typically Brahmins and the non-Brahmin patrons supported the view of India as being fundamentally Brahminic.[75] Most of the students of the *samaj* in the early years of the twentieth century were Brahmin. By 1919, there were 558 Brahmin boys and nine Brahmin girls listed as students, followed by 393 non-Brahmin Maratha boys and one girl. During the same period there were four Muslim students, one "native Christian" student, and five from the "depressed classes."[76] For an overwhelmingly Brahminic society, that there would be one more student from the "depressed classes"—the euphemistic term for the most oppressed of caste Indians—than from the Muslim community speaks volumes, given traditional Brahmin abhorrence of contamination, in which even the shadow of impure persons, whether widows or untouchables, was considered anathema. The GUM and PGS may not overtly have preached an exclusionary rhetoric, but they implemented one all the same.

We might imagine that Muslim musicians would themselves have formed their own music appreciation societies. But the link with educational reform is key to the formation of such associations. Muslims were not targeted for educational reform by an association such as the SLSS in Bombay, just as the offspring of Muslim musicians were not asked to join these societies as key members. The lack of a Muslim Gayan Samaj is not an accident nor, as it is claimed, a result of the community's secretiveness and unwillingness to share musical knowledge. In the face of the juggernaut of musical modernity and an overwhelmingly Hindu public sphere that received colonial approval, perhaps the reticence of Muslim musicians can be read not as inexplicable but as an understandable withdrawal from a movement that so pointedly ignored them. Of course, this raises the question of whether music was a problematic issue in Muslim modernity. The Muslim bourgeoisie in Bombay was Ismaili and Bohra, and while their involvement in education—and female education in particular—is well documented, more work needs to be done related to the question of music and other cultural activities.

The SLSS, GUM, and PGS were all part of an interconnected effort that set the tone for an emerging cultural sphere. While there is no historical evidence to suggest a conspiracy in this effort, the emergence of the public sphere as Hindu was no accident but dovetailed with larger political trends. Aggressive Hindu religious organizations such as the Arya Samaj (1875) took as their agenda the task of making Hinduism a systematic modern religion replete with its own Ten Commandments and proselytizing mission. Others, such as the Sanatan Dharm, also reformist in its agenda, aimed to return Hinduism to its "eternal" truths. Cultural associations such as the SLSS, the GUM, and the PGS, were not, in that sense, unique in their efforts, but they were distinct in picking music as the object through which a larger social and cultural ideology could be championed. Moreover, this ideology about music was furthered through the publishing ventures of the two music appreciation societies. The PGS was one of the societies that published the writings of native scholars who responded to the challenges posed by colonial commentators in their perception of Indian music as lacking in scientific principles or order.

The History of Marathi Proscenium Music Theater: 1843–1933

In the last section of this chapter, I turn to Marathi theater, to return full circle to the beginning of this chapter: Hirabai Barodekar and the road to respectability. The PGS in the twentieth century boasted among its members and teachers artists the likes of Balkoba Natekar. Theater was not as acceptable to K. N. Kabraji, who found it abhorrent. Marathi theater in the late nineteenth and twentieth centuries elicited a range of responses. For women like Hirabai Barodekar, it was captivating. For musicians like her father, it was reprobate and immoral. For an artist like Bal Gandharva, it was his road to stardom. Marathi theater brought together the world of princely states with music appreciation societies and performers who wanted to break free of preexisting molds.

In the early part of the nineteenth century, traveling troupes performed folk theatrical forms such as *bhaand* (mimes), *lalit* (shows given on auspicious occasions), *bahuroopi* (impersonations), *bharud* (allegorical talk drama), *gondhal* (sung and danced ritual performance), *chayanatya* (dance form), *kalsutri* (puppet shows), and various kinds of *khel* and *tamasha* (light-hearted theatrical productions) for spontaneous audiences in village centers and wealthy homes.[77] Many of these productions drew their inspiration from the bhakti poets of Maharashtra, in particular Eknath (1533–1599), who conveyed spiritual, moral, and ethical messages to people through the medium of folk theater.[78] The ideological thrust of most bhakti-inspired messages was aimed at Brahmin domination and control of the means of spiritual salvation. The productions were not theatrical in a classical sense, but rather performances in which the audience participated. Although the space in which the actors performed was separated from the onlookers, the audience surrounded the performers and actors, except in the case of a *tamasha*, where they faced them. Additionally, devices other than a curtain were used to signal entrances and exits, beginnings and ends. Either the *sutradhar* (the storyteller) sang a couplet or even a limerick to move the narrative along, or else a *pati* (a length of cloth held up horizontally as and when needed) was used to screen some actors from the onlookers. These theatrical productions were held in town squares, temporarily constructed *pandals*, or large private courtyards typically constructed to allow a surrounding audience.

The birthday of formal Marathi theater is celebrated as November 5, 1843, when the ruler of the small princely state of Sangli, Chintamanrao Patwardhan, ordered Vishnudas Amrit Bhave, a talented sculptor and craftsman, to stage a production of *Sitaswayamvar* (Sita's marriage, adapted from the Ramayana). He greeted the idea with great enthusiasm.[79] Bhave had been much impressed with a troupe from North Karnataka, Bhagwat Mandali, which had come through Sangli in the same year. Concentrating on puppetry until then, he was inspired by the performance of the Bhagwat Mandali, expanding and developing theatrical productions based on Puranic mythology.[80] The prose dialogue was not scripted, and a great deal of it was delivered impromptu by the actors. Bhave's theater audiences in rural areas were not distant, silent, and anonymous masses. They exclaimed loudly when the demon appeared on stage, advised the actors how to proceed, and sometimes threw themselves into the action, so the lack of scripted dialogue did not stand in the way of effective drama. Moreover, Bhave's productions were not viewed as plays (*natak*), but referred to as *khel* (a term used to denote lighthearted entertainment as opposed to formal theater) for much of his professional life. His name and troupe became associated with Puranic and folksy entertainment, and as the director he wore many hats: he was scriptwriter, narrator, choreographer, and coach. He was also a shrewd manager who recognized that his success had encouraged many artists to found their own companies; among his many pioneering contributions to the transformation of folk theater was the inauguration of the formalization of the relationship between the actor and the "company" in writing. In Marathi, this modern exchange was (and still is) literally spoken of as the "giving of paper" (*kagad dene*), and it meant that a written promise to adhere to a set of rules had been given by the actors to the director.

Bhave devised a ten-year contract with severe terms. Actors had to attest that they had voluntarily [*rajikhushi*] and in full possession of their intelligence [*akkal-hushaari*] agreed to "behave as they were told, take only that which they were given, accompany [Bhave] wherever he went and as he ordered, and do so without complaint; accept whatever percentage of the show's proceeds as Bhave deemed fit, and if he offered nothing, then to accept that as well and without complaint; keep no gifts given to them but hand them over to Bhave; engage in no acts of deceit; teach no other actors what Bhave had taught them."[81] The contract commingled modern stipulations with village gods and spirits. These gods and spirits were not the remnants of a precolonial or premodern past but rather part and parcel of the entailments of modernity. Bhave understood well that he needed to hang both an emotional and financial sword over the actors' heads to ensure that they behaved in accordance with their contracts. The actors swore, in writing, by their hereditary goddess [*kulaswaminichi shapath*], to observe the promises in the "given paper." The punishment for breaking such a vow lasted all their lives. They had to sign an agreement not only to pay a fine to Bhave but to remit to him a portion of their proceeds for an indefinite period if they struck out on their own. These were terms, notwithstanding Bhave's prescience in recognizing that competition was close at hand, that could not possibly be adhered to by the signatories. Even the curse of an ancestral village goddess could not avert the probability that unreasonable contractual clauses such as lifelong indebtedness would simply be ignored. However, the terms also suggest the growing popularity of Bhave's theater. He was not alone in recognizing the newfound popularity of this modern entertainment in an emerging public sphere. If Bhave felt compelled to assert his rights over the labor of his troupe through draconian contractual terms, the actors asserted their rights to the proceeds of their labor by simply reneging on their agreements.

In 1855, fourteen of Bhave's students declared their intention not just to found their own company but to stage around the country the very plays they had learned from him. Bhave's patron had died in 1851, and the new ruler of Sangli had no interest in theater. Bhave complained bitterly about the treachery of his troupe to the new ruler without any real hope of redress:[82] "I have labored for thirteen years to put before people plays of Ram and Ravan, etc., and have trained all these children. They even signed their agreement on paper to behave in accordance with my rules. But now they claim they are ready with their own show and are planning to deceive me and take my play on the road without my permission."[83] Bhave urged the ruler to "prevent them from leaving the town," but it was too late. Within a decade of Bhave's first production, eight more theater troupes came into being, and by 1879, there were as many as thirty-five different theatrical troupes all over Maharashtra.

Most early Marathi theater companies took their names from the cities to which they were affiliated, such as Ichalkaranjikar (Ichalkaranji) Natak Mandali, Mumbaikar (Bombay) Natak Mandali, Punekar (Pune) Natak Mandali, Waikar (Wai) Natak Mandali, Kolhapurkar (Kolhapur) Natak Mandali, and Sanglikar (Sangli) Natak Mandali. The fare offered by each company was slightly different. The Sanglikar troupe was renowned for dance, whereas others tended to focus on acrobatics. A famous wrestler, Narharbua, headed the Kolhapurkar Natak Mandali. His troupe was known by the unpronounceable yet descriptive name *Chittachakshuchamatkritinidhan Samayrang Rasodbhav*, which advertised their fare: "quasi-magical, incredible feats that astonished both the mind and the eye."[84] Bhave's troupe was known for staging Puranic theater; faced with increasing competition from these other companies, he embarked on tours—but this time with a difference. He took his show not to village squares and aristocratic homes but into a new, modern venue—the world of colonially influenced city theater auditoriums in the two major cities of Bombay and Pune. In these two cities, as in others around the country, a new cultural sphere was emerging, one that was more bounded and focused on "entertainment" that attended a new conception of "leisure time" for the urban elite.

The city of Bombay in the early nineteenth century was home to a merchant community of hereditary traders and bankers who had established links with the outside world through commerce. Gujarati was the lingua franca of the city, spoken by members of the Hindu Gujarati, Muslim Bohra, and Zoroastrian Parsi communities. Until 1818, when the East India Company defeated the Marathas, Pune was the political and cultural center of the Marathi community. Pune would remain the center of Marathi Brahmin culture and the city in which the glories of the *peshwai* were claimed as a cultural legacy. After 1818, however, Bombay became a metropolitan and cosmopolitan center rivaling Calcutta, and a city that acquired great importance not just for Hindu and Muslim Marathi speakers who thronged to the city from Pune and the coastal areas of Konkan, but also for the Gujarati and Parsi communities.[85] In the mid-nineteenth century, the development of Bombay's public culture was supported and encouraged by leading industrialist figures such as Bhau Daji Lad, Jagannath Shankersheth, and Sir Jamshetjee Jijibhoy, all of whom welcomed the transformation of folk into bourgeois theater.[86]

Theater was one of the high points of respectable public entertainment in Bombay, with a colonial history going back many years. In the late eighteenth century, the army made up the largest number of Englishmen in India; newly constructed theaters served, in large part, the entertainment needs of military personnel. Officers with dramatic talents could indulge their thespian desires in theaters such as the Bombay Theater, founded in 1770.[87] It was a theater built and designed to stage English plays for the entertainment of Bombay's European population and was maintained mainly by subscription and the funds raised by occasional performances. The other theater in the early nineteenth century was called the Artillery Theater; in 1820, all "Bombay Society, including the Governor, flocked there to witness a performance called 'Miss in her Teens and the Padlock.'"[88] In 1867, spurred on by suggestions that native Indians should focus on indigenous theater, the Kalidas Elphinstone Society staged *Shakuntala* in English and three years later in Sanskrit.[89] Additionally, a Gentleman's Amateur Club offered small theatrical productions in which men performed women's roles. Around the same time Parsi students of the Elphinstone College started a dramatic company that staged Shakespeare's plays.

Bombay's well-known banker Jagannath Shankersheth built his own new theater house, the Grant Road Theater, in 1842. It acquired fame for staging the skits of one Dave Carson, who excelled in caricaturing "native Indians"— mainly Parsis and Bengalis—and their accents.[90] Carson's fame rose to its peak during the furor over the Ilbert Bill, and his caricatures were designed to bring out the absurdity of having a "Bengali babu" as a judge who could try a European subject. But unlike the strictly colonial theaters, Shankersheth's theater was willing to stage "native" productions as well, and Grant Road became the new theater district of Bombay. In the years between 1853 and 1931, as Kathryn Hansen has shown, Bombay became the center of a polyglot theater, drawing interchangeably from the Parsi, Gujarati, and Marathi stage. Bhave was keen to stage his own productions in this new public forum, as it promised better remuneration than impromptu village performances. In 1853, his troupe performed two ticketed Puranic-based mythological plays at the Badshahi Theater on Grant Road.[91] Between 1852 and 1862, Bhave conducted seven tours of the region (the modern Indian state of Maharashtra) and wrote fifty-two narratives (*akhyan*), which were published in 1885.

Bhave's *akhyan*s inaugurated yet another moment in the transformation of Marathi theater from folk to proscenium. The profession of the modern playwright emerged in concert with the efflorescence of modern Marathi literature between 1858 and 1874. Theater companies not only promised their audiences that the actors would deliver their lines *exactly* as they were written in distributed playbills, thereby devaluing an earlier spontaneous and unpredictable performance, they also expanded the repertoire of the Marathi stage to include plays about historical figures such as the Peshwas. In 1862, the Ichalkaranjikar Company staged the first "bookish" play, written *as* a play by Vinayak Janardhan Kirtane, which featured Madhavrao Peshwa, a late-eighteenth-century ruler known for his military victories. The Ichalkaranjikar Company performed in Baroda and received a letter signed by forty-two leading citizens, one of whom was the earlier *dewan*, Madhav Rao, endorsing its move away from folk theater to somber entertainment: "These days, once the play gets going, the main objective of the theater which is to put before the audience the true condition of mankind is obscured by the troublesome roaring of the demons [*rakshas*] . . . or by the relentless singing of the story-teller [*sutradhar*] or the crafty irritations of the comedian [*vidushak*]. . . . We are happy to see such nonsense slowly recede from your theater in favor of newer fare suitable for intelligent audiences."[92] The letter writers had praised the Ichalkaranjikar Company for moving away from popular theater and for having recognized the need for a rebirth [*punarujeevan*]of drama along more enlightened lines. The public was redefined with every staged success.

In 1875, Balwant Pandurang Kirloskar, who had apprenticed with the Kolhapurkar Natak Mandali, famous for staging spectacular productions, moved on to establish his own Bharatshastraottejak Belgaonkar Mandali (Renaissance-of-India's-Culture Theater Troupe) in Belgaum in the southern Deccan. In September 1875, he staged the first performance of *Sangit Shakuntal,* a musical and Marathi adaptation of Kalidasa's play *Shakuntala.*[93] Three years later, he moved to Pune, took up employment in the revenue department, and, in 1880, resumed his theatrical career with the staging of the better-known and -discussed Pune performance of *Sangit Shakuntal.* It marked the decisive moment for the commingling of "classical" music with Marathi bourgeois theater. The play was written as a musical, and actors were given parts to sing. To expand his audience, Kirloskar invited a senior British military officer, Major General Hewett, to the play. In a letter to Kirloskar, he praised the performance: "That I was thoroughly pleased, you, I trust feel sure from the fact of the great interest I was taking in the performance the entire evening and the attention I was devoting to each act [as] it was being performed. To my idea it was faultless. So well was everything done."[94] The letter served to promote the play and, in 1883, Kirloskar followed with yet another resounding success in the staging of *Sangit Saubhadra,* adapted from the *Mahabharata.*

On the one hand, Marathi music drama maintained its connection to an oral tradition of storytelling by drawing from the *Mahabharata.* However, it dropped the populist politics of bhakti along the way in favor of a new classicized and Sanskritized form of storytelling that was upper-caste Hindu in the issues it raised, even in the plays that addressed social reform. New playwrights of the Marathi theater were middling civil servants who pursued their interest in theater and music on the side, but with greater success than they would ever see in their main professional occupations. They would successfully produce a new high culture. They mined Sanskrit literature for dramatic material, adapting from Kalidasa, Banabhatta, and the Puranas, also borrowing freely from Shakespearean plays. In 1891, Ganpatrao Joshi's Kolhapur-based Shahunagarvasi Natak Mandali staged G. B. Deval's Marathi adaptation of *Othello, Zunzarrao*, becoming an overnight success. Vasudevrao Kelkar translated and rewrote *The Taming of the Shrew* as *Traatika*. Gopal Ganesh Agarkar, who cofounded the Marathi nationalist newsweekly *Kesari* with Bal Gangadhar Tilak in 1886, translated *Hamlet* (*Vikarvilasit*) and Shivram Mahadev Paranjpe did the same with *Macbeth* (*Manajirao*). Othello and Macbeth were so effectively turned into characters from Maharashtra's princely history that when their connection to Shakespearean figures was noted it evoked more surprise than recognition. Kalidasa's and Shakespeare's Marathi counterparts held (and still hold) sway over the Marathi stage for many years as the alternative to the more dominant music drama inaugurated by Kirloskar.

Marathi music drama did not tax its audience with technical virtuosity but maintained, nonetheless, a connection to "serious" music. Most singer/ actors, such as Balkoba Natekar, Bhaskarbua Bakhle, Ramkrishnabua Vaze, Krishnarao Phulambrikar, and Govindrao Tembe, were trained by *gharana ustads*, and many of the new musical compositions devised exclusively for theater showed evidence of such training. In the last decades of the nineteenth century, even as musicians might have felt their music being diluted and foreshortened in this new medium, many of them recognized that theater music had its basis in precisely the music they knew well. Instead of performing one or two ragas, musicians sang shorter and more up-tempo compositions. The compositions themselves required trained musicians to sing them, even though directors like Kirloskar deliberately stayed away from the melismatic embellishment [*galebaazi*] characteristic of the slow expositions of ragas. Music theater in Maharashtra ushered in a markedly new form of music—publicly performed, semiserious, and popular, catering primarily to a middle-class and "respectable" audience. Women were central to the construction of this new audience. With very few exceptions, there were no more *lavani*s or *gondhal*s on the stage, associated as they had become with bawdy and lewd entertainment, and even when some of the music of these forms permeated newer compositions, it was not acknowledged as such.[95] (The place for *lavani*s would be the new Marathi cinema of the twentieth century.) What was much more important was the setting of a new code of dress, mannerism, and behavior by, paradoxically, the leading cross-dressing Marathi singer, Bal Gandharva (1889–1975), who was acclaimed as having the most melodious female voice and wiles on the Marathi stage of the early twentieth century and whose debut performance as an actor/singer was in the production of *Shakuntala* in which he played the lead role. Bal Gandharva's style—how he draped his sari on stage, the jewelry he wore, and even the way he walked—set the standard for bourgeois women of the period.[96] Hansen argues that it was precisely the fact that these standards were set by men that made it acceptable for women to move around in public.

Fifteen additional *natak mandali*s were founded following the production of *Sangit Shakuntal*. Some advertised themselves as nationalist, others as Puranic, and still others affiliated themselves with major musicians.[97] The growing acceptability and audience of Marathi theater attracted young nationalists like Vishnushastri Chiplunkar and Bal Gangadhar Tilak, who began to use the theater to propagate anti-British sentiments in Marathi.[98] Tilak added his name to the masthead of the Aryodwarak Mandali, and Mahadev Govind Ranade, the liberal counterpart to Tilak, urged the Kirloskar Natak Mandali to stage plays that addressed questions of social reform.[99] In 1913, Govindrao Tembe, Bal Gandharva, and Ganeshrao Bodas left the Kirloskar company, where they had been hired as actors, to found their own theater, the Gandharva Natak Mandali, which went on to become almost as famous as the Kirloskar company, mainly on the strength of its exquisite music.

The middle class made theater's fortunes at the same time that theater, in mimicking colonial theatrical productions, dropped the relative populism and nonurban feel of *khel, lavani, gondhal,* and *tamasha* in its drive to attain bourgeois approbation. Nationalist politics entered Marathi theater with the depictions of the Brahmin-dominated *peshwa* period of Maratha history and plays based on the life of Shivaji. While the *peshwai* was represented as rife with intrigue, its structure was held up as the exemplar of a "native" order that had been overtaken by colonialism. Issues related to social reform were also addressed in the early life of the Marathi theater. In 1899, *Sangit Sharda* depicted the unspeakable difficulties faced by a young girl who was coerced into marriage with a man old enough to be her grandfather, clearly referencing the storm around the Age of Consent controversy. These early plays—*Sangit Shakuntal, Sangit Saubhadra,* and *Sangit Sharda*—maintained their popularity for decades. The content of the reformist plays was restricted to those subjects that were relevant to the middle and upper classes, and more radical caste-based politics would not take center stage in the Marathi theater until well after Indian independence from British rule.[100]

Marathi music drama was immensely popular but not immediately hospitable to women as actors. This is not to suggest that women were absent from the theater. In 1867, a theater troupe named the Vibudhjanachittachatak Swativersha advertised itself as a company in which women acted female roles. But "due to the prevailing social conditions," as Ashok Ranade has noted and explained in a pithy if vague formulation, "they came from the prostitute class."[101] In 1873, the Altekar Natak Mandali had advertised different rates for housewives and women of ill repute (they had to pay more) suggesting that all women were allowed into the theater as consuming members of the audience, but respectable women were not allowed on the stage as actors whose performances were publicly consumed.[102] Although respectable women were initially shut out of the world of public performance, some were able to push themselves into visibility, as Hirabai Barodekar would do, at the same time that others were moved out of sight, categorized, and segregated. There were a few women playwright/composers such as Hirabai Pednekar, who wrote *Jayadrath Vidamban* (1904) and *Damini* (1912). She was supported by the maverick playwright Shripad Kolhatkar, perhaps the only dramatist of his time to combine populist musical forms such as the *lavani* (an overtly bawdy form of music-theater dance) with relatively progressive gender and anti-elite politics in his plays.[103] On the whole, however, the social moratorium against women actors was not lifted until the third decade of the twentieth century. The first breaching of this social taboo had all the flavor of the scandal routinely associated with musicians, princely courts, and theater.

Hirabai Barodekar was the first Marathi woman to act and sing on stage. Her father was Abdul Karim Khan, the famous lyrical *khayal* vocalist and doyen of the *kirana gharana*. We will meet Abdul Karim and Hirabai at some length in the last chapter of this book, but for now, these important figures index the emerging ties between princely states, musicians, and the emerging world of theater. Abdul Karim Khan had spent four years in Baroda, from 1894 through 1898, where he held Maula Baksh Ghisse Khan responsible for having blocked his attempt to secure permanent employment.[104] During his short-lived stay at the court, Abdul Karim became romantically involved with Sardar Mane's daughter. Mane was a high-ranking court official, and it is unlikely that he would have seen an impoverished, married, Muslim musician as an attractive matrimonial catch for his daughter. Abdul Karim Khan and Mane's daughter eloped (the story as commonly told in Marathi is that Abdul Karim Khan ran away with her) and the couple had five children, two boys and three girls. When the marriage broke up, two of the girls took as their surnames the word Barodekar, meaning "of or from Baroda," a common practice in Maharashtra, while one of the boys took Mane, his mother's maiden name, as his surname. Abdul Karim Khan never publicly acknowledged his relationship to his daughter, who referred to him only as her teacher (*guru*). Years later, and against the father's wishes, Hirabai Barodekar and her brother, Sureshbabu Mane, founded the Nutan Sangeet Vidyalaya and added a branch devoted to the teaching of theater in 1929. In 1930, Hirabai Barodekar acted in the play *Saubhadra* and, in 1933, Jyotsna Bhole made her debut in *Andhalyachi Shaala* (*School for the Blind*) and Padmabai Vartak acted in *Natyamanvantara*. The taboo against women acting on stage was not completely gone, but these three women were demonstrating that it was possible for respectable, married, Marathi women to act on stage.

Marathi theater remained in the space of a reworked Sanskritized and classicized music drama well into the first four decades of the twentieth century. To its credit, it offered musicians a different venue and an alternative mode of employment than that of the princely courts. It was, however, a regional theater, even if it performed nationalist themes, as it was monolingual and often had as its principal concern the commemoration of Marathi heroes. It was also weighted in favor of upper-caste Hindu themes. This meant that quite apart from the distaste with which musicians such as Abdul Karim Khan viewed theater, those who did not read and speak Marathi would not find theater welcoming. *Ustad*s would find in early Marathi theater a forum dominated by bourgeois Hindu religiosity on the one hand, and colonial mimicry—albeit with a strongly Marathi overtone—on the other. Even though this theater was overwhelmingly music-oriented, very few Muslim vocal musicians were invited into its inner sanctum. While Ahmed Jan Thirakwa (a *tabla* player) and Ustad Kadarbux (a *sarangi* player) did play significant roles in theater, they were instrumentalists in a theater dominated by vocal musicians. While senior Muslim vocal musicians who were secure in their court appointments, such as Alladiya Khan, showed scant interest in the theater, there were many others who could have been gainfully employed by this new forum. While they were certainly not prominent in earlier forms of theatrical performance, it is nonetheless striking that in a new forum that purported to reach out to a more "refined" audience, Muslim vocalists were absent. The new Marathi theater was practically defined into existence as music drama and borrowed freely from the vocal music conventions of the time; yet the predominant vocalists of the period, who were mostly Muslim, were not visible in it.

Later modernizers, such as Pandits Bhatkhande and Paluskar and *ustad*s such as Abdul Karim Khan, would try to dissociate their efforts to classicize music from the "low-brow" and overly popular musical fare offered by the stage. But the success of the Marathi music theater in fact aided their efforts in its heralding of the Brahmin bourgeois takeover of music in Maharashtra. With the arrival of women like Jyotsna Bhole and Padmabai Vartak on the stage, more and more women studied classical music, not necessarily with the intention of becoming full-fledged classical performing musicians, but with the possibility of performing on stage. India's most famous popular singer, Lata Mangeshkar, who sang playback for movies for five decades, received her musical training from her father, Dinanath Mangeshkar, known as Master Dinanath, another famous Marathi stage personality. Even a few *ustad*s— Abdul Karim among them, despite his initial distate for theater—recorded select compositions from Marathi theater.[105] More than any other medium, Marathi theater appropriated high art music and made it respectable for the middle classes.

Marathi theater came into its own as a modern form of entertainment largely by shedding all that was seemingly coarse and uncouth from its performative history. In keeping with this agenda, music, too, was cleansed in order to be performed on the stage. While theater was engaged in this task of autocleansing, in education reform societies and music appreciation societies, something else was happening: music was being linked to a gendered morality, India's antiquity, and an all-encompassing religiosity. Many patrons of the early Marathi stage were members of these voluntary associations, and some of the actors on the Marathi stage supplemented their incomes by teaching at schools set up by these societies. While women were finding a way onto the Marathi stage by mimicking Bal Gandharva, they were simultaneously being created as sensitive, refined, and pure consumers of music by voluntary associations. The focus on women's musical education was taken up first by education reform societies and later by music appreciation societies that advocated bourgeois women's musical education for a different reason, one that had less to do with consumerism and more to do with companionate marriage.

Conclusion

I began this chapter with Sir William Jones, whose early recognition of the significance of Indian music was so clearly tied to his own sense of India as a classical Hindu civilization, an observation that took root in modern times in extremely powerful ways. I then linked the development of colonial religiosity to the cleansing of Marathi stage theater, a process that reached its apotheosis in the music drama of the Kirloskar Natak Mandali and the Sanskritized Marathi music-play *Sangit Shakuntal.* Theater aficionados, directors, and actors were active members of yet another move into the public sphere set in motion by educational reform societies and music appreciation societies. In the GUM and PGS, one sees a further cleansing of music along with the consolidation of new connections between music, women, and religiosity. What is most compelling about the activities of these associations is not merely that they were elitist, but that they used projects of respectability and civilization to displace the traditional role of Muslims, for unlike other areas of reform such as education, the key performers of music were overwhelmingly Muslim. Unlike other areas of social reform where the argument marshaled against and about Muslims was that they were not interested, in the sphere of music, this was manifestly untrue. Yet colonial writings on music emphasized nation, Hindu/Vedic religion, and notation as the three sine qua nons of classical music. In the publications of the PGS and other early works, all three concepts were picked up without difficulty, but while notation fell short of its proclaimed aims, music did become irrevocably tied to ideas of nation and religion, ideas that themselves coalesced under the newly revitalized, and redefined, categories of Hinduism and Brahminism.

To understand this history of the relationship of Hindu nationalism to music, we need to examine how and why religion entered the public sphere of music at all. It is not the case that all Indian music was religious; such a theory is easily disproved simply by looking back at the range and variety of music performed in Baroda's court during the nineteenth century. In Baroda, devotional music—as opposed to "religious" music, which is to say music that was expressly linked to understandings of religion as scriptural, congregational, and institutional—was one among many kinds of music performed. Going further back in Indian music history, one can see the same range and variety of music performed during the late Mughal period. It is only when British colonial writers saw *all* Indian music as religious that a significant transformation took place. A Hindu religious nationalism was provided with the terms by which it could declare triumphantly that Indian music was just as religious, and as easily textualized, or notated, as the more sophisticated music of the West.

Jones's conception of religion was not the same as those of his successors. By defining Indian music as religious, subsequent colonial writers betrayed their overwhelmingly Christian view of the world even as they arrogated to themselves the conceit of progressive secularism. All aspects of Indian life—social, economic, and cultural—were viewed through the lens of a British Christian understanding of religion. Once such an understanding was brought to bear on music in early writings debating the merits or demerits of the music itself, the relative merits and demerits of the different religions were discussed as if they were cognate with musicological questions. Islam represented a far greater threat than the heathen, pagan, and childlike practices of the Hindus. It also meant that the definitional parameters were set in such a manner that if native writers were to persuade colonial administrators that their music was music per se, they had to do so in the language of a Christianized religion and declare that Indian music was indeed fundamentally religious. Indian music's purity was linked to women, educational reform, companionate marriage, and emerging notions of bourgeois religiosity.

This was the epistemological prelude to the recruitment of music for a national agenda. The activities and publications of the music associations and educational reform societies were limited in scope and regionally focused in this early period. Interestingly, early societies and theater companies in the Deccan region looked to South India for inspiration and connections. The Poona Gayan Samaj established a branch in Madras and solicited the patronage of rulers of Mysore and Hyderabad, as well as local military personnel. These activities were not thematized in terms of a pan-Indian cultural nationalism even as they were viewed as quintessentially Hindu and Indian. Only when key modernizers, and here Bhatkhande and Paluskar are the two primary actors, took up the charge of nationalizing music across northern and western India did music come to be inextricably aligned with the language of modern nationalism.

❈ THREE ❈

THE CONTRADICTIONS

OF MUSIC'S MODERNITY

Vishnu Narayan Bhatkhande

The year was 1922. Music had been in the public eye for close to two decades. Princely states were still providing the major source of both employment and economic stability for musicians, but independent schools for teaching music had been founded in cities in all three presidencies. In Bombay Presidency, music appreciation societies in Pune, Bombay, Satara, Sangli, and elsewhere had begun conducting classes for select groups of young men and, occasionally, women, and the process by which musical education for a middle-class public would become systematic seemed under way. It was a time that an interested contemporaneous observer might have described as one of progress. And yet, no less a figure than Pandit Vishnu Narayan Bhatkhande, a renowned musicologist and scholar, wrote in a letter to a friend that he felt as if he were witnessing the impending demise of music.

The recipient of Bhatkhande's letter in 1922 was his close friend and colleague Rai Umanath Bali, a *taluqdar* from Daryabad, close to Lucknow. Rai Umanath would have read this lament: "Poor music. I really do not know what sins music has commit[t]ed. No protector comes forward to champion its cause. Nobody appreciates its great utility. People will certainly have to repent one day. The next decade will kill most of the leading artists and scholars

96

and by the time the people wake up there will be only fifth class musicians left to please them."[1] This premonition of loss seems extraordinary, voiced as it was by Bhatkhande, already well known by then as a protector and champion of Hindustani music.

When Bhatkhande spoke and wrote, he did so mainly about North Indian vocal music, and within that subfield of Indian music, his accomplishments were many and wide-ranging. By the second decade of the twentieth century, he had excavated and made public a large number of old manuscripts. He had collected and notated thousands of musical compositions that he had subsequently compiled in many pedagogical volumes. He was a prolific writer of historical and musicological treatises on music in Sanskrit and Marathi (his native language) and an influential theorist and historian. A few years after writing the letter to Rai Umanath Bali, the two of them collaborated with another wealthy *zamindar*, Nawab Ali, to found a college of music. Toward the end of his life, he was sought after by rulers of princely states to explain the intricacies of music, by leaders of the nationalist movement to establish departments of music in newly founded universities, and by high-ranking officials in the provincial governments to proctor examinations and evaluate teaching methods and curricula in new schools of music.

Bhatkhande's accomplishments had all been in the service of music.[2] He had spent the first two decades of the twentieth century actively involved in bringing music to the forefront of public consciousness, advocating the need to make music easily available in terms of access to both musical performances and musical learning. And yet, in 1922, his lament sounded heartfelt. Had something changed between when he began his career in music in the early years of the twentieth century and a mere two decades later? Had something gone wrong? There was a clear sense of an impending failure, alluded to in his letter, and indeed, as we shall see, his own failures were quite real. In the literature about him, biographical and historical, these failures have all but disappeared. Because of his successes Bhatkhande is considered an icon not just in the modern Indian state of Maharashtra, but also in the larger world of Hindustani music in India.

In this chapter, the focus is both on Bhatkhande's accomplishments and on what is left out of the extant literature: his disappointments, failures, and flaws. He is presented as a flawed secularist, as a failed modernist, and as an arrogant nationalist. This may seem an odd way to proceed, but a close look at his failures enables one to disentangle his tripartite understanding of music—

modern, scholastic, and secular—otherwise occluded by hagiography and dismissal. At a time when music and faith were being successfully soldered together by musicians like Pandit Paluskar, Bhatkhande insisted that music and religion be kept apart. When South Indian music was carving out for itself a unique place in Indian history in which its origins were being posited as untouched by and unlinked to North India, Bhatkhande advocated the integration of North and South Indian music. Without it, he believed, a new nation would sing not in a unified chorus but in differentiated cacophonies. In the course of his travels, he met a number of eminent musicians and scholars who spoke of Indian music's undoubted antiquity. He responded to these charlatans, as he perceived them, with disdain. For him, late-nineteenth-century music had a young, two-hundred-year genealogy, which meant that India's music, as he saw it, was fundamentally modern, not ancient, but its youth did not detract from its status as national classical music. Put another way, even though he argued that a nation, any nation, needed a system of classical music, his argument did not assume the necessity of an ancient pedigree.

Nationalism in and of itself was not Bhatkhande's sole focus, and national politics, whether Gandhi's noncooperation movement or Ambedkar's and Periyar's anti-Brahmin causes, were not his concern. His letter to Rai Umanath Bali made no mention of the noncooperation movement, Chauri-Chaura, or Gandhi's arrest in March 1922, something that had happened a few months before he penned the letter. There was no such evasion when it came to music's national future as Bhatkhande envisioned it. Music, in order to be nationalized, had to be institutionalized, centralized, and standardized. It had to be put into a national academy to which everyone could have access. But before that could happen, it needed a demonstrable and linked history, one with a text or a few key texts that explained foundational rules, theories, and performance practices. This history also required a historical point of origin, but unlike his contemporaries, Bhatkhande had no particular investment in putative ancient Vedic origins. Music's history could do as well with a foundational text from the sixteenth or seventeenth century.

This vision of a modern yet Indian music nationalized and instituted in a recognized academy never acquired quite the successful punch Bhatkhande hoped it might in independent India. Indeed, the music college that he founded began to founder almost as soon as it began. These failures are juxtaposed against the overwhelming success of his contemporary, Pandit Paluskar, about whom we shall read in the next chapter. And it is this vision that seems particularly relevant today, when the institutionalization of national classical music, North or South Indian, appears inextricable from all that Bhatkhande questioned, such as the mutually exclusive trajectories of North and South Indian music; the uncritical worship of one's teacher, who was assumed to be a spiritual guide; the imputation of spirituality to the performance of music; and the maintenance of secrecy and suspicion, in particular, around questions related to easy access to primary sources, documents, letters, and the like.

For all that Bhatkhande maintained a radical perspective on music for his time, he is also one of Indian music's most contentious, arrogant, polemical, contradictory, troubled, and troubling characters. It may be better to view him not as a charlatan or a savior, but as a tragic figure, one who was his own worst enemy. All through his writings, there is ample evidence of elitism, prejudice, and borderline misogyny. In the pages to follow, a few of the most egregious examples of his contempt, his anti-Muslim prejudice, his Brahminic elitism, and his privileging of theory over practice as it relates to music are offered without camouflage or disavowal. Yet nothing Bhatkhande wrote or said was uncomplicated, and he constantly qualified his most troubling assertions. As a result, there is simply no way to box his life and its trajectory into simple categories or directions. Every anti-Muslim utterance, every elitist claim, and every arrogant dismissal was qualified by what remained a constant throughout his life—an obsession with textual authority. What motivated him was a modern and modernist pursuit: the search for proof, demonstrability, documentation, history, and order. His classicism was modern, his prejudices were not restricted to any one group, his elitism was qualified by a powerful desire for egalitarianism, and the austerity he demanded of musicians was amply lived by him as example.

Bhatkhande made three compelling and radical claims. First, respectfully but firmly, he rejected the authority of the Vedas. Second, he was unfailingly skeptical not just about the *Natyashastra* but also about most texts from the ancient period, settling instead on a seventeenth-century South Indian text as the only one that had any real bearing on contemporary music. Third, he believed in the concept of secular music, meaning that the performance and pedagogy of music should be rejuvenated in the modern period, untouched by a discourse of religion or spirituality. Not one of these ideas has taken hold in the world of performing arts, whether in performance or pedagogy. Sixty-odd years after Bhatkhande's death, much of classical music is suffused with sacrality, held up by the notion of the ancient *guru-shishya parampara*. The

Vedas and the *Natyashastra* are routinely assumed to hold the secrets of Indian music's performative origins. This state of affairs bears little resemblance to Bhatkhande's actual work and writings.

As befits a tragic figure, the unwitting saboteurs of Bhatkhande's dreams, desires, and vision have not been his competitors or even their students. For a man who spent his life making music visible, scholastic, and secular, the most ironic of his failures is a posthumous one, effected by his own devotees and students, who have done exactly the opposite of what he advocated. People who were acquainted with him or his students police the documents that would allow a critical history of his life to be written. Scholars are greeted with skepticism, even suspicion. The archive is closed to the public, and many students, men and women, begin their lessons by prostrating themselves at their teacher's feet and do not question why this should be so.

At the turn of the millennium, there was a music gathering in Bombay dedicated to Bhatkhande. One of the leading musicians in the city, a student of one of Bhatkhande's students, presided over the occasion. At the base of Bhatkhande's portrait, adorned by a marigold garland, stood a silver incense stand. The proceedings began with a speech about his greatness. There was deep respect for his memory at the gathering, and the atmosphere was reverential. No one made a mention of his radical claims or his prejudices, and while there were occasional questions, vigorous or polemical debate was out of the question. A leading historian and scholar of music, Ashok Ranade, spoke of a future of music in which students would be obligated to question their teachers, a future in which music teachers might perhaps learn from their students. But even he spoke of this future as something still to happen. "Yenaar aahe vel," he said in Marathi, "the time is approaching." Close to seventy years after Bhatkhande's death, it has not yet arrived. How did it happen that a vision that began with scholastics, debate, and secularism culminated in garlands and incense? To some extent, Bhatkhande has to be held accountable; in order to do that fairly, we need to begin with Bhatkhande's life, where he was born, his early years, and his education, then move with him through his musical tours, writings, institutional success, and, finally, his last days.

Vishnu Narayan Bhatkhande was born on August 10, 1860, into a Brahmin family in Bombay. His father worked for a wealthy businessman. Neither of his parents was a professional musician, yet he and his siblings were taught music; this was not unusual in a family of his class background. At the age of fifteen, he began receiving instruction in sitar and shortly thereafter began studying Sanskrit texts on music theory, a field of inquiry that would remain with him as an obsession all through his life.[3] In 1884, he joined the Gayan Uttejak Mandali, the music appreciation society whose history was detailed in chapter 2. The Mandali exposed Bhatkhande to a rapidly expanding world of music performance and pedagogy, and for the next six years, he studied with musicians such as Shri Raojibua Belbagkar and Ustad Ali Husain, learning a huge number of compositions, both *khayal* and *dhrupad*.[4] However, music was still a sideline for him. He received his BA from Elphinstone College, Bombay in 1885. In 1887, he received his LLB from Bombay University and embarked on a brief career in criminal law. He abandoned it to turn his full attention to music after the death of his wife in 1900 and his daughter in 1903.[5]

The first thing Bhatkhande did was to embark on a series of musical research tours, the first of which was conducted in 1896 (when his wife was still alive). During this tour he traveled to the provinces of Gujarat and Kutch. In 1904 (the year after his daughter's death) Bhatkhande traveled extensively in South India. He resumed his touring in 1907 with visits to Nagpur, Hyderabad, Vijayanagar, and Calcutta, and concluded in 1908 with a tour of Allahabad, Benares, Lucknow, Agra, and Mathura.[6]

He traveled with a series of questions—one hundred of them. His major project was to search out and then write a "connected history" of music, and it began with these tours, which he believed would give him some clues to help recover some missing links. In the course of his travels, he got some clues, and had to abandon others. How he coped—ideologically, affectively, and intellectually—with what he found is a large part of this story. The ostensible reason for the tours was to visit religious sites and see the country, but Bhatkhande was less interested in those objectives than in meeting music scholars. A single-mindedness of purpose dictated his approach in each city. He refused offers of introduction to professional lawyers and businessmen, claiming that he had no desire to trade superficial comments on the weather but wanted to get on with the business of meeting scholars of music and musicians.[7] Aside from an occasional compliment to some monument, his diaries are devoted solely to his musical pursuits.

In his reliance on random interlocutors, there was an ethnographic quality to Bhatkhande's approach to his research. Mornings in new cities always began the same way. After waking up, he set out in search of scholars and patrons of music. He found them by asking people on the streets if they knew the names of famous people who had an extensive knowledge of music. In this question alone, one can locate the success of music's move into the cultural sphere. A layperson on the street could now be approached to provide information about music and musicians. With this information, acquired at random, Bhatkhande set out to locate the residences of the people whose names he had found. Once he arrived, he used his letters of reference and introduction, bluntly stated his purpose, and set up appointments to meet and talk. If he happened to attend a music performance he considered it a serendipitous event, but his primary interest was to meet other scholars of music, not spend all his time listening to music. A curious way to write about music, one might think. But Bhatkhande was interested less in the actual performances of music than in the theory that underpinned the education of the musician.

Bhatkhande kept several diaries of his tours. The status and location of the originals is unknown. The person entrusted with them, a self-styled student of Bhatkhande's by the name of Prabhakar Chinchore, reportedly found them squirreled away in an old library, following which he kept them secret for years. Here and there the odd musician or the occasional critic was allowed a sneak peek at parts of this "authentic archive," but in general, and far more than the archive of his rival, Paluskar, Bhatkhande's materials have been kept away from the public. Prabhakar Chinchore had contracted Alzheimer's disease by the time the research for this book was conducted, so at this point, the origins of the diaries are unknown. Three of the four diaries had been copied in handwritten cursive Marathi. They could certainly have been doctored, but given the paradoxical reverence with which Bhatkhande's students treat his memory, it is likely that the master's words were simply copied word for word, a document of greatness for distribution among the believers. At any rate, they are considered authoritative, and that is itself significant even if experts agree that the copies in circulation are not in Bhatkhande's handwriting. Since these texts are considered authoritative by the cognoscenti, they have a special place in the archive of music.

In one of these diaries, Bhatkhande referred to his potential readers (*vachak*),[8] suggesting that even in a format as seemingly private as a diary, he was writing for a future audience, not just noting down personal memories for family members alone. The diaries were not merely accounts of his travels, but also the blueprints for his future writings. Along with recollections of the day, he worked out both musicological minutiae and the narratological style he would adopt in his more formal texts—in particular, in the five-volume *Hindustani Sangeet Padhati*. People he talked to in his travels reappear as figures in his formal texts. He kept notes for himself and wrote parenthetical comments that draw the reader into a private exchange regarding his interlocutors.

Bhatkhande did not interview the people he met so much as he interrogated them, seeking out what he judged to be their ignorance. He always began with deference and compliments and then moved on to gentle questioning, which became increasingly aggressive. The interview culminated with him having maneuvered his interviewee into a situation where the only possible response to a technical question was to confess ignorance. In all these encounters, Bhatkhande met only men. He had little regard for women musicians and did not believe he could learn anything from them. This was not because they were women but because, given the condition of music at the time, women were less likely than men to have access to the kind of information he believed would set music free.

Bhatkhande used this barrage of questions even with well-known authors of texts on music. While the diaries provide evidence of an extraordinary intellect focused on a singular project, they also point to Bhatkhande's high opinion of his own scholarship. Somewhere in the middle of an interview with a music scholar, he would ask, "Do you read Sanskrit?" Shortly thereafter, the questions would take on a patronizing tone: "Are you sure you understand Sanskrit?" He would ask it again. "Are you sure you have understood what you've read? Because I don't think you have." Invariably, his interviewee, a musician, would confess ignorance of Sanskrit. Confession, however, was not enough. Bhatkhande would often confirm his diagnosis. "So, you don't understand Sanskrit, cannot sing any of the ragas in the *grantha*s you claim to have read, and have not understood the *grantha*s themselves?"[9] Bhatkhande then corrected his interviewee, set his knowledge of Sanskrit straight, and even offered to sing parts of music that were written about in the *Sangit Ratnakara*,[10] the text about which he had just received the confession of ignorance from his browbeaten subject.[11]

In this attempt to expose the lack of textual and theoretical understanding of music, he questioned not only scholars and patrons, but musicians as well. He asked them the same questions over and again. "On what authoritative text or source (*adhaar*) do you rely for your musical knowledge and performance? Which books have you read in music? Which texts were you told about by your teacher? Have you ever seen those texts? Can you show them to me?" Their response was usually that they had not read anything, had never seen these texts, and had received instruction without asking their teachers all the questions Bhatkhande believed were vital to their education. A tradition (*parampara*) was in place, and they had abided by it. He reported such encounters with no apparent awareness that his techniques might not have been greeted with warmth. Instead, Bhatkhande wrote that his efforts to reeducate people had met with great appreciation![12] On occasion, he apologized for his forthrightness but qualified this with the suggestion that since both he and his interlocutor were engaged in the same noble pursuit—the search for the foundations of music—he hoped no offense would be taken. From the hostility he generated, it is clear that offense was taken and offered in equal measure. Bhatkhande was not popular among musicians or among other scholars, who found him arrogant and aggressive.[13]

In the course of the musical tours described in his diaries, Bhatkhande met many people—scholars, musicians, and others. This chapter will deal with three exemplary conversations: with Sri Subbarama Dikshitar, a well-known authority on South Indian (Carnatic) music in Etaiyapuram in Tinnevelly District; with Raja Sourendro Mohun Tagore, a well-known authority on North Indian (Hindustani) classical music in Calcutta; and with Karamatullah Khan, a sarod player in Allahabad. These conversations reveal a bit about Bhatkhande's personality, opinions, aspirations, and desires. They also point to a sense of disquietude, an ambivalence that would not go away.

On December 17, 1904, in Etaiyapuram, Bhatkhande met Sri Subbarama Dikshitar (1839–1906).[14] Dikshitar was the author of *Sangeeta Sampradaya Pradarshini* (one of the first notated compilations of Carnatic music compositions, published in 1904) and, at the time, one of the most celebrated of Carnatic music scholars. Initially Dikshitar was reported by Bhatkhande as akin to an "ancient sage whose face shone with wisdom" and whose knowledge of music equaled his own.[15] Bhatkhande's narrative begins with Dikshitar as a humble but learned man who acknowledged at the outset that he was not familiar with Sanskrit per se even though he had a great many couplets (*shloka*s) from the *Sangit Ratnakara* memorized. This is, by itself, a curious comment, since the Dikshitar family was well known for its proficiency in Sanskrit. So what Bhatkhande presented as honesty on Dikshitar's part could well have been simple modesty. Dikshitar answered, if not always to Bhatkhande's satisfaction, his questions about the use of the chromatic scale in Carnatic music, the use of only twelve microtones (*shrutis*) as opposed to the twenty-two in the original text, and the genesis of the seventy-two *melakartas*. He also agreed to procure for Bhatkhande what would have been for him a priceless gift, a copy of a seventeenth-century text, Venkatamakhi's *Chaturdandi Prakashika* (c. 1660). Dikshitar claimed that it was a more recent and authoritative source for Carnatic music's orderliness than the *Sangit Ratnakara* and offered to explain it to Bhatkhande.

By the end of the conversation, Bhatkhande remained unimpressed by the singers of Carnatic music, but awed by its impeccable system. Here one can get a preliminary glimpse into his agenda: he had begun formulating what would become his own system of Hindustani music.[16] But systematizing music was a far easier task than finding a "connected *itihaas* (history)." This kept eluding him. Instead of connections, he got fragments and inconclusive answers. He wanted material links between texts and current musical practices, but few existed. He maintained the hope that someone (else) would investigate the links between the fixed scale in Vedic chants and current music, yet it was not an interesting intellectual quest for him or the sole focus of his search. Had he been so invested, he might have prejudged the music differently and moved on. Instead, he heaped scorn on most assertions that contemporary music could be traced back in a straight line to the Vedas. He returned to his search many times and asserted that music was an ever-changing art. And in one of his most radical assertions, Bhatkhande stated that music as it was then performed had a history going back only two hundred years, not two thousand. Therefore, and because it changed constantly, music had to be viewed as a modern form. This assertion won him no friends among his music contemporaries, many of whom were equally concerned with emphasizing that music was, by definition, timeless and eternal, yet derivative of the Vedas. What Bhatkhande was searching for was textual authority, one or two Sanskrit texts that could serve as benchmarks for contemporary musical performances. For him, these texts would enable the writing of a history of change, not a history of stasis or of civilizational continuity. But even with Sanskrit texts, in particular the one he was most taken with, Sharangdeva's *Sangit Ratnakara*, he could not in the end make them fit the bill as the urtext; neither could any other scholar.

These were not his only problems. He wanted to establish a link between the *Sangit Ratnakara* and Carnatic music so that he could use it to bridge the gap between the *Sangit Ratnakara* and North Indian music. He had hoped that "with the help of this music I can identify where the missing links are between an earlier music and contemporary music."[17] He believed that the *Sangit Ratnakara* was the closest textual source for North Indian music performances, but if now, as Dikshitar had told him, the *Chaturdandi Prakashika* was more relevant than the *Sangit Ratnakara*, the historical time frame he was working with was closing, approaching the seventeenth century as a starting point rather than the thirteenth. This should have made his historical project easier, and his conversation with Dikshitar may have been the reason he would assert in his writings that contemporary "classical" music had a two-hundred- rather than a two-thousand-year history. While he acknowledged that the sources exercised a "veto power" over his desire for a connected history, he never fully let go of this ideal.

But if texts were disappointing, Bhatkhande also had no real aesthetic appreciation for Carnatic music:

> In the South, the emphasis on tala [meter] has diminished the wonder of melody . . . all singing here is bound to each beat of the tala. There is a jerk per *maatra* [beat] and this "yaiyy yaiyy" style of singing—if they sing like this then I will in all honesty rate their style quite low. If you calculate the number of beats between two *aavartan*s [cyles] and if you emphasize through jerks each beat while waiting for the next one and then pounce on it like a hungry cat, I am afraid I cannot find such music appealing. . . . This is my prejudiced opinion, and singers here will not be happy with it nor do I expect them to be. . . . They will say their music is popular, but popular music is not necessarily good music.[18]

He turned to Carnatic music mainly for its formulas and order.[19] His desire to establish a Sanskritic base for Carnatic music was propelled by an instrumental purpose. If such a base could be established that met with his scholastic approval, he intended to use it to systematize North Indian music. His criticism of Carnatic music was balanced by his dislike for the arbitrariness and lack of order in North Indian music, where tradition and performance dictated the rules of music rather than the other way around. His desire to know the intricacies of Carnatic music was governed by a drive to affix a system of similar rules (*niyam*) that would be understood by all practitioners, students, and connoisseurs of North Indian music.

The most important result of his conversation and meeting with Subbarama Dikshitar was the idea that Venkatmakhi's *Chaturdandi Prakashika* might be useful in restoring order to the current disordered state in Hindustani music. Here one also sees his desire to have "throughout the country one style of music." Some years later, in 1916, at the first All-India Music Conference held in Baroda, he would voice a hope that if both systems of music could be integrated, the nation would sing in one voice. The imperative was a unifying one, and he saw his task as fraught but necessary. "My efforts will initially meet with great disapproval, but after an age the road I have chosen will appeal to succeeding generations, in particular an educated society, this is my hope . . . God has chosen to relieve me of my householder responsibilities, perhaps in one sense this is the reward for that pain."[20] However, before such nationwide systematization could happen, one major hurdle needed to be overcome: "First the rules of ragas have to be fixed once and for all just as they are here."[21]

Following his southern tour, Bhatkhande went to Calcutta in November 1907. If Etaiyapuram had cost him one link but given him another, Calcutta, by way of his conversations with its residents, gave him confirmation of his credentials. For many years, Bhatkhande had admired Raja S. M. Tagore (1840–1914). Tagore was not only a wealthy *zamindar* but also a notable authority on Hindustani music. He had authored, edited, and published several books on the subject.[22] Trained in music at an early age, he received instruction from famous musicians such as Kshetra Mohan Goswami and Sajjad Hussain. Bhatkhande was eager to meet Tagore and narrated his meeting with warmth, directing his readers to Tagore's generosity, dignity, and knowledge. He noted how quickly he had established a sympathetic friendship, finding in Tagore's views on music and history confirmation of many of his own. It was, as one reads from his other narrated conversations, the only worthwhile meeting for him in Calcutta. Tagore even arranged for Bhatkhande to receive copies of several old treatises on music.

Most of his other conversations in Calcutta had been frustrating mainly because he reported that people he met asserted far too easily and without proof that all Indian music was divine since it hailed from the Sama Veda or the Atharva Veda (1000–800 B.C.). They also invariably claimed knowledge not just of Sanskrit but also of Western classical music. Bhatkhande narrated these declamatory conversations with barely concealed exasperation. The figure of the pedantic pandit was one he would use in his writings as a key symbol of what he called *nirupyogi panditya*. And it was in Calcutta that he would come to the sense that it was vitally important to keep music separate from both religion and politics, the latter understood as high-level governmental negotiation and conflict. Perhaps this is why, despite the nationalist tumult around him, his diaries bear no mention of Gandhi, Nehru, Jinnah, or Ambedkar, and it is only in the occasional personal letter that he lets slip a comment that reveals any knowledge of or interest in the political happenings of the time. His sense of the need for an unsacralized music can be seen from his account of a conversation with Raja S. M. Tagore's brother, Gaurihar Tagore, in which Bhatkhande had responded to a question with this answer: "Yes (I am), indeed a Brahmin," and "it is not that I don't have faith in God," but "I consider faith and music to be separate subjects. I believe that in the twentieth century they should stay separate. If that is not done, it will amount to a disrespect for music."[23]

Bhatkhande shows here his acute sense of history. It is "in this century" that music needs to be kept away from faith. By itself, the demand does not seem unusual, except when compared to the wishes of his contemporary, Pandit Paluskar, for whom the crisis of contemporary music was resolved by fusing faith and religiosity with the performance and pedagogy of music in the belief that this fusion was the essential element that set Indian music apart from the West. By contrast, Bhatkhande's critique of music seems distanced from any deep engagement with the nature or capabilities of Western music. Bhatkhande had no interest in showing that Indian music and musicians could do all their Western counterparts were capable of, such as assembling bands and orchestras. Indeed, he not only had no knowledge of Western classical music, he had very little interest in it, and as a model for Indian music, the only aspect of it that was relevant was the bar system, which he used to notate meter. But even there, the only accomplishment of that borrowing was to divide tala into compartments. As such, we get no sense from his work that he was in competition with the West, and his sense of urgency was propelled by a local and located unease about the current practices of musicians, which, in turn, lent heft to his belief that without his intervention, the future of music would falter. When he looked for models either to oppose or mimic, he looked to North and South Indian music. His sense of order came from South Indian music and his sense of aesthetics from North Indian music. Indian music, by definition, could be systematic, old without being ancient, and unlinked to faith without sacrificing its native quality.

Although Bhatkandhe's conversation with Gaurihar Tagore was useful as a way of expressing his secularism, it was not as directed as his dialogue with S. M. Tagore. There he brought up the question of his elusive connected history. From the beginning of the conversation, the question of an adequate history plagued him. "Is it even going to be possible to write a history of our music?" he asked him. "If it is possible, how should it be written? Where does one start? Where and how can one establish a reliable chronology? In Akbar's time, Tansen was famous, but he has left behind no written record."[24] Even if history does not march forward in a straight line, where music was concerned, it had taken too many undocumented detours. Tagore was the only figure in Bhatkhande's diaries who escaped being damned by faint praise or caustic criticism, because Bhatkhande was able to have a scholarly conversation with him about textual sources. Even though Bhatkhande would go on to write that Tagore's written works were themselves scholastically weak, he recollected his meeting and conversations with him with unqualified pleasure, gratitude, and regard.

In Allahabad, on the last leg of his tour, Karamatullah Khan, a sarod player from Allahabad, presented Bhatkhande with one alternative to his imagined connected history. Bhatkhande was unreceptive. He had a deep-seated suspicion of musicians as a group, but he had also reasoned that a textual foundation was essential to the writing of his history. He could not accept that musicians were the living archive of music's theoretical history, even if they were his resource for its performative history. Karamatullah Khan had come to meet Bhatkhande, having heard about him as the great intellectual of musical history. He had written his own small work on music and wished to talk to Bhatkhande because he admired him. In the course of the conversation, he raised the possibility of a different way to understand music's past and Bhatkhande bridled in response. Bhatkhande already believed that musicians would resist his attempts to order Hindustani music, and the reason for that would emerge as a refrain in subsequent works, namely, that "this work is very difficult and because our music is in Muslim hands it has become even more difficult. Those people are for the most part ignorant and obstinate and will not like new rules imposed on them, this is my experience."[25] It is not clear whether he meant musicians as a group or Muslim musicians in particular, but at any rate, he was skeptical even before the conversation commenced.

By way of introduction to this conversation, Bhatkhande wrote, "By and large, I don't like discussing music with professional musicians. They know little but like to fight a lot. They spend a little time with us, learn just a little from us, and then say they have known this all along. They claim our knowledge is only bookish, not useful for skillful practitioners. I suppose one should just accept that they are the ones who are virtuous, skilled, can play instruments and sing, and so we should just acknowledge what they say as the truth." Not an auspicious beginning, it would be fair to say. But perhaps what was emerging was also a process of demystification, a sense that one could treat a practitioner as someone with whom a reasoned conversation about music was at least conceivable. The comment also addressed the divide between a history and theory of music, on the one hand, and its practice, on the other. This divide was one that Bhatkhande wanted not to maintain but to bridge. The conversation proceeded:

Karamatullah Khan: What have you decided about Teevra, Atiteevra, and Atikomal Swaras?

Bhatkhande: Khan Saheb, you must have addressed all of this in the book you wrote.

K: Yes, I have.

B: Which text did you use as authoritative for your work? Or did you write whatever came into your mind?

K: Of course not, how could I have written without textual authority?

B: Tell me the name of one Sanskrit text if you can, please, so that we can then talk about that text.

K: What is the need for a Sanskrit text? Why only Sanskrit? It is not as if there are not many other texts. I have thought carefully about a lot of them before writing my own.

B: Were those texts in Sanskrit or Prakrit?

K: No, what is wrong with reading in Arabic and Persian, there are no lack of texts there. There is one beautiful text after the next on music in these languages. Music as an art was not confined solely to Hindustan. Arabia, Iran, these countries too had music. They too had ragas and raginis, their children and wives, such compositions can be seen for example in "Arabi" raga, I worked through the 52 notes given and came up with our "Bhairavi" or our "maakas" is the same as your Sanskrit "Malkauns." I studied all of this and then wrote my book and I will give you a copy. (He does this immediately.)

B: Khansaheb, are you claiming that your Musalman Pandits translated our Sanskrit texts and then *took* them to their respective countries?

K: No. Not at all. Nothing like it. Music belongs to all countries. I went to the Paris Exhibition and heard music from all over the world. I talked at length to various scholars of music there and then came back and wrote my book.

B: I do not completely follow your meaning, perhaps. Are you possibly claiming that scholars from Arabia and Iran *took* their music from our country's ragas?

K: No, not at all. I am saying those countries had ragas/music right from the beginning. Whether they *took* it from here or Hindus *took* it from there, who is to decide? Perhaps the concept of ragas traveled from there to here. It is possible.

[Bhatkhande noted to himself, "This answer in particular made me a little angry. Ragas from *our* books are turned inside out, twisted around in *their* books, yet we have apparently stolen music from them, this is what this Khansaheb is declaring." (Emphasis mine.)]

B: Khansaheb, which is this book, can you tell me its name and year? Was it *Sarmaay Ashrat*? [sic]

K: No, No. That is not the book I mean, that is a recent book. I am talking about books going back hundreds even thousands of years back, one of which is Tohfat-ul-Hind, a very important work.[26]

Bhatkhande broke off the conversation here, writing: "Forget it. There is no point in arguing with this Khansaheb."[27]

The arrogance is unmistakable in this conversation, as is Bhatkhande's hostility. What we are given in this account is a judgment on a musician followed by a conversation that confirms the indictment. The question of theft is central, going to the heart of Bhatkhande's project: What are the origins of Indian music? The immediate impression this conversation conveys is that of an expansive musician in conversation with an arrogant, prejudiced, and irate pedant. Moreover, it appears that Bhatkhande was simply lapsing into elite Hindu prejudice against "low-class" Muslims and rejecting an alternative history simply because it had been suggested to him by a Muslim musician. We can concede that Bhatkhande's prejudice is buttressed by his arrogance; what we also see in this conversation is his exasperation, once again, with throw-away historical claims made by musicians. Bhatkhande calls off the conversation when Karamatullah Khan refers to a text dating back thousands of years. He had responded similarly in Calcutta with people who cited the Vedas as references. There is no question that Bhatkhande had in place a conception of "our" music, which is Indian, of Hindu origin, to which Arabic or Persian could have contributed, but for which a Sanskrit text might be decisive. Yet, had he simply prejudged the question of history as either Hindu or Muslim, he would have stopped with this interview and gone no further in his inquiry. And in the course of his years-long inquiry, his exclusion of performers as informants was not carried out exclusively on the ground of caste or religion or gender per se, but as a result of his obsession with scholasticism and the creation of a modernized, national, cultural institution. This does not, needless to say, preclude a hybrid origin for Indian music, so one is left with the question: Why could he not conceive of one?

Karamatullah Khan was in effect stating that it did not matter whether ragas had come from Iran or Arabia to India or the other way around, or what the origins of raga were—music belonged to all countries and people. This was quite a remarkable argument, open-ended and flexible, but it was not precise. Had Bhatkhande accepted it, it would have necessitated closing the inquiry into origins, but much more important, it would have meant that it did not matter whether or not music was, or could be, demonstrably classical. From the vantage point of the late twentieth century, Karamatullah Khan was voicing a prescient and progressive claim against national, ethnic, and religious essentialism when it came to music. But Bhatkhande was looking for a "classical" music that existed in his time, not one that used to exist in ancient times. References to "thousands of years ago" were routinely met with characteristic irritation. The confusion and ignorance of musicians bothered him, because if they were singing a "classical" music, there was no consensus among them about the sign or the proof of the classical. There were no agreed-upon texts or authorities, and every musician was free to cite and interpret the "tradition" exactly as he chose. Moreover, there was no agreement even as to which were the basic or foundational ragas. One of the frequent criticisms leveled at Bhatkhande was that he did not know the basics of ragas—Abdul Karim Khan, for instance, dismissed him as an ignorant pedant, as we shall see in chapter 6. What bothered Bhatkhande was not simply the question of nomenclature, but also the issue of standardization. Having conducted the research, he bridled when a practitioner of the art told him his history was too limited and exclusionary and usually turned away when told he did not know the basics. This is why even the wonderful fluidity of music's origins as suggested by Karamatullah Khan had to be rejected. The suggestion that it did not matter where ragas came from or whether they were demonstrably Persian or Arabic was not something Bhatkhande could accept, whether it was suggested to him by a Hindu musician or a Muslim one.

Bhatkhande was not unique among late-nineteenth- and early-twentieth-century nationalists in caring deeply about a classical and pure past. Once the origins of music had been decided by Bhatkhande, its future could be pulled out of the contemporary morass of sectarian divides and familial jealousies. All nations ought to have a system of classical music. He would have accepted that there was a certain measure of give and take between different classical music systems. He would perhaps even have agreed that there was, or ought to be, a Persian classical music. What he could not accept was that the foundation or system of Indian music was uncertain. Bhatkhande had rejected the claims that music could be traced back to the Vedas and that the *Sangit Ratnakara* was authoritative. He had stated that the *Natyashastra* was not useful for the study of raga-based music. Given all this, it would be hasty to conclude that anti-Muslim prejudice alone governed his course of study. Yet, as we have seen, he could not accept that contemporary music had a non-Hindu or non-Sanskrit origin.

While this combination of sentiments locates Bhatkhande squarely as a Hindu nationalist, it does not, by definition, make his vision for music exclusionary. The question of origins related to history, not to contemporary or future practice. While music needed a clear and precise historical trajectory, the future of music was not closed but open, available, and accessible to all. This is precisely where we see a difference between him and other musicians such as Paluskar. Even when he precluded a non-Hindu origin for music, he had no desire to turn contemporary musical performance and pedagogy into something recognizably Hindu. Paluskar assumed that music was Hindu in the past and Hindu in the future. Bhatkhande had no investment in a Hindu music as it was defined for him, whether in Pune, Calcutta, or Tanjore, but was interested in a national music. For all his prejudice, then, his judgment against musicians was not based on religion alone or on the sense that Muslims were foreign to India, but on the grounds of documentation, demonstrability, and a sense of secular nationalism.

I bring Bhatkhande's travels to a close with one last meeting. In 1908, in Mathura, he met a Mr. Ganeshilal Chaube, who raved and ranted at Muslims for their obdurateness, thievery, and ignorance.[28] Bhatkhande suggested to the irate Mr. Chaube that Hindus should share some of the blame for having allowed their music to decline. Chaube is important here neither for his tirades against Muslims, nor for his claim that he learned music directly from the heavens. Bhatkhande describes him as similar to scholars he had met on his southern tour. Chaube and others could "rattle off various Sanskrit quotations out of context to intimidate people but it should not be surmised from this that they actually understood what they were saying."[29] The ability to recite Sanskrit by rote was not scholarship. Chaube, as well as others who made claims on behalf of "music and texts that go back thousands of years," was pilloried in caricature and as the epitome of pedantic and useless knowledge (*nirupyogi panditya*) offered by charlatan pandits.

Bhatkhande's Solution: Texts and a Connected History

By 1909, Bhatkhande had finished his tours and was ready to embark on his own writing projects. By now he was familiar with most of the major Sanskrit texts, such as Bharata's *Natyashastra* (dating from the second century B.C. to the second century A.D.), Sharangdeva's *Sangit Ratnakara* (a thirteenth-century work), through Ahobal's *Sangit Parijat* (seventeenth century). From our location in the twenty-first century, the obsession with Sanskrit texts might appear part of an early, elaborated ideological sympathy for a future *Hindutva*. Yet to see Bhatkhande's focus on Sanskrit texts as part of this ideology might not be giving him enough credit and would certainly mean ignoring a great many of his assertions. For one thing, his scholasticism would have inevitably led him to Sanskrit texts on music theory. It would not be possible to ignore Sanskrit texts even if there could be no straight line from the *Natyashastra* to the present. Crooked as the line might be, there was a corpus of texts on music written in Sanskrit, translated on occasion into Persian, such as Faqirullah's *Rag Darpan*, that could not be ignored if Bhatkhande was serious about writing a complete history. The texts could be deemed irrelevant or inaccurate, as Bhatkhande argued, but to not delve into extant treatises on music that predated those in Persian or Arabic would be unthinkable. What set Bhatkhande apart from his contemporaries in the world of music, then and now, was a lack of investment in arguing that music's origins could be traced straight back to and through only a Sanskrit text. Nor did he quickly collapse *Sanskrit* with *Hindu* and then *India*. Bhatkhande lived in the period of an emergent nationalism, when all nations search for a hoary past to legitimize themselves, as Benedict Anderson has reminded us.[30] But Bhatkhande's search was not a simple Hindu nationalist search. He consistently emphasized that music as it was currently being played and sung belonged to a different period, one that was constitutively modern and adequately different from previous periods so that any reliance on texts such as the *Dharmashastra*s as a guide for everyday life was seen by him as romantic at best and anachronistic at worst.

Bhatkhande rejected the idea that the claim for an unbroken history of music could be sustained merely by asserting that Hindustani music could reach back into antiquity, to the Sama Veda chants, as the origins of contemporary music (*prachaarit sangit*). He also came to discover that music's relationship to texts more than two hundred years old was difficult, if not impossible, to prove. The 36,000 couplets of the so-called Gandharva Veda, supposedly composed by the god Brahma and assumed to be the first text on the arts in ancient India (the title of Veda suggests that its origins were not human but divine), were not available in transcribed manuscript form, and all knowledge of it was based solely on references to it in other Sanskrit works.[31] While he regretted not having done research on the Sama Veda, chants which were claimed to be the origins of Hindustani music,[32] he also advised his students not to believe that "our" music derived from the Sama Veda unless and until someone demonstrated how it came together with the origins of Gandharva music, as suggested by the *Natyashastra*.[33]

The *Natyashastra* had not shown itself to be of much use or relevance, and Bhatkhande summed up why this was so. "Bharat's *Natyashastra* has been recently published and become famous," he wrote, "and *shruti* [microtone], *grama* [ancient scales], *murchana* [scales sung in rapid ascending and descending order], *jaati* [possible precursor to raga]—on these subjects there is some description but not of our ragas."[34] He had concluded that *shruti*, as described in the *Natyashastra*, was not useful in determining the fixed scale of Hindustani music. He had not found adequate demonstration of the relationship between microtones and pitches in the *Natyashastra*, and in his subsequent writings he expressed sarcasm and contempt for the wasted efforts of writers on the subject.[35] In other words, music's inescapable modernity—and its unverifiable interreferential historicity—was both apparent and, to some extent, acceptable.

Furthermore, on the subject of music's modernity, Bhatkhande expressed consternation as to why his colleagues avoided recognizing it. "If ancient music is now no longer visible, what is the harm in saying that plainly?" he wrote. "Look at the texts on music in the West, you will find nothing in there that maintains people's confusion and ignorance."[36] The issue was clarity, and there was an abundance of confusion in Sanskrit texts. Bhatkhande had asked scholars during his touring: "Do you think it is possible to revive any of the Sanskrit raga rules? If not, where will be the superiority of a scientific or theoretical musician over an ordinary illiterate, practical singer? Both would be without foundation." Furthermore, "if there is a dispute, what work is to decide? Who is to judge? Will you leave such an important point to the arbitrary tastes of ignorant musicians?"[37] If there was no consensus among musicians themselves about aesthetic standards, what was to be done? The answers he received confirmed for him that the paucity of authentic, original (*mool*) *grantha*s and the irrelevance of available ones to contemporary musical performances had produced a situation where the only possible solution was for someone to produce an authoritative text. Such a text had to be foundational, explaining both the rules and methods of current musical practices. This text could be used as a standard-bearer in the matter of adjudication of quality, as well as in the evaluation of historical change over time. "If music is conceded to be moving constantly, has not the time [arrived] when a new systematic treatise on the current ragas (including Mohammedan additions, of course) is desirable, if not indispensable, for the guidance of the public? In view of the possibility of getting the help of the best musicians, . . . attached to native courts and in view of the facilities. . . . the phonograph, don't you think it practicable? Our ancient Pandits at one time did the same, they made a good collection of ragas. Will not such a step at least arrest future degeneration and mark a stop [make a stamp]?"[38] The solution was simple. Someone needed to collect, annotate, and compile the ragas, and write an authoritative, decisive, historical, and theoretical text. Who better than Bhatkhande himself, given the time and effort he had spent in learning compositions and languages and conducting tours?

Over the course of one year, 1910, Bhatkhande composed hundreds of Sanskrit couplets in which he outlined his theory and history of Hindustani music. He named his text *Shrimallakshyasangeet* (hereafter *SLS*). He also wrote *Abhi-*

nava Raga Manjari and *Abhinava Tala Manjari*, Sanskrit treatises on raga and tala. With the authorship of these three texts, Bhatkhande wrote himself into a long line of music theorists ranging from Sharangdeva to Ahobal. Tradition was now invented with a classical yet modern genealogy. This modern genealogy, in Bhatkhande's view, was what made Indian music classical, because it had a system, a method of adjudication, order, and stability. In other words, the condition for music to be classical was that it was modern. And insofar as Bhatkhande could not simply dismiss Vedic texts or the *Natyashastra*, he did what modern historians do; he accommodated them into his narrative as texts of faded importance but not direct relevance. By doing so, he kept the concept of antiquity vital to a conception of nationalism, but he did this without falling prey to the nationalist seduction of drawing a straight line back between current music and ancient texts. The gap between theory and practice that "illiterate musicians" had fostered now had a bridge, but a self-aware and modern one. By 1928, at the age of sixty-eight, he had written eighteen musicological works—compilations, textbooks, treatises, and booklets. In none of them is there an uncritical celebration of India's ancient wisdom, or of the Vedas as the source of all knowledge for music.

Bhatkhande's Major Works: Sanskrit and Marathi, *Hindustani Sangeet Padhati*

Bhatkhande wrote initially in Sanskrit, which had prestige but limited accessibility. Given his project, this may seem curious, because his interests were democratic and egalitarian, but it is understandable. A modern national classical music needed a classical language. Furthermore, there was a scholarly precedent for him in Sir William Jones's evaluation of Indo-Persian musicological treatises, many of which were translations of Sanskrit treatises. Even though both Arabic and Persian had been used as spoken and written languages far more recently than Sanskrit, Bhatkhande did not consider them adequate for a history of music.[39] They were translation languages, in his view, not authorial ones. In such an understanding, he followed an established colonial and elite pattern of prognosticating about India's future by asserting the primacy of Sanskrit, and thereby a Brahmin understanding as well, as the only authentic window into India's past without which no competent history of her future was imaginable.[40] Bhatkhande's deference to Sanskrit was not unrelated to the authority conferred on it by European Orientalist scholarship. Many scholars have written on the role of colonialism in rendering Sanskrit and the Vedas integral to an understanding of India as Indian.[41] Yet Bhatkhande's deference to Sanskrit was also tactical, strategic, and slightly cynical. B. R. Deodhar, founder of a school of music in Bombay and student of Bhatkhande's rival, Pandit Paluskar, had asked Bhatkhande about why he'd written in Sanskrit in a conversation with him. His response was candid. "People do not accept anything unless it can be backed by Sanskrit quotations . . . the only way the public can be persuaded . . . is by producing a Sanskrit book which gives the new rules."[42]

However, he also wrote a number of important texts in his mother tongue, Marathi, including four volumes of explicatory texts, which he named *Hindustani Sangeet Padhati* (hereafter *HSP*). They were published between 1910 and 1935. Of all his writings, these volumes offer the clearest glimpse into his politics. The first three were finished quickly, between 1910 and 1914.[43] The fourth volume took much longer, and although he completed it in 1929, it was published only in 1932. The conditions under which he wrote it were not perfect, as he wrote to Rai Umanath Bali, explaining the reason for his long silence: "I was busy finishing the fourth volume of my Hindusthani Sangit Paddhati (the work on the theory of music). Thank God, I have been able to finish it somehow. The noises in the head still continue but I do not worry on that account. I am trying to get accustomed to them and hope to succeed in accomplishing it."[44] The years between the publication of the first three volumes and the last one were busy ones for Bhatkhande. He had organized five music conferences, established in 1918 a school of music in Gwalior, and in 1926 cofounded the Marris College in Lucknow.

In these works, Bhatkhande wrote in colloquial (as opposed to literary) Marathi, in the form of conversations between student(s) and teacher in a music classroom. Each volume was one uninterrupted conversation. This format would have been available to him from a number of sources. His colonial education would have introduced him to Plato's Socratic dialogues. He would have known the Pune Sanskritists, at least by reputation, and might have had on hand the *shastra/prayog* distinction available from contemporary writings on the Upanishads. He would also have had a sense of *shastra* that could be translated as both science and classicism. Lastly, the dialogue format was common as well to Persian and Arabic texts, familiar to many scholars.

The main objective of these volumes was to explicate Bhatkhande's Sanskrit treatise, *Shrimallakshyasangeet* (*SLS*), and *Abhinava Raga Manjari*.[45] But there seems to have been another objective, which was to offer *SLS* as the only text that could satisfy a genuinely scholastic student. When Bhatkhande referred to *SLS* in these four volumes, which he did a great deal, he did so by naming the author as one among the writers of the canon without revealing that he was writing about himself. In other words, if one did not have advance knowledge of the fact that Bhatkhande was the author of *SLS*, one would not know by reading the four volumes of *HSP*. *HSP*, thus, was not only self-explicating but also self-aggrandizing.

The four volumes were intended as pedagogical texts, emphasizing dialogue between teacher and student, but Bhatkhande used the first three to write on a variety of subjects: Indian history and historiography, Sanskrit texts, Muslim musicians, the Vedas and their relationship to music, colonial writers, princely states, Westernization, colonialism, nationalism, the superiority of *dhrupad gayaki* over *khyal gayaki*, and the need for notation. Distrustful of all but a few musicians and skeptically respectful of all texts composed in Sanskrit, he gave full voice to uncommonly strong criticisms of musicians, princely rulers, ignorant audiences, intellectual charlatans, and half-baked ideas. In other words, his criticism cast a wide net, unrestrained by hierarchy, class, caste, or religion. Most of these criticisms were voiced through anecdotal caricatures, so there is no way of knowing if the events and people so unflatteringly described were fictional or corresponded to actual meetings, but the ghosts of Karamatullah Khan (the ignorant musician) and Ganeshilal Chaube (the fake Pandit) hover over many of the narratives.

The main characters in these texts are the teacher and the student. The teacher is cautious, humble, benign, and learned. The student is curious, quick, skeptical, yet respectful. Both characters epitomize the virtues of their respective subject positions. The teacher is patient and slow to anger, even though in all conversations with musicians, he is always at the receiving end of ignorant and arrogant abuse. Insofar as they reveal the author's interiority, these texts, as much as the diaries, can be considered Bhatkhande's autobiographies.

These chronicles criticized the dominant hagiographical tradition. Bhatkhande's method of instruction could be seen as similar to that of the neo-traditional exchange between student and teacher (*guru-shishya parampara*), but significant modernizing touches set it apart. In his narrative constructions of a dialogue between the exemplary student and the wise teacher, truth triumphed over ignorance, the first represented by the teacher in the course of his travels, the second represented by musicians and charlatan scholars.

The narrative advances through questions and clarifications, interspersed throughout with anecdotes and reminiscences. The student expresses ignorance through doubt, denunciations of texts or myths, or demands for additional explanation. The teacher responds by proffering either an anecdote, a brief lecture on history, or a first-person remembrance of an encounter. The narrations are sophisticated versions of Bhatkhande's diary reports of conversations with Karamatullah Khan in Allahabad, Babu Chatterjee in Calcutta, or Ganeshilal Chaube in Mathura. Each anecdote concludes with a moral, such as "beware those who come bearing false knowledge."[46] In other instances, the teacher attends a performance, at the end of which he asks the singer, with strategic humility, the rules and textual foundations of the raga he has just sung. All through these accounts, the teacher/narrator creates with his students a community of cognoscenti allied in a battle against those who would mystify the pursuit of real knowledge.

While *SLS* is the metatext that presides over the volumes, it is revealed as the final authority on music only after a whole range of texts in Sanskrit and English are explained. Bhatkhande believed that students of Hindustani music should master seventeen major texts,[47] in addition to the two foundational texts, *Natyashastra* and *Sangit Ratnakara*. In fact, he wrote of the two authors as one, BharatSharangdeva. Each volume had lists of texts the student was expected to read and memorize, along with the libraries in which they were to be found throughout the country. He did not restrict his teachings to Indian languages, referring to two watershed texts in English, C. R. Day's *The Music and Musical Instruments of Southern India and the Deccan* (1891) and Augustus Willard's *A Treatise on the Music of India*, written originally in 1793 but published as a book only in 1834. Other English writers, from Sir William Jones to Raja S. M. Tagore, were also quoted at length, and the quotations were followed by Bhatkhande's critical opinions.

On Muslims and Colonial Beneficence

If Bhatkhande was an extraordinarily complex visionary in so many areas, he was also a man of prejudice. When writing about the decline of music, he suggested that colonial interest in texts was preferable to "Badshahi" (Mughal rule) benevolence: "Some people assert that the condition of music is such because our music fell into the hands of Musalman singers."[48] But for Bhatkhande, it was the inattention to order and system that distinguished the Badshahi. "There is nothing novel in the fact that under Musalman rule, Musalman singers were encouraged [that is, patronized] and given importance. But who was going to teach those singers anything about the correct way of singing and about Sanskrit *grantha*s?" Added to that, a justifiable pride in religious exclusivity interfered with learning. "Those people were also proud of their religion, and there was no possibility that they would learn from Hindu Sanskrit pandits. To say that that period was not a great one for music would not be unusual." From here, he moved on to the British:

> Muslim rulers were not as interested in our ancient knowledge as our present rulers are. Today it would not be unusual to find many Westerners who have studied our religious texts very well. Those sorts of examples are not frequent in the time of the Badshahi. I know of no Musalman pandit who has written a Sanskrit *grantha*. I don't even know of one who understood a Sanskrit music *grantha*. Musalman singers liked music, they were very creative, one can say this, but they had no interest in learning the ancient texts, this too can be said. Even singers like Tansen left no written texts behind. Even to prove that they understood music *grantha*s well would be extremely difficult.

Bhatkhande was willing to concede creativity to "Musalman" singers, but this was all. These singers were ignorant of texts and neglectful of both the order and the historical condition of the musical tradition.

Bhatkhande expressed no view that he did not almost immediately contravene or contradict in subsequent pages. The mode of expression for Bhatkhande was to relay an opinion or judgment and then immediately qualify or retract it. I cite here the most egregious passage about Muslims as one example of many in his four volumes, so as not to evade the depth of his prejudice. The teacher/narrator explains to his students the difference between the four kinds of pitches associated with a raga—*vadi, samvadi, anuvadi,* and *vivadi*. To do so, he uses the metaphor of a conservative middle-class Hindu household:

> The *vadi swar* is the father, the *samvadi* his first son, who had less status than his father but more than anyone else in the house. The *anuvadi swar*s are the servants, whose sole function is to facilitate the

work of the father. Finally, the last category, *vivadi*, are not useful. They are *bhandkhor* and *tondaal* [eager to pick a fight, aggressively hostile, and loudmouthed]. There are those who believe that using a *vivadi swar* in very small quantities is sometimes necessary, even desirable; then one can perhaps see how to do this using a different principle or analogy. Sometimes in Hindu households there are Muslim servants, but it is necessary to affix limits on where they may enter and how much freedom they should have. Of course, I am only using this example flippantly, I don't need to say that.[49]

Flippant or otherwise, the sense is clear. Discordant pitches ought best to be discarded, but in a spirit of accommodation, the teacher grants that if they are to be used at all they should be carefully monitored and controlled, much like Muslims in a Hindu household.

When not being prejudiced Bhatkhande was often dismissive, pitying "poor Muslims who were intimidated by 'our' Sanskrit texts and knowledge."[50] He wrote of them as childlike, often using the adjective *bechare*, which could literally mean poor or with bad luck, worthy of pity, beguiled, or unschooled.[51] He ridiculed Muslim singers for their pretensions to *granthi* knowledge[52] and represented them as ever willing to pick a fight, abusive, polemical—similar to the hypothetical servants in his earlier example. Having written of Muslims as aggressive and in need of surveillance and control, he went on to indict Hindus as well, arguing that they should bear a fair share of blame for having let what was rightfully theirs fall into the wrong hands:

If our current music is not the same as that of the music writers' period, it is no fault of the writers. If *our* educated people did not value music knowledge and knowingly let it pass into the control of the Miansahabs [a term used for Muslims], and in their company *our* music changed, then who should be held accountable for this? Now however much *we* may repent this takeover it is not, in my opinion, going to be very useful. It would not be wrong to state that just as it would not be possible to have Manu's views be dominant in society today, in the same way it would not be possible to use ancient texts on music. It is not my view that Muslim singers have ruined music. Their only fault was that they did not write down all the changes they made to the music. But there may have been many of them who could not read or write.

This is an important passage. Bhatkhande condemns both Hindus and Muslims, but the reasons are not clear. His irritation is directed at musicians, singers, and instrumentalists—not because of their religious affiliation, but because as performers they did not pay adequate attention to posterity nor, for that matter, to the future. In this sense, Bhatkhande's search for origins was not simply nostalgic. Had it been so, he would not have so quickly dismissed the relevance of the *Dharmashastra*s to contemporary life or the Vedas to music. Indeed, his contemporaries like Paluskar embraced a nostalgic and reconstructed ideal of Hindu life in accordance with Manu. Bhatkhande's project, however, accommodated an understanding of historical change. Muslims might be blamed for their illiteracy, but not for their faith.

The passage continues in an ironic tone: "Our love and respect for Muslim singers should be apparent in this, that within our community [*amchyaat*] any Hindu singer however excellently he sings, if there is no Khansaheb [Muslim musician] in his musical tradition, we consider him only a *bhajani haridas* [a singer only of devotional music]!" He admits, in other words, that devotional music is aesthetically inferior to that which is taught and authenticated only by Muslim musicians. Moreover, "Where do we have the right to think less of Muslim singers? We are truly in their debt. If we were to tout the fact that Tansen's guru was Swami Haridas, even so if someone were to ask us which is the text he left behind, what could we say? Even if this is the condition, don't squander your respect for ancient texts. They are not altogether useless. When you read them then you can decide, calmly, what their value is."[53] Having denounced Muslims for being aggressive, ignorant, and illiterate, he does not altogether reverse his opinion but acknowledges that music's aesthetics are indebted to its Muslim history. But is its history not indebted as well? *Thaat* (grouping of ragas) was Hindu, and there were two kinds of performances and ragas, Hindu and Muslim. "We sing *miyan-ki-malhar, miyan-ki-sarang, miyan-ki-todi, husaini todi, darbari todi, bilaskhani todi, jaunpuri, sarparda, saazgiri, shahana, yamani, navroz,* . . . and if we were to say they are supported by ancient texts, would it do us credit? Some might ask, what if we left aside these Musalman varieties, there are other ragas that are in our *grantha*s, are there not? Yes, but who even sings those today?"[54] This is not necessarily a lament but also an observation that the focus on *grantha*s misses the point. Contemporary music, however one felt about it in the early twentieth century, was that which was sung by Muslim musicians. He continues, "We break the rules given in the *grantha*s and mimic Musalman singers. In so many cases we do not even acknowledge the *thaat*s that are given in the *grantha*s. Even in the singing of well known ragas like *bhairav, bhairavi, todi* we follow none of the *granthi* rules, will it not beg the question, then what is our *shastra.* '55 This is an important question for a nationalist like Bhatkhande. He continues with an imperative: "Understand my point correctly. I have no desire to criticize present day music or musicians. *I will go so far as to say that our Hindustani music is only just being classicized. The texts on music that are being written today are all establishing new rules for music's classicism.*"56 This statement can be read as Bhatkhande's most emphatic declaration that music needed to be classical in order to be modern. It can also perhaps be read as his injunction to his students to stay away from an uncritical nostalgia for the *grantha*s. Bhatkhande was clearly aware that in order for music to be called classical it needed established rules, but he was also aware of the fact that particular rules were themselves an inextricable part of the modern world in which he was firmly located, without nostalgia.

Classicization, seen in this regard, was instrumental and went hand in hand with nationalization. The *gharana*s could not fit the bill—not because they were Muslim, but because they were disorderly. Moreover, they were not public institutions. Access to them was restricted, there was no public arena of discussion and debate, and instruction was selective. The reason Muslim musicians had to be excluded was not simply because they were Muslim, but because they, like the Kshetra Mohan Goswamis and Ganeshilal Chaubes, did not possess the knowledge to create and sustain a modern academy of classical music. The academy had to be built from scratch, which Bhatkhande recognized in his comment that "Hindustani music is only just being classicized." The *ustad*s and *gharana*s could not serve the academy's needs, nor could the *bhajani haridas* (a veiled reference to Paluskar), because in spite of their creativity, they did not understand what the "classical" was in their music. For Bhatkhande, classicization meant at least two things: system, order, discipline, and theory, on the one hand, and antiquity of national origin, on the other. Of course, these requirements equally define the very character of modern music. The first set of elements he could not find in contemporary practice, and he had toured the country in search of them. He found confusion, not order, and an emphasis on spontaneity rather than disciplined performance. So he set out to impose order on contemporary music. His liberal nationalism allowed him to include "Muslim" ragas, such as *malkauns,* *darbari*, and *miyan-ki-malhar*. But they all had to be integrated into a body of rules, constructed according to a national canon of musical theory.

The rules in his writings cautioned his readers against believing that mere voice training (*galyaachi taiyaari*) was all that was needed for good performances, insisting that performers needed to know the rules of music (*sangeetache niyam*) as well.[57] In one of the lengthiest anecdotes of all five volumes, he narrates a detailed story—in the nature of a *panchatantra katha*[58] or an Aesopian fable—of a gifted but undisciplined singer who believes that with a little bit of music education he can join the ranks of famous musicians. The singer starts out with a traditional teacher (*guru*) who demands of him all that Bhatkhande would demand of his students, but tires quickly of such discipline, in which he is required to notate what he learns and focus on perfect pitch (*swar*) and theory (*raga agyan*), rather than vocal acrobatics (*tanabazi*). Unhappy with the rigor of this training, he switches to a musician maestro (an unnamed *Khansaheb*). The contrast between the two is clear. The Muslim *Khansaheb* smokes tobacco (*hookah*), chews betel nut (*paan supari*), disparages him publicly, teaches him very little, and tricks him out of his money.[59] Bhatkhande's disparagement was clear: without true knowledge, which is to say rule-bound, bookish knowledge, students were liable to fall into the hands of ignorant practitioners.

Along with his dismissal of ignorance, Bhatkhande advocated a healthy skepticism concerning pandits and singers who believed that the texts in their possession were written by the gods themselves.[60] He took pains to dispel popular myths about the power of ragas to influence climates and seasons.[61] Society, he noted, was too ignorant and childlike at the time to understand fables as mere fables. One should not try to dispel such ignorance, he cautioned, but pity it instead.[62] This was not real history, and students needed to know that even ancient texts could be challenged.

This was difficult advice. He commented wryly that "it is a great crime (*mahapaap*) in these days to state that writers of ancient *grantha*s had made a mistake in their theorizing or that music as it was performed is no longer possible to perform."[63] And indeed, criticism of his works came flying at him from musicians and scholars. The first group believed his writings were simply irrelevant to their performance; the second, in unlikely sympathy with the former, accused him both of trying to reduce music education to mere mechanical understanding and of denying its divine history. Bhatkhande addressed such criticisms directly. "Those writers who have abandoned the muddle of *murchana* and *grama* and written their texts using contemporary music as their foundation should be admired and applauded,"[64] he wrote. Yet he wrote in Sanskrit because he understood that, otherwise, he would not be recognized as a classical writer.

Sanskrit had more than a merely instrumental function. Throughout the volumes of the *HSP* texts, there is a tension between Bhatkhande's desire to make music modern and accessible and his unshakeable belief, despite his erudition, that Urdu, Persian, and Hindi texts on music were not scholarly enough for the task at hand.[65] Here he shared the sentiments of Sir William Jones, who admired the complexity of Sanskrit for its ability to tackle the first principles of music. Unfortunately, such a classificatory logic had too great a potential to take on a divisive character in its very formulation, given the historical circumstances of the time: Hindu music was made essential, natural, and ancient; Muslim music was thus made lacking in foundation, aberrational, and new.[66] Inasmuch as this may not have been the logic that Bhatkhande was working with, it provided the ballast other lesser scholars could use to put into practice a partitioning of the cultural sphere (and of music) into Hindu and Muslim.

In addition to his other writings, Bhatkhande also compiled 1,800 compositions, collected during his travels from hereditary musicians, in six volumes titled *Kramik Pustak Malika*. These were originally composed in Marathi and later translated into Hindi. This was and remains an extraordinary compilation. On the one hand, it brought together for the first time, in one series of texts, virtually the entire corpus of popularly sung ragas and compositions. This meant that students no longer needed to participate in the elaborate rituals of admission into a guild in order to learn music. The compilation was itself the culmination of a concentrated effort to make famous musical compositions accessible, notated, and easy to learn under the supervision of a reasonably trained musician. It did not, in other words, require a maestro to teach ordinary, everyday people the rudiments of music. Because of Bhatkhande's unceasing efforts, the compilation could be considered part of the national canon of musical compositions—the property and treasure of all. On the other hand, the compilation managed simultaneously to detach the compositions from their Muslim *gharana*s. This meant that the role of the *gharana*s in compositional authorship was erased from the newly created record of music's history in the pursuit of a neutral and nonreligious corpus. What it did, therefore, was to write Muslims out of musical history as authors. This move did not wipe them out of music's history entirely, but it did not allow their contribution to be considered as authorial or authentically authoritative. And worse still, it paved the way for other, less secular Hindu nationalist musicians and scholars to climb atop Bhatkhande's foundational work and claim that what was primarily sung by Muslims from within a familial tradition now needed to be installed in a primarily Hindu home. This home, now guarded by new notions of Sanskrit knowledge, barred access to "illiterate musicians" who happened mostly to be Muslim.[67]

Last Days

The fourth volume of *HSP* was Bhatkhande's final writing project. His failing health and the noises in his head grew burdensome, but his devotion to music never flagged. In 1923, he had been asked by the ruler of Indore, Tukoji Rao Holkar, about the superiority of singers over instrumentalists. His response had been careful and prompt: singers were superior, he claimed, and he had it on good Sanskrit authority that this was so.[68] In 1931, the zeal to answer any question about music, no matter where or how, had not diminished at all, as one sees in his correspondence with his old friend, Rai Umanath Bali. This time the issue at hand was not conferences but high-school music textbooks for the schools of the United Provinces (UP). In what seems to have been a somewhat tense correspondence, he wrote, "I am sorry to learn that the Allahabad people have successfully stolen a march over you in the matters of School text books. It appears they worked secretly in the matter and managed to get their books approved."[69] By Allahabad, he was referring to a rival music institution. In Bhatkhande's identification of the problem, Bali had been tricked because the UP government had simply gone about producing textbooks the wrong way. The Bengal provincial government, on the other hand, had done it correctly. What was the difference? In the same letter, Bhatkhande wrote "they appointed a committee of music knowing people to consider the whole subject and then asked publicly writers to submit their work. Even a man living in Bombay like myself was put on the committee. *My* views on the Hindusthani System were accepted by that Govt. Rev. Popley will tell you all that happened in Calcutta. Prof. Mukerji of Lucknow knows about it.[70] *My name* was suggested to the Bengal Govt. by Dr. Rabindranath Tagore himself. In his own institution at Shanti Niketan, *songs* *from my book*s were taught by his music teachers. Bhimrao Shastri and Dr. Rabindra Nath Tagore know me personally and also know of *my work*" (emphasis mine). Boasts apart, Bhatkhande was once again bothered by the lack of a nationalized system by which music curriculum was to be determined.

Obviously peeved at being passed over, Bhatkhande expressed restrained annoyance to Bali:

> I must state honestly here, that you never asked either myself or Shrikrishna [his student, and principal of the Marris College, Shrikrishna Ratanjankar] to prepare small textbooks for the schools of the province. If you had done that we could have finished the thing in a couple of weeks. . . . Our college textbooks are enough to supply material for 50 books if necessary at a moment's notice. The fact is that you yourself did not know what was being done behind the Purdah in Allahabad and failed to ask me to prepare the books. How can you then blame either myself or Shrikrishna for negligence in the matter?

Putting aside his ire, he volunteered to help get the books published, suggesting ways to popularize them quickly, but he was not pleased by his friend's suggestion that he needed to secure favorable opinions of his work.

> You want me to go round to important people and obtain their favorable opinions on my books and notation! At this time of the day it would look rather awkward on my part to make an attempt like that. I used to receive hundreds of letters from people appreciating my books but I have not preserved them. I always wanted to stand on my own merits. I do not think I shall be able to approach big people now after writing for 25 years for favorable opinions. I shall consider it below me to do it. The very fact that our books are now taught in (1) The Benares Hindu University, (2) The Madhav Sangit College and its branches (Gwalior), (3) The schools of Nagpur city, (4) The Baroda School of Indian Music and its branches, (5) In the Hindu Women's University and its affiliated Schools in Surat, Ahmedabad and Baroda, Satara, etc., (6) In all the 200 primary Schools of Bombay in the control of the Bombay municipality, will be enough recommendation for the books and the Notation in them. For me to now approach big men who understand nothing about the subject, soliciting favorable opinions would look a bit ridiculous.

Finally, putting an end to this part of the conversation, he declaimed, "[my] books are looked upon as standard authorities on the subject." Not even his competitor Pandit Paluskar had been quite as rigorous in the imposition of standards. "None of Digambar's pupils has cut a good figure before our Gwalior boys trained in our system which speaks for itself." He was arrogant, no doubt, but also upright. "We do not work underground for success," he wrote to Umanath Bali, apropos of Allahabad's secretiveness, "but work in the open and leave the public to judge. Even if Allahabad books hold the field for a time, be sure the success will be short lived. . . . Have faith in God and try your honest best and leave the rest to him."

Bhatkande had spent most of his life after the death of his wife and daughter roaming around the country conducting music examinations and inspecting music schools. His travels came to an abrupt end in 1933, when he suffered an attack of paralysis that left him bedridden for almost three years.[71] In February 1933, he wrote to his student Shrikrishna Ratanjankar, "Life has reached the end of its journey. . . . I have done whatever I deemed my duty. Whatever material I could collect I have recorded and protected it. I have full faith that in future, there will be worthy people to use it suitably. While writing sometimes with over enthusiasm I have used sharp words in discussing the theory of music. But believe me, it was not intended to hurt anybody's feelings."[72] On September 19, 1936, at the age of seventy-six, Bhatkhande died in Bombay.

Conclusion

Bhatkhande had cofounded the Marris College with Rai Umanath Bali in 1926. He was neither robust nor healthy at that point. He had begun to suffer from high blood pressure and, as a result, heard "singing noises" in his head all day and night.[73] He had also suffered a severe hip injury and needed sedatives to tackle his unrelieved insomnia. His physical discomforts notwithstanding, he remained involved in the administrative affairs of the Marris College and embroiled in a power struggle with an old friend, Nawab Ali, over the hiring of a music teacher and the firing of an unpopular principal.

Bhatkhande had lived for the previous twenty-five years without either the comfort or the financial and emotional responsibilities of married life. He traveled incessantly even when his health did not permit it, but as he wrote to Rai Umanath Bali,

> You need not worry about my health. My chief complaint is loud head noises which prevent sleep. . . . They have increased my deafness considerably. . . . I shall never allow my health to come between me and my duty to the College. I would rather die in the College than in a sick bed here. I eat well, take fair exercise, and with one grain of Luminol get enough sleep. An old and deaf man has necessarily to go through these difficulties and I have no reason to complain.[74]

Had he been given a choice, he would have chosen one of two sacred sites in which to die, sites that he had kept apart—either Kashi (Benares) or the Lucknow Music College. As it happened, he died in Bombay, the city of his birth, ten years after the founding of his college.

With Bhatkhande's death, a newly formed practice of music scholasticism seems to have died as well. Not only had he laid out a theory and history for Hindustani music that musicologists, musicians, and historians would need to contend with seriously in any further study of the subject (more than any other musicologist of his time or since), he had set the terms for rigorous, erudite scholarship on music. Bhatkhande not only documented all he wrote, he made his sources public. In so doing, he established a standard for music scholarship that, regrettably, has not followed his example. Instead, letters, diaries, original compositions, and rare books have been kept hidden for decades, rarely shown even to research scholars, and mostly made available only to a deeply entrenched insider community that accepts hagiography as the sole acceptable mode of historical writing. On occasion, fragments of primary sources are published but no citations are given; this makes it impossible for anyone else to have firsthand access to them. Such secrecy would have been anathema to Bhatkhande.

Bhatkhande was by no means alone in his desire to bring some order to the performance and pedagogy of music, but his genius lay in the curious mix of his approach. He blended high-minded scholasticism with rigorous attention to citation, documentation, and proof, always driven by a desire to make music more accessible to a larger public. Bhatkhande's textbooks facilitated the teaching of music out of as many homes as there were teachers and in as many homes as there were students. The early decades of the twentieth century witnessed a large middle-class expansion of music appreciation and learning. Given the growing respectability of music—already set in motion by other music reformers, music appreciation societies, and public performances—musical learning became not only acceptable but a required component of a certain middle-class education, particularly for young women, as we shall see in a later chapter. Lastly, Bhatkhande's sense of the nation extended beyond the boundaries of his native region.

Bhatkhande argued this cause in impassioned prose: "The leaders of the Nation who are for the present engrossed in saving the political future of the country should lend some portion of their energies to the regeneration of this art, so as to bring it within the vision of the nation and to rescue it from the decay which ends in death. The New India must be a full blown entity, and it would never do to omit the regeneration of our music from the programme of our workers."[75] Music, he claimed, had "metabolic value" and would be "the best tonic for reviving the energies of our hard-worked nation-builders, some of whom have themselves remarked to me that they would have been much better equipped for their exhausting work if they had this natural tonic and restorative to fall back upon." For Bhatkhande, music was both medicine and magic.

Bhatkhande's commitment to music allowed for a random practice to be disciplined by a connected history, a stern typology, and a documented musicology. These are not mean achievements, but they are predicated on the assumption that musicians qua musicians had destroyed music. The same performing artists who had organic and embodied knowledge of their art (and its craft) and in whose families music had resided and flourished for generations were the main problem confronting music. Perhaps it had been caused by their Muslimness, perhaps not. Bhatkhande alludes to this possibility but leaves overt assertions about Islam unsaid. He is clear, however, about the solution to the problem: namely, to impose on these practices a nationalized and textual solution. The solution was as incongruous and ill-fitting as the initial claim was preposterous. Despite his desire for an "Indian" music, it is precisely Bhatkhande's connected history that might have given people like Paluskar the needed weight to turn classical music into Hindu music.

What then, can we make of this complex man? For all his egalitarianism and high-minded secular approach to musical pedagogy and performance, we cannot ignore the fact that his politics included overt and disquieting prejudice toward musicians as a group and Muslims as a community. Hundreds of

Muslim musicians thronged the halls of the All-India Music Conferences, but within twenty years of the last All-India Music Conference in Lucknow in 1926, the numbers of Muslim musicians declined sharply. Bhatkhande had himself bemoaned the fact that all "first class musicians were rapidly dying out,"[76] but what, if anything, had he done to maintain their claim to music's historical heritage? Instead, the narrative history of music is couched in evolutionary terms as the inevitable "transfer of power" from feudal Muslims to national Hindus. What responsibility might we place at Bhatkhande's doorstep for the decline in the number of Muslim musicians? And how might we assess the cost of the rebirth of national music in the terms he laid out for modern India?

In the course of conducting research for this book, I posed the question of the possible decline in the number of practicing Muslim musicians to a few musicians and musicologists. My interlocutors consistently gave me one of three answers, all of which placed the blame on Muslim musicians. The first was couched in terms of inadequacy and insecurity: "Muslim musicians were uneducated and secretive; once the music was made available to everyone, they could no longer maintain their self-importance." The second answer focused on the deficiencies of Islam and the community of Muslims: "They have always been fanatical and backward. It is because of them that music almost came to an end in this country." The third response was simply to disagree about the decline in numbers by listing the names of Muslim musicians in India; proponents of this line of thought advised me not to overread "communalism" in my historical analysis.

All these answers, including the so-called liberal one stressing that Muslims were by no means absent from the current field of musical performance, can be drawn from Bhatkhande's corpus, yet he never made any one of these claims with such absoluteness. Still, one does see repeated iterations of the idea of something he identified as "our" music in his work to which Muslim musicians had, at best, contributed. If the practitioners of music were seen as so ill suited to dealing with the forces of modernization, why then were they not better protected by music's self-proclaimed saviors? Instead of blaming musicians for their poverty and illiteracy, why did Bhatkhande and others not lavish attention on their recuperation? Had there been as many Hindu musicians as there were Muslim musicians, would Bhatkhande and others have approached their demise with such indifference? Instead of paying attention to these questions, music's reformers sought rather to liberate music from the musicians. Such a violent transformative separation could hardly have been inevitable or natural.

In the very deliberate particularity of Bhatkhande's choices lie some of the troubling answers as to why, despite overwhelming evidence to the contrary, his historical narrative of music developed as it did. Had he been able to incorporate, in some fashion, the legacy of the *gharana* system without appropriating it, he might have had greater success. His many exclusions, not just of Muslims but of women, South Indian music, and musicians, except in the most instrumental terms, can be seen as the inevitable and unintended consequence of a flawed project that could not relinquish the desire for a single origin of music. In theory, Bhatkhande's academy would belong to all Indians irrespective of religion or caste or gender. But while he could claim that his work was known by stalwarts of India's rapidly expanding nationalist movement, the national academy never took shape except in bits and pieces. In that light, if one were to read Bhatkhande generously, one can see his most vituperative statements as prescient expressions of frustration at being thwarted in his desire precisely by the *gharana*s that survived the onslaught of modernization and classicization.

Bhatkhande was unpopular during his lifetime, and his writings were criticized immediately upon publication. A certain kind of failure was a very large and intrinsic part of his success. In 1931, at the age of seventy-one, in another letter to Rai Umanath Bali, he could claim countrywide fame without sounding boastful.[77] In 1926, Bhatkhande had met and advised Gandhi and Rabindranath Tagore on how to teach music in their respective institutions.[78] In 1929, Pandit Madan Mohan Malaviya, a leading Hindu nationalist, had invited him to inspect the music teaching at Benares Hindu University.[79] Having secured the respect of such prominent nationalist leaders as Gandhi, Tagore, and Malaviya, Bhatkhande could state matter-of-factly and with good reason that Hindustani music scholars and patrons from Bengal to Gujarat, the United Provinces to Maharashtra, recognized him.

For all his fame, musicians disliked him intensely for presuming to instruct them on the rules of music when he himself was not a performer.[80] Scholars such as K. B. Deval and E. Clements, whom he criticized—whether about the appropriateness of the harmonium as an accompanying instrument for vocal performances, or about the accuracy of their scientific calculations about microtones—were not well disposed toward him.[81] Pandit Paluskar, his rival, dismissed his notation system and pedagogy and kept his distance from him. And this is precisely where the question of failure and success and the attendant politics of both men need to come into dialogue. The fundamental distinction between the two men lay in the actual countrywide success of Paluskar's agenda, a success markedly different from Bhatkhande's. Bhatkhande had dispelled spiritualism, religious rituals, superstition, and sacralization from his agenda. With Paluskar the exact opposite prevailed. The culture of sacrality was everywhere in his schools. The musician was transformed into a spiritual teacher, and the students were incorporated into a reworked *gurukul.* Women had been harnessed to play the roles of the "inside" proselytizers.

It is ironic—against Bhatkhande's wishes but not without resonance in his method and manner—that Hindu music was further turned back into what he most disliked, namely, a music linked to spiritualism and divinity. He claimed he was not averse to Hindu music being changed, merely to the change not being recorded for posterity. The ostensible issue at hand for him was history, not religion or politics per se. Nonetheless, the distinction between the performers and national owners that had been allowed to fall into the wrong hands creates a separation between a Hindu "us" and a Muslim "them." When one adds Bhatkhande's many other assertions about Muslims, one is presented with a politics that appears far more contradictory, troubling, and narrow than has been conceded so far.

Given the many prejudiced assertions made by Bhatkhande, can one rest on the tired cliché that some of his best friends were Muslim, and that he had nothing against Islam qua Islam but merely against musicians who merely happened to be Muslim and who expressed their Muslimness in antiprogressive ways? Can one justify Bhatkhande by saying that he merely reflected the politics of elite Hindu Brahmin males of his time? Alternatively, should one agree with Vinayak Purohit, who lambastes Bhatkhande for being a colonial collaborator and an arch communalist?[82] None of these claims combines an in-depth critical examination of Bhatkhande's enormous contributions with his opinions. How does one put his writings on Muslims in a historical perspective that is neither presentist nor apologist? If this is a difficult question to ask, it is all the more difficult to avoid. And yet, with the exception of Vinayak Purohit, whose diatribe is so sweeping that it cannot be seen as a serious attempt to understand the man or his music, not one of the commentators on Bhatkhande writing in English, Hindi, or Marathi has brought to public attention any of the passages cited in this chapter. If nothing else, I hope to bring to the fore undeniable evidence of Bhatkhande's own anti-Muslim sentiment without making this the only part of the story.

Bhatkhande was not popular in his native state and believed he had been misunderstood, mistreated, and unjustly criticized by his fellow Maharashtrians.[83] In the years between 1881 and 1936, when Bhatkhande had acquired a name for himself, the Marathi nationalist newspaper *Kesari* reported only that Professor Krishnarao Mule, author of a book on Hindustani music, had noted that Bhatkhande's system of *thaat*s was without a solid foundation.[84] Pandit Paluskar, on the other hand, could count on the paper to report his every activity, act of nationalist defiance, conference, and dispute with another musician.

In addition to his unpopularity, the college Bhatkhande founded never lived up to his ideals. In fact, three years after its founding, the college confronted virtual bankruptcy, and Bali, who ran its day-to-day affairs, considered handing it over to the university.[85] And in retrospect, if by some stroke of prescience Bhatkhande could have witnessed his future students and supporters paying homage to his memory by garlanding his photograph with flowers and laying beside it a stand of *agarbatti* (incense) before doing *namaskar* to his painting, his lament about the direction and future of music might have been even more intense. Bhatkhande believed that all the ghosts and spirits that were part of music's performative culture needed to be exorcised. The future of music lay in order, systematic pedagogy, archival depth, and classical learning.

The accolades Bhatkhande received posthumously also might have troubled him greatly. The Marris College was renamed the Bhatkhande Sangeet Vidyapeeth in 1947, the year of India's independence from British colonial rule.[86] That might not have bothered him, but two years later, in 1949, a leading Hindi journal of the arts, *Sangeet Kala Vihar*, published his horoscope and reproduced a letter written by him in English to a noted scholar of music, Professor G. H. Ranade, under the heading, "The late Pandit V. N. Bhatkhande's handwriting."[87] The letter was reproduced with no apparent intent other than to provide a sample of his handwriting. In 1967, the government of India issued a postage stamp in his name. At last, he had received nationwide recognition, even though most of his projects would have disappointed him had he lived to see them through the next few decades.

The spotlight of this chapter has been Bhatkhande's many Pyrrhic successes. However, we need to remember that he was and remains a figure of enormous national importance to the fortunes of Indian classical music, seen as the icon of music's theoretical modernity. In a fundamental sense, Bhatkhande believed he was affirming music, and in the process he would make it available to all Indians, regardless of caste, religion, and gender. Bhatkhande's supporters rightly tell us that he did what he did for the larger glory of Indian music, and without him, India would have lost part of its cultural heritage. That would not be untrue. All the same, to highlight Bhatkhande as a failed visionary, we need to turn to his competitor and contemporary, who oversaw the unqualified successful completion of the Hindu agenda for music. We turn now to another musician who shared a first name with Bhatkhande but was frequently a thorn in his side: Vishnu Digambar Paluskar.

❋ FOUR ❋

THE CERTAINTY OF MUSIC'S MODERNITY

Vishnu Digambar Paluskar

Bhatkhande's career in music, as we saw in the previous chapter, offers us a retrospective look at the contradictions within a scholastic, historicist, and fundamentally liberal Brahmin agenda for music—one that did not quite succeed institutionally. In the next chapter, we shall have occasion to look more carefully at his institutional shortcomings and at the notion of music as part of a national agenda. In this chapter, in direct contrast with Vishnu Narayan Bhatkhande, who can be seen as a tragic figure, we spend time with his counterpart, Vishnu Digambar Paluskar, who comes to us over the course of history as a triumphant figure. Pandit Paluskar was the neotraditional counterpart to Bhatkhande. His understanding of music was simple, straightforward, contained few contradictions, and focused on the simple, spiritual, and public duties of music over the arcane and intellectual. Vishnu Digambar, as he was known in his time, rejected the courtly life of princely states in favor of a more peripatetic career, had close ties to Hindu reform associations, was active in the nationalist movement, and, toward the end of his life, retreated into spiritualism, *bhajan*s, and *Ramayana pravachana*s.

Paluskar's mission for music—and it was a mission in the religious sense of the term—was threefold. The first was to raise the status of musicians by ridding music of its association with entertainment and linking it, in its stead, to the performance of devotional music in the context of highlighting religious themes. The second was to form a number of institutions for the spread of musical education around the country. Lastly, and perhaps most importantly, Paluskar reinstated a modern version of a bhakti-based, but Brahminized, understanding of the *guru-shishya parampara*. This bound students to him in a lifelong relationship of devoted obedience and loyal fealty. Students included women, who were crucial to his program, especially through their responsibility to initiate their offspring into a religious understanding of music. Unlike Bhatkhande, Paluskar had no secular pretensions. The separation of God and music was not for him. Paluskar not only publicized his faith as the expression of a personal relationship to the divine, he also yoked it to a programmatic agenda for music. Music was not simply a lost and misguided form that had fallen into the wrong hands and needed to be rescued, corrected, and then made available to all, as it was for Bhatkhande. Music for Paluskar was a live agent. He believed music had an important task to perform: returning the attention of the public to the true and only faith of the land—the Hindu faith.

Paluskar made it possible for an ease of understanding to settle into an emerging middle class's understanding, certainly in Maharashtra but across northern India as well, about the natural inextricability of Indian art from Brahminized Hindu sacrality. As an instrument of this mission, music performed its assigned task under Paluskar with much more success than Bhatkhande could claim, his nationwide recognition by nationalists notwithstanding. The schools established by Paluskar and his followers—the Gandharva Mahavidyalayas—still teach students in the thousands. They maintain, with some degree of variation of inclusion, the same spirit of the curriculum as Paluskar conceived a century ago, and have made it a matter of routine in music and dance schools around the country for students to forge a lifelong relationship of devotion to their gurus, more generally associating the performing arts with the divine.[1]

The intertwining of music and dance with the divine—and with a so-called traditional guru—along with the prominence of prayers, chants, key deities, and Puranic mythology, can be seen as a determined move against colonial assertions of Western, national, superiority. It can also be seen as a consciously nationalist effort to recuperate and recover, for use in the colonized present, a precolonial sense of music, religion, and cultural life. In their critiques of secularism, many scholars have pointed out that for any authentic narrative of Indian history, a disenchanted history must be replaced with one in which gods and spirits occupy their rightful space. There are sound reasons for this concern. But when confronted with the success of a figure like Paluskar, the move from a critique of colonial history to an affirmation of the traditional poses several problems, chief among which is the old-fashioned problem of politics. For one thing, in linking music with religious devotion, Paluskar was being not recidivist but modern. His understanding of Hinduism as a proselytizing force dovetailed neatly with the agenda of Hindu revival organizations such as the Arya Samaj and the Sanatan Dharm. The modern character of Hinduism is not by itself the issue. What we see with Paluskar is bhakti nationalism, which, in his linking of music with faith, performance with religiosity, and pedagogy with worship, brought along with the gods and spirits a few uninvited demons.

To reveal the demons as well as to accept the gods and spirits as part of music's history has implications for a larger history of Indian cultural nationalism. Paluskar's success and Bhatkhande's failure provide not only a quick corrective to the celebratory conceits of liberal and secular modernizing movements, but also a sobering look at the politics of an equally modern, neotraditional, conservative religious agenda. A vast critical literature has demonstrated the inherent religiosity within the concept of the secular and repudiated the concept altogether for its intolerance and inadequacy. Indeed, some features of that critique hold true for Bhatkhande's "secular" project as well, as we have seen in the previous chapter. As the flip side of Bhatkhande's secular and failed project, Paluskar's project can be read in terms of a resistance to the forces of colonial epistemology and power, but might also be seen in broader terms that bring out the dangers of an affiliation of a national religious tradition with any effort to resist or escape colonization.

Before I begin with Paluskar's early years, something should be noted about the sources used in this chapter. Lala Gurandittamal Khanna wrote the earliest of Paluskar's biographies in Hindi, *Gayanacharya Shrimaan Pandit Vishnu Digambarji Paluskar ka Sankshipt Jeevan Vrittaant,* which was written while Paluskar was still alive and his only surviving child was nine years old.[2] He wrote of Paluskar's belief in a Hindu pantheon, his devotion (bhakti) to God, his exquisite rendition of *kirtan*s (devotional songs), his renunciation of the world, and his clarity of vision. In Khanna's narrative, Paluskar is turned into a saint who, by his efforts for the "Hindu race," entered into the very pantheon he worshipped. The same style was used by Paluskar's other biographers as well. Paluskar's most well-known students, Vinayak Narayan Patwardhan and B. R. Deodhar, wrote their devotional remembrances of him in Marathi: *Mazhe Gurucharitra,* in 1956, and *Gayanacharya Pandit Vishnu Digambar,* in 1971, respectively. Additionally, N. R. Pathak, Paluskar's confidant and student in Lahore, wrote articles in Marathi in which he recounted the tenor of everyday life while at the Gandharva Mahavidyalaya.

All these accounts are somewhat adulatory. Moreover, every writer has insisted that his narrative has an authentic "truth" not found in any other. In this corpus, hagiography and ethnography feed each other's truths. The objective proof of Paluskar's godly and otherworldly nature as a guru is demonstrated through some miraculous event, narrated by an author who always claimed to witness the event himself (for example, when Paluskar addressed a deity while in a trance or moved mountains by the force of his devotional singing). In Deodhar's account, which is the most recent, sources such as the school's magazine are cited, but for the most part, the biographer's presence and memory suffice as the sources for irrefutable documentation. Although all these accounts read like predictable hagiographies, it is clear that in Paluskar's case, he actively played the role of a saint and wished to be portrayed as one. Additionally, both he and his students were committed to cementing a culture of sacrality around the history of music and its devotees. Given the difficulty of locating primary sources in music, I have treated these biographies both as motivated hagiographies and as ethnographies of the past, archival sources and cultural documents that help explain the contemporary culture of music in modern India.

Meraj to Lahore: The Start of a Career, 1872–1898

Vishnu Digambar Paluskar was born on August 19, 1872. He was exposed to the world of musical performance at an early age. Paluskar's father was the favored *kirtankar* (devotional singer) of Dajisaheb Patwardhan, the ruler of Kurundwad, a small court in South Maharashtra. Rulers of small princely states were more like large *zamindars,* but nonetheless maintained the ritual protocols of kingship, including employing a *darbari gavai* (court singer) and maintaining a court. Many poor families depended on *rajashraya* (princely patronage) for their survival. Paluskar's was one such family; he and his brother often provided the instrumental accompaniment for their father's musical performances of *kirtan*s and *bhajan*s, thus receiving hands-on musical training even if they were not getting systematic instruction. At a local religious festival, Paluskar had an accident with a firecracker that permanently damaged his eyesight. He was still in school at the time, but the doctor in attendance believed that reading would further ruin his eyes, so the family decided that since he was musically gifted, they would send him away to train as a performing musician. Before he left home, his parents arranged Vishnu Digambar's marriage to Vithabai Kelkar, sister of the postmaster of Kurundwad. He was fifteen years old at the time and she was ten.[3] The couple moved to Meraj where Paluskar began his "official" musical training in 1887.[4]

Fourteen miles north of Kurundwad, Meraj was a princely state ruled by Balasaheb Patwardhan.[5] Its court was famous because its *darbari gavai* was Balkrishnabua Ichalkaranjikar. Balkrishnabua was, at the time, the foremost singer in Western India of *khayal*, which he was credited with having brought into western India from the north.[6] Paluskar began his training with him under the terms of an unwritten and unspoken agreement in which he was required, along with the other students, to engage in household chores, including washing clothes, gathering firewood, and keeping the house clean. Students were also expected to look after their guru's children and run all errands as their guru saw fit. Balkrishnabua's method of teaching music was similar to that of other *ustad*s. He taught his students without once telling them the name of the raga they were learning. He taught them compositions, but not the underlying rules of the raga.[7] Students, in their turn, could not expect or voice any demand that they be taught the next bit of music, sequentially or otherwise. Balkrishnabua's students could not ask questions, and disagreement, voiced or even hinted at, was dealt with by swift dismissal. The single greatest prohibition was against writing down what had been learned. Notating a composition was simply out of the question. One learned music by patiently doing one's duty at home and committing to memory whatever the maestro chose to dispense as instruction.[8] It is no coincidence that one of the first things Paluskar did in his attempt to standardize musical education was to come up with a system of notation for music.

By 1896, Paluskar's training was more than adequate for him to secure a job at another princely court as the appointed musician. However, he chose to leave the world of princely patronage altogether. According to Deodhar, it irked him to witness his teacher's constant humiliation at the hands of aristocratic patrons who neither knew music nor appreciated a musician's worth.[9] Balasaheb Patwardhan, Paluskar's benefactor and patron, bestowed a great deal of preferential treatment on him but treated his teacher very badly. He often corrected Balkrishnabua in public on elementary musical matters regarding the use of *sur* (pitch) and *tala* (meter), interrupted him in midperformance demanding that he sing a different raga than the one he had begun, and frequently asked visiting singers to sing after him.

The order of performance (then and now) was not just a simple matter of arrangement according to convenience. Virtuoso, famous, senior musicians performed after junior, less accomplished musicians had completed their performances. Seniority was determined not merely by age but also by reputation. Biographies of musicians contain narrations of feuds that date back to a ritual insult, often signified by a request to precede a less accomplished performer. The order of performance functioned as a system of identification and ranking that informed the audience about the precise category in which to place the performing musician—as apprentice, child prodigy, senior student, junior musician, or senior musician. Musicians on tour treated each performance as a test or duel in a larger struggle for reputation. One secured victory over an opponent by asking a question he could not answer, singing a raga he could not identify, engaging in vocal gymnastics that defied easy imitation, or by currying favor with the princely ruler. Students of the vanquished or insulted musician often took it upon themselves to avenge their guru's honor by "defeating" on another occasion, through the use of similar techniques, either the victorious musician himself or one of his students. This competitiveness ensured the maintenance of familial feuds and the rigidity of kinship practices within music families.[10] Musicians sang as representatives of their particular style of performance, or as heirs to a specific tradition.

Given the protocols of such a system, if a princely state ruler ordered a visiting musician to sing after the court-appointed musician, as happened frequently with Balkrishnabua, it put both musicians in a difficult predicament. Since remuneration depended on the ruler or his *dewan,* as we have seen in an earlier chapter, the visiting musician had to either obey or forfeit compensation, and the court musician, under contract, would have no choice but to swallow the insult. Paluskar, according to Deodhar's biography, was worried that if he stayed in Meraj, given how much he was favored by Balasaheb Patwardhan, he would one day be asked to sing after Balkrishnabua, which would put him in an untenable position. Rather than wait to deal with a future possibility that might require him to choose, in public, between obeying his *annadata* (patron) or honoring his guru, Paluskar left Meraj with two other students and struck out on his own.[11] Eschewing several offers to become a court singer, Paluskar traveled around the country performing *kirtan*s and *bhajan*s at temples in Oundh and Satara and at the courts of Baroda, Kathiawad, and Junagadh to earn money, gathering a following and acquiring fame as a skilled musician in his own right.

Of the cities and small towns in which Paluskar performed, Junagadh had a special significance: it is the location of the foundational myth about the origins of Paluskar's success. In Junagadh, he is said to have had a formative encounter with a man described as a *siddha purusha* (enlightened man) and a *bairaagi* (one who has renounced the world). Paluskar's first biographer wrote simply that the *bairaagi* told him to go to the Punjab, found his school there, and not worry that he hailed from a different part of India. Paluskar's most authoritative biographer, B. R. Deodhar, has a more complex account. He wrote that Paluskar wished the truth of his encounter with this *siddha purusha* to be kept hidden from his followers until after his death. Deodhar himself only heard the story from Narharpant Pathak, Paluskar's confidant. Pathak had studied music with Paluskar between 1905 and 1907, had heard the story directly from him, and had pledged to keep it silent until after his death. In conformity with his wishes, he broke his silence to a select gathering of the bereaved, Deodhar among them, only after Paluskar's death in 1931.[12] Two mythic characters emerge out of this narration: Pathak the storyteller and Paluskar the scribe.

The story itself is as follows. Close to a *jagrut* (live) temple of Dattatreya atop a hilltop near Junagadh, Paluskar met a sage who demolished his egoism and arrogance by showing him the limitations of his musical abilities.[13] The sage advised him that true musical knowledge was available only for those who had the strength to renounce the world and all its material trappings and dedicate their lives to God, meditation, and music. Since Paluskar could not do this, the sage directed him to continue with his work on music and instructed him to head to North India, where he would find his fate and fame. Finally, the sage told Paluskar to eschew arrogance and reach out to the public.

This story, despite the buildup, the storyteller, and the scribe, gives one pause. It does so not because it is fascinating or surprising, but because it is neither. Why then was the story constructed in a narrative form that offers a climactic buildup to a posthumous revelation? None of Paluskar's biographers make clear what element of the story necessitated its being kept hidden or why Paluskar wanted to do so. What we do know is that Paluskar aspired to the life of a saint, believed one should live in the fashion espoused by India's ancient sages, and accepted as part of everyday life the material reality of epiphanies, miracles, visions, premonitions, and other experiences that escape rational understanding. The historical details, then, of the actual meeting between Paluskar and the *bairaagi* are unimportant. The release of the story of the encounter is far more important, stage-managed as it seems to have been, by Paluskar himself, as a "secret gift" to be bestowed upon a select group in order to perpetuate the myth of his sainthood.

Returning to his early life, Paluskar apparently took the *bairaagi's* advice and in 1897 hosted one of the first public performances of music, in Gwalior, where he printed and sold tickets for the show. From Gwalior he went on to Delhi, Jullunder, Amritsar, Lahore, Kashmir, Rawalpindi, Bharatpur, Jodhpur, and Okara. In Okara, he began creating what would have horrified his old teacher: a notational system by which he could teach students. From Okara, he went to Lahore in 1898, and began to formulate his scheme for a school of music. Far more than Bhatkhande, Paluskar's early years were spent in character as a musician. He led a peripatetic life and acquired, in that sense, a more grounded understanding of what music pedagogy needed to be successful. The first place where he tried out his institutional experiment for music was in the northern city of Lahore, where Punjabi, Urdu, and Hindi were spoken. He was far from his native Kurundwad and did not speak any of the languages spoken in Lahore. For the next decade, however, Lahore would be his home.

Lahore and the First Gandharva Mahavidyalaya, 1901

The first thing Paluskar did when he moved to Lahore was publish his notational system (Figures 4.1, 4.3). He could not start a school without money, so he spent three years raising funds, soliciting patronage, and networking with key members of the Hindu community. His desire to found a school for music that would return music to its traditional, unsullied origins endeared him to the leading lights of Hindu reform and revival organizations outside the sphere of music, such as the Arya Samaj (which had a stronghold in Lahore) and the Sanatan Dharm Sabha.[14] Din Dayalu Sharma, the leading light of the Sanatan

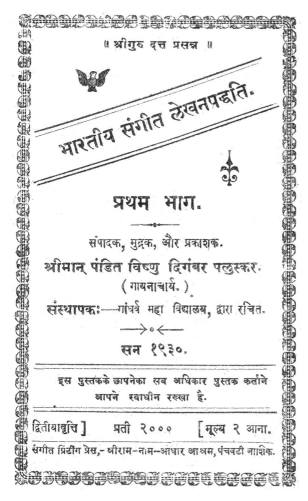

॥ श्रीगुरु दत्त प्रसन्न ॥

भारतीय संगीत लेखनपद्धति.

प्रथम भाग.

संपादक, मुद्रक, और प्रकाशक.

श्रीमान् पंडित विष्णु दिगंबर पलुस्कर.
(गायनाचार्य.)

संस्थापकः—गांधर्व महा विद्यालय, द्वारा रचित.

—>०←—

सन १९३०.

इस पुस्तकके छापनेका सब अधिकार पुस्तक कर्तांने
आपने स्वाधीन रख्खा है.

द्वितीयावृत्ति]   प्रती २०००   [मूल्य २ आना.

संगीत प्रिंटींग प्रेस,- श्रीराम-नाम-आधार आश्रम, पंचवटी नाशिक.

FIGURE 4.IA. Book of notation published in 1930.

Dharm Sabha, suggested to Paluskar that he name his new school of music
the Gandharva Mahavidyalaya (hereafter GMV). The term *Gandharva* is important. It refers to the mythological singing and dancing of celestial beings
in the heavenly court of the god Indra in Vedic mythology. It is also the name
of an *upa veda* [ancillary Veda] of the Sama Veda.[15] In the contemporary
world of music in Maharashtra, the term *Gandharva* is also added as an honorific title to certain musicians deemed to be of the highest caliber.[16] In the

क्रमिक (Series) पुस्तकें.

गांधर्व महा विद्यालयके संस्थापक श्रीमान्
पंडित बिष्णु दिगंबर पलुस्करजीने संगीत
विद्यापर भारतीय लेखन पद्धती में आज
तक जो पुस्तकें लिखी है उनके
नाम और किंमत.

		भाग	रु.	आ.	पै
भारतीय संगीत लेखनपद्धतां	(हिंदी)	१	०	२	०
बालोदय संगीत	(हिंदी)	१	०	२	०
बालोदय संगीत	(हिंदी)	२	०	३	०
,,	(हिंदी)	३	०	४	०
	(मराठी)	१	०	४	०
महिला संगीत	(हिंदी)	१	०	२	०
,,	(हिंदी)	२	०	४	०
संगीत तत्वदर्शक	(हिंदी)	१	०	८	०
अंकित अलंकार.	(हिंदी)	१	०	६	०
संगीत बालप्रकाश	(हिंदी)	१	०	६	०
संगीत बालप्रकाश	(हिंदी)	२	०	१०	०
संगीत बालप्रकाश	(हिंदी)	३	०	१२	०
संगीत बालप्रकाश	(मराठी)	१	०	८	०
,, ,,	(गुजराथी)	१	०	८	०
स्वल्पालाप गायन	(हिंदी)	१	१	०	०
स्वल्पालाप गायन	(हिंदी)	२	१	४	०
स्वल्पालाप गायन	(हिंदी)	३	१	८	०
स्वल्पालाप गायन	(हिंदी)	४	१	४	०
संगीत बालबोध	(हिंदी)	१	१	०	०
संगीत बालबोध	(हिंदी)	२	१	०	०
संगीत बालबोध	(हिंदी)	३	१	८	०
संगीत बालबोध	(हिंदी)	४	२	०	०
संगीत बालबोध	(हिंदी)	५	२	०	०

[कन्हर पान ३ देखना.]

FIGURE 4.1B. A list of Paluskar's notated publications, provided in each one of his books.

importance placed on Vedic Hinduism at the end of the nineteenth century, both the Arya Samaj and the Sanatan Dharm explicitly maintained a reformist understanding of Hinduism, though the latter was much less organized than the former. Both organizations called for the forsaking of bad habits, such as eating meat and drinking alcohol, and both targeted Christianity and Islam as proselytizing evils. The belief that Islam and Christianity would destroy India's true Hindu culture also had its parallels in music.

Paluskar's efforts to align music with a Hindu reform agenda were noted with approval. The Marathi nationalist newspaper, *Kesari*, had a correspondent in Lahore who reported his activities for a Marathi-reading public in Pune and elsewhere. The *Kesari* and its English counterpart, *Mahratta*, had been co-founded in Pune in January 1881 by Bal Gangadhar Tilak (1856–1920) and Gopal Ganesh Agarkar (1856–95). *Mahratta* was initially under Tilak's control, while Agarkar directed the *Kesari*. Within a year of the founding of both

प्रस्तावनिका.

भारतीय संगीत लेखनपद्धतिः—इस पुस्तकका बनानेका मुख्य उद्देश यह है कि संगीत विद्या की लेखनपद्धति तमाम दुनियांमें प्रचलित हो जिस देश देशान्तरकी गायनपद्धति तथा वादनपद्धतिको जानना संहेज हो सके और संगीतके नेता जो है उनको यदि संगीतकी मधुरता अधिक बढानेके लीये कोई स्वर या लयकारीको घटाना बढाना हो तो अनुकूलता हो सके ऐसा होनेसे संगीत विद्यामें हरप्रकारसे उन्नति करनेमें सुलभ होगा और संगीत विद्या लोगोमें सहेज प्रचलित होगी अब तक इस लेखनपद्धतिके बारेमें हर प्रकारसे खुलासा मेंने बनाई हुई संगीत तत्वदर्शक पुस्तकमें था. अब उसमेंसे लेखनकाही केवल भाग अलग करके इस पुस्तकके नामसे प्रकाशीत कीया है जीसे लोगोंको खरीदनेमें सुलभता हो (कारन तत्वदर्शकका किंमत आठ आना और इस पुस्तकको केवल दो आना हैं) और अलग अलग भाषामें इस लेखनपद्धतिको प्रकाशित करनेमें हमकोभी सुलभता हो. इस लेखनपद्धतिको अलग अलग भाषामें प्रकाशित करनेकी बडी आवश्यक्ता मालुम होने लगी है इस पुस्तकमें संगीतलेखनमें जीन बातों की आवश्यक्ता है और वो आवश्यक्ता पूर्ण करनेमें मेरे शक्किके अनुसार जितनी युक्ति या हो सकता है उतना प्रयत्न करके चिह्न नियत कीये हैं. इस पुस्तकको विचारसे पढके जो सज्जन संगीतका अभ्यास करेंगे उनकों इस संगीत लेखनसे अत्यंत लाभ होगा. और अनुभवसे यह देखा गया है यह लेखन संगीत पद्धति प्रथम १९०० में मैंने प्रारंभ की तबसे दिनपर दिन सज्जन स्त्री पुरुषोंको गायनवादनका बहुत लाभ हो रहा है. और आगेभी इससे सज्जन लाभ उठावेंगे.

ता. १०-१-३०]   भवदीय,
विष्णु दिगंबर.

FIGURE 4.1C. Preface to book of notation published in 1930 in which Paluskar recalls that he began notating music in 1901.

papers, the editors were involved in a libel suit and became famous throughout the Deccan.[17] They did not stay coeditors for very long. Disputes between them in other venues highlighted their differences on liberal reform subjects such as women's education, leading to a decisive split in 1888. After 1888, Agarkar relinquished all control of the *Kesari* and founded another Anglo-Marathi newspaper called the *Sudharak* (Reformer). By 1890, both the *Kesari* and the *Mahratta* were entirely under Tilak's editorship and could rightly be called his mouthpieces, voicing a particularly Tilakite point of view, most notably in editorials voicing powerful anti-Muslim sentiments and inveighing against social reform.[18] The argument that music was in the hands of people who were liable to destroy it by their negligence—Muslim musicians who performed it for the dissolute entertainment of indolent princely state rulers—was expressed on a number of occasions in the *Kesari*. Paluskar's activities consistently received mention in the paper, from the beginning of his career with the founding of the Lahore GMV until his death in 1931.

The formal announcement of the opening of the new GMV in Lahore was held on May 5, 1901, in Raja Dhyansingh's *haveli* (traditional home). Lala Hansraj, Arya Samaji principal of the Dayananda Anglo-Vedic College, attended the event, and Din Dayalu Sharma made a trip from Darbhanga especially for the event.[19] Readers of the *Kesari* would have read this account of the event from Lahore. "For the past three years, Vishnu Digambar Paluskar has been here. Because he is skilled in his art, the rajas of various small and large princely states are applauding his talent and he has become well known. . . . The maharaja of Jammu summoned Vishnupant to him and gave him clothes worth a thousand rupees and an additional thousand rupees for his school."[20] The maharaja of Kashmir gave Paluskar both a personal gift of money and donated Rs. 1,500 per year to the school. Maharajas, in Lahore and other cities in colonial India, were centrally important for people like Bhatkhande and Paluskar, since they were, aside from industrialists, the only people with deep financial pockets; without their financial assistance, early attempts at institutional training would not have been possible. It was rare to receive a free gift, and the maharaja of Kashmir was not being altogether altruistic. He donated the money on condition that Paluskar establish a branch of the GMV in Kashmir and sing in his *darbar* every year.[21]

In the beginning, Paluskar rented a decrepit and dark building for thirteen rupees per month, all he could afford. For fourteen days, no student came forward to enroll, but within a month, the school had twenty students,

FIGURE 4.2. GMV building in Lahore.

and the number increased steadily after that. By August, three months after the founding of the school, the *Kesari* reported that "there are now five or six teachers and all told about 60/70 students. In this manner, this school for music has been founded here and its business is proceeding apace. This is a matter of great pride for us Maharashtrians."[22] The article combined regional pride with an acknowledgment of lack. "Unlike the English, our Maharashtrian music does not have notation. When Vishnupant saw this, he came up with new signs that make it possible to notate our music. This notation is absolutely new. We did not have it before this time and because of it anyone can use it to learn how to sing and play." Paluskar was also commended for having taken his mission, so to speak, into the belly of the beast—into Muslim North India—where, because "music is in the hands of illiterate and debauched hands, its foundation in purity and classicism is rapidly disappearing and [Paluskar] is deeply committed to the renaissance of the principles and truths that form the basis upon which our *rishi*s [sages] founded this music." The *Kesari* published no such accolades to Bhatkhande, perhaps because *rishi*s and *muni*s were not quite as prominent in his agenda.

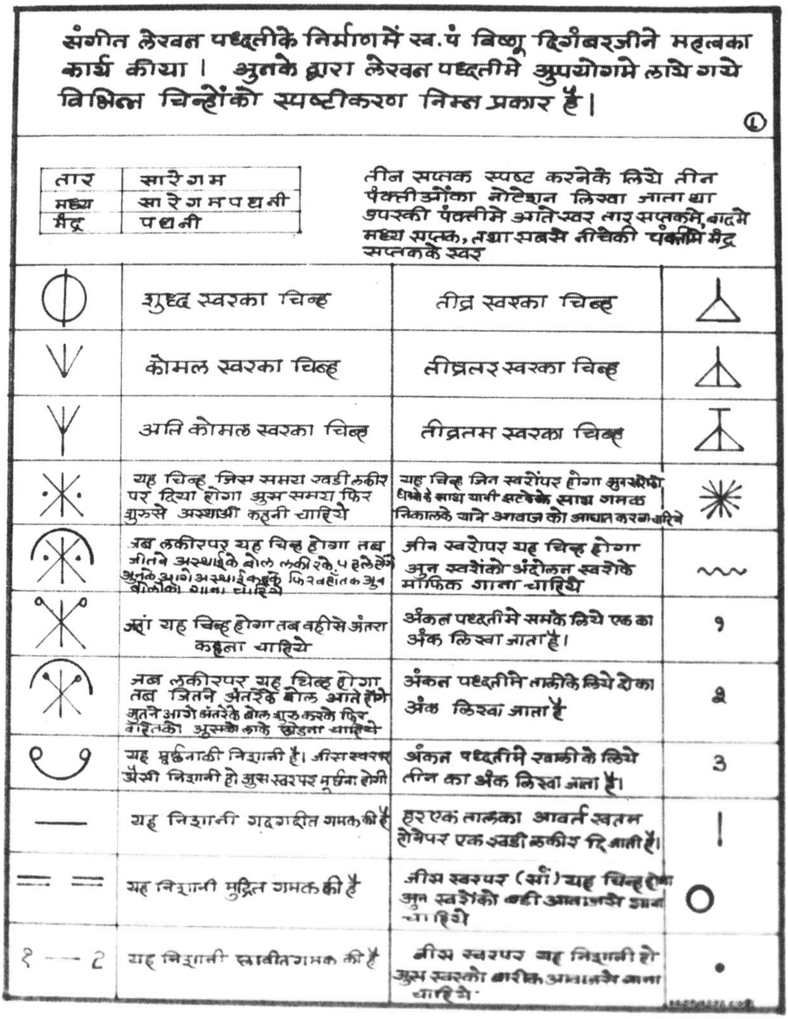

संगीत लेखन पद्धतीके निर्माणमें स्व.पं बिष्णु दिगंबरजीने महत्वका कार्य कीया । अुनके द्वारा लेखन पद्धतीमे अुपयोगमे लाये गये विभिन्न चिन्होंको स्पष्टीकरण निम्न प्रकार है।

①

FIGURE 4.3. Paluskar's musical notation.

Paluskar rejuvenated the principles and truths of the ancient sages by filtering his music through a sternly paternalistic, traditional, and unambiguously Hindu religious pedagogy. The full course of study of the Lahore GMV lasted nine years, the last three of which were devoted to the study of music theory and teacher training.[23] This rule was relaxed as the school expanded. A few years after its founding, the GMV began offering courses that required only three- or six-year bonds. The GMV had a rigid curriculum, strict rules about the numbers of hours that a student had to spend practicing music, and a code of behavior, including a dress code, that legislated how students were expected to comport themselves in public. Miscreants were punished, and corporal punishment was considered par for the course. No student in Paluskar's school could take musical instruction lightly. Students were repeatedly told that they were involved in a process of *tapasya* in service to the goddess of music. This was no laughing matter, and even silly pranks that students engaged in, no doubt to enliven the overwhelmingly ponderous atmosphere of religiosity, were swiftly cut short and the students castigated.[24]

The original GMV building proved inadequate for a growing student body and Paluskar moved the school to a larger dwelling. The new building—for which the rent was Rs. 30 per month—was said to be cursed. Soon after moving, a series of deaths and illnesses befell his staff and their families, and Paluskar accepted that the building was inauspicious. He moved again, this time to temporary lodgings. Finally, in 1904, Paluskar bought a plot of land and built a permanent home for the school. In the same year, he started the *Upadeshak* class, intended for students who could not afford to learn music through the regular curriculum. For these students, Paluskar waived the Rs. 101 entrance fee and housed and fed them at his own expense.[25] In return, instead of training them to become professional musicians, he taught them how to teach music for a living. The first *Upadeshak* class had eight students, all of whom committed to a nine-year period of study.[26] In order to ensure that they did not treat their musical education lightly, Paluskar issued bonds in Hindi, Marathi, and Modi. These bonds were not just symbolic agreements, but serious contracts. If a student reneged on the agreement, he could leave the school only after he had paid the full penalty stipulated at the time of signature. Here is an example of such a bond: "I hereby write to the Principal of the Gandharva Mahavidyalaya that my younger brother, Omkarnath is 14 years old. He is a Brahmin by caste. I am placing him in your school to learn music in accordance with your rules, and I guarantee this by the terms of a nine-year bond. The rules of the Upadeshak class are acceptable to us. Because we are poor, we are not able to pay the fees of the school, which is why I am placing him in the Upadeshak class. If for some reason, I wish to remove my brother from the school before the nine years are over, then the fine due us rated at Rs. 15 per month, from the day he was entered until the day he leaves, will be paid by us without delay."[27]

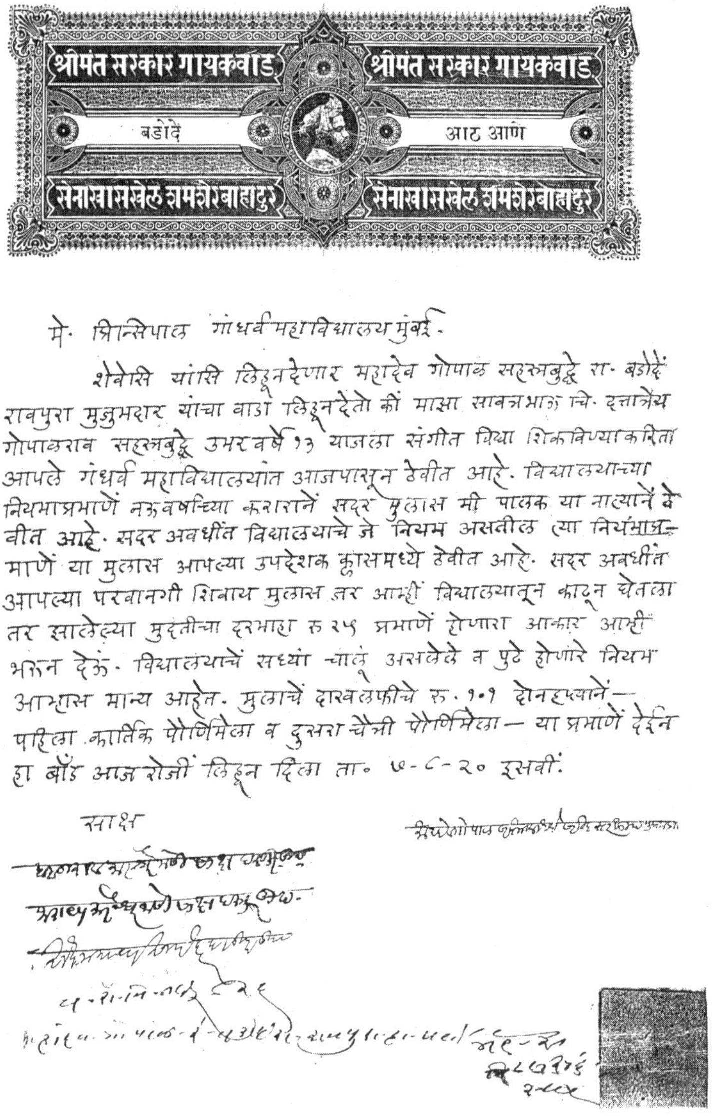

श्रीमंत सरकार गायकवाड श्रीमंत सरकार गायकवाड
बडोदे आठ आणे
सेनाखासखेल शमशेरबहादुर सेनाखासखेल शमशेरबहादुर

मे. प्रिन्सिपाल गांधर्व महाविद्यालय मुंबई.

शेवेसि यांसि लिहून देणार महादेव गोपाळ सहस्रबुद्धे रा. बडोदे रावपुरा मुजुमदार यांचा वाडा लिहून देतो कीं माझा सावत्रभाऊ चि. दत्तात्रेय गोपाळराव सहस्रबुद्धे उमर वर्षे १३ याजला संगीत विद्या शिकविण्याकरिता आपले गंधर्व महाविद्यालयांत आजपासून ठेवीत आहे. विद्यालयाच्या नियमाप्रमाणें नऊ वर्षांच्या करारानें सदर मुलास मी पालक या नात्यानें ठेवीत आहे. सदर अवधींत विद्यालयाचे जे नियम असतील त्या नियमाप्रमाणें या मुलास आपल्या उपदेशक क्लासमध्ये ठेवीत आहे. सदर अवधींत आपल्या परवानगी शिवाय मुलास जर आम्हीं विद्यालयातून काढून घेतला तर झालेल्या मुदतीचा दरमाहा रु २५ प्रमाणें होणारा आकार आम्हीं भरून देऊं. विद्यालयाचें सध्यां चालू असलेले व पुढे होणारे नियम आम्हास मान्य आहेत. मुलाचें दाखलफीचे रु. १०१ दोन हप्त्यानें — पहिला कार्तिक पौर्णिमेला व दुसरा चैत्री पौर्णिमेला — या प्रमाणें देईन हा बाँड आज रोजी लिहून दिला ता० ७-८-२० इसवी.

साक्ष

FIGURE 4.4. Example of a bond.

Clearly, Paluskar was able to tap into an extant interest in music as a career, and the decision to make separations between the kinds of music taught in his school showed a mixture of altruism and shrewdness. In 1930, the year before his death, he could claim as the success of his public mission the release of three hundred *Upadeshak*s into the larger world of India, all devoted to Paluskar and to teaching music as he had taught them. He was no ordinary music teacher. His aim was not just to train musicians, but to produce a musically educated listening public that would associate music not with entertainment or pleasure, but with religious devotion. The combination also allowed him to facilitate entry into his schools of people for whom music was already linked with the performance of bhakti in the form of *bhajan*s and *kirtan*s. By giving music's performance and pedagogy an overtly religious tint, its previous reputation for disreputability could now be considered a thing of the past.

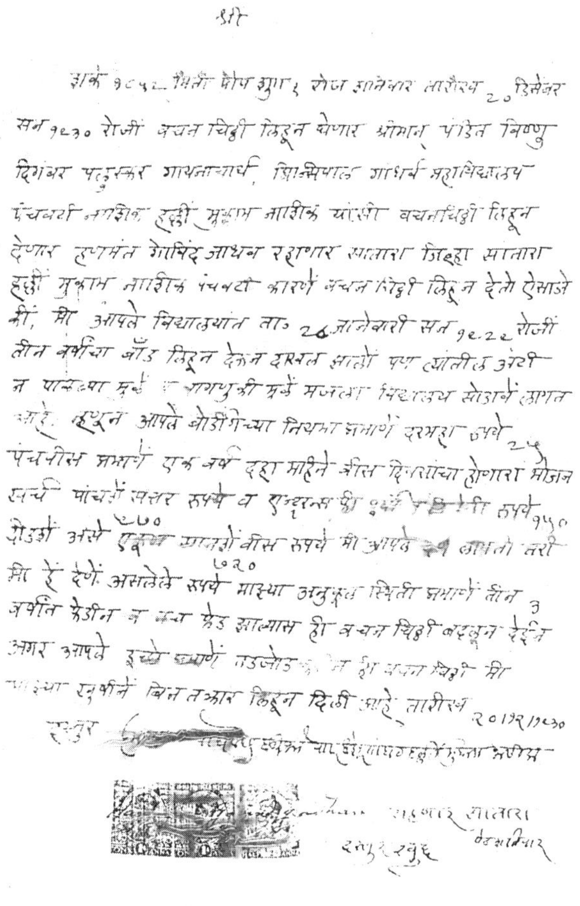

FIGURE 4.5. Note from a defaulter.

All students, from both the *Upadeshak* and regular classes, participated in the culture of sacrality that Paluskar naturalized in his school. Religious rituals and devotional singing were institutionalized as a necessary part of the curriculum. All mornings began with communal prayers, devotional music was sung at all gatherings, and classes were cancelled on religious festivals. There is no evidence to suggest that Paluskar cancelled classes in his Lahore school on days other than those that caste Hindus found auspicious. He went so far as to treat days that were considered merely auspicious, such as Vasant Panchmi and Shivaratri, as if they were full-fledged religious holidays. On such days, either Paluskar himself or an instructor at the school did *puja* in the mornings, conducted prayers, and sang devotional songs in the evenings.[28]

Devotion, however, could not fund the school, and Paluskar needed money to keep it going. He was that rare artist whose enterprising sense of business mixed well with his religious sentiments. The school staged public concerts on weekends, and the musical services of the students were made available to the public for a fee of Rs. 100, payable to the GMV.[29] As was reported in the Annual Report of 1904,

> The Vidyalaya has introduced the innovation of sending out musical parties to outstations on auspicious occasions like marriage and thread ceremonies [a ritual ceremony conducted for young boys of all *dwija* castes, which is to say upper castes alone, as an initiation into the first phase of life]. A party is generally composed of one professor and two or three students of the normal class with a set of musical instruments for accompaniment. Any gentleman requisitioning a party is required to contribute Rs. 50 to the permanent fund of the institution and pay intermediate fare to and back from Lahore.[30]

Six such parties were dispatched in 1904, netting the institution a grand total of Rs. 300. It is possible Paluskar could have made even more money, but he set limits on the kinds of events to which he was willing to dispatch a musical party, avoiding "secular" entertainments in favor of thread ceremonies and weddings, events that had the sanction of religion.[31]

Since coming to Lahore, Paluskar had made a serious effort to learn Hindi and had also come to believe that it ought to be the national language. In 1905, the GMV began publishing a magazine in Hindi called *Sangeet Amrit Pravaha*, which was issued on the second Sunday of every month. On its first page, it displayed a picture of the goddess Saraswati (the

deity of knowledge), whose musical instrument was the *veena*. On one occasion, the magazine published a notated version of the Afghan National
Anthem with the following short news item: "We have heard that when His
Majesty Amir Kabul comes to India, he is greeted by the Indian Band playing his own national anthem. This is so because when he came to the soil
of India, he insisted that he be greeted only by his own national anthem.
Witness the power of Independence. Does our national anthem greet any of
our Princes and Kings?" *Sangeet Amrit Pravaha* published short explanatory
articles on music-related subjects.[32] It also gave its readers news related to
the school, particularly the activities of the musical parties that traveled the
country performing at weddings and thread ceremonies.[33] Paluskar's entre-
preneurial activities did not stop with the magazines. Through the printing
press affiliated with the school, he also released pamphlet-sized textbooks on
instruments such as the harmonium (a relatively new and controversial
instrument, similar to the accordion), the *mridang* (a South Indian percussion drum), tabla, and the sitar. He built a workshop in which he hired
workmen to repair and build new harmoniums, *tanpura*s, *veena*s, tablas, and
*mridang*s.[34]

By 1904, the school had seventy-five students, a few more than the sixty
or seventy students reported in the *Kesari* for 1901, and four full-time instructors. Financially, it faced a small but significant deficit, but Paluskar managed
to keep the school going.[35] His activities were being reported in the *Kesari*,
but he had not yet received national recognition for his work on music. In
1906, a *darbar* was held to celebrate the birth of George V's son, heir to the
British throne. Paluskar was determined to insert a short "Indian music"
recital into the entertainment program. He was able to do so and sang for fifteen minutes in the presence of a large audience gathered to commemorate,
ironically, the momentous birth of yet another potential colonial ruler.[36]
Paluskar proclaimed his participation in the 1906 *darbar* as the success of his
project to elevate the status of music. As he saw it, if the ruler of England—
not to be confused with the colonial state—gave Indian music his patronage,
there could be no stopping its progress now.

Paluskar's performance at the *darbar* was not antinationalist by any
means. In 1905, Paluskar published poems in *Sangit Amrit Pravaha* in support
of the Swadeshi (self-reliance) movement, calling upon his readers to participate.[37] Rousing stanzas such as "How did wealthy nations acquire their
wealth? By preventing indigenous income from leaving its boundaries," and

"The true daughter of India is that young woman who scorns all foreign clothing altogether," exhorted women to be true to India at the same time that they publicized a nationalist argument against India's drain of wealth. However, if Paluskar had no embarrassment about the colonial *darbar*, his students, in their retrospective biographies, were alert to how it might seem to a new generation, explaining it away by listing a series of Paluskar's nationalist activities, such as his popularizing the patriotic song "Vande Mataram" at all political gatherings in Lahore. For Paluskar himself, as for others, there was no contradiction in using *Swadeshi*, incendiary nationalism, along with a colonial *darbar*, to popularize his project.

By 1907, the Lahore GMV was well established. It held public performances of music, both Hindustani and Carnatic, and expanded its curriculum to include flute classes.[38] The following year, Paluskar left Lahore for Bombay, but the school continued to run. In 1909, Paranjpe Dattatreya Sharma, who had assumed the stewardship of the school from Paluskar, published this account of the decline of music and the related goals of the GMV: "Even though *Sangeet Vidya* [the science/wisdom/knowledge of music] originates with the Vedas, in the time of the *Yavan* (Muslim) rulers, this *Vidya* went underground. And whatever little of it spread among the people, even that is rapidly disappearing. But our institution, ever since it has been founded, has given it new life and is making it available to the common man." The article went on to state that "even though there are a great many *grantha*s on music available in these modern times, the common man has not benefited from them. This has many reasons, one that there were singers who knew no science, and scholars who had no experience of music. But because of our institution, where we have both scholars and musicians, we can now be sure that this knowledge will spread among the people."[39] Paluskar and the GMV were already being accorded legendary status as the man and the institution bringing together musicians and scholars.

It was not altogether an empty boast. The Lahore GMV was a fountainhead in more ways than one. In addition to teaching music, it hosted variety entertainment programs, such as magic shows, chess matches, and card games. All informal events were held in the school temple, and no entertainment program was complete unless it began and concluded with communal prayers. *Sangit Amrit Pravaha* described one such gathering on November 19, 1911: "The program of the gathering began at 2 pm and lasted until the evening. To begin with, all students and teachers at the school joined in singing prayers. After the prayers were finished, various other activities commenced." Even after Paluskar's departure from Lahore, the school maintained his emphasis on devotional music and included it as part of all its programs.

In 1911, the GMV conducted exams in vocal and instrumental music and published the names of forty-one of the eighty students who had secured first- and second-class grades in each of the three years of the course.[40] Twenty-three of these forty-one were Maharashtrian, twelve were Parsi.[41] Sixteen women, including eleven Parsi women, received honorable mention for their excellence in the school.[42] In articles written by his fans in the fifteenth-anniversary commemorative issue of the school's publication, Paluskar's North Indian beginnings had already acquired the flavor of a chronicle that began with his arrival in Punjab, moved into his time of hardship, and culminated in the triumph of his unique perseverance and discipline. As one of his followers wrote, "If one thinks about the last fourteen years and the tremendous success achieved by the Gandharva Mahavidyalayas, then one would have to say that it is all the result and just reward for Pandit Vishnu Digambar's musical excellence, his strict discipline in the school, his pedagogical style, emphasis on vice-free behavior, punctuality, vision and persistence, all rare qualities in these days."[43] Paluskar returned to Lahore for its twenty-fifth anniversary, and the school continued to function as a subsidiary branch of the Bombay school until the partition of the subcontinent into India and Pakistan in 1947.

When Paluskar went to Lahore in 1908, he entered a world that differed greatly from his own cultural milieu. Lahore had been a difficult city for him, but he had done what he set out to do, which was to make a mark for himself on the national scene. He had lived there as long as necessary, but once the school was able to function smoothly on its own, he left. He had proved his credentials well outside his native state and could now go home—or at least close to home, for there was one last stop. Paluskar headed to colonial Bombay, a city that was cosmopolitan, colonial, and parochial all at the same time.

Paluskar's Corporate Phase: Bombay, 1908–1918

Paluskar had deputed his student, V. A. Kashalkar, to go to Bombay before him and scope out the possibility of opening a school. On earlier visits to the city, Paluskar had also performed at the Gayan Uttejak Mandali, at

Bhatkhande's invitation, and garnered the support of a group of leading industrialists and political figures. This advance work allowed him to found the Bombay GMV almost as soon as he arrived in the city. The school was immediately successful, and he was feted among the musician community and even welcomed into the tangential world of music drama as a musician and luminary. He no longer needed to prove his credentials, and his fame in North India helped him establish himself quite quickly. He shifted his financial headquarters to Bombay and turned the Lahore school into a subsidiary branch, as it remained until it shut down. He moved the printing press, all the funds, and many of the staff from Lahore and, from 1911, published both the Hindi *Sangit Amrit Pravaha* and Marathi *Gandharva Mahavidyalaya* from the Bombay GMV.

In Bombay, Paluskar considerably expanded his repertoire of talents. He held public performances, expanded the curriculum to include instruction in instruments such as the violin, and put together an orchestra composed of his students. He also became an impresario of public events and held social gatherings, convocation ceremonies, awards ceremonies, and music competitions. He celebrated every birthday of every branch of the GMV, and doubled his student body. He opened a medical dispensary, gave lectures at Wilson College on the state of music, and continued to dispatch musical parties to sing at weddings, naming ceremonies, and thread ceremonies.

In 1911, Paluskar engaged in a number of activities that showcased his strategic understanding of public relations even as they continued to underscore his strategic relationship to nationalist politics. If the *darbar* in 1906 had put Paluskar on the national map, his speech at the 1911 coronation *darbar* reveals his shrewd understanding of the need to maintain a high profile in public and manage its contradictory aspects at the same time. "The ascension to the throne of King George V and Queen Mary," he proclaimed, "was an event in Indian history that should be noted in gold letters everywhere for their beneficence and grace to Indian subjects." King George had attended a ceremony at the Bombay GMV, gave sweets to 27,000 children, and allowed himself to be sung to by 1,200 GMV students who had been granted an audience with him. Paluskar went on in the speech to predict that in the reign of George V, music would climb to such heights as it had attained in the Vedic period.[44]

At the same ceremony, Paluskar demonstrated superb showmanship in his orchestration of a "variety entertainment" show, a form that became standard fare in modern bourgeois India. He also displayed his ability to strategically juggle the demands for entertainment of an emerging public audience with the necessity of keeping both nationalists and royalists appeased. The assembly first prayed for the health of the King. Then two Muslim students sang the national anthem. Following this, one hundred Marathi students sang a Marathi song set to "God Save the King," and the so-called *Swadeshi* band gave a recital of instrumental music. The band was followed by a vocal recital by four women students in raga *kaushiya* and then a sitar recital, and the whole event closed with Pandit Paluskar singing a *bhajan* and calling the assembly to prayer.[45] Paluskar, in effect, choreographed a new kind of mixed musical entertainment for the lay public. Instead of the performance of a single raga alone, he put together a performance of classical music consisting of short sound bites, thereby augmenting its popularity and altering its public perception.

Having participated in *darbar*s in Lahore and Bombay, Paluskar proceeded to stage them himself, fashioning a range of official "functions" that served to celebrate and publicize his institutions and agendas. In 1911, he inaugurated the first awards ceremony for his school. The *Kesari*, his longtime supporter, reported that "the overall preparations were beautiful, everything was in good taste and decorum, but more than this the event had the style of a *darbar* and for this we have to applaud the principal of the GMV, Pandit Vishnu Digambar Paluskar and his staff."[46] Fueled in large part by radical journalism in support of the *Swadeshi* agitation, circulation figures for the *Kesari* were close to 20,000.[47] Those readers would have read the following description:

> It gives us great pleasure to report that on Tuesday, January 3, 1911, at the Framjee Cowasjee Hall, the Governor Sir George Clarke presided over the GMV's award ceremony which was conducted with great pomp and style. The Governor was accompanied by his wife, Lady Clark. Also in attendance were Mrs. Chandavarkar, and some European, Parsi and Hindu women. Notables such as the ruler of Miraj, Shri Balasaheb Mirajkar, the ruler of Kurundwad, Shri Dajisaheb Kurundwadkar and his son, Justice Sir Narayan Ganesh Chandavarkar, Justice Ganpat Sadashivrao, Sir Bhalchandrakrishna, Seth Manmohan Ramji . . . Magistrate Dastur, Dr. Ranade, . . . Narayan Viswanath Mandlik, etc., and members of all classes of society had come to the event.[48]

The list of attendees in the article points to Paluskar's calculated cultivation of the wealthy and powerful elite in Bombay, including two leading industrialists, three justices, and the two rulers of the two princely states where he had begun his career.

This elite unanimously supported Paluskar's musico-religious agenda. Justice Sir Narayan Chandavarkar began his welcome address by reminiscing about his conversations in England about music and religious education in India. Someone had asked him if religious instruction and musical education were readily available in India, to which he had responded by claiming that both were assiduously taken care of in the home. In fact, he claimed, one was taught through the other. Children were taught religion through the music sung to them by their mothers. Justice Chandavarkar went on to endorse Paluskar's agenda by stating that "our music today is in degenerate hands and since it is merely a means of seeking pleasure it will not progress. Whether it is man or the nation, unless the foundation is correct, all will come to naught. This is the same for music. When the Gandharva Mahavidyalaya was founded two years ago, its principal had vowed to me that the music that would be taught in this school would always be devotional music in the service of God. Two years later, his vow can be seen to be true."[49] His approbation was seconded by the governor, who recommended Indian music's modernization on the lines of Western choral singing, since it brought people together, and "voiced his approval that in the Gandharva Mahavidyalaya devotional music, the songs of different saints, Kabir's *doha*s were being paid particular attention . . . since music in India had been recently most neglected."[50] Paluskar held his awards ceremonies every year following the inauguration with equal pomp and show. The steps he had taken to institute a culture of sacrality around the performance of music in Lahore grew into a confident stride in Bombay with the securing of elite and colonial approval, and his school curriculum's religiosity became even more pronounced.

The Bombay GMV's typical day began with devotional supplication. In Deodhar's description,

> As the clock struck 7 am, the morning prayer began. All students and teachers had to be present for these. . . . First the Sanskrit *shloka* "gururbrahma gurur vishnu gurur devo maheshwara" was sung in some raga or the other. Then the Hindi prayer "racha prabhu tune yeh brahmaand sara" [you are the creator of the entire world] was

sung in raga *bhairavi* by everyone. Then the patriotic religious Hindi song "dharma dudh se mata tum humko paalo" [mother, nurture us with the milk of faith] was sung by the leader of the prayer. Then everyone sang the first part of "racha prabhu," then the prayer leader sang "nimakar prabhu shees binti hamari" [please listen to my prayer, oh lord] which was repeated by the whole group, then we all sang "saraswati sharda vidyadani dayani" [a prayer offering obeisance to the goddess of knowledge] in raga *bhairavi* which concluded the morning prayers.[51]

A little later in the narrative, Deodhar mentions that the Bombay school did not attract very many students from the Muslim community, but that Parsi students were taking very well to Indian music.

In 1911, the Bombay GMV had some funds in reserve. This was a far cry from the small deficit under which the Lahore school was running. In fact, the Bombay GMV subsidized the Lahore school by assuming its debt, which reduced its surplus from Rs. 2,000 to Rs. 1,200, still a reasonable sum of money. In 1911, the Lahore school had eighty-one students who took exams. By contrast, the Bombay GMV had a total of 792 students on its roster, of whom eighty-eight were women.[52] In little over a decade, Paluskar had gone from a modest institutional beginning in Lahore to institutional success in Bombay, where the number of female students alone outnumbered the total student body of the Lahore school.

Paluskar, however, was not content merely with staging *darbar*s and running a school. His agenda included an aggressive competitiveness with the "West." As he put it,

> Up until today, there has been a resolute belief in the West that Indian music does not have harmony such as exists in the West. This is given as the reason we do not have bands [orchestras]. To prove this incorrect, our school has engaged in tireless effort and shown them how wrong they are by producing two new Hindustani bands, which have been performing at various *jalsa*s in Bombay and deputations elsewhere as well. In our bands we have a minimum of ten and occasionally as many as sixteen members playing as many different instruments. When we play, we sound almost exactly like a European band. . . . Indeed, we are going to try and put together a band using ancient instruments as well.[53]

This kind of competitiveness set him apart from Bhatkhande, who had no interest in Western orchestras. Paluskar, in contrast, seemed to want to let both a colonial government and the British monarch know that, his flattery notwithstanding, Indian music was completely capable of doing everything that Western music could do.

He was aware that neither the national spotlight nor religious devotion could pay the bills. He issued appeals to donors in his magazines, and to reassure them of his progress, he published annual reports, news about a constantly expanding curriculum, and a list of the magazines available to students in the newly formed library, including them in his vision of the future: "Our aim is to have branches of the school all over India. It will spread liking for music throughout the country and produce more instructors of music to further the spread. In the same manner, it is imperative that we educate women from good families about music. It will ensure for our Hindi people that music will be taught to the children from the very beginning, otherwise we all know the danger that we shall lose our music forever."[54] Paluskar also explained why he emphasized only devotional music, both in the school and when his students performed in public:

> The reason we do this is that up until today, because of the prevalence of *ustadi gayaki* [music sung by *ustad*s], music has been used to emphasize only the *shringar rasa,* and in order to distance music from pleasure and turn people's attention to God, we decided to host *jalsa*s [musical events]. These *jalsa*s, if held on days such as *ashaadi ekadashi* or *Krishna jayanti*, days that religious people spend all night in prayer, then it gives us the opportunity to not only educate people about bhakti, but also to augment the fees of the school.[55]

The strategic importance of this appeal should not be underestimated. Paluskar knew that the conservative Hindu industrialists in Bombay had pockets deep enough for his purposes, so he included, along with this righteous appeal, a balance sheet and a financial report on the last three years, perfectly matched, right down to the last paisa.[56]

The finances never worked very well, but for a while at least the school did fine. In 1912, Paluskar opened a branch of the GMV in Pune, which admitted eighty students in the first three months. In the same year, he opened a second branch of the school in Bombay.[57] The Bombay GMV eventually ran into financial trouble, because in order to expand and accommodate his rapidly increasing number of students, Paluskar borrowed money to house the school in its own building rather than a rented one. Often his ambitions exceeded his wallet. In order to pay off his debts, Paluskar embarked on a number of music tours between 1910 and 1912. At a conference of the Sanatan Dharm in Lahore, he was given a copy of Tulsidasa's *Ramayana,* which increasingly became central to his public performances. Not only did he use parables from it to turn the history of the GMV into a legend, he used it to proselytize and instruct people on the need for musical education.[58] In addition to his usual repertoire of *kirtans* and *bhajans,* Paluskar began giving lectures on the *Ramayana* as well, and hit his musical stride for good with the *pravachans.*[59]

By 1915, Paluskar started losing financial control of the Bombay school, but his success in other ventures continued to grow. He had begun publishing notated compositions in *Sangit Amrit Pravaha* as early as 1905 and had supervised and written forewords to a steady stream of publications until four years before his death. They included eighteen little books on different ragas, fifteen small textbooks, and many other texts on a variety of subjects including exercise music.[60] His notation was in use in women's schools, such as the Jullundar Kanya Vidyalaya, and in key nationalist educational institutions such as the Benares Central Hindu College, Pune Ferguson College, and the New English School, which included Tilak on its faculty.[61] However, even the *Ramayana* could not help him with his increasingly mounting debt, so though it may have occupied him spiritually, he had to make some material adjustments to the daily activities of the school.

The first two casualties were the magazines. In 1916, he terminated both *Sangit Amrit Pravaha* and *Gandharva Mahavidyalaya.* The magazines were expensive to print, had small circulations (about one hundred readers each), and he no longer needed them to publicize his activities. He also virtually stopped performing "classical" music and personally tutoring students, particularly those for whom music was a hobby rather than a vocation. He spent more time touring the country in 1916 and 1917, giving performances so that he could pay off his debts. When he returned to Bombay, he displayed what seems a stubborn resolve in the face of financial disaster, embarking on further building projects that could not be subsidized completely by his performances. On September 2, 1917, Paluskar opened a boarding house for students with customary pomp and show, hardly an activity that would have helped him lower his debt.

In 1916, Bhatkhande had convened the first All-India Music Conference, which Paluskar attended, and two years later, in 1918, Paluskar convened his own conferences. They were different from Bhatkhande's in that they were overtly musician-centered events. In 1918, the first of a series of five conferences was held in Bombay. Paluskar's biographers insist that he was not financially shortsighted but simply too engrossed in the *Ramayana* to pay close attention to the school. But in 1918, his activities seem not to have diminished so much as his ambitions had expanded. The larger stage of all Indian nationalist politics captured his attention, and at annual sessions of the Indian National Congress, Paluskar had an audience, in both numbers and kind, to whom he would pitch his distinct combination of religion, nation, and music.

From Nationalism to Withdrawal: 1918–1931

When Gandhi returned to India from South Africa in 1915 and nationalism began to acquire an all-India character, different from the late-nineteenth-century regionalist nationalisms of Tilak in Maharashtra or Surendranath Banerjee in Bengal, Paluskar was one of the many who supported him. In 1918 he delivered a lecture in Pune titled "The Present State of the Art of Music," presided over by Abbasaheb Muzumdar, a key member of the Poona Gayan Samaj. In that lecture, he asked that the "demands of the nation should all be voiced in one language. In Ireland, as all nationalists at nationalist gatherings join in one heart and in true pitch and at the same sing their anthem, so too, should all Indians demanding *swarajya* [self-rule] say in one voice, *Bharat hamara desh hai* [Bharat is our nation]. . . . These days in Hindustan there is a fight afoot for *swarajya*. Once we have it and peace is restored, music will spread far and wide, we see signs of it even now."[62] This was a claim Paluskar could make with comfort. By 1917, students from his *Upadeshak* class had established music schools in the Paluskar tradition in Benares, Allahabad, Kanpur, Jullunder, Sindh, Hyderabad, and Meraj.[63]

There were many articles in the *Kesari* about events on the national front, but between 1918 and 1923, there were no articles on music. With Tilak's death in 1920, the newspaper lost its leader, but not its focus on nationalism.[64] The period between 1919 and Gandhi's arrest in March 1922 saw widespread, intermittent, frequently violent mass mobilization against the British, along with Gandhi's increasing control and leadership of a peasant-supported nationalist movement. During this time, Paluskar toured the country giving performances of his *Ramayana* and grew increasingly committed to Gandhi's nationalism. In 1921, he apparently parted a throng in Ahmedabad that had prevented Gandhi from entering the convention hall at the annual session of the India National Congress (INC). The crowd was apparently mesmerized by his rendition of the first few couplets of the hymn "Raghupati Raghav Raja Ram," and he announced that he would continue his singing only after they had allowed Gandhi easy passage. At the session itself, he had led the singing of "Vande Mataram."[65]

In the same year, Paluskar had also done a *Ramayana pravachan* for four months at a well-known temple in Panchvati, close to Nasik. He spent more and more time in Nasik, where he acquired a following, and in September 1922, became involved in setting up an ashram in front of the temple where his *Ramayana pravachan* had received a warm welcome. Increasingly, he preferred *pravachan*s in temples over performances in secular venues and adopted the vestments of a *sadhu* (one who has renounced the world and spends his time in meditation and prayer). He refrained from singing secular classical music, except on rare occasions or when his singing ability was challenged.[66] But by now, he had also nearly doubled his debt in Bombay, which meant that his desired disengagement from the material world was simply not possible until he had discharged his financial obligations.

Before he left Bombay for good, he made one last splash on the national scene, at the INC session in Kakinada in 1923. His outburst became the occasion for the second mythic story about him, on par with his encounter with the Junagadh sage. Muslim leaders had protested the playing of music outside mosques, an issue that had long been an incendiary one and that had caused riots in Bombay as early as 1870 between members of the Parsi and Muslim communities. While other singers at the INC had performed without the use of musical instruments, Paluskar took it upon himself to protest what he saw as an unfair infringement of Hindu rights and shouted down no less a nationalist figure than Mohammed Ali, president that year of the INC, a leader of the Khilafat movement and friend of Gandhi. The episode is narrated differently by each of his biographers and by newspaper accounts.

The *Kesari* reported the event as follows:

When it came Paluskar's turn to sing, he took with him the absolutely necessary instruments such as the *haathpeti* [harmonium],
fiddle, tabla, etc. when he was told that there was a ban on the use of
instruments. He would not accept this. When it came his turn to
sing his couplets once again there was a furor raised about his using
instruments. He asked [Maulana] Mohammed Ali about it, and was
once again told about the ban. For this Marathi Panditji, this insult
could not be borne! He also understood very well the nature of the
slight. He replied to Mohammad Ali in a crystal clear and commanding voice. Panditji said, "A national session is not a Musalman
mosque. As the national session belongs to Muslims, it belongs as
well to Hindus and others. At a nationalist session you demand that
instruments not be used, what is the meaning of such an outrage?
You yourself have arrived at this session in great style to the playing
of various instruments and drums, why was the ban not instituted at
that time? To institute it at the time when singers are to sing is to insult those less important than you."[67]

Paluskar was permitted to perform with musical accompaniment and after his
outburst, the *Kesari* reported that there was no more talk about a ban on
music.[68]

Paluskar's first biographer used the Kakinada session to refute the uniden-
tified charge that he was so taken with devotional singing as to forget his duty
to the nation by stating in no uncertain terms that "the truth is that from the
very beginning [Paluskar has] been engaged in constant *desh-seva* [patriotic
service to the nation]. In particular, for the Hindu *jaati* [community/fold/
race]."[69] His subsequent biographer narrated the same account, concluding
that Mohammed Ali was so persuaded by the truth of Paluskar's argument as
to have recanted his views and accepted his error.[70] And B. R. Deodhar, the
most authoritative of all his biographers, wrote, "Even the Muslims had not
liked what Maulana Mohammad Ali had insisted upon, but who was to say
anything to the president of the Congress session? However, everyone was
very happy with the manner in which Panditji stood up to him and applauded him with thunderous clapping."[71] None of Paluskar's biographers
see any contradiction in their assertion that Paluskar was "withdrawing" from
the world when he was so manifestly moving onto a larger stage than that of
the administration of music schools alone. Instead, from the first biographer

to the last, we have a tale that begins by defending a charge that he was not adequately nationalist and concludes with an account of Paluskar's Hindu pride, which inspired everyone at the national session.

Pride, however, was also Paluskar's downfall. By 1923, the bill collectors were hounding him to repay the over Rs. 2 lakhs he owed them. The debt, although enormous, could have been managed had he been willing to register the Bombay GMV, but against even Gandhi's advice he refused. Registration would have allowed a financial bail-out by investors and left him in charge of the day-to-day running of the school without the financial burden of keeping it going, but the more he was pressed to do so, the more stubbornly he dug in his heels.[72] His refusal eventually cost him the building in which the school was housed and, as a result, the school itself. His *Ramayana pravachan*s had gained immensely in popularity, and through repeated performances, he was able to fend off bankruptcy a few times, but the end was near.

In 1924, he could hold out no longer; the Bombay building was auctioned and sold to the highest bidder. The money from the sale went a fair distance toward reducing his debt but did not do away with it altogether. The same year he moved permanently to Nasik, which he had already begun putting down roots. He moved the furniture and all the musical instruments from the Bombay GMV to his new home in Nasik, from which he returned periodically to Bombay, mainly to convene or attend conferences on Marathi music.

So ended a remarkable pedagogical career. In fact, the dissolution of his Bombay GMV allowed Paluskar a certain measure of freedom. Released from institutional obligations, he traveled almost compulsively. In 1924, when he returned to Bombay, he lived in a *dharmashaala* (free boarding house) and met his various students mainly to find out what they were doing. In 1925, he attended the INC session in Belgaum and held a *Ramayana pravachan* in his old hometown of Meraj. In July 1925, his student B. R. Deodhar founded his own music school in Bombay, which was intended to replace the original GMV, and invited Paluskar to attend the inauguration ceremony.[73] By 1926, Paluskar was on tour again, beginning with a two-month stay in Amritsar, going to Karachi and back to Lahore for the jubilee celebration of the twenty-fifth year of the original GMV. In all these cities, he was feted by his old supporters, the Arya Samajis, and he performed *kirtan*s, *bhajana*s, and *Ramayana pravachan*s. In 1927, he presided over the opening of another school by one of his students in Pune and attended the INC session in Madras. He also traveled to Burma and Sri Lanka. He tried once more in 1929 to restart the Gandharva Mahavidyalaya in Bombay but could not attract many students, and the school came to a sputtering end in a few years. However, his mission was complete. His students had accepted his mandate and were running their own schools all over the subcontinent. He was nationally famous and in his waning years could give himself up to the music he had first learned as a boy. In 1931 he fell ill, and his old patron arranged for him to move from Nasik to Meraj. On August 21, he died in the same city where he had commenced his musical training, looked after by the same patron who had set him on his path to fame. Hereafter, he was mourned as the *sansaari sadhu* (worldly monk) whose name would always be associated with the *prachaar* (spread) of music.[74]

In 1932, the year after Paluskar's death, his senior students Narayan Rao Khare, V. A. Kashalkar, Shankarrao Vyas, V. N. Patwardhan, and others founded the Gandharva Mahavidyalaya Mandal at Ahmedabad. Their intention was to further Paluskar's vision by both founding additional schools and establishing a system of affiliation whereby institutions of music around the country could tie in with the main Gandharva Mahavidyalaya for exams, degrees, and curricula.[75] The *mandal* was registered in 1944, and in 1946, the prefix *Akhil Bharatiya* (All-India), was added. The Akhil Bharatiya Gandharva Mahavidyalaya Mandal (ABGMV) today is an enormous bureaucratic organization that oversees the running of all GMV affiliates, administers nationwide music examinations, and houses all archival material related to Paluskar's life and work.[76]

To this day, music instructors around the country, even those in institutions not formally affiliated with the ABGMV, can requisition, for a small fee, the Mandal's copyrighted guidelines, forms, and exams for their own students. For the Mandal, every such request counts toward the continuing success of Paluskar's program. Each student is individually tested and the examiner uses a set formula, according to which a candidate for the exam is evaluated for proficiency in various aspects of music: meter, pitch, raga recognition, music theory, and so on. Beginners undergo a ten-minute examination, more advanced students take a thirty-five-minute examination, and candidates for a degree are examined for ninety minutes and are also required to perform in public for half an hour. Additionally, the Mandal administers examinations in various forms of dance—Kathak, Bharatnatyam, and Odissi—and in Carnatic vocal music and percussion. Students of vocal music are expected not only to know their classical repertoire, but also to demonstrate their ability in semiclassical (theater music and devotional songs) as well as what is termed "light" music.[77] Such is the success of the ABGMV that, in the 1970s, over ten thousand students from music schools other than the Gandharva Mahavidyalayas registered to take the exams.

The ABGMV also houses Paluskar's papers. The archive was built up by Balwantrao Joshi, Registrar of the GMV. Over the years, he collected a comprehensive storehouse of primary source material associated with Pandit Paluskar. Joshi did this as a labor of love, traveling the country at a moment's notice to locate and retrieve primary source material for no reward other than to be associated with Paluskar's mission. Such is the loyalty Pandit Paluskar still commands.

The main branch of modern India's foremost school of music, the Gandharva Mahavidyala (GMV), is located in Vashi, two hours away from the center of Bombay. The apartment on the top floor belongs to Pandit V. R. Athavale, senior professor of vocal music.[78] Athavale had been one of Paluskar's students and referred to him as "Maharaj." "It is his vision, his work that we are furthering. I've been doing it all my life," he told me. "Maharaj was among the ten greatest people in Maharashtra, along with Tilak, Agarkar and others. He dispatched us like Shivaji's *senapati*s [warriors] to Allahabad, Kanpur, Karachi. As soon as we had learned the basics, he sent us all over the country to set up Gandharva Mahavidyalayas."

Balwantrao Joshi, registrar of the GMV, added, "He had the ability to know people and the limits of their musical knowledge. So he was able to recognize that even if someone was not going to be a great performer, he might be a good organizer and he was able to utilize people's talents very well." Nana Bodas, professor of music, added, "He held convocation ceremonies, awarded degrees, held music conferences—we still have all of that today. But to have it then?"[79]

Indeed, Paluskar demonstrated an organic understanding of what the national cultural sphere meant, and he went about aggressively transforming that part of it pertaining to music. He understood without the benefit of a colonial education that he needed to make his agenda sound as if it could be all things to all people—Hindu, Marathi, nationalist, religious, supportive of women, inclusive of minorities, anticolonial, and pro-crown. By 1918 Paluskar had schools all over the country and was a player, though a minor one, in nationalist politics. But we might ask: having so established his music, what exactly did his success mean to the people in whose name he carved out such a distinctive share for himself in the country's cultural history?

Music and Community: Women, Muslims, Parsis

Paluskar's success is trumpeted by his students as a success for *all* Indians. And indeed, it is precisely in those terms that his agenda needs to be evaluated, given the success of his project in so many cities across India. However, if we begin with his foundational schools and examine the demographic constitution of students, key inclusions and exclusions come to the fore. In Paluskar's Lahore and Bombay schools, Hindu and Parsi students outnumbered all others. In 1912, the Bombay GMV had 1,304 fulltime students—1,074 male and 231 female. In the fourth annual report, Paluskar classified his students into caste groups. Of the incoming 174 male students, there were 70 Brahmins, 74 non-Brahmins (24 Kshatriya, 25 Prabhu, 25 Marathi), and 30 Parsis. In other words, the single largest unified group was Brahmin, followed by Parsis. In the case of women, this statistic was reversed. Parsi women outnumbered Brahmin and other female students by well over twofold. Of the incoming 68 women students, there were 35 Parsi women, 15 Brahmin, 10 Prabhus, and 8 Kshatriya. Parsi women and Brahmin men were in the clear majority of the student body. The largest number of these incoming students enrolled in the voice classes (116 men and 29 women), followed by enrollment in the harmonium classes.[80] In 1917, the *Kesari* reported that the Bombay GMV now had 200 *kulin* (Brahmin) men and women students registered, double the number from 1912.[81] These numbers bring up three immediate questions. First, what explains the presence of Parsis in the school? Second, what did Paluskar's pedagogy for women really amount to? And most important, why were there no Muslim men and women in the school? The last is a question linked to the first two.

Paluskar often proclaimed that his desire was to elevate the status of musicians. Since the field of music at the turn of the century included large numbers of preeminent Muslim musicians, one might expect that Paluskar would have included them in his project precisely because they were musicians, and would have recruited their talented progeny into his school. Such a move would have ensured him the success of both his missions: elevating the status of musicians and preventing music from dying out in debauchery. This would seem even more appropriate in Lahore, a city with a large Muslim population. Yet Paluskar's Lahore GMV had no Muslim students.

There are a number of reasons that might explain the attendance of Parsi men and women in the Lahore and Bombay GMVs. As we saw in an earlier chapter, the Parsi Gayan Uttejak Mandali in Bombay had taken the first steps to make music appealing to women of bourgeois families. Perhaps influenced by their community's actions in Bombay, they had decided to try learning music. There is also a history of the conjoining of conservative Parsi and Hindu communal sentiment against a perceived history of Muslim oppression in Persia and India. Moreover, the Parsi community, relative to the Muslim community, was smaller and financially more prosperous. Additionally, Zoroastrianism, given its nonproselytizing character, represented no threat to organizations such as the Arya Samaj, whereas Islam and Christianity did. Indeed, the Parsi community has typically been pointed to as the model minority community—one that unsettles no part of Indian life. The attendance by Parsis in the GMV was noted both in issues of the school's magazines and by Deodhar in his biography to proclaim the inherently inclusive policies of the school.[82]

In his speech at Paluskar's Bombay GMV in 1911, Justice Chandavarkar reportedly asked, "Through this music, Hindus can sing their devotional songs, so can Parsis, why should women not use the music for the same purpose?"[83] In keeping with the speech, Paluskar's *Mahila Sangeet,* a sixteen-page Marathi pamphlet on women's music, taught women to use their musical training for devotional purposes and for such purposes alone. The pamphlet included a brief introduction to the benefits of learning music, written in the form of a conversation.

"What benefits does one accrue by learning music?" is the question with which the conversation begins. "There are four kinds of benefits" is the answer: "Emotional, Physical, Societal, and Religious." The first was a happiness that purified the mind. The physical benefit was the expansion of one's breath and the forestalling of chest afflictions, as well as calmness of mind and sleep. The societal and religious benefits were interlinked and "similar to the effect on people of the wisdom of ancient sages as heard through the singing of their *shloka*s [couplets], *bhajana* [devotional songs], and *kavita* [poems]. In much the same way, when women sang devotional music, they influenced people to enhance their faith with devotion and keep them on the path of truth."[84] Thus women were to be trained not as performing or professional musicians, but as the carriers of religious ideology and the upholders of truth. Here and elsewhere, women were elevated to the same status as that of India's ancient sages, even as they were told by Paluskar to stay at home and teach their children and other women about devotional music. This is not to sug-

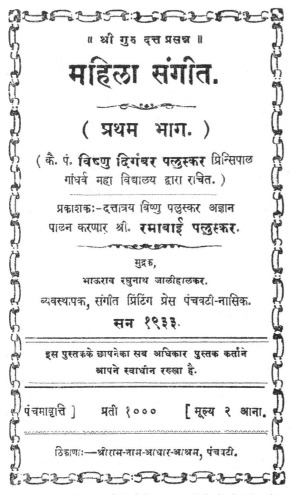

॥ श्री गुरु दत्त प्रसन्न ॥

महिला संगीत.

(प्रथम भाग.)

(कै. पं. विष्णु दिगंबर पलुस्कर प्रिन्सिपाल
गांधर्व महा विद्यालय द्वारा रचित.)

प्रकाशकः–दत्तात्रय विष्णु पलुस्कर अज्ञान
पालन करणार श्रीं. रमाबाई पलुस्कर.

मुद्रक,
भाऊराव रघुनाथ जालीहालकर.
व्यवस्थापक, संगीत प्रिंटिंग प्रेस पंचवटी-नासिक.
सन १९३३.

इस पुस्तकके छापनेका सब अधिकार पुस्तक कर्तांने
आपने स्वाधीन रख्खा है.

पंचमावृत्ति]   प्रती १०००   [मूल्य २ आना.

ठिकाणः–श्रीराम-नाम-आधार-आश्रम, पंचवटी.

FIGURE 4.6. Cover of *Mahila Sangeet*, Paluskar's Marathi pamphlet on women's music.

gest that women could not or did not resist such a construction; it simply highlights the deliberateness and comprehensiveness of Paluskar's demolition of any spatial demarcation between the public and private spheres, between sacred and secular domains. Women were not encouraged to leave the private space of the home to go out into the world. Rather, they were being trained to carry the burden of ancient cultural and religious purity within the home and, through their role in new forms of household education, for the benefit of the world as well. They were in the home, in other words, for the sake of the religious nation.

In Paluskar's formulation, Parsis were the model minority and women were the noble upholders of nationalist ideology. Both organizations that supported Paluskar, the Sanatan Dharm and the Arya Samaj, had identified Islam and Christianity as the evils against which a new Hinduism had to defend itself.[85] It seems unlikely that it was a coincidence that there were no Christian or Muslim students in his schools, and there are some answers buried in Paluskar's pedagogy as to why this was so. Given the GMV's emphasis on Hindu *pujas*, the suspension of classes on Hindu festival days, and Sanskrit prayers, which were sung on all occasions including informal gatherings, it is reasonable to postulate that Paluskar had founded not just any music school, but a Hindu music school. By placing religiosity at the forefront of his pedagogy, Paluskar institutionalized a Brahminic Hinduism as the modal cultural form of Indian music. Musicians thought of themselves first as artists and inheritors of a particular performance-based tradition. How might they have responded to Paluskar's foregrounding of Hindu religious beliefs in his musical pedagogy? Might it have been the case that knowingly or otherwise he had alienated most Muslim musicians and their talented progeny, as well as Muslim students from nonmusical families who might have been interested in learning music? Yet, against the charge of such foreclosure, Paluskar could always point to the attendance of Parsis in his school to demonstrate the inclusiveness of his program, as his biographers have done on his behalf. Parsi willingness to learn Indian music was both a shield and ploy. Against Parsi participation, the absence of Muslim students could now be explained as their own stubborn unwillingness to participate in music's nationalist modernity.

In the years after Indian independence in 1947, a handful of reputable Muslim musicians became the advertisement for the secularism of Indian classical music, and, I would argue by extrapolation, also for Hindu nationalism, without naming it as such. I use two word-of-mouth accounts here with caution, not with the intention of claiming them as proof but to pose questions about the nature of Paluskar's success on a large scale. The renowned *Shehnai* maestro, Bismillah Khan, is considered an exemplary musician, not simply because of his genius but also because he prays at the temple overlooking the Ganges in Benares every morning. Alladiya Khan, doyen of the Jaipur/Atrauli *gharana*, referred to himself and was known in the profession as the "sacred-thread wearing Muslim"; in other words, the Brahmin Muslim.[86] Let me present a few ways in which these accounts might be understood.

Court and temple musicians in earlier periods had participated in sanctified rituals in both directions, Hindu and Muslim, without that participation interfering with their religious self-definition. Indeed, religious self-definition was by no means the primary identity for musicians. Seen in this light, the participation of Muslim musicians in Hindu forms of religiosity could be viewed simply as the continuation of an earlier performative practice. Alternatively, participation in the ritual could be seen as resisting the exclusionary dictates of nationalism or as positing the fundamentally unthreatening connection between forms of religiosity and musical performance. In my affiliating both the musician and the ritual with a contemporary understanding of the terms *Hindu* and *Muslim*, I could be accused of making separations where none existed earlier. If Muslim musicians were participating in so-called Hindu rituals, or, as in the case of Alladiya Khan, holding on to both identifications—Brahmin and Muslim—would that not necessarily imply that the labels themselves had exhausted their usefulness? But it should also be noted that forms of religiosity particular to South Asian Islam do not seem quite as visible in the world of music as do Brahmin chants and rituals at musical performances. *Sura*s from the Koran, for instance, are not routinely recited by Hindu musicians. Instead, rumors circulate, sotto voce, about how the famous musician Pandit Kumar Gandharva refused to sing ragas like "Miyan ki malhar" on the grounds that they were connected to Muslims. This may lead to questions about the role of music in South Asian Muslim modernity that are beyond the scope of this book, but it is striking that these perceptions bring together a range of nationalist ideological opinions. Viewed in this manner, music comfortably serves opposing nationalist agendas without contradiction. Music can be secular, inclusive, Hindu, Muslim, religious, ritualistic, resistant to the forces of colonialism, and still possess a history of continuity. Both conservatives and progressives can celebrate Indian classical music as offering the right nationalist mix because it alone has resisted the forces of colonial modernity.

Here, I offer, polemically, a different reading. What we see through Paluskar's achievements is the emergence of a national cultural sphere in the early years of the twentieth century, long before the nation itself was in sight, in which Muslimness needed to be hidden from view, toned down, or reformulated. It had to *demonstrate* (what it might previously have both accommodated and welcomed) its participation in Brahminic ritual, prayers, *bha-jan*s, *kirtan*s, and *abhang*s, and attendance at temples as proof of its right to membership in the Indian nation. This inaugurated the structural and systemic difficulty of being a musician in the public world of music without participating in Hindu forms of religiosity. In light of this, and in this new era in which Hindu nationalism was on the rise, might it be possible to take a different view of Bismillah Khan's and Alladiya Khan's assertions of "faith" or of Brahminic lineage? Might they be strategic gestures that made visible the changed context of the time, gestures that now seemed necessary to protect their futures as musicians in a predominantly Hindu public world of cultural performance? By offering this as a possibility and in stressing the national success of Paluskar's recognizably Brahmin, Hindu agenda, my aim is to shake the comfort of the view that Indian classical music, however defined, transcended contemporaneous history and politics. Indeed, I assert here instead that music was critical to the development of this new cultural sphere, exposing its contradictions in these subtle if significant ways.

Bhatkhande and Paluskar: Competitiveness and Complementarity

Paluskar and Bhatkhande finally met in Bombay sometime between 1911 and 1912. In 1908, when Paluskar was commencing his move to Bombay, Bhatkhande had sponsored his performances at the Gayan Uttejak Mandali, a Parsi-founded music appreciation society that staged semipublic performances of music, but did not actually meet him then. Initially, Bhatkhande was not averse to having Paluskar among his interlocutors, but the two of them never became friends, unsurprising given their differences in perspective, ideology, religiosity, and musical approach. In fact, their first meeting dissolved into acrimony and their relationship remained distant, if civil. Bhatkhande approached Paluskar with a proposal for a series of lectures he could give at the Bombay GMV. Paluskar opposed the format and the intellectualized content of the proposed lectures, and the meeting dissolved.[87] The animosity between them continued. Paluskar was contemptuous of Bhatkhande's highly intellectualized understanding of music and Bhatkhande, in turn, was persuaded that Paluskar's methods would reproduce precisely the problem he had undertaken to correct: the training of musicians without educating them in music's history and theory. Both were correct in their perceptions of each other, but neither yielded and each remained wedded to his own point of view.

The animosity and competitiveness between Bhatkhande and Paluskar, once begun, never waned. Paluskar was interested in the intellectual aspects of music, but they had never really been a major focus or concern for him. Yet, in the *Gandharva Mahavidyalaya* journal issues of 1916 (the year of Bhatkhande's first All-India Music Conference), technical articles about *swara* and *shruti* were published along with detailed mathematical exegeses. The magazine also published articles that translated and explicated Sanskrit texts on music, and one can surmise that only his competitiveness with Bhatkhande would have spurred such publications.[88] Bhatkhande noted in a letter to a friend that none of Paluskar's students were particularly impressive and Paluskar's students commented critically on Bhatkhande's overintellectualized music and emphasis on education.[89]

Paluskar's biographer and student V. N. Patwardhan, for instance, lambasted Bhatkhande for using his first conference in 1916 to show off his personal genius, disparaging his use of pseudonyms. He narrated his account with metaphors and fables to conclude the story with Bhatkhande's ultimate defeat:

> Pandit Bhatkhande used pseudonyms such as *chaturpandit* [clever pandit] in his writings on music. By this he tried to suggest that *chaturpandit* was a writer from a bygone period. But just as truth can never die, untruth can never live. The sun can never be prevented from rising in the sky even if the roosters who crow are covered in dark cloths. At his own conference, the famous *beenkar* [instrumentalist] Mangeshrao Telang came forward to place the truth before the entire assembly that what Pandit Bhatkhande was saying about himself was utterly untrue.[90]

Patwardhan also lectured his readers about the "superiority complexes" of overeducated people who had no regard for musicians and preferred to deliver speeches at conferences in English. This was clearly a reference to Bhatkhande's 1916 conference, at which Paluskar had not only delivered his address in Hindi but chastized the organizers for their emphasis on English.

Both Bhatkhande and Paluskar believed strongly that music needed to be adopted as a cause by nationalists. The difference between them on this subject lay in the overt connections that Paluskar stressed between music, nation, gender, and modern Hinduism, whereas Bhatkhande wished music to be kept aloof from religion, politics, and women. Bhatkhande wished to nationalize music; Paluskar wanted music to be nationalist. Bhatkhande's historicism required him to find some way of accommodating what his intellectual and scholastic research revealed about Muslim authorship of music, and his agenda simply ignored women. Paluskar, on the other hand, had no such ambiguous relationship to India's Muslim heritage. At its worst, this heritage existed for him as a travesty of history. At its best, Muslim musicians functioned as an entrenched status group. Furthermore, women had a definite role to play in Paluskar's notion of the future of music. It was a role of propaganda, not progressive education, but by giving music the patina of bhakti, he made it attractive to an emerging bourgeoisie that could envision the prospect of sending their daughters to his schools.

The attitude toward religious instruction is notable not merely as the most visible of the differences between the two men but also in terms of their understanding of Indian cultural modernity. Bhatkhande's modernity lay in an expressed separation between religion and music, even if he occasionally felt the need to be defensive about his skepticism regarding the lore and fables that abounded in the understanding of music in his time. He rejected the sentimental and unnecessary worship of one's guru and believed in dialogue (albeit with imaginary students and solely on the pages of a text) and debate. Paluskar's modernity was camouflaged under the cover of a so-called traditionalist argument. However, his was a shrewder understanding than Bhatkhande's since it involved the material takeover of a public sphere through the deployment of a mannered national religiosity. Music was the instrument through which a public sphere was to be not merely expanded but brought within a larger Hindu fold. For Bhatkhande, modernity was an intellectual project; for Paluskar it was an institutional one in which music provided the means, the method, and the message. In Paluskar's successful cooptation of the public sphere, one sees clearly how the commingling of religious instruction with musical education cemented the identification of the culture of the bourgeoisie as Hindu. In Paluskar's understanding, Indian culture was Hindu culture, and his unapologetic and triumphalist project of returning music to tradition placed music under the umbrella of Hindu culture.

Moreover, Paluskar was not as aloof or remote as Bhatkhande, who had an impossible intellectualized demand that all serious students of music be knowledgeable in four languages, master seventeen arcane texts of music, and know its complete history before they could be permitted to perform. Paluskar made music instruction far simpler and understood an emerging modernity far better than Bhatkhande who, in retrospect, despite his exhortations, indulged in a desire for a renaissance scholar to come forward, and when no one did, came forth himself. In Paluskar's case, indeed, it may have been precisely the deemphasizing of a depth model of education that facilitated the speed of his success. As soon as his students reached a basic proficiency in music, he sent them off to found a school. Bhatkhande's demand that his ideal student needed to plough through Sanskrit, Persian, Telugu, and the occasional Bengali text seems abstruse by comparison. Indeed, even the curriculum for the Marris College needed to be simplified because its demands were too unreasonable. As recently as 1999, the relative successes and failures of the two men of music were dramatized once again. While Paluskar's students were implementing their plan to move their headquarters from Meraj into a brand new facility in Bombay, Bhatkhande's Marris College of Music (renamed the Bhatkhande Sangeet Vidyapeeth) was involved in a struggle with the state government over accreditation.

Paluskar's devoutness is not by itself the issue any more than is the genuineness of his faith. The real issue lies in the commingling of music and sacrality in modern India, not as the expression of individual private faith but as a paradigm of public culture. Paluskar's program elaborated what became the modal form of cultural modernity, the very form against which one has to see Bhatkhande's modern, historicist agenda as the one of the complementary alternatives. By showing Paluskar's mission as modal and Bhatkhande's agenda as the alternative that failed, I wish to bring into even sharper relief the alternative possibility for musical history that Bhatkhande rejected.

The religious nature of culture, operating under the sign of national secularism and emblematized in a figure like Paluskar, was integral to Hindu self-fashioning. This point is made through two narrations, one documented, the other perhaps apocryphal, both issuing from the same source, Dr. Sharatchandra Gokhale, one of Maharashtrian music's most critical scholars. He wrote in praise and defense of Paluskar, "It is said that he despised Muslims but there is little truth to that rumor. He truly believed that the method of teaching *arya sangeet* [ancient music] was destroyed by the Muslims, that they annihilated its science, defiled its purity, and for their own pleasure enhanced the numbers of singing girls. This view was mistaken, but because it was such a fixed belief he saw everything through its gaze. Even so, he had nothing but appreciation for *any* talented musician. His student Deodhar started learning Western music, and he encouraged him, even renting him a piano!"[91] The second story, told to Dr. Gokhale by B. R. Deodhar, was as follows. Paluskar apparently told his students to listen as many times as they could to the singing of the great *khayal* musician, Abdul Karim Khan, for what they could learn from him about virtuosity and sweetness of voice. However, he reportedly confessed to the great singer himself at a conference, "It is indeed true that you sing well, but what is to be done? You're a Muslim."[92] Both these stories are narrated as proof of Paluskar's appreciation of all music, even that sung by Muslims. In the previous pages, I have tried to lay out the material, social, and structural history of music's institutionalization to show how it is possible for even a critical scholar such as Dr. Gokhale to simultaneously acknowledge and deny Paluskar's prejudices. Like Bhatkhande, Paluskar was set on rescuing a music that held for him no relation, other than a negative one, to the majority of its practitioners. Unlike Bhatkhande, he was successful in institutionalizing the relationship in programmatic fashion.

The similarity between the two men of music in the end is a negative one. Neither of their visions could structurally accommodate minorities, aside from those who were willing to assimilate (the Parsis or the Hinduized Muslims) or behave merely as docile bodies of difference (women). Yet both genuinely believed that their programs were inclusive and nationalist in the best and most enlightened ways. Perhaps this places the liberal secular and the religious conservative understanding of music on equal footing. My point here, however, has been to show that any easy condemnation of the first must be rendered far more complicated in light of the latter, as both are equally implicated in the contradictions of colonial modernity. While this recognition precludes the comfortable celebration of either, it is important to recognize that, at least in the sphere of music, Paluskar was far more successful, and influential, than Bhatkhande. And therein lies the rub.

❀ FIVE ❀

MUSIC IN PUBLIC AND

NATIONAL CONVERSATION

Conferences, Institutions, and Agendas, 1916–1928

By the end of the first decade of the twentieth century, music was taught in schools in addition to private homes. Musicians performed in public halls as well as in aristocratic drawing rooms. Bhatkhande had published his major works on music theory, and Paluskar's two schools, in Lahore and Bombay, were well established. Furthermore, Paluskar's students were well on their way to founding additional music schools modeled after the Bombay GMV in cities around the country. However, even more than schools and texts a new format, the All-India Music Conference, would convert music into a subject worthy of national attention, not in the manner in which Jones had spoken of it, but as part of a modern, anticolonial project.

In convening All-India Music Conferences (hereafter AIMC), Bhatkhande (and Paluskar) did not invent a new format as much as he adapted the principal mode of the Indian National Congress. Between 1916 and 1926, Bhatkhande and Paluskar each convened five music conferences. Bhatkhande's first conference was restricted to musical experts, but at subsequent conferences, tickets were sold to the public daily and musicians' performances at the close of the day's discussions were held in large and crowded venues. Daily discussions about music tended to be quite technical, and in this new and open forum musicians, musicologists, critics, writers, and connoisseurs passionately and knowledgably argued about and discussed a number of subjects related to music, ranging from the intricate mathematics of different pitches to the development of a national music. Often, questions of science and music were themselves linked to discussions about the new national music.[1] Early musicologists used an array of scientific techniques to prove and document the existence of a superior understanding of classical music in India's ancient texts at the same time that they argued about the minutiae in Sanskrit texts on subjects such as the correct order of pitches in a given raga. Rulers of princely states continued in their roles as patrons, hosting conferences rather than *jalsas* in their state capitals, donating money, and "lending" the services of their court musicians. Musicians who attended did so not only to perform in the evening but also to lend a hand to the conference participants by providing practical demonstrations of various subjects for discussion, such as the dominance of particular pitches in a given raga or variations within a raga.

As with all other matters related to music, key differences marked the two sets of conferences. Bhatkhande convened all of his conferences in North India. In addition to musicians and scholars, the Western-educated elite of the cities in which they were held and some princely state rulers attended them. The rulers came to the conferences with their state bands in attendance and made speeches about the need to rescue music and make it available for the nation, while Bhatkhande's friends and supporters presented papers on the fine points of music's theory, notation, and practice. Most papers were delivered in English, and those that were not were translated into English. The reports were published in English with appendices in Hindi and Urdu and, for the third conference, in Bengali. The conferences themselves were not held every year; there was a six-year gap between the first three conferences and the last two. The first three conferences (held in 1916, 1918, and 1919) were mainly preoccupied with founding a national academy for music, and the fourth and fifth (in 1925 and 1926) were convened to establish a college of music in Lucknow, after plans to found a national academy came to nothing. All five conferences advocated the creation of a national system of notation and a uniform description of ragas.

Paluskar, by contrast, convened his conferences neither to discuss the founding of music institutions nor to debate the merits of different notational systems. He had already established the Lahore and Bombay Gandharva Mahavidyalayas and could point to their success with pride. Nor did he need to ponder the differences between systems of musical notation, since the textbooks of notated compositions published by the Gandharva Mahavidyalaya in Bombay had been in use for over a decade by the time he convened his first conference. Consequently, many of the issues that occupied center stage at Bhatkhande's conference were simply passé for him. Paluskar's conferences were much smaller and intimate affairs ostensibly devoted to questions concerning musicians. Although both conferences addressed questions related to the standardization of ragas and *shrutis*, they were very different in tone, substance, and performance. Participants at Paluskar's conference spoke in Hindi or Marathi, not in English. Prayers took up a good bit of time at Paluskar's conference, and the participants were mostly musicians and musicologists. No rulers came to his conference with their state bands in attendance.

Bhatkhande convened the first All-India Music Conference in Baroda in 1916, the second in New Delhi in 1918, and the third in Benares in 1919. He tried to hold the fourth conference in 1922 in Indore, but after the ruler withdrew his financial support, he had to hunt for a new venue and a new patron. In 1925 and 1926, he convened the last two in Lucknow, culminating in the foundation of a school of music named after the colonial governor of the United Provinces, Sir William Marris.[2] He considered another conference in 1928, but soon lost interest. In any case, his health had failed him, and by 1932, he considered himself an old man whose active life had ended.[3] Bhatkhande was a major figure at the All-India Music Conferences and the driving force behind them, but since he did not have the backing of an institution, he had less freedom to determine when and where they ought to be held. Paluskar, on the other hand, had complete independence in deciding the venue and dates for his conferences and convened one every year under the aegis of the Gandharva Mahavidyalaya in Bombay between 1918 and 1922.

As Bhatkhande and his cohort listened to each other's lofty speeches and formulated plans for a National Academy of Music, Paluskar rested in the quiet comfort of having already accomplished all that the speakers were planning to tackle. Consequently, when it was his turn to speak, he grandstanded, chastised the conference organizers for their exclusiveness, and declared most issues that were of importance to them irrelevant. He had done all they were setting out to do many years ago. He had captured the musical mainstream by setting up small, local, music schools. At the conference, participants discussed in detail the problem of bringing simplified music to the masses. Not only had Paluskar implemented such simplification through the publication and distribution of his music textbooks, he had also succeeded in recruiting women to his schools. He had brought together a modern religiosity with musical nationalism, both of which were better served by encouraging women to become part of the program rather than excluding them on the grounds that they were incapable of understanding the rarefied essence of music, as Bhatkhande believed. Bhatkhande wanted a grand national academy of music that would stand as the nation's fountainhead for music education. While Bhatkhande talked about giant organizations, Paluskar had made significant headway in controlling large chunks of the nation's musical education by going at it piece by little piece. By the fourth conference, Bhatkhande and his friends publicly conceded that a national academy of music was an idea both too large and too far ahead of its time. Paluskar, at much the same time, celebrated his institutional and pedagogical success by convening a conference of all his students who had been members of his *Upadeshak* class, founded in 1904, to train music instructors. In 1930, when Bhatkhande's college of music faced bankruptcy and internal strife, Paluskar claimed that he had placed three hundred music instructors all over India who had implemented his agenda in little schools. Consequently, there was little intellectual jousting at Paluskar's conferences, merely an air of comfortable success. Finally, in Paluskar's conferences, there was certainty about India's music history; at Bhatkhande's, history continued to haunt certainty about music.

These two sets of conferences highlight not just the differences between the two men of music, but also the issues that came to the fore when music was discussed at a national level. Paluskar's conferences were local, small-scale, "indigenized," and characterized by comfortable celebrations of his manifest success; Bhatkhande's were national, "Westernized," and grandiose, designed to create the basis for his ultimate triumph. Yet the point worth making here is that for all that they were a showy stage of princely grandeur and benevolence, they were also genuine forums for intellectual arguments about music's history and theory.

Contentious debates were integral to Bhatkhande's conferences, and indeed controversy was a vital part of all his endeavors. While such incendiary conversations confirm what we know about his arrogance and belligerence, they also point to his conferences as a public and interregional space within which it was possible to air alternative understandings of music's history or origins. These viewpoints, voiced by a few participants at Bhatkhande's con-ference, suggesting that India's musical origins lay in Persia, Arabia, or Turkey, had no place in Paluskar's conference. In the light of the politics of Paluskar's bhakti nationalism, Bhatkhande's contentiousness can perhaps be seen as affording, if nothing else, one possible opportunity for a different un-derstanding of music's future without discounting either his dismissals of these alternatives or, for that matter, his altogether inadequate secularism. With Bhatkhande there was the possibility of debate about music; with Paluskar there was none. This distinction between contentious and flawed open-mindedness and closed comfort is apparent not just in the differences between the conferences but also in how the two men founded their res-pective institutions of music learning. Paluskar's institutional success bespeaks his conservative clarity. Bhatkhande's failures are the result of a nationalizing imperative and a historicist confusion. In imagining what music's future might have looked like had Bhatkhande achieved greater success with the Marris College, we may perhaps see a different possibility for music's moder-nity via an alternative pedagogical and nationalist route. This recognition of the "road not taken" by Bhatkhande—his failure to implement his agenda nationwide—is crucial for my argument. I emphasize it in order to consider the question of the politics of music's modernity in broader terms in the con-cluding chapters of this book.[4]

Bhatkhande's All-India Music Conferences, 1916–1926

In keeping with the format of the INC sessions, participants at the first AIMC delivered their speeches in English, and the conference's standing committee was created to include a representative each from "Southern Maratha country, Baroda, Tanjore, Gujerat, Masulipatan, Mysore, Madras, Madura, Bengal, Lucknow, Nagpore, and Karwar."[5] Immediately, we see the interregional focus of this conference. Unsurprisingly, most of the major par-ticipants were men, with the notable exception of Atiya Begum Fyzee Ra-hamin, noted authority on music and wife of the famous Bombay artist Abalal Rahamin. Nineteen performers "rendered useful assistance" at the con-ference. Of these, fifteen were Hindustani musicians and four were Carnatic musicians who had come to Baroda from Vijayanagara, Tanjore, and Madras. Of the fifteen Hindustani musicians, fourteen were Muslim. Sayajirao Gaekwad of Baroda, chief patron of the conference, had "lent" seven of his musicians to the conference, including the famous vocalists Faiyaz Khan and Faiz Mohammed Khan, and the others had been sent by the rulers of Udaipur, Alwar, Jaipur, Indore, and Tonk.[6]

None of these musicians attending the conference was included in the list of formal theoretical commentators or major speakers. Instead, they were deemed "practical artists" by the organizers, and if a dispute arose about the mathematics of a particular pitch, for instance, one of the musicians was called upon to sing or play in order to help the theorists with their scholarly evaluations. Musicians like Abdul Karim Khan, about whom we shall read in the next chapter, had by then begun collaborative projects with other musicologists. What they lent to the scholarly enterprise was the expertise of their artistic performance as well as a musician-centered theory, but in general they were seen at the conference as artisans and craftsmen, not theorists. As soon as the musicians had concluded their practical demonstrations, the scholars continued with their conversation. Occasionally, one of the musicians would interject a dissenting point of view, but they were not formal presenters at the conference.

By 1916, Bhatkhande had concluded his four tours and had a well-established reputation as an authority on music theory. On his tours, he had spoken to as many musicians as he thought necessary. Like contemporary ethnographers, the "native informants" had given him information but not interpretation. The ethnographer's intellectual interlocutors were other ethnographers, not the native informants. This was true for Bhatkhande as well, although he did not think of himself as an ethnographer per se. He had extracted from his native informants—the musicians—all the information he needed, and at the first AIMC he was not interested in speaking with them so much as debating the finer points of the mathematics of *shruti* and the accuracy of Sanskrit translations with other scholars.

In a curious turn of events, the content and tone of the conference had been decided three months before its participants congregated in Baroda. In December 1915, Sayajirao Gaekwad had sent a letter to a sessions judge from Dharwar, Mr. E. Clements: "I want you to help me; and I have spoken to my Munshi [finance minister] to arrange for a meeting of gentlemen like yourself, who take interest in or understand Indian music. The object of this meeting is to discuss and find out what can be done to revise and improve Indian music. I have come across a few people besides yourself, who are interested in the cause."[7] Bhatkhande and Paluskar were among the "few people" who were to be part of the first AIMC and the two men, in the course of their careers, had agreed unequivocally on very few matters, except for one. Both of them disliked and mistrusted Clements. The AIMC's chief patron had perhaps unwittingly united Bhatkhande and Paluskar by issuing their worst enemy a warm invitation to the conference.[8]

On the face of it, both Bhatkhande and Paluskar had reason to support parts—if not all—of Clements's agenda. Like earlier Orientalist scholars before him, Clements was enchanted by India's ancient history, and his desire to establish a Brahminic origin for Indian music might well have endeared him to Paluskar. Relatedly, his interest in scientific research might reasonably have appealed to Bhatkhande. However, Paluskar thought him too "Western"— not for any intellectual reason, but because of his notational system—and Bhatkhande found his emphasis on antiquity intellectually unsustainable and his scientific experiments bogus. Even though they had themselves "borrowed" from Western notation for their own compilations of musical compositions, Paluskar believed his system was entirely derived from ancient India, and Bhatkhande disagreed with Clements's recommendation to simply map onto Indian music an unmodified notational system taken from Western classical music. Moreover, Clements was championing the *shruti* harmonium in place of the *sarangi* and the tempered harmonium, a substitution both Paluskar and Bhatkhande adamantly opposed. Nonetheless, despite their dislike of him, they both also recognized that he was a powerful figure in their world, with influential rulers like Sayajirao Gaekwad as his supporter and musician friends like Abdul Karim Khan.[9]

The first issue of contention had to do with science, mathematics, and the proper definition of Indian music. In 1885, the English physicist, Alexander J. Ellis, had delivered a paper in London on Hermann von Helmholtz's *Sensations of Tone*, which had been published a year earlier.[10] In this paper, he challenged Helmholtz's evolutionary conclusion that the Western tempered scale was the natural culmination of all other primitive scales in existence, arguing instead for a relativistic understanding of the construction of scales around the world. His article came to be known as the Ellis Report, viewed as making the case that the Indian musical scale, as one of the so-called primitive scales, was neither natural nor scientifically based.[11] These were fighting words. A deputy collector from Satara, Raosaheb Krishnaji Ballal Deval, had responded in 1910 by publishing *The Hindu Musical Scale and the 22 Shrutees*, in which he had demonstrated the complex mathematics of the commonly used pitches in order to prove Ellis wrong about his statements concerning the lack of science in ancient Indian music.[12] Clements had written a complimentary foreword to Deval's publication, praising it for its comprehensiveness, acuity, and most of all for establishing the unquestionably ancient and scientific basis for Indian music.

Bhatkhande, however, had not been impressed. "Mr. Dewal [sic] is personally not a musician," he wrote to his friend, Nawab Ali, taluqdar of Akbarpur (Faizabad District) in the UP, and moreover "finds fault with the attempts of all his predecessors including all European scholars and professes to lay down the correct notes as a brand new and original arrangement. He goes the length of saying that his arrangement is the most ancient one (2000 years old) and so forth."[13] As we have seen, Bhatkhande reacted particularly badly to unfounded historical claims. Here he reacted in character:

> He is neither a good Sanscrit Scholar nor a good musician although he quotes from Rag Vibodha & Parijat which books are his only authorities. Both these he seems to have misunderstood. He is a friend of mine. I showed him the ridiculous conclusions deducible from his arguments and he is nearly convinced. The principal fault I find in the arrangement is that he is wrong in calling it the most musical scale of the Sanscrit books. It may be a good modern scale (if Abdul Karim's notes are quite correct) but when you begin to lay it down as Rag Vibodha and Parijat Scale you are positively wrong.[14]

In keeping with his other claims, Bhatkhande had no objections to identifying the scale as modern, but he could not support the claim Deval was making about it being authentically ancient. Deval and Clements had as their close collaborator a musician with whom Bhatkhande had many disagreements: Abdul Karim Khan, the famous kirana gharana vocalist.

Of Abdul Karim Khan, Bhatkhande wrote, "I am not an admirer of Abdul Karim. . . . In Poona he seems have developed into a great authority. Mr. Dewal wanted some Mahomedan musician to back him and flourishes his name throughout . . . Mr. Dewal writes these modern notes against the ancient Shrutis which is the rotten part of the theory." Bhatkhande wished him to be more direct about his scholarship. "When you write new names against the Shrutis, say that you are making a new arrangement according to the ancient method, that would be more honest and more consistent," demanded Bhatkhande (emphasis mine). "You do not sing a single ancient Rag in its ancient purity, why then this show of putting modern names on ancient shrutis. . . . He has Abdul Kareem and others to constantly sing or play to him and then a retired civil engineer to work out the calculations."[15] Once again, Bhatkhande rails against poor historical practices. He does not dismiss Abdul Karim per se. Abdul Karim was a *khyal gayak*, and Bhatkhande's personal taste in music ran to *dhrupad*. Nonetheless, given his opinion, Bhatkhande could hardly have been pleased that the chief patron of the AIMC had invited Deval's chief champion, E. Clements, to the conference. To make matters worse, Clements came to the conference with both Deval and the engineer, Nilakant Chhatre, who had, according to Bhatkhande, worked out all of Deval's calculations.

Deval's book was not the sole cause of Bhatkhande's irritation. In 1911, Deval had cofounded with Clements the Philharmonic Society of Western India in Satara, which claimed in its manifesto that it was engaged in serious scientific research relevant to music.[16] In keeping with the stated aims of the society, Clements and Deval modified a version of the American organ and promoted it as a replacement for both the tempered harmonium and the *sarangi*. Bhatkhande did not like the harmonium, but he did not dismiss the *sarangi* as did Clements. Paluskar did not care for the harmonium either but had close ties with the Marathi stage, where it was gaining in popularity, sometimes using it to teach members of the stage in his schools. By dismissing both instruments in favor of their own "Western" organ, Clements and Deval had once again managed to alienate both Bhatkhande and Paluskar equally. In inviting Clements, Sayajirao was throwing the debate on music wide open by forcing Bhatkhande and Paluskar into conversation with their most contentious competitors.

Thakur M. Nawab Ali, the friend to whom Bhatkhande had written about his criticisms of Deval, was president of the conference. He was perhaps aware that even in a gathering as august as the one before him, tensions could run high because of deep-seated disagreements among the participants. In his address, he announced both the problem confronting the conference and its solution: "No one will deny that the Music of the country is at present in the hands of an ignorant and illiterate class and that it is essential to rescue it from the possibility of complete destruction and place it on a scientific basis."[17] This was a claim against performers as a group, not against Muslims per se. In effect, Nawab Ali was endorsing both Bhatkhande and Paluskar in urging that music needed to be "rescued" from its practitioners. But he knew that any reformulation was fraught, so he cautioned that "the deliberations of the Conference should be conducted in a friendly spirit in order that a definite step forward may be taken and the cause of Indian Music substantially advanced."[18] Despite this warning, the conference began with an intellectual duel.

Bhatkhande read the first paper, "A short Historical Survey of Hindustani Music and the means to place it on a scientific foundation with the view to make its study as easy as possible." His title encapsulated all that his friend, Nawab Ali, had elaborated as the goals of the conference. For music to march into the future, it had to incorporate within itself both history and science. It also had to transform and simplify its pedagogical practices. But who was to decide music's "scientific foundation"? Clements and Deval had earlier already staked their claim to such authority and repeated it at the conference. Clements argued that his scale was the same as that of Sharangdeva's in the *Sangit Ratnakara*.[19] Deval, for his part, postulated in "The Theory of Indian Music as Expounded by Somanatha" that Somanatha had demonstrable knowledge of superior harmonics.[20] Furthermore, they had brought with them their rigged organ, called the *shruti* harmonium, to demonstrate not just their theories about *shruti* but also the superiority of their instrument over the *sarangi* and the tempered harmonium. The demonstration fell flat. Clements and Deval had taken their argument deep into Bhatkhande's territory, and at the start of proceedings, the next morning, they faced a formidable group of his friends who rallied to demolish their theories and demonstrate that their new instrumental invention was the work of foolish and ignorant minds.

D. K. Joshi of Poona, a longtime associate of Bhatkhande's, began by challenging Deval's knowledge of Sanskrit.[21] Shankarrao Karnad, Bhatkhande's closest friend, argued that Clements could not possibly claim that his scale was the same as that of the *Sangit Ratnakara*, since it was not in practical use by any musician, and in any case, Bhatkhande's classificatory system and base scale was the best system by far. The same afternoon, the musicians were recruited to help demonstrate that the *shruti* harmonium was altogether wrong. They banded together and the report noted that "after two hours trial and interesting discussion, the Conference came to the conclusion that the scales suggested by Mr. Clements for the Kaphi, Khamaja, and Bilawal Ragas did not tally with those sung by the practical artists as going by those names in current practice."[22] Using a different argument, Mr. Mangeshrao Telang claimed that the *Sangit Ratnakara* was an inappropriate text for North Indian classical music and that Bharata's *Natyashastra* was better suited. When Clements countered with the argument that there was no inconsistency between the scales in the *Sangit Ratnakara* and the *Natyashastra*, Telang replied that he did not wish to be interrupted any further.[23] For the next two days, the debate continued, with Deval and Clements on one side and Bhatkhande and his friends on the other. Time was spent dealing with mistranslations and misunderstandings of Sanskrit texts, referring Deval and Clements to independent Sanskritists, and subjecting their historical and theoretical scholarship to criticism.

The conference grew increasingly contentious. As soon as Telang finished chastising Clements for interrupting him, he called Bhatkhande a charlatan and a liar for publishing his Sanskrit work *Lakshya Sangit* under a pseudonym. Telang accused him of doing so "with the evident object of palming it off on the public as an old authoritative book on Northern Indian Music."[24] Bhatkhande's solicitor friend, B. S. Sukthankar, rushed to defend him and the day ended without further attacks. The next day passed without acrimony until the evening. When Paluskar took the stage late in the day, he upstaged everyone who had preceded him by addressing the audience in Hindi. While the conference organizers had arranged for presentations made in languages other than English to be translated for the benefit of the discussants, it was also the case that most musicians did not speak English. By addressing the gathering in Hindi, Paluskar made two key points. First, he separated himself from the conference organizers by highlighting his own expertise as a performing musician who knew how and in what language to speak to fellow musicians. Second, and more important, he made it clear that his nationalism was more genuine—by not using a Western language—than that of the conference organizers. His polemics earned him the applause of the musicians. Even if the South Indian musicians did not speak Hindi, Paluskar was standing up, as it were, for the rights of musicians to be heard and spoken to at a conference about music.

Paluskar's intervention concerned a competitive and controversial issue: the notation of music. As noted in the report, "He spoke on the subject of Notation and remarked that the ancient Sanskrit treatises contained sufficient material on which suitable symbols could be founded, and recommended the merits of the system of Notation invented by him."[25] In other words,

Paluskar was letting people such as Clements know that in his opinion, Indian music had all it needed in Sanskrit texts and required nothing from the West. This deliberate, politically motivated, and vocally nationalistic abnegation of the "West" was a theme that Paluskar used to inaugurate his own conferences. The issue had to do with whether or not notation itself had anything to offer Indian music.

Those who supported notation wanted their own to become the standard bearer. Clements countered Paluskar's argument by championing his own cause and "placed before the audience his own suggestions for noting Indian Music by making suitable alternations in the European Staff Notation."[26] Those who did not support notation, including for example Atiya Begum Fyzee Rahamin, believed that no notation—Western or otherwise—could ever faithfully reproduce Indian music, suggesting that it destroyed artistic creativity. Other participants worried whether notation should be Western or Indian. Should it be part Western or all Indian? Should it be done on two lines, as Clements suggested, or three, as Paluskar advocated? The one person noticeably silent on the subject was Bhatkhande.

Notation was an issue also because of a related and larger concern about musical education. Paluskar was the one participant at the conference who had already received accolades for his institutional success. For this reason, he may have provoked some competitive anxiety on the part of those participants who were just beginning to get their feet wet in the realm of institution building. In the literature on Paluskar, there is a widely reported story about his conversation with Atiya Begum Fyzee Rahamin at the first AIMC. According to B. R. Deodhar, Paluskar's biographer, Begum Rahamin challenged Paluskar to document his prowess as a music teacher by letting the gathering know how many Tansens (legendary musician in the court of the Mughal emperor, Akbar) *his* school had produced. Even Tansen had not been able to reproduce himself in his students, retorted Paluskar, but in his Gandharva Mahavidyalaya he had done more than Tansen had done. Paluskar claimed to have trained scores of *kansen*s. The neologism *kansen*—where the word *kan*, meaning "ear," replaces the first three letters of the name Tansen—was used to denote musically trained listeners. Paluskar's retort was factually accurate. Even if his pedagogy had not produced any nationally famous musicians, it was certainly true that by 1916 he had already trained more students than Bhatkhande and his friends could imagine.

While Paluskar was perhaps the most dramatic speaker at the first AIMC, two other participants, Maulvi Abdul Halim Sharar, author of a famed historical book about the glories of old Lucknow, and Tassaduq Hussain Khan, a musician from Baroda, made speeches that were just as memorable.[27] Sharar's speech was translated into English and read to the gathering.[28] In his address, Sharar separated music into "our present Hindustani" and "Indian music." He was reported as having argued that "our present Hindustani Music is the result of the blending of Mahomedan Music with pure Aryan Music," and as for Indian music, "he had little more to say than that the ancient Sanskrit treatises up to and inclusive of Ratnakara were now entirely incomprehensible. As for Arabian Music, he said that the music which the Mahomedans brought to India was not purely Arabic, but was a mixture of Arabic, Persian, Syrian, Roman, and Greek."[29] The paper was telling: in the entire conference, it was one of the few assertions of a different conception of music. Sharar was arguing for music to be understood as neither purely Arabic nor Sanskritic, but as a live, syncretic, hybrid, and dynamic art that had no need of a Sanskritic cover of authority or authentication.

Tassaduq Hussain Khan, a singer from Baroda, made the second intervention along the same lines as Sharar.[30] The report stated that "it was . . . his personal opinion that the current music of Hindusthan had considerably outgrown the Sanskrit literature on the subject and that being so, he would always desire that all conferences where music was being discussed would make it a point to induce the practical artists of the day to join in their deliberations." Tassaduq Hussain Khan noted that artists had contributed to the most important changes in the "old Sanskrit music of the country and that entitled them to that confidence." In the conclusion of his address he also "assured the members of the conference that the practical artists in the country were in no way hostile to the reform and uplift of Indian Music, but were, on the contrary, very anxious to take their own share in the work of evolving a workable uniform music system for the whole country."[31] Abdul Halim Sharar and Tassaduq Hussain Khan had in different ways made two heartfelt appeals not to straitjacket the future of "Hindustani" music by limiting its history or its participants.

These two Muslim speakers had, in effect, argued that music's origins should be seen as hybrid, its essential character as dialogic, and its fundamental nature as syncretic. In so doing, they were arguing against the entire tone of the conference, whether voiced by Bhatkhande, Paluskar, or Clements, even if all of them had different concerns with music's purity or foundation. Maulvi

Abdul Halim Sharar had allowed for the idea that many authors writing in languages other than Sanskrit contributed equally to a musical tradition shared by all Hindustanis. Tassaduq Hussain Khan had suggested that musicians were themselves the authors of changes in "Sanskritic" music. It was simply unimportant, these two men suggested, to hammer away at textual purity, whether Arabic or Sanskrit, when music was played, sung, and authored by musicians in a number of ways, none of which fit an accepted definition of either authorship or purity. However, their joint entreaties were not what the conference participants would take home as their mandate for the future. Instead, they left Baroda with the voice of Sirdar Jagmohunlal of Alwar in their ears, for he had reportedly "exhorted the audience to remember that it was the sacred duty of each and every one of them to prevent it (music) from degenerating," saying that "Indians must never lose the nationality of their music."[32] The precise nationality of music was unclear, but nation and religion had come together to dominate the terms of the conversation.

The dynamics of the first conference were unique. A small gathering of intellectuals and musicians, with a few rulers of princely states in attendance, it had the flavor of an occasion at which questions about music were actively debated, with Paluskar, Bhatkhande, Deval, Clements, and Maulvi Abdul Halim Sharar as the principal interlocutors. Successive conferences had fewer intellectual fireworks and the reports bespoke none of the excitement of a new convention. In the first conference, Bhatkhande was pushed into conversations and debate with those who were published authors in their own right. At the second conference, there was neither tension nor exchange. Issues about music's history and theory seemed already resolved and the aim of the second conference, held at the Congress Pandal in New Delhi and boasting the patronage of members such as Gandhi and Rabindranath Tagore (both of whom were too busy to attend but lent it their support), was to found a national academy of music. In the two years between the first and the second conference, a bureaucratization had begun, setting a new tone that would seep into all discussions about the national academy. Bhatkhande and his cohort busied themselves with drafting guidelines and rules, assembling provisional committees, and writing memoranda. Because of this, the conference proceedings read more like the minutes of a meeting at which music's functionaries gathered, rather than the proceedings of a conference in which intellectuals sparred over historical and theoretical issues.

Bhatkhande claimed that the first conference had "opened the eyes of the whole country to the real needs of the situation and inspired them with confidence, that the problem of reviving, uplifting, and protecting Hindusthani music was after all not so difficult to solve, given the necessary sympathy and cooperation of the educated classes."[33] He was targeting the elite as music's potential saviors, and with good reason, since from the list of attendees, the second All-India Music Conference was clearly the place to be if one was a "maharaja" interested in the arts. The list of patrons included numerous *taluqdars* and rajahs from various princely states, and one after the next they endorsed the resolution for the founding of the academy. In one sense, it was a grand and spectacular gathering of the rich and powerful, who by their presence attested to the importance of founding a national academy. In another, despite the princes' oratory, it was a shallow simulacrum with little material promise, since very few of these princes reached deep into their pockets to donate money for the agenda about which they had just voiced abundant praise. Seven lakhs of rupees were needed to found the national academy. Given the wealth of the princely state rulers, it made sense for Bhatkhande to solicit their support. But the donations fell far short. Only the Nawab of Rampur, known for his generous patronage of the arts, made a sizeable contribution. His official title, Col. His Highness Alijah Furzand-Dilpazeer Daulat Inglishia Mukhlusudaulah Nasirulmulk Amirulmra Nawab Sir Syed Mohammed Hamid Alikhan Bahadur Mustaidijang, G.C.I.E.G.C.O.V., A.D.C. to His Imperial Majesty the King Emperor, was as long as his pockets were deep. He donated fifty thousand rupees and was nominated as the president of the second AIMC.

That so many princes should have gathered at this conference attests to the status that conferences had acquired in the public eye. The AIMCs were one of the few national(ist) venues in which the princes could hold on to their old roles as the patrons of music. Yet they could neither make the transition into a national sphere nor augment their vocal flourishes with material support. They came to the conference since it positioned them as the benevolent and longstanding patrons of art; they made speeches but did not in fact provide adequate patronage any more than they had done in the old days. Music as an adornment of the court was patronized, but this was music as a national art. When it came to funding a genuinely national activity, most of them retreated to the comfort of their native states without donating any more than a paltry sum of money. The idea of public philanthropy, even when it was couched in the language of nationalism, was new to them and perhaps unwelcome as well. At any rate, they were not forthcoming in anything other than ceremonial protocol and show. When it came to actually contributing large sums of money, it was the merchants rather than the princes who came to music's aid.[34]

The princes, however, made the speeches. The Nawab of Rampur, president of the second AIMC, reminded the gathering of the role music would play in the nation's future. In his welcome address he told them all to keep in mind that "if music has to fulfill the noble mission . . . you should put forth all your efforts to keep it pure and undefiled" and declared, "apart from the fact that music is the highest expression of art, it has a national significance. Every nation has its own music, which expresses the soul of the nation and denotes all the national culture, its characteristics and the peculiarities of its refinement."[35] Such rhetoric was not limited to him alone. Speaker after speaker noted that the artists were the major impediment to music's progress and that only nationalism could rescue music from its dire straits. Dr. M. A. Ansari noted "it was a standing shame that India had no National Anthem, that music was the index to social and general advancement of a nation, and that India should reorganize her music and prove to the world that she was not neglecting any detail in the process of nation-building."[36] K. N. Shivapuri, joint secretary of the second AIMC, wrote apropos of musicians that "their inborn prejudice and narrow-mindedness which prevents them from parting with their art must be conquered" and "they must be made to realize the superiority of a national interest over a private interest."[37] This theme remained constant. On the one hand, there was the nation's need for music as a symbol of its modern status and ancient history. On the other, there were illiterate, prejudiced, and narrow-minded artists. At least forty-one of the fifty-one artists at the second conference were Muslim, yet many speakers noted that music had fallen into degeneracy during the "Mohomedan" times.[38]

The academy was seen as the solution. At the new academy, they would use what Bhatkhande called a "good workable raga system employing all the ragas now sung in Northern India."[39] Consequently, a great deal of time at this second conference was spent in standardizing the ragas commonly sung and played at the time. Bhatkhande supervised the next day's debate about fifteen or so ragas with an eye to marshalling consensus about the pitches that were used or discarded in each raga. In keeping with the spirit of rendering ragas systematic, Mr. M. Fredilis, director of music from Baroda state, made the following recommendation about notation: "I recommend the Western notation be adopted for India, but the names of the Notes with their Symbols should be translated into all Indian languages by a committee of Pundits, and I can safely say without prejudice, that the Western Notation is the most complete in the world, and I, as a professional, am of opinion that it is the only notation capable of producing those musical phrases which is the very life of Indian Music."[40] Fredilis's notions about notation were not that different from those suggested by Clements, both of which used the Western bar system and a modified staff to notate music, yet Bhatkhande was able to work with Fredilis. As it turned out, not coincidentally perhaps, Bhatkhande's own notation system was found to be the best of the lot, so his mandate for both ragas and notation was considered acceptable for the academy.[41]

Since the academy was to be "national," it had to satisfy a number of different constituencies. Because of this, a long-lasting relationship between bureaucratic niceties and elite organizers of music conference was inaugurated. Resolutions, votes of thanks, notes of appreciation, and readings of support were all first formally announced, after which, through a series of motions, they were seconded, approved, drawn up, voted upon, passed by, and written down. Reception committees, permanent committees, standing committees, subcommittees, selection committees, advisory committees, and provisional committees were convened to handle all the work. Whether the subject was notation or starting a music magazine, nothing could now happen unless a motion was drawn and underwent a series of procedures. Music, in all its facets, was put through a bureaucratic mill.

At the close of the second conference, the agenda for the third conference was published as an appendix to the report. The promotion of the new academy had topmost priority, after which the organizers agreed that they would also consider the founding of a museum, a library, an orchestra, and a standardized notation system. Plans for the national academy were laid out in detail and the organizers calculated that they would need at least twelve lakhs of rupees to get started, an additional three lakhs to set up a museum, library, and so on, and it was determined that a modest goal should be set down: raising five lakhs in a year.[42] Thus by the end of the second conference the price of the academy had gone from seven lakhs, already an unreachable goal, to fifteen, and it would go up even further at the third conference held in Benares in 1919.

Bhatkhande was elected president of the third conference, at which Atiya Begum Fyzee Rahamin, who had been a key participant at previous conferences, author of a history of Indian music, and intimately connected to the world of modern Indian art, spoke passionately about the academy. She had just returned from a trip to Europe and was generally irate about the West. She spoke in the language of Gandhi's *Hind Swaraj*:

> We know from bitter experience that the so-called Western civiliza-
> tion is no civilization at all—but (the) destructive force of a nation
> that has never known any real culture—but has ever been led by ma-
> terialism. They can give us nothing but we can give them everything
> to make them human and yet it is our misfortune that placed as we
> are today we are perforce obliged to keep in touch with what is hap-
> pening in the other side of the world—for the sake of self preserva-
> tion and for the wrong to be righted.[43]

She had been most angered by the representations of Indian music in the West, and she urged everyone to press ahead with plans for the academy. However, her calculations (twelve lakhs as the endowment fund for the academy, seven lakhs for the buildings, three lakhs for "books, instruments, paintings and for incidental expenses," and a reserve fund of two lakhs) exceeded earlier estimates by double. The academy's costs, just as a plan on paper, had gone from seven to fifteen to twenty-five lakhs in one year alone.

As with the second conference, the academy was the most important item on the agenda, followed by the issue of notation. Paluskar had not attended the second conference but came to the third despite Bhatkhande's ttempts to keep him away.[44] Once again, he grandstanded in familiar ways. In his comfortable role as the successful institutional and corporate musician, he was re-
ported to have said that "the Conference was uselessly adding to its burden by trying to create a system of Notation—as the Notation which he himself ha[d] invented and [was] using in giving instructions in his Academy is suited to all purposes."[45] And once again, he chastised the organizers as he had done at the first conference. The report notes that "he also said that the use of foreign languages and systems of Notation, in discussions relating to Indian Music was wrong and that only Indian Notation should be used."[46] Paluskar spoke from a comfortable position, as he had already accomplished all that they were debating in Benares, without bureaucracy, without debate, without dissent, and with spectacular success.

Perhaps Bhatkhande and his friends would have been better off had they listened to Paluskar. His success certainly made him a reliable authority on how to found schools and publish notated textbooks of music. Instead, they went ahead with their plans, registered the national academy in New Delhi in 1920, and set up an office run by another one of Bhatkhande's friends, Mr. Koul. Shortly after the academy was founded, some members of the organizing committee proposed that they move the headquarters to Benares and affiliate themselves with the Bharat Kala Parishad (Society of Indian Art), whose objectives matched those of the academy.[47] Thakur Nawab Ali was on the committee of the *parishad* and agreed with Bhatkhande and Rai Umanath Bali that the academy should remain independent.[48] Bali wrote to Bhatkhande that while he agreed that "Benares has been and still is the seat of learning" and that "we would have every facilities for the organization and propaganda of our scheme," he was still worried that "if the academy is affiliated to the Parishad, I am afraid its individuality would surely be lost."[49] Bhatkhande wrote back,

> I quite agree with you that the question of transference is a very important one and no hasty decision should be come to in such a matter where the question of the life and death of the great institution is involved. Nobody is overfond of the amalgamation or rather the affiliation but the difficulty is how to collect funds to continue. Koul says we have about 500 Rs. in the bank and nobody comes forward to help. The office of the academy will have to be closed sooner or later if this state of things continues.[50]

The state of affairs did continue, and the academy was dead soon thereafter. The first three conferences had basically come to nothing.

In May 1922, Bhatkhande wrote again to Rai Umanath Bali about the possibility of holding a fourth conference in Lucknow. It had been three years since the Benares conference, and plans for a conference in Indore had fallen through after the ruler withdrew his support. Perhaps Bhatkhande recognized that a national academy was premature without either a state to fund it or a nation to predicate it, and he decided to downscale his institutional ambitions. If not an academy, then perhaps a college might not be a bad idea. "What became of your idea of starting a music class or School in Lucknow?" he wrote to Bali.[51] Bali had tried to push forward a proposal at all three conferences for a school in Lucknow to which neither Bhatkhande nor Nawab Ali had paid any mind.[52] However, now that Bhatkhande had conceded his failure to establish an institution of music in Bombay or Delhi, he was willing to consider Lucknow. But first, they had to have a conference about it. With the establishment of a music college in mind he wrote, a "conference in Lucknow is a good idea too. I shall try to help you as far as I can. I believe Baroda, Gwalior, and Indore would certainly send their artists. . . . Lucknow can with its great Rajahs and Taluqdars easily put together 10000 Rs. if she has a mind to do it." The Benares conference had cost only Rs. 8000. And finally, he wrote, "I am told Lucknow is a Shia stronghold and Shias don't encourage the art. They say it is haram! I hope it is not true. We may let alone the Shias and stick to Hindus and Sunnis only. . . . Music has nothing to do with politics." But, of course, it did, and Nawab Ali recognized it as Bhatkhande may not have. "Personally, I am very doubtful about the success of the music Conf. at Lucknow," he wrote to Bali. "Apart from the difficulty of collecting funds for the purpose, I am afraid of the mujtahids of Lucknow. You know Lucknow is the center of the Shia community and our priests are very orthodox in these matters. Perhaps you remember that the Ulemas of Lucknow tried their level best to dissuade H. H. or Rampur to go as President the 2nd Conf. at Delhi." He warned Bali and, indirectly, Bhatkhande, too, that "by holding the Conf. at Lucknow, you will be storming their citidal [sic] and rest assured they will not tolerate this invasion. I am therefore afraid of an organized and systematic religious propoganda [sic] against the Conf. at Lucknow." And finally, he proposed, with some puzzlement, "Why not have it in Cawnpore if you are so keen on holding the Conf. [in] this cold weather in the U. P [sic]?"[53] Despite these worries, the fourth conference was held in Lucknow, at Kaiser Bagh Palace, with the stated objective to establish a college for training in music.

Once again, the elite came together and made speeches in exalted prose invoking the same things they called for in previous conferences. Bali, the general secretary of the fourth AIMC, declaimed that "culture is the foundation of nationalism," and "the ancient Indian social ideals whose exalted individualism gave birth to melody are being transformed under stress of world forces . . . a nation is evolving whose collective soul is crying for rhythmical utterance in musical harmony."[54] In almost parodic fashion, in addition to a return of exalted prose, there was a repeat performance of the intellectual battle between K. B. Deval and Bhatkhande. Deval delivered his familiar lecture on *shruti* and championed his *shruti* harmonium despite the drubbing he and his coconspirator, E. Clements, had received at the first conference. Not only did Deval put forth the same arguments as before, the same band of Bhatkhande's friends refuted his claims as they had done in Baroda. They went further than they had in Baroda at the first conference and Mr. Karnad, who had disputed all of Deval's claims earlier, now attempted to have him silenced through bureaucratic measures. He moved that "the Srutis expounded by Mr. Deval in his paper and alleged to be those of the Sangeeta Ratnakara, were as a matter of fact not the Srutis of the Ratnakara, which resolution was seconded by Mr. B. S. Sukthankar." A great deal of ad hominem firepower was leveled at Deval. The report notes, "In the course of the discussion, many of the scholars present asked several pertinent questions to Mr. Deval, but he was not able to give a satisfactory answer to a single one of them. He was saying all the time that he was not there for being examined, but the Chairman ruled this as out of order, and said that as he had come forward with certain theories, he had to answer all pertinent questions which were put to him if he could." Deval was finally leveled with a one-two punch. "Mr. M. S. Ramaswamier [Ramaswamy Iyer] pointed out to him that if he was not prepared to answer questions, he should retire from his lecture just as he had retired from his Deputy Collectorship."[55]

Despite the drama and Bhatkhande's recognized position of authority at the conference, money remained a problem. The princely state rulers attended the conference but, once again, they were less than forthcoming with money. They had come to attend an event. By their presence, they positioned themselves as the time-honored patrons of ancient art. But even wealthy rulers such as the maharajas of Baroda and Jaipur, for all their rhetorical support of national music, donated only paltry sums of money for the conference: Rs. 500 each. The agenda of the conference, namely, to raise money for the new school of music, was a notional one for the princes. Bhatkhande acknowledged years later that he and others had been barking up the wrong tree.[56] All of his calculations for the conference and the school were unrealistic. He had believed that the total cost of the conference would be close to Rs. 10,000, but it was more than double, a little over Rs. 26,000.[57] The total amount raised for the school of music in Lucknow was Rs. 37,500, less even than the amount raised at the Benares conference for the national academy.[58] Despite such an unpromising financial start, Bhatkhande did finally found a college of music, one over which he believed he would exercise control.

The Marris College: September 16, 1926

The Marris College of Hindustani Music was founded in September 1926. It was named after Sir William Sinclair Marris, governor of the United Provinces. Rai Rajeshwar Bali, Umanath Bali's older brother and minister of education in the United Provinces, gave a speech at the opening ceremony at the Kaisarbagh Baradari on September 16.

> The greatest masterpieces of Indian Music are almost in the exclusive possession of people who can hardly distinguish between the formula and the spirit whose highest conceptions of the musical language are confined to its grammatical inflections. They are like the pandits who can recite at a moment's notice, or sometimes even unconsciously, the whole volume of Panini's Sutras, but who have never had a glimpse into the real beauties of literature. To our *ustads* in general there need hardly be any rational connexion between the strain of a song and the sentiment expressed in the words therein. And I hardly wonder. Indeed I wonder how, even among men of their education, surroundings and mental vision, it is sometimes possible to come across an artist of true calibre.[59]

Rai Rajeshwar Bali went on to say that the Marris College had been founded because musicians were unable to "make our music respond to the altered circumstances of our national life, to reverberate with the new beatings of heart and the throbbing hopes and aspirations which accompany the rebirth of a nation to a life of fresh endeavor and activity." He continued, "Let the educated people do today what the Rishis did of old," for he could not believe "that Bhairava and Kedar can ever be the product of the brain of a mercenary professional." He concluded that "this is the justification for founding an All-India College of Music." Earlier at the conference, Bali's brother, Rai Umanath Bali, had wanted to "address the crying needs of an emerging nation," and in the founding of the college, he believed they were doing so.

In September 1926, when the college began, the founding members had about Rs. 50,000 at their disposal, and the colonial government had agreed to "sanction an annual grant of half the recurring expenses of the college up to the maximum of Rs. 8,000."[60] The first prospectus of the college announced that "high class Hindustani Music" would be taught, both vocal and instrumental.[61] Bhatkhande's *Kramik Pustak Malika* and Nawab Ali's *Marfulnagh-mat* were used as textbooks. The syllabus was rigorous: in five years, students were expected to learn fifty ragas and twenty-five *talas*, and if they stayed for an additional year, they were expected to learn thirty additional ragas in one year. Bhatkhande instituted his list of seventeen major treatises as necessary reading for all students, who also had to attend lectures on the texts as part of the curriculum. At least 125 students were admitted in the first year and, by 1930, the college had 130 students on its rolls.[62]

The College did fairly well, but Rai Umanath Bali found he was alone in running its daily affairs. His two cofounders, Nawab Ali and Bhatkhande, visited Lucknow periodically and gave him plenty of advice, but both of them had other matters on their mind. They both also had distinct opinions, not always the same, about who should teach what kind of music at the college. Nawab Ali was mindful of Muslim sentiment in the city and was clear about his musical preferences. Bengali music, by which he meant the singing of *dhrupad*s, was not at all to his liking and he saw no need to placate Bengalis in Lucknow. Bhatkhande, on the other hand, preferred *dhrupad*s to the more lyrical *khayal*. Since Nawab Ali had power and money, Bhatkhande often acquiesced to his wishes and advised Bali to do the same. Bhatkhande directed Bali in letters from Bombay about which musicians to hire and how much to pay them, expressing his opinion of their attitudes. "These old fogies have exaggerated opinions about their own merits," he wrote about Umrao Khan, a *khayal* singer from Gwalior, and he was skeptical about Alabande Khan, a *dhrupad* singer from Alwar. "Will he teach classes and sing every week? He again carries an intoxicated head over his shoulders. He may not come down from his residence in the clouds."[63] Such problems beset the early years of the college. Musicians were terribly disconcerted by these newfangled pedagogical methods and made demands that seemed preposterous to Bhatkhande. Shrikrishna Ratanjankar, a student of Bhatkhande's who had been appointed as a music teacher at the college, wrote to him complaining about a *khayal* singer, Ahmed Khan, who refused to have his songs notated in the class he was teaching. But since Ahmed Khan had been appointed at Nawab Ali's behest, Bhatkhande could do nothing directly and recommended that Bali take up the matter of Ratanjankar's complaint directly with Nawab Ali. This shuttling back and forth between Bhatkhande and Nawab Ali would eventually exasperate Bali, whose thoughts turned quickly to shedding himself of the responsibility of managing the college.

To complicate matters further, personnel problems began to take on an even more complex tone. In 1928, Bhatkhande was aware of the prevailing political atmosphere not just in the city of Lucknow but more generally in the region and country.[64] He wrote to Bali, noting that

> sooner or later, the whole of the Musalman element in the college
> will leave us and we shall have to go in for Hindu element both in
> the teaching staff and in the students. . . . If Ahmed refuses in your
> presence to allow his songs to be taken down, give him notice to
> leave and advertise for a good khyal singer. Also write to D. K. Roy
> and ask him to look out for a Dhrupad singer (a Bengali gentleman).
> We need not then care about the Moslem feeling and should do our
> duty fearing God and no man. Our poor country is doomed and all
> that on account of these differences and internal trouble. I thought
> music would at least escape the misfortune but no! Even a music col-
> lege must share the general fate of the country.[65]

Bhatkhande finally had his college of music and, to give him his due, had made a good-faith effort to implement a more genuinely inclusive and secular curriculum than was used in any of Paluskar's schools. He had included both Sanskrit and Urdu works as required reading, mandated knowledge of an-cient texts and music's modern history, and had done all of this in the belief that his music college could escape the political turmoil in the rest of the country.

Politics at the college were made more complicated by the lack of fund-ing. One year after the college began, Bhatkhande wrote to Bali: "Baroda is really a disappointment. But who can help individual opinions and tastes. H. H. has a School of Indian Music in his own city and perhaps wishes to re-serve the whole of his sympathy for it. We shall not quarrel with people whose tastes and views differ from ours and who do not find their way to sympathise with our effort."[66] Princes, as Bhatkhande realized, had not wel-comed the spirit of national philanthropy. In addition to the financial short-fall, there was another problem. Bhatkhande had appointed his old friend M. K. Joshi to be the first principal of the college, but within a year of his appointment he had alienated both the students and the teaching staff, and Bali wanted him to resign. In May 1928, Bhatkhande wrote back to Bali. "Your last two letters have really put me into a great difficulty. I mean those in which you ask me to obtain the resignation of Mr. M. K. Joshi of the Principalship of the Marris college of Music. You will be good enough to remember that I myself brought him to Lucknow at your request and installed him as Principal."[67] Bhatkhande was concerned for his friend, but at the same time he acknowledged his shortcomings as a principal. "He is a graduate, a Government Pensioner and a musician knowing fairly well the music system taught in the College. I do not doubt he has his weaknesses which have made him an unpopular principal. I know also that he has not given you the satisfaction you expected from him and his treatment of the teachers under him and the students again has given rise to some dissatisfaction. The way he kept his registers and other papers in his charge leaves much to be desired." Yet Bhatkhande pleaded against replacing him in highhanded manner. "Dear Rai Saheb, D. K. and M. J. belong to my caste and have been my friends for a long time past . . . Do you expect me to tell him that he is found incompetent, negligent, unsocial, and unpopular and therefore unfit for the principalship?" Bhatkhande prevailed, and M. K. Joshi was allowed to stay on as principal until December 1928. There were other problems related to M. K. Joshi. A few months earlier Bali had received an anonymous letter accusing Joshi of treating students and teachers in "a way that makes the Mahomedan teachers dissatisfied."[68] Bhatkhande responded by cautioning Bali against taking such letters seriously. "Big officers always get anonymous letters. Such letters always exaggerate little weaknesses here and there and make them look large. The best way is to keep cool and quietly investigate the complaints and put things right if they are amiss, but under no circumstance be led away by them."[69] However, even after Joshi was replaced by Ratanjankar, troubles continued, and in May 1929, it came to Bhatkhande's notice that Bali was so fed up with the college and the lack of support he received that he was considering turning the college over to the state university.[70]

Bhatkhande did not want to ask for financial aid from princes, having already been disappointed on that score by the rulers of Indore and Baroda, and he urged Bali to keep at it without despondency. By 1931, his correspondence with Bali betrayed clear signs of frustration on both sides. Bali felt abandoned by Bhatkhande, who for his part believed that having done the leg work, it was not his responsibility to keep the college running. Besides, Bhatkhande was busy publishing his fourth volume on music history and could not be too concerned with administrative matters. On September 3, 1932, he suggested to Bali that he approach Pandit Madan Mohan Malaviya and have the college be remanded under the protection of the Benares Hindu

University if the government of the United Provinces was unwilling to come forward.[71] "You accuse me of neglecting the interest of the College," he wrote to Bali, "[but] what can a poor old Brahmin do?" he asked. "Where the question of money has to be faced all the personal service that was possible for me to undertake I have already rendered," he wrote, advising Bali to "cut down expenses and live within your income until better times come." He assured Bali as well, "They will surely come. Selfless work never passes unnoticed by God." In conclusion, he acknowledged that Bali would not find this terribly helpful. "Dear Rai Saheb, you will say my letter is only dry sympathy—but what else have I got to offer?" By now, Bhatkhande was old and referred to himself as such. He had no more interest in additional conferences and advised Bali against holding any more. The conferences themselves had been Bhatkhande's major successes, but he had also given Bali a tremendous gift. Shrikrishna Ratanjankar, Bhatkhande's devoted and loyal student, was more than willing to work tirelessly and diligently with Bali. Bali was a magnanimous man. Despite his frustrations, he chose to honor the grand old man of music after his death in 1936 by establishing a postgraduate university of music in 1939 and naming it the Bhatkhande University of Music, mainly to organize examinations and postgraduate teaching. The Marris College became its constituent college. After Indian independence in 1947, the college was renamed the Bhatkhande Sangit Vidyalaya, and the university was called the Sangit Vidyapeeth.[72] Ratanjankar and Bali kept the college independent until 1957, when it was finally turned over to the state government.

Paluskar's Conferences: 1918–1922, 1926, 1931

If difficulties and conflict marked all of Bhatkhande's endeavors, comfortable concordance of views permeated Paluskar's gatherings. Paluskar's first conference was called not the All-India Conference but the Gandharva Mahavidyalaya's Sangeet Parishad, and this was a crucial distinction. From the very beginning, it was clear that this was a conference designed for two reasons. The first was to celebrate the GMV's success in a public statement that announced to the country that it was the leader in music's modernization. The second was to increase the GMV's influence and plan such augmentation with various members of the different schools. The objectives of the conference had been confidently announced in an advertisement.

All of us at the Gandharva Mahavidyalaya have worked tirelessly for the past seventeen years on behalf of Indian music, and we see our increasing success with every passing day. . . . There are numerous branches of the Gandharva Mahavidyalaya's students who have been trained in the Gandharva Mahavidyalaya and have decided to make music their social reform cause, lay people who have learned music in the Gandharva Mahavidyalaya tradition—through all this our music has spread throughout the country in unprecedented ways and beyond our expectations. . . . All of us at the Vidyalaya have decided to hold a three-day conference to discuss how to increase our influence even further.[73]

Paluskar's conference began thus, with a public celebratory statement of institutional success and a call for participants to help the Gandharva Mahavidyalaya increase its already substantial influence on music in the country.

Paluskar gave the first speech in Hindi. The conference report noted that he addressed the gathering by claiming that in his seventeen years at the GMV, this was the first time he felt the urgent need to host a conference. Why? Was it only competition with Bhatkhande that led him to convene his own conferences? Apparently not. Paluskar was concerned about the lack of unity among musicians, and his conferences were designed to resolve this problem. He sought to privilege musicians and their needs in marked contradistinction to Bhatkhande's more intellectualized undertaking. Paluskar focused on the theme of unity in his speech. He called first for unity among musicians but also encouraged national unity against Westernization. "Let's take the example of a band," he was reported as having said. "We can have a *deshi* [native] band as good as a foreign band; in fact it can be better than a foreign band. But we have disunity in our band, so it cannot come together. This conference is designed to replace that disunity with unity."[74] This was a red herring, however, since after making such a salutary claim, unity was never raised again as a subject, nor was anything concrete planned to implement any such bringing together of musicians. Instead, Paluskar's supporters took this public occasion as an opportunity to congratulate him for his success and to dispense in their turn bits and pieces of advice that complemented his mission. Clearly, there was more than the unity of musicians in the minds of those attending the conference.

Barrister M. R. Jayakar, nominated as the president of the conference, cautioned the gathering against believing that genuine music instruction could be in any way foreshortened.[75] "Keep music's true knowledge alive," he advised; "it is better to have twelve truly trained musicians than 200 badly trained ones," referring perhaps to both the speed with which GMVs were training students, and to new music appreciation societies that offered short courses in music. Jayakar went on to distinguish between the two prevalent systems of music in India—North and South Indian. "North Indian music's older tradition, on account of a great deal of mixing with Mohamadan singing, has been destroyed. My first piece of advice to you is to restore the classicism in music by spreading education through an organized society. Us educated people have to take up this task. We have to get to the absolute origin of this classical tradition and we must first understand its history. Each raga has its own history . . . we must understand the biography of our classical music."[76] This was a rather different and straightforwardly Hindu nationalist argument about history. At Paluskar's conference, history was self-evident. It did not require critical examination or skeptical challenge. Instead, music's history was to be nationally and nationalistically supported. "There are in Bombay today about 85 institutions for the teaching of music," said Jayakar, advising the principals of those institutions that they not forget that "*gayan shastra* [classical science of music] is an integral part of *hindi sanskriti* [Hindi civilization]. When working for the progress of tradition one must never let *hindi sanskriti* be destroyed. Western innovations like the harmonium and the gramophone have wantonly taken over and the essential *hinditva of hindi* instruments is being destroyed. We must not let a beggarly and negligible Western science defile our tradition. Discard it like it were poison. Our music *has* a history. Never forget that each and every raga has its own history." Such was the theme for history that was set at the GMV Sangeet Parishad. Hindi (the language) and Hindu (the category) seemed to come together under the banner of civilization. There could be many reasons for this. The writer of the report may have noted down "Hinditva" instead of "Hindutva." It is possible that Jayakar meant "Hindi" to stand in for "Hindu," though we cannot be sure. The superiority of a pure *Hindi* civilization over a "beggarly" Western civilization was to be not debated but asserted confidently. Here we see the key difference between Paluskar and Bhatkhande. For Paluskar, a conference was not a coming together of interested intellectuals and skeptics, wasting their time discussing the best possible notational system for music. He had pulled together the first Gandharva Mahavidyalaya

Sangeet Parishad under the aegis of his fountainhead school of music, and the main issue at hand for him was to make a public statement that identified him and the GMV as the rightful vehicle for the preservation and dissemination of the nation's Hindu music.

The conference opened the following morning with an exhibition of Indian musical instruments. There was no discussion of music-related questions until the evening, and even then, the first item on the agenda was the question of how best to ensure the continued implementation of the Gandharva Mahavidyalaya's mission in all its branches. Narayanrao Khare, one of Paluskar's students, gave a speech in which he yoked the ideals of *Swadeshi* ideology to music's future. Protect the craftsmen from the encroachment of foreign goods, Khare advocated, linking economic nationalism to music's purity. "We have done this in the Gandharva Mahavidyalaya, in fact, we are the leaders in music's revolution," Khare proclaimed. The revolution's project was now that of reviving and popularizing Indian instruments and protecting the Indian craftsmen who made them. Shankarrao Vyas and Omkarnath Thakur supported such sentiments in their speeches, bringing the second day of the conference to an end.

On the last day of the conference, after the usual congregational prayers, a photographer took a photograph of all the participants. Paluskar spoke grievingly of the death of the vice principal of the GMV, V. N. Patwardhan, and then various participants, mostly Paluskar's students, gave lectures and speeches on subjects such as how to promote the GMV's notation system further, and how to keep the link between religious instruction and musical education strong.[77] It is not clear why Paluskar called his gathering a conference, since many of the activities bespoke the documenting and publicizing of the GMV's success rather than the discussion of unresolved issues.

At the second conference, Paluskar's revered guru, Balkrishnabua Ichalkaranjikar, gave the plenary address, in which he spoke wistfully of bygone days when princely state rulers treated musicians as if they too were royalty. He reminisced about singers whose voices were so enchanting as to compel even princes to stop in their tracks for ten hours at a time. He remembered instances when musicians were so well regarded as to be brought from their homes to the court for their scheduled performances using a highly prestigious, although dreadfully uncomfortable, mode of transport: the backs of royal elephants. None of Ichalkaranjikar's nostalgic reminiscences bore any relationship to fact, since we know that he himself was not very well treated by his princely patron, nor indeed were most princely court musicians, most of whom occupied the same status as other entertainers. However, without dishonoring a musician's memories, it would be useful to follow the narrative to examine what might have been at stake in maintaining such inaccurate memories in the face of modern change. Following Ichalkaranjikar's speech, Paluskar's students gathered to discuss the early years of the Lahore GMV, to promote the GMV's notational system, and to congratulate one another for having been part of such a moment in music's history.

Only on the last day of the conference were theoretical questions related to music raised. Narayanrao Khare, who had earlier proclaimed the GMV as revolutionary in its field, delivered a comprehensive lecture lasting hours in which he explained numerous Sanskrit couplets dealing with pitch and microtone. Intellectual proceedings for the day concluded with one more lecture on *shruti*, and that was that. There were no other talks, debates, or contentious matters, and at the closing ceremonies the following day, prayers and votes of thanks were offered, and on that note the second conference adjourned.

If conferences were designed for intellectuals to come together and air their differences, then Paluskar's invocation of Bhatkhande's rubric was a misnomer. His focus was instead on reviving authentic Hindu musical instruments, setting up workshops for their repair, and promoting his own notation system. The GMV conferences brought together Paluskar's disciples to worship and pray, not to argue or debate. His students congregated to reminisce, retell the "Lahore origin" and the "Deonar sage" stories, and to exchange memories of their teacher. Those who had not had the privilege of learning with Paluskar attended to participate vicariously by being part of such a gathering, even if they were not among the chosen students.

Paluskar convened five consecutive conferences in Bombay between 1918 and 1922, but after the first three the attendance dropped significantly, and for the fifth conference he was unable to sell all the tickets he had printed. However, within a few years of the failed fifth conference, GMVs around the country convened their own regional music conferences. The *Kesari* reported an All-India Music Conference in Belgaum in January 1925, which was attended by Pandit Madan Mohan Malaviya.[78] The GMV had a tenth music conference in 1928 in Mandalay, following which Paluskar traveled to Rangoon for another regional conference.[79] In 1928, Paluskar also convened a conference for music teachers in Panchvati (Nasik) after he closed down his Bombay GMV. At this conference, all the students of his *Upadeshak* class gathered to talk about their success in teaching music. Finally, in November 1929, he participated in a one-day conference convened solely for women musicians, at which he gave a speech encouraging women to pay close attention to how they taught music, advocating that they eschew teaching instrumental music and high-pitched singing until their students were ready.[80] In other words, even if Paluskar had abandoned convening any further music conferences of his own, he was still busy attending, participating, and presiding over a great many such events, up until two years before his death in 1931.

Conclusion

From the outside, Paluskar's conferences all seem to have been rather dull and self-centered affairs in which a number of his students got together solely to celebrate the corporate success of the GMVs. For one thing, there were none of the intellectual duels that make reports of Bhatkhande's conferences interesting historical documents. For another, despite Paluskar's declaration to unite musicians, his statement might be seen, at best, as a public declaration of support for musicians and, at worst, as yet another example of the grandstanding he did so well. Unity was certainly not a programmatic agenda that he implemented in any shape or form, and he may have made such statements solely to mark his distinctive difference from Bhatkhande. But why did Paluskar, a showman and impresario of public events, convene such lackluster events? Had his heart been in convening grand conferences on music, it is likely that he would have spared no effort, perhaps even to the point of bankrupting himself. The significance of Bhatkhande's achievement in convening his All-India Music Conferences must then be read through Paluskar's decision to follow suit, even if Paluskar's aims were entirely different.

In keeping with the general theme of Paluskar's success and Bhatkhande's failure, this apparent reversal within the context of the music conference demands some comment. Even though Bhatkhande's conferences—as academic, theoretical conferences—were more successful than Paluskar's, Bhatkhande failed to capitalize on this success. Bhatkhande's subsequent institutional endeavors were all failures, such as the collapse of the prematurely founded national academy or the eventual lapse into musical mediocrity by the Marris College, as was widely perceived to have happened following its takeover by the state government. By contrast, Paluskar's students went on to build bigger and better institutions than he himself had set up. Although Bhatkhande's All-India Music Conferences might have crowned him as the true leader of music's modernity, Paluskar had cornered the market, the audience, and the students for himself. If his conferences seem dull in retrospect, they were hardly failures. Rather, Paluskar's conferences served to make public statements of his national success. Then he let his students do the rest.

A few final points of difference need to be underscored. Two decades after the conferences and following Indian independence from British rule, one institution of music learning did indeed acquire national significance. It was not the Marris College, despite all of Bhatkhande's efforts to turn it into a secular liberal institutional ideal of modern musical pedagogy, but the Gandharva Mahavidyalaya in New Delhi, housed in a seven-story building and run by one of Paluskar's students. Had the Marris College or some branch thereof acquired the same status as that of Paluskar's GMV, it is possible that India might have had a national school of music whose curriculum, policies, and understanding of history could have maintained some connection to its founder's liberalism, flawed and incomplete as it was. Instead, sacrality is comfortably ensconced in Paluskar's Gandharva Mahavidyalaya, where prayers, worship, and ritual play an easy role in the quotidian affairs of music and dance.

Paluskar stayed ahead of Bhatkhande at every stage. On every entry on a balance sheet of success between these two extraordinary men of music, Bhatkhande would find Paluskar to have stolen the march on him. While his notational system prevailed over Paluskar's more complicated three-line system and is used in both the Marris College and in informal schools of music around the country, it is also the case that the GMVs and their affiliated institutions train more students in music than virtually any other single institution of its ilk. While Bhatkhande certainly authored impressive volumes of music theory and history, something Paluskar showed no interest in pursuing, it is also the case that although the volumes were translated into Hindi, they were reprinted in Marathi only in 1999. In other words, his magnum opus was unavailable for almost sixty years in his native language and is not widely read. While there are a few books about the music teachers at the Marris College and a couple of biographies of Bhatkhande, there is no organized collection that compares to the institutional archive built up by Paluskar's students.

Perhaps the most telling demonstration of the two men's relative success and failure lies in the material understanding of modern history as shown by their followers after their deaths. Even now, Paluskar's students recognize and understand that all documents related to his life should be made readily available to the public, and they are willing to do so and forthcoming with information about him. All documents related to Paluskar are centrally located in the Akhil Bharatiya Gandharva Mahavidyalaya at Meraj, soon to relocate to a new and spacious building in Vashi on the outskirts of Bombay. Bhatkhande's students, on the other hand, in a final ironic indignity to his memory, have guarded his letters and papers with the jealousy reminiscent of the older musicians against whom he argued for much of his life. The secretiveness of musicians was something Bhatkhande abhorred. In a curious twist of history, his acolytes have embraced exactly what he despised and hoard with all the suspicion of their predecessors the documents related to the past as if they were hereditary musical compositions. The ghost of Bhatkhande's nemesis—secrecy—haunts and hinders all present-day efforts to pry open music's past for historical airing. Bhatkhande's "collectors" hid his letters for years and continue to reveal only some of them, and those only to an inside group. This select group in its turn put together an uneven and motley collection of hagiographical reminisces, letters, exam assessments, and the like, doing so without any notice of where the original documents might be found. The collection, titled *Bhatkhande Smriti Grantha*, is notoriously difficult to acquire in India. It was published not by a centralized national authority but by the Indira Kala Sangeet Vishwavidyalaya in the town of Khairagarh in Madhya Pradesh. A few copies of the collection are available for purchase, but it is impossible to simply send away for a copy or engage in any of the otherwise normal and routine procedures by which one can locate most of the papers related to Paluskar from the Akhil Bharatiya Gandharva Mahavidyalaya.[81] Those who were fortunate to purchase a copy of the collection when it was published refuse to lend it or allow one to look through it. The one copy available in a library in Bombay was borrowed years ago and is now considered lost for good.

This story of secrecy hides other secrets as well. Bhatkhande's acolyte, Prabhakar Chinchore, who found his diaries squirreled away in a library, guarded them for over fifty years, circulating them to only a select few. He chose to keep them in his possession rather than relinquishing them to a national or state archive or even a library's rare-books collection. As a result, one volume of the diaries is untraceable despite manifold rumors. Letters that

Bhatkhande wrote to Rai Umanath Bali, Nawab Ali Khan, and others are also in private hands, and serendipity or the random whim of the owner of the collection are all one can hope for if one wants to see them. For all his understanding of modernity, Bhatkhande could never institute it or formalize a fundamentally modern acceptance of the protocols of history writing among his followers, barring a few exceptions. By and large, his followers perpetuate a culture of secrecy and hagiographical worship that would seem more appropriate for Paluskar than for Bhatkhande. No strangers to modernity, Paluskar's followers continue to make enormous strides in expanding the purview of the Gandharva Mahavidyalaya, while Bhatkhande's Marris College struggles to maintain its accreditation in the face of state government disapprobation.

The irony of Paluskar's success and Bhatkhande's failure lies not just in the institutional character of their own personal missions but also in their legacies. Paluskar's bhakti gods have prevailed over the now ghostly possibility of an alternative future for music's modernity, both because of inherent flaws in Bhatkhande's peculiar historicism and because of a fundamental institutional failure that has been compounded by his followers. In retrospect, however flawed his secular and remarkably open liberal nationalism might have been, his radical integrity was one viable and possible alternative to Paluskar's bhakti gods, not to mention the attendant ghosts of modernity who canonized Paluskar's religiosity and undermined Bhatkhande's secular vision. In this sense, Bhatkhande's failure allows us to see the possibilities that could have emerged in a modern reinvention and reinvigoration of Indian classical music in a way that Paluskar's success has made all but unthinkable. And yet, my point is not to choose between the two men of music as much as to view Bhatkhande against the grain of Paluskar's spectacular accomplishments. By viewing the two side by side, we can evaluate both paths as examples of the tragic history of colonial modernity. And we can further appreciate the extent to which Paluskar's success in installing a traditional practice of music was deeply implicated in this modernity and successful only because of his vigilant understanding of the modern institutional and political contexts of his day.

It is against this backdrop, however, that I wish to recall the different road that music might have taken. Music's modern history could have been written into India's cultural history more generally, as had been proposed to Bhatkhande, first by Karamatullah Khan, the *sarod* player from Allahabad, and then by Maulvi Abdul Halim Sharar at Bhatkhande's first All-India Music Conference in 1916. Both men urged him to relinquish his obsession with music's origins. In one sense, he did so by constantly emphasizing that music's "true" ancient history was unrecoverable. However, he never embraced the proposition that music had hybrid origins and its history was traceable back to multiple cultural locations in Persia, Arabia, and Turkey. He would have accepted the argument that each one of those countries had their own classical music, but at the same time he retained his conviction, even if he couldn't establish it, that Indian music's origins had to be exclusively Indian and Hindu. His honesty lay in acknowledging that such an origin could never be satisfactorily proved, which is perhaps the only reason he abandoned the search as futile. This is not to say that he was willing to accept anything else in its stead. Had he paid greater attention to Karamatullah Khan and Maulvi Abdul Halim Sharar, he might well have taken music down a different road, moving in a direction that would have led him far afield of his search for music's modern yet classical genealogical history. This would have required him to welcome the company of those musicians and scholars who told him that Indian music's hybrid origins were a sign of its vitality—not the cause of its decline—and that Muslim musicians were the authors of their own art and indeed their future. This history was available to him as a real alternative. That he did not choose it is music's loss.

However, even as Bhatkhande's failure might also be seen as tragic when contrasted against Paluskar's success, we need now to turn now to the group most affected by these two men, namely, hereditary musicians. How did *ustad*s react to the changes around them? In the next and last chapter of this book, I come full circle, to Abdul Karim Khan, a *kirana gharana ustad*, who was well loved in Maharashtra for his *khayal gayaki*. How had Abdul Karim dealt with the challenges posed to him personally and to his profession more generally by Bhatkhande and Paluskar? How did his daughter come to take her mother's maiden name and abjure her relationship to her father? How did she become the darling of middle-class Marathi domestic circles and still acquire the fame she did as a stellar performer? For some answers, we turn now to the last chapter.

❀ SIX ❀

THE MUSICIAN AND *GHARANA* MODERN

Abdul Karim Khan and Hirabai Barodekar

In 1894, a young musician named Abdul Karim Khan and his brother, Abdul Haq, came to Baroda. They were sons of a Delhi musician and, for close to a decade, they had performed in numerous courts and cities—including Meraj, Meerut, Mysore, Jaipur, Junagadh, Kathiawad, and Malwa. Now they came to try their luck in Baroda. It was a court well known for its patronage of music as well as for its famous musicians. Abdul Karim and Abdul Haq came to hear those musicians sing, perform in the court if invited, and to uphold the *kirana gharana* tradition to which they belonged.

Soon the brothers were the talk of the town. Baroda musicians debated their controversial musical performances, and their fearlessness pleased the ruler, Sayajirao Gaekwad. Their accomplishments might have led to a long career as Baroda court musicians, but instead their stay came to a precipitous end. In 1898, four years after his arrival, Abdul Karim stole out of Baroda under cover of darkness. By itself, this stealthy departure does not leave any wrinkles on the fabric of music's history. What turns Abdul Karim's departure into one of Hindustani music's most loved scandals was that a young woman, Tarabai Mane, went with him.

Tarabai and Abdul Karim's elopement required stealth. She was Hindu, young, and the daughter of a Baroda court *sardar*, Marutirao Mane. He was a Sunni Muslim Pathan, already married, and a struggling, poor musician to boot. The couple ran off to Bombay, where they lived together for a year before getting married. Following their marriage, they had seven children, five of whom survived. Each of the children had two names—one Hindu, one Muslim. Two of those children, their son Abdul Rahman and their daughter Champakali, were musical prodigies and, like their father, began performing at a young age. All seemed to be well; the couple founded a school for music, taught, and performed, but in 1918, after twenty-two years together, Tarabai left Abdul Karim, taking the children with her. None of them ever saw him again.

Abdul Karim died in 1937, after a long and illustrious career as a *kirana gharana* singer. A decade later, his estranged wife passed away as well. After her separation from Abdul Karim, she had put all her energies into promoting the musical careers of Abdul Rahman and Champakali. They would be known in Maharashtra not as Abdul Rahman and Champakali, but as Sureshbabu Mane and Hirabai Barodekar (although her nickname was Champutai). Hirabai's *khayal gayaki* propelled her to fame as one of Maharashtra's most well known and beloved singers. Critics would often remark that her voice was very much like that of her guru, Abdul Karim Khan. It was never publicly voiced that he was also her father.

Religion, caste, and gender come together in this story about a *gharanedar* Muslim father and his Hindu musician daughter. What makes Abdul Karim's story stand out is its beginnings in scandal; his daughter's life, by contrast, is a study in the excising of scandal. Abdul Karim's career also travels alongside that of Bhatkhande and Paluskar—sometimes tangentially, often in conflict, always in conversation. Buffeted between their differing aspirations for music, he encountered, as a Muslim musician in the city of Pune, the weight of Brahmin prejudice.

The lives of Abdul Karim Khan and Hirabai Barodekar also recapitulate the basic themes of this book. Both of them sang in Baroda—Abdul Karim in the late nineteenth century, Hirabai in the third decade of the twentieth century. If the father preferred performing in princely states to other venues, the daughter did not. Abdul Karim reviled music theater; Hirabai was one of the first women to pick it up with tremendous enthusiasm and to great acclaim. For the former, music *natak* represented the betrayal of serious music;

for the latter, it offered opportunities for respectable women. In the span of a family's life, music theater moved from disreputability to gendered respectability. Additionally, both father and daughter had dealings with Bhatkhande and Paluskar. Abdul Karim argued with Bhatkhande and was insulted by Paluskar's claim that Muslims had destroyed music. Hirabai Barodekar was honored by Paluskar's request to sing at his first conference and did so against the wishes of her guru, a *kirana gharana ustad*.

Up until now, I have not written directly about performing artists, even though I have addressed them as a group. Having laid out the institutional, social, and epistemological conditions that paved the way for the nationalization of music, the logical question would be: What were the effects of all these transformations on the actual musicians? How had women, newly brought into the purview of music, responded to that opening of the cultural sphere? How had *gharana*s and *ustad*s responded to the new set of demands made of them by a larger and different audience than they were used to? Through Abdul Karim's life, we see that musicians were not powerless witnesses to the transformations enacted by others to their pedagogy and performance. When we turn to Hirabai, we see how a *gharana* musician's daughter rebelled against her father's wishes and still became the exemplary figure of upper-caste Hindu respectability. The interconnections between the chapters in this book and the lives of Abdul Karim and his daughter are many, and through them, I retrace key milestones in music's history. Lastly, I note that a new kind of pedagogy and performance emerged in the twentieth century, visible in its early shape from the accommodations and adjustments made by musicians like Abdul Karim.

Hagiography, Biography, and History

In writing about Abdul Karim and Hirabai Barodekar, I have used Marathi biographies of the two artists. The authoritative source on Abdul Karim to which one is referred is the biography written by Balkrishnabua Kapileshwari, one of his early Brahmin students. It is an important source not only given Balkrishnabua's longstanding and intimate acquaintance with Abdul Karim, but because he used numerous additional informants, all of whom contributed their own personal story or anecdote about Abdul Karim, many of which are included in his account. Kapileshwari's biography, in that sense, was both singly and multiply authored. Hirabai's brother's son-in-law wrote one of her biographies; the other was written by one of Hirabai's own students.

It would not be altogether inaccurate to label the three biographies as hagiographies, because all of them depict the two musicians as *sant manu*s (saintly people). As Milind Wakankar has pointed out, the bhakti archive has produced (as its effect) the emanation of the aura of the *sant* (Mirabai, Kabir, or Tukaram) as a uniquely individual personality, one who struggled in his or her own time and whose struggle helps us envision how we might live our own lives within set communities. In the corpus of musician biographies written in the late nineteenth and twentieth centuries, the auratic nature of such a *sant manu*s is transferred to the musician depicted as a guru who teaches by his or her own behavior in both the performative space of a *jalsa* (music recital) and the everyday world of domestic life. When students of famous musicians have written biographies of their teachers, they have usually done so as a ritual offering of gratitude to their gurus, as *guru dakshina*. As a result, the behavior of musician teachers is depicted by their students as free of blemish.

Yet musicians like Abdul Karim Khan engaged in various secular struggles as well, dealing with matters related to pedagogy, schools, and publications. Genius, therefore, is indexed in the narrative as the combination of a relentless (but eventually triumphant) struggle in the secular world alongside spectacular music performances.[1] This is not a narrative style unique to Kapileshwari alone, but the defining characteristic of a genre of biographical writing that brings together in a singular narrative the living personality of the artist who has to live in the world but whose life is animated by the aura of the transcendent *sant manu*s. Indeed, we are asked to infer from these biographies that without a powerfully spiritual dimension to one's character, being or becoming a musician would be impossible. The precise quality of this spiritual dimension is left unspecified, except insofar as it is adumbrated as distance from the messiness of everyday life. Music, in the form of *riyaz* and *tapasya,* allows for the requisite distance from the messiness of everyday life, and the musician/performer copes with the pettiness of wives, the hostility of competing musicians, and the vicissitudes of change by rising above all of it. The ability on the part of a musician to exercise such distance is attributed to his or her inherently auratic character. This suggestion is made over and over again, and it is the dominant hagiographical haze through which one has to read history, ideology, and the politics of everyday life.

Hirabai Barodekar's biographers present her as constantly beset upon by travails, but eventually triumphant. Tarabai (not Tahirabibi) manages the family finances and her daughter's career. Abdul Karim is a guru by osmosis because he taught Sureshbabu, who in turn taught Hirabai. Tarabai is central to the narrative, whereas Abdul Karim flits through it on occasion. By contrast, in Abdul Karim's biography, the scandal that is erased from Hirabai's biography is recreated as a saintly legend. Kapileshwari's biography, written in postindependence India, aspires to epic status. His characters are obliged, as a result, to index the monumental struggles between good and evil in a rhetorically simple, sentimental manner, absent of nuance, humor, or irony. Here Tahirabibi (not Tarabai) is a villainess who hoodwinks Abdul Karim for twenty-two years before showing her true colors.

Though these hagiographies are transparent in their attempts to beatify the two musicians, we get from them a powerful and unique sense of twentieth-century history. Kapileshwari's text, as a generic example of such writing, is particularly instructive. The text reads tediously because we are given episodic accounts of one performance after the next, and at all of them Abdul Karim demonstrates not only his talent but also his sterling character. Nonetheless, Kapileshwari forces us to pay attention to what mattered to musicians. The linear narrative of Indian nationalism does not matter here. Events like Tilak's release from Mandalay, Gandhi's *satyagraha*, and the 1923 INC session are all merely the occasion for another *jalsa*. Conventional Indian history is turned into background noise, and in the foreground we have the performances, how they were received, whether they were well staged or perhaps even sabotaged by other musicians. We are made aware of a very particular sense of history that is well ensconced within the space of the modern, but in which the only meaningful chronology is the chronology of performances. Furthermore, the text's rhetorical and stylistic simplicity allows for clear moments of crisis to poke through the surface of the text, disturbing the complacency of the otherwise inexorable trajectory to self-realized genius. In these moments, the messiness of history, ideology, and politics makes its appearance, if not always in straightforward ways.

Take, for example, Kapileshwari's positioning of Abdul Karim's life as a struggle against a pervasive Brahminism. In and of itself, Kapileshwari does not lay out a critique of Brahminism, which is for him a liberal ideal of intellectual depth, epitomized by R. G. Bhandarkar, the famed Pune Sanskritist. Yet, when Abdul Karim is attacked by Pune Brahmins for presuming to recite

Sanskrit *shloka*s, Kapileshwari describes Brahminism as a culture of harassment. But the critique is not a systemic one. In keeping with his ideal, he gives us Abdul Karim Khan as the exemplary Brahmin himself! In moments such as these, the characters (and the roles in which the author casts them) index a complex historical tension. Able to best Brahmins on their own terms by singing their *sloka*s with attention to *laya* and *sur,* Abdul Karim demonstrates the musically correct way to sing the *Gayatri Mantra.* We are invited to see him in such accounts as the model Muslim musician: eclectically devout, neither doctrinal nor dogmatic, and deeply respectful of Brahminic Hinduism even when its practitioners treat him badly. It is in precisely such narrations that a contrapuntal reading suggests that, instead of the saintly musician, a Muslim musician forced into situations requiring him to accommodate Brahmin prejudices, makes concessions to elite Hinduism, and finds a way in between and against the agendas of powerful people like Bhatkhande and Paluskar.

Throughout this chapter, I have translated or paraphrased the stories written by these three biographers. In order to make the text readable, I have omitted most of the "according to Kapileshwari" or "in the words of Hirabai's biographers" sentence constructions, but my selections of anecdotes and stories are all taken from the three biographies. While I have followed a roughly chronological account of first Abdul Karim's and then Hirabai's lives, I have also broken the chapter up thematically. Because Abdul Karim's life is contemporaneous with Bhatkhande's and Paluskar's, I focus more on him than on Hirabai. In keeping with the larger historical account of music's transformation in the nineteenth century, my story ends with Abdul Karim. The mid- to late-twentieth-century account of music that would include Hirabai's trajectory is a story of the working out of processes set in motion by musicians such as Abdul Karim, on the one hand, and by Bhatkhande and Paluskar, on the other.

Before the Scandal: Was Music Political?

In 1894, Abdul Karim and his brother came to Baroda. At their first performance, they made quite a stir. They sang a composition, *piya gunavanta,* in raga *puriya,* tuning their *tanpura*s to the *pancham* not of the *mandra saptak,* but of *nishad,* two pitches higher. This unconventional tuning allowed for the emphasis on the *nishad* and *gandhara,* thereby bringing out the real spirit of the raga.[2] It was an important victory for the young musicians, since they showed off their musical prowess and as a result were asked to stay for a while in Baroda. The same year, two famous singers, Aliya and Fattu Khan, were invited to the city. Their performative style was quite spectacular. While singing, they tugged at the carpet on which they were sitting cross-legged, ground the heels of their feet together while leaning back with arms outstretched, hurled their bodies from side to side, gesticulated wildly, and emphasized the *sam* with a loud clap. Taken aback, Baroda musicians suggested to them that they significantly reduce if not altogether delete the flamboyant content when singing for the ruler.[3] Baroda's court culture was in the process of being overhauled and streamlined. Aliya and Fattu Khan's performative exuberance was not as acceptable as it used to be.

A subdued Aliya and Fattu Khan performed for Sayajirao Gaekwad, and at that performance, three sets of musicians, separated from each other by seniority, employment, and fame, were brought together in a moment of historical crisis. The Khan brothers finished their recital with the expectation that no musician would sing after them, given their stature and fame. This was an accepted norm, both then and now. Senior, famous musicians closed out performances while junior, lesser-known musicians began them. But Sayajirao Gaekwad wanted to showcase the talent of his own *kalavant*s (the artists of the *kalavant karkhaana*) perhaps even to measure, by contrast, their caliber against Aliya and Fattu Khan. His *kalavant karkhaana* employed many musicians, and he demanded that one of them sing after the famous duo. He was stunned that none would comply with his order. Only two visiting singers, Abdul Karim and his brother, dared breach Hindustani music's protocol and agreed to perform, thereby averting one type of crisis but precipitating another.

Sayajirao Gaekwad, in fact, spent most of 1894 abroad.[4] Yet it seems unnecessary in this case to investigate whether Kapileshwari got his dates wrong or if the encounter he narrated even actually happened. As historical readers, we get from this account a dramatic sense of the cultural milieu of late-nineteenth-century musical performances as remembered by a key musician in whose company Kapileshwari spent a great deal of time. We hear in a musician's voice what mattered to other musicians, or at least three different sets of them. In the face-off between Aliya Khan and Abdul Karim, there was the question of respect, and of the breach in protocol, but there was also more at stake than either employment or courtly entertainment.

All musicians gathered at the court recognized the norms that bound their larger community. Aliya and Fattu Khan were senior and famous, and the court *kalavant*s chose to brook the ruler's disfavor rather than go against them, but Abdul Karim and his brother did the opposite. By singing last, they made the court musicians appear pusillanimous; earned the ire of Aliya Khan, who declared that he would turn upside down the upstarts who had upset him; and risked alienating the musician community at large by their youthful confidence.[5] Perhaps they were currying favor with Sayajirao in order to secure permanent employment. Yet, it may also be seen as marking a key moment in which a small but symbolically large adjustment was made by a young *gharana* musician who recognized that something new was afoot. Abdul Karim was shaking loose of both princely courts and a restrictive community sensibility.[6]

Artists like Abdul Karim, in any case, navigated a difficult course in the pursuit of their careers. Performances were competitions (*mehfils*) to be won or lost. Arguments over musical matters—which *sur* was incorrectly used in which raga, how raga *gujari todi* could be sung using *pancham*, which *gharana* had stolen a composition from which other, and who had flaunted which tradition—made up the material reality and the everyday politics of music. From the outside, these may have looked like small squabbles, but in the world of music, performance was the motor of history, and its grease the competitive, and often hostile, arguments about musical matters. The grease, in some cases, could be as sticky as glue. Arguments between musicians were rarely forgotten and often generated lifelong enmity.

While at Baroda, Abdul Karim antagonized Maula Baksh Ghisse Khan, superintendent of the *kalavant karkhaana*. They disagreed about musicology, history, and music theory. Maula Baksh used *shankarabharanam* as the first raga in his schools, deeming it foundational, while Abdul Karim understood it as *bhoopali* (from the Hindustani tradition) by another name. There were other disagreements between them, as well, for example, about Maula Baksh's instrumental use of notation to prevent musicians from securing permanent employment at Baroda. As a result of the hostility, Abdul Karim came home one day, fell ill, and was sure that Maula Baksh had tried to kill him using *jadu tona* (black magic). This would not be the last time Abdul Karim would believe the worst of a fellow musician. In the course of his life, he routinely thought he had evaded one spell or had another cast upon him by a jealous musician, or that he had been poisoned, later deciding to eat only food cooked for him by an intimate friend or family member.[7]

Abdul Karim's conviction about *jadu tona* can be approached symptomatically. We could accept that a large number of gods and spirits, both malevolent and benevolent, were unexceptionally within the imaginative horizons of modern musicians like Abdul Karim. If we do not see Abdul Karim as an exemplary figure representative of an alternative or resistant modernity, history can enter the picture to rewrite his role not as saint, but as a politician jousting for position in a changing milieu in which the semirational sat comfortably with the nonrational or irrational. In such a situation, the recurrence of *jadu tona* and poison in the narrative alerts us to the pervasive anxiety in the daily lives of traveling musicians.

Under these circumstances, it would have been less fraught for many musicians to stay at home. However, travel performed a vital pedagogical function in the early career of a musician. It expanded his musical repertoire because he heard other musicians perform, it tested his own mettle since performances were jousts to be won, and it facilitated word-of-mouth publicity. Even so, constant travel, giving performance after performance from court to court, exacerbated anxiety, not least because it increased the opportunities for discord. As we have seen in previous chapters, a welcome reception could never be taken for granted, and there was always the risk, no matter how limited the venue, that one's compositions could be stolen and reperformed under a different name by a hostile musician.

In this milieu there were two stakes: the archive and the future of music. These were linked because performers were the literal embodiment of both. The archive of music was housed, literally, inside the physical body of the musician—or rather in his memory—since there was no written music. An attack on the body of the musician could potentially eliminate both the performer and his archive. A heightened sensitivity about one's body and health, and thus the fear of poison, bespeaks a pervasive professional anxiety. Only by performing what one had heard or learned from a musician now long gone could one demonstrate both historical knowledge of music and the depth of one's deeply personal archive. As Abdul Karim acknowledged, musicians were not well educated. They could often neither read nor write, and their music was memorized. But in this absence of a written record of compositions and musicology, the space of performance was neither exalted nor abstractly aesthetic. Musical or musicological arguments were not neutral nor did they pertain solely to the question of *ilm* (knowledge). A performer had to demonstrate theoretical and musical skill to impress an audience of musicians but also withhold enough knowledge to avoid being plagiarized. And by the late nineteenth century, an already fraught world was now charged by the air of change as well.

Many musicians adapted to the change. Whether arguing with Maula Baksh or singing after Aliya and Fattu Khan, Abdul Karim was showing signs that he was politically savvy. Spiritual he may or may not have been, but his activities were certainly those of an astute musician, willing to engage, challenge, and contest those more powerful and established than him. For all that, he was faithful to his *kirana gharana* tradition, and even though his hackles rose when its historical lineage was challenged, he accepted and accommodated himself to the modern and used its tools to envision a new kind of *gharana* pedagogy and performance, as we shall see. After leaving Baroda, he founded a school, published compositions, gave ticketed performances, tried his hand at notation, and engaged in musicological debates with other musicians. But he was not ready to leave Baroda just yet. His departure was not yet assured. For that to happen, he first had to meet Tarabai Mane.

The History of the Scandal: Tarabai Mane

Marutirao Mane was a *sardar* in Baroda's court. The Mane family originally came from Rahimatpur but moved to Baroda as part of the entourage of Sayajirao Gackwad's first wife. A singer, Hirabai Govekar, someone who would be called a *baiji,* who had been patronized by the family, came with them. In Baroda, Hirabai Govekar studied music with Faiz Mohammed Khan (Maula Baksh's competitor and rival), took her patron's last name, and called herself Hirabai Mane.[8] Marutirao and Hirabai Mane's daughter was Tarabai Mane.

Sardar Mane heard Abdul Karim sing, and impressed by his knowledge of *bhajan*s, he bestowed his protection on the two brothers, asking Abdul Karim to teach music to his daughter. In 1894, when they first met, Tarabai was fifteen years old and Abdul Karim was twenty-two. She was a promising singer, and her first public music performance was given in the court at the invitation of Sayajirao's mother, the *rajmaata*. From Kapileshwari's narration, we get the distinct impression that the Baroda court and everyone associated with it was steeped in religiosity. Sayajirao Gaekwad had ordered that all religious ceremonies at the court had to be conducted strictly according to Vedic protocol. Accordingly, we read about Tarabai's performance as an event that conformed to what the court believed was Vedic Hindu tradition.

Tarabai began by doing *namaskar* to everyone assembled, starting with her guru, Abdul Karim. She sang only devotional compositions. When the *rajmaata* needed a break, everyone was offered sweet warm milk flavored with nutmeg. When the performance resumed, Tarabai sang selections from different ragas, and at the close of her recital, the entire gathering was beckoned by the court priest to a communal *aarti*, which concluded with Tarabai's chanting of prayers. Everyone then received *teerthaprasad,* and an overwrought Tarabai collapsed in her mother's lap.[9] In this account, religiosity and music come together in a performance that carries in its telling the hefty weight of gendered sanctity.

Kapileshwari published his biography in 1972, years after Bhatkhande and Paluskar had passed away. His narrations of princely courts, and of their rulers and families, are similar to the Puranic stories told in the illustrated series *Amar Chitra Katha.* There is a powerful romance with royalty in which *sardar*s, *rajmaata*s, rajas, and *rajputra*s are all exemplary figures. But in the biography of Abdul Karim, the romance with royalty is put together with a Brahmin, Marathi, middle-class male imagination of the ideal modern young woman. It is remarkably similar to the ideal that Paluskar put forth in the 1920s, a half century before Kapileshwari wrote his book. In Paluskar's view, devout women needed to learn music in order to teach it to their children. Music, for Paluskar, was sacred, not sexual. Women were restrained in their behavior and affect and their musical performances privileged devotional bhakti, not sexual desire. Three-quarters of a century after Tarabai's performance, Kapileshwari portrays her in keeping with Paluskar's ideal of musically talented women.

Tarabai Mane's portrayal cannot be accidental. Music was an extraordinary modernizing force in Maharashtra, in particular for women, many of whom took advantage of it. Because of Bhatkhande and Paluskar, it was respectable for middle-class women to learn music, and many of them did, becoming performers in their own rights. Paradoxically, by the 1950s, a whole generation of *baiji*s had been replaced by upper-caste women singers, who were respectable, chaste, and asexual in their affect. Hirabai

Barodekar, Abdul Karim's daughter, was certainly one such performer, but in Kapileshwari's narration, the success of Paluskar's agenda reaches back into history to cast her mother, Tarabai Mane, as devout, childlike and asexual. Abdul Karim is similarly portrayed as distanced, somber, and equally asexual.

Yet this couple ran away together, giving Hindustani music lovers a scandal to talk about for the next century. Readers of the biography might be tempted to assume that the two eloped because they fell in love. Kapileshwari quickly puts that impression to rest. The libidinal energy and excitement of a romance is nowhere to be found in the narration. Abdul Karim and Tarabai come together solely for noble reasons. There is no love, passion, laughter, or any suggestion of lightheartedness about this young couple or what they may have felt for each other. Instead, on her part there was worship, devotion, and duty, and on his, distanced protection. The only reason this nonromantic alliance came to a head is because of a dramatic moment of epic tragedy. The young Tarabai's mother passed away and her father, who had turned to drink, made her life a living hell by accusing her of complicity in her mother's possible betrayal of him. Paranoia, jealousy, cruelty, and intoxication come together to produce for a hapless and desperate Tarabai an intolerable situation. It is solely to rescue his student from this situation that Abdul Karim takes time out of his *riyaz* to bestow upon her a noble and passionless act of protection.

For a full year after running away to Bombay, Abdul Karim and Tarabai did not get married. Put even in such bland terms, the scandal ought to be leaping off the page. Even if Tarabai was the granddaughter of a courtesan, and marriages between musicians and *baiji*s were not altogether exceptional, their elopement suggests transgression. Abdul Karim was married, Muslim, a poor though gifted musician; she was Hindu, single, and the daughter of a high-ranking court official. Not only did she run off with Abdul Karim, she might even have lived with him for a year before getting married. But in Kapileshwari's pages, there is a prohibition against taking any pleasure in a taboo-breaking act. Nor is Tarabai depicted as a young woman of courage and strength, both of which she must have had in abundance to do what she did. In place of any recognition of an affective relationship, we are offered a sanitized, asexual union that culminates in a marriage ceremony seemingly scripted by a national liberal secularism incorporating Hindu, Muslim, and Christian rites all in one. Tarabai takes her vows with her hand on the Gita, Abdul Karim with his hand on the Koran.

Kapileshwari's pen is formulaic in both its rescripting and proscribing of scandal. The text is disinfected of the euphoria and mess of human life, but the disinfectant does not completely do its job. Sharatchandra Gokhale, music critic, writer, and a friend of Kapileshwari's, chuckled wickedly while narrating his memory of their elopement. His story was full of passion and taboo, of rule breaking and border crossing, encapsulated in a pithy statement: *Abdul Karim ni Sardar Manyaanchi mulgi palavli* (Abdul Karim ran off with Sardar Mane's daughter). Perhaps it ought to stay so, despite Kapileshwari's beatificatory prose, as a taboo-breaking, interfaith love affair that in its early years had all the characteristic qualities of important scandals that subsequent narrations attempt to remove. It is a scandal that captures the full aspirations of nationalist modernity, only to end up narrativized in a text that hushes up and undoes those very aspirations.

Early Married Life

In the early years of their marriage, Abdul Karim traveled incessantly, giving *jalsa*s in different cities. A prodigious musician, he could play the tabla, the *sarangi*, the *jaltarang*, and the *been*, and sing *khayal, thumri, dadra, bhajan*s, *garba*s, and Sanskrit *sloka*s. He sang in princely courts, music appreciation societies, and private gatherings—a year or two in Solapur, a short while in Kolhapur, a year in the Carnatic, and travels to Dharwad, Bagalkot, Solapur, and Hubli. Tahirabibi (as Kapileshwari refers to her after her marriage) went with him. Their children were all born in different cities. Abdul Rahman/Sureshbabu was born in Belgaum (1902); Champakali/Hirabai in Meraj (1905); Gulabkali/Kamalabai in Sholapur (1907); Abdul Hamid/Krishnarao in Hubli (1910); a son who did not survive, in Pune (1912); Sakina/Saraswatibai (1914); and a daughter who also did not survive, in Meraj (1917).

During these years, Abdul Karim came to be recognized as a singer who took cities by storm. Sharatchandra Gokhale remembered that Abdul Karim could "pay a casual visit up to the *ati taar shadja* and then, in one quick movement, race down to the *mandra saptak* but always with grace and sweetness, never with a jerk."[10] His was the act, a fellow musician once noted, no smart musician ever followed.[11] In the course of Abdul Karim's career, he taught artists like Kesarbai Kerkar, argued with Vishnupant Chatre over the purity of *gharana* pedigrees, and sang for Balkrishnabua Ichalkaranjikar (Paluskar's guru) and Annasaheb Kurundwadkar (ruler of Kurundwad).[12]

These were his successes, but one student, Rambhau Kundgolkar, shows us what he was up against.

Bamman Gavaiyya

Since marrying Tarabai, Abdul Karim had not set eyes on his first wife, who also had come from a musician family. On occasion, he ran into her relatives, who voiced their disapproval. A nephew by his first marriage, Abdul Wahid, also accused Abdul Karim of teaching only *bamman* (Brahmin) students. When Abdul Wahid claimed that he wanted nothing to do with Brahmins or their caste politics, Abdul Karim responded that music was not about caste but about *ilm* (knowledge), and not an issue that had any bearing on families, relatives, or *gharana*s. But his interrogators persisted. Why, they asked, did he teach Brahmins and their children to the exclusion of Muslim children? This partiality to Brahmins enraged the community, complained Abdul Wahid, when Muslim children in so many cities were not even allowed access to public water. Why should Muslim *gharana* children do all the work and Brahmin children reap all the rewards?[13]

These were tough questions, and at the time, Abdul Karim had offered bland responses, claiming that music was all that mattered, not caste or religion. But when Abdul Karim returned to Pune, he instituted a change at home. He insisted that his daughters dress with the modesty that behooved proper Muslim girls, give up travel and learning music, stay at home, and acquire an Islamic education from a *qazi*. But the question Abdul Wahid had asked him had nothing to do with his domestic life. It pertained to his behavior as a professional musician, a *gharanedar* and *khandaani ustad,* and in those roles, his favoritism to Brahmins was inexplicable. A better answer to Abdul Wahid's questions can be deduced from Abdul Karim's rage at a Brahmin student, Rambhau Kundgolkar, who was lured away from serious music by Marathi theater.

In the mid- to late nineteenth century, there was a large expansion in the number of music theater companies in Maharashtra. Many of these companies folded quickly, but they signaled a new interest on the part of a growing public. The companies also offered performers possibilities for travel that were more interesting than the alternative of waiting in a princely state for days on end until they were asked to perform. With a theater troupe, one could expect more performances, more money, regional fame, and recognition. Unsurprisingly, a number of musicians joined these theater troupes as lyricists, composers, and performers willing to try their hand at both singing and acting. One such musician was Rambhau Kundgolkar.

Rambhau Kundgolkar, who became famous on the Marathi stage as Savai Gandharva, had started his *taleem* (training) with Abdul Karim but left it to find his fortune on the Marathi stage. Abdul Karim was furious. Not only did this mean that Rambhau would now train with other musicians and *ustads*, but in his early years, Abdul Karim was contemptuous of the theater. Later in life, he would record a Marathi theater composition (*chandrika hi janu*, Dev Gandhar, released in a 78-rpm recording), but in the late nineteenth and early twentieth centuries, theater was not simply low-brow and immoral, it also posed a threat to masculinity. Kapileshwari remembered Abdul Karim describing what Rambhau was planning to do in lieu of serious music: he was going to abandon serious music (*tambora chodkar*), shave his face (*much-dadi nikaalkar*), cross-dress (*aurat jaisa bankar*), and cavort—not act—on stage (*natak mein nachega.*) There was a clear concern with masculinity and emasculation in this utterance. But *gharana* morality as exemplified in Abdul Karim also found theater immoral. In his opinion, only disreputable people sang and acted on the stage; serious musicians stayed away. Years later, when against his wishes his children would act on stage, Abdul Karim found it impossible to accept that his son and daughter could act as husband and wife. It cemented his sense that the theater was the home of immorality and degeneracy. There is, however, an addendum to this story.

Abdul Karim was furious with Rambhau not just because he had abandoned music or had cost him a talented and promising student, but for another reason as well. Rambhau was a Brahmin student, and Abdul Karim had trained him so as to make a statement both political and professional. In the text, Abdul Karim is remembered as having expostulated in anger at Rambhau's desertion, "Bamman gavaiyyon ke saamne bamman gavaiyya hi taiyaar karna tha [I wanted to train a Brahmin student *right in front* of Brahmins]."[14] Even though in his encounter with Wahid Khan he had claimed that music had nothing to do with caste or religion, Abdul Karim had clearly noted Rambhau's caste and, in training him, he was making a very specific point. He might have consciously picked Rambhau as a Brahmin student whom he could throw up as a shield to deflect Brahmin disapproval. His expostulation itself has a defiant tone, suggesting that he wanted to make, literally, a frontal assault on Brahmins by showing them what he could do in their presence. What it came down to was betrayal. Rambhau, in opting for Marathi theater instead of serious music, had scuttled Abdul Karim's plans.

This was the second decade of the twentieth century. Bhatkhande's countrywide project to write a textual, classical, and connected *itihaas* for music, and Paluskar's project to expand his already burgeoning network of Gandharva Mahavidyalayas, were both well under way. The Poona Gayan Samaj and numerous other music appreciation societies were up and running in Satara, Sangli, and Meraj, all cities in which Abdul Karim had performed. Paluskar had instituted communal prayers in Sanskrit in his Gandharva Mahavidyalayas, and all Hindu holidays were ceremonially celebrated. His students had been dispatched, as V. R. Athavale remembered, like Shivaji's *senapati*s to found schools all over the country. Abdul Karim himself was spending a fair amount of time performing in Maharashtra, where Brahmin dominance was powerful, and it would be unlikely that he would be unaware of the Hinduizing rhetoric of organizations such as the Hindu Mahasabha, for instance. More than all of this, Kapileshwari alerts us to the question of Brahminism. He stays away from commenting on politics in his biography, but as soon as he begins to write about Abdul Karim's public performances, he remarks that there was Brahmin opposition not just to Abdul Karim, but to Muslim singers singing Hindu devotional music in general.[15]

In the expostulation "Bamman gavaiyyon ke saamne bamman gavaiyya hi taiyaar karna tha," we have one answer to Abdul Wahid's question to Abdul Karim about the latter's favoritism to Brahmin students. We also get a sense that Abdul Karim was aware that in order to stand up to it, he would need to engage with Brahminism as a powerful force. It might mean picking more Brahmin students instead of Muslim students and making adjustments to his pedagogy, both of which he was willing to do. But his rage at Rambhau tells us that he had lost a vital weapon in his struggle. Abdul Karim would go on to train many other Brahmin and other upper-caste students in the 1920s, but a decade earlier, Rambhau would have been one of the early students, clearly bound for fame, who could have helped him demonstrate the opposite of what Paluskar claimed. Muslim musicians had not destroyed music, and some of them, like Abdul Karim, had even trained the best Brahmin musicians of the future. Perhaps then he would have felt able to counter Paluskar's claim to him, some years later, that Muslims had destroyed Indian music.

Gharana Modern and the Arya Sangeet Vidyalaya

In 1907, Bhaskarbua Bakhle and Khamiyajaan competed at the Aryabhushan Theater, Pune, in a ticketed performance attended by Abdul Karim. He began to follow their lead.[16] His first ticketed show was in Sholapur, replete with advertising, showmanship, and financial remuneration. Like Paluskar, Abdul Karim produced variety entertainment shows that concluded with his own recital as the star attraction. Unlike Paluskar, he had no interest in music as an instrument of proselytizing. His shows were not *Ramayana pravachans*, as were Paluskar's, nor did he speak of using music to turn the attention of the public to the true faith of the land. Instead, he used music to showcase his musical pedagogy, technique, and skill.[17]

A year later, again in Sholapur, Abdul Karim actually met Paluskar for the first time. Paluskar had recently moved back to Bombay from Lahore and had come to Sholapur for the inauguration of another Gandharva Mahavidyalaya. He came not just as a famous performer but as a committed proselytizer, and his performance combined *bhajans* with stories from the *Ramayana*, along with disquisitions on the current state of music. Abdul Karim, sitting in the audience, heard him claim that "our ancient music has been destroyed by these Muslim singers and I am devoted to wresting our music back from them and need your help to do so."[18] Abdul Karim stayed quiet at the time but responded to the accusation by founding his own school of music.

In order to raise funds for the school, he announced a *jalsa* in which two child prodigies would demonstrate their musical skills. The prodigies were his own children, Abdul Rahman (Sureshbabu), aged seven, and Champakali (Hirabai), aged four-and-a-half. At the *jalsa*, he announced the name of the raga, following which one child sang the *sargam,* and the other sang the *aalaap.*

For Abdul Karim, as a *gharana* musician, to openly announce the name of the raga at a public performance was to take a rather large step into the future. The standard charge leveled at *gharana* musicians around the turn of the century was that they taught in bits and pieces without telling even their own students the name of the raga. *Gharana* pedagogy, its critics asserted, trafficked a little too much and a little too deliberately in obfuscation. By announcing the raga his children were to sing, Abdul Karim ensured that no such charge could be leveled. If he had wanted to, he could have fooled the audience. He could have announced the name of one raga and had his children perform another. None other than the true cognoscenti of music would have been any the wiser. But Abdul Karim did something different. He recognized that it was increasingly important for a new audience to know the raga being performed, and so he announced it.

By revealing the name of the raga he was accepting, presciently, the character of a new, national, middle-class audience for whom the appreciation of music began with a certain level of technical knowledge—in this instance, the identification of the raga. But more important, he was stripping the naming process of the power it held over musician and audience alike. In hindsight, it could even be seen as an almost contemptuous gesture to an audience that insisted on knowing the name of the raga. Abdul Karim followed the announcement with his children singing the *sargam* and *aalaap*. Perhaps his gesture was intended to show the audience that knowing the name of the raga added nothing to their knowledge of music other than just a name. The name alone, without a thorough knowledge of *sur* and *laya*, in a sense, conveyed nothing other than an identity tag.

The importance of his announcement lay less in the present than in the future. Musicians, he might well have been saying, did not need to traffic in extreme secrecy about either their pedagogy or their knowledge. They needed to come out into the open, and even trumpet their expertise for all to see and hear. In this *jalsa*, Abdul Karim advertised his own expertise while also recognizing a historical shift manifest here in the form of a new audience, to whom he announced the name of the raga. Even more to the point, the demonstration by his children showed other musicians that true musical virtuosity made secrecy obsolete and transparency unthreatening.

After all, naming a raga in public, even if it bothered musicians to do so, did not disturb the upper echelons of *ustadi* performance or appreciation. The truly knowledgeable cognoscenti, comprised of a very small group of musicians and their students, never needed to be told what raga was being performed, since it was basic knowledge for them. But the cognoscenti was only a small part of a new audience. An emerging middle-class audience was beginning to come into its own and was showing signs of becoming invested in the whole process of naming, categorizing, and identifying: the *gharana*, raga, and tala all became part of the public discourse of music appreciation. It was no longer enough to claim to have heard a tremendous performance by a maestro of music. In the years to come, a performer's *malkauns* would be compared to another's in the newspaper and written about in books. In naming the raga at his *jalsa*, Abdul Karim might have shown that the cognoscenti had nothing to fear, but he had also recognized a discursive shift.

In the mid–twentieth century, musicians would often voice their contempt of this middle-class desire to know the name of the raga. What difference could it possibly make to a real understanding of music? The true connoisseur never asked such questions, indeed the true connoisseur never needed to ask. It was also the case that Bhatkhande's musicology and Paluskar's *pravachan*s did not ever displace the *ustad*s, who commanded as much the same respect as they did earlier. The *ustad*s could still instruct their students that their talents lay in their throats (*galyaat ahe*) and not in their heads (*dokyaat nahi*), and that they needed to sing (or play) without worrying about anything else like nomenclature and questions of typology. But the key difference in the late nineteenth century was that, for the first time, questions about nomenclature, names of ragas, and families of ragas were all being published in books and becoming available for an interested public.

It was through such publications, schools, and music appreciation societies that a new midlevel, musically knowledgeable population had emerged. This was a new audience that included the *kansen*s of Paluskar's schools and the students of Bhatkhande's musicology, who understood music even if they did not perform it. There were undoubtedly the exceptionally talented students who graduated with music degrees only to begin their *taleem* all over again with an *ustad*. But even there the situation had changed; the anxiety level had dropped. It no longer mattered quite as much in the mid-twentieth century as it used to in the late nineteenth if a student was not told the name of the raga. Because of Bhatkhande and Paluskar, there were published typologies, notated compositions, and musicological works. This meant that musicians had to deal now with students who came to them with some base knowledge, and better prepared intellectually than they used to be. The *ustad* could challenge, dismiss, or disregard all previously published works, but he could not make them disappear. In addition to a changed student body, basic-level music training could now be purchased in schools, through books, and through using notation. It was not accessible only to those who aspired to a career as a professional musician.

These were the changes Abdul Karim could not have foreseen at a *jalsa* in 1908. But in naming the raga so publicly, he was coming out confidently, without acquiescence, buttressed by the knowledge that in revealing the name of the raga, nothing of great musical importance was given away. Also, without revealing any significant details, he had advertised the success of his peda-gogy, in which the science and technique behind any given raga had to rest on a thorough knowledge of *sur* and *laya*.[19]

Two years later, on May 10, 1910, at the founding of his Arya Sangeet Vidyalaya in Belgaum, Abdul Karim made a speech directed at Paluskar. Muslims, he insisted, had encouraged music, not destroyed it. He agreed that music was in a state of decline, because of its association with indolence and vice. He had no quarrels with the attempt to cleanse it and turn it respectable again. Musicians had a profession to protect, and its association with de-bauchery was not something they wished to maintain. In the opening of the school, he was showing the absurdity of Paluskar's claim that Muslims qua Muslims had destroyed music not simply by railing against Paluskar, but by engaging him, actively, with the recognition that if schools, ticketed perform-ances, and greater transparency were the order of the day, he could do as well as Paluskar. He could found a school, train Brahmin students among others, notate compositions, and still perform magnificent music.

Brahmins and Pune

In 1912, Abdul Karim moved his school to Pune and was immediately con-fronted with many difficulties. Pune was a Brahmin city where the orthodoxy monitored the public use of water and opposed a Muslim musician teaching Hindu boys.[20] Tarabai and he decided to entrust the Brahmin students to draw water from the well and bring it home for others to use. The strategy did not work. Even though the students were Brahmin, their appearance at the well was still challenged. Pune's orthodox Brahmins viewed all of Abdul Karim's students as contaminated because of their intimate association with him. Even an appeal to a reformer like Gopal Krishna Gokhale was met with the unsatisfactory response that reform took time and that change always moved at a gradual pace. At most, Dr. Bhandarkar, an eminent Sanskritist, sent his daughter, Malini, to study with Abdul Karim, and in a show of soli-darity, the famous writer N. C. Phadke and Acharya Atre joined the school as well.[21] The orthodox population of the city was not the only problem Abdul Karim faced. Two other schools of music competed with Abdul Karim for students.

In this cantankerous and competitive milieu, Abdul Karim and Tarabai, with Raosaheb Deval's help, met with measured success. Abdul Karim was reluctant to turn his school into a "warehouse" for performing musicians.[22] He insisted that it be a *gurukul* and would take on only a few students at a time. Despite all the difficulties the school stayed afloat, not least because Abdul Karim's fame was increasing. He received more invitations to perform than he could accept, and because of his *jalsa*s in city after city, both the *kirana gharana* style of singing and Abdul Karim himself became well known. While he traveled, Tarabai ran the daily activities of the school. In time, Abdul Karim cut back on his private performances, opting to do more public, ticketed recitals, which also helped the school's finances.

Two years after Abdul Karim and Tarabai moved to Pune, Tilak returned to the city after his release from Mandalay. Abdul Karim's friends arranged to meet him with the intention of bringing to his attention the difficulties Abdul Karim's students, even Brahmins, faced in Pune. Tilak was told that Abdul Karim did not believe in caste distinctions, encouraged his students to be religious, ran a *gurukul*, fed and clothed all his students, and taught Indian classical music, paying full and respectful attention to the *Gayatri Mantra* (sacred Hindu verse). In the gathering, a few orthodox Brahmins asked Abdul Karim's friend and collaborator, Raosaheb Deval, why he accepted a Muslim singing such verses. Dr. Bhandarkar stepped in to respond:

> I know the *Dharmashastra*s and the *Veda*s well because I am a Sanskrit scholar. Even if Khansaheb is Muslim and has been singing the *Gayatri Mantra*, I do not believe that either our religion or the *Veda*s have been violated. We are not here to argue about the *Dharmashastra*s. A worthy Muslim singer does not even allow his Brahmin students to ask for *madhukari* [alms] but instead, for the sake of our Indian classical music, leaves not just his *gharana* base but also the patronage of the Baroda court to settle here in Pune. We should applaud his efforts not belittle them.[23]

In other words, Tilak was given additional reassurance that Abdul Karim posed no threat to high Brahmin Hindu culture. The biography does not tell us how Tilak responded to this exchange, but a few days later when Abdul Karim sang for him, he is reported to have told Raosaheb Deval that "if foreigners like Governor Wellington and Clements take such interest in our Indian music, then so must I. Furthermore, what you all are doing is work for the nation and I support it fully."

In his attempt to portray Abdul Karim as the unthreatening Muslim, Kapileshwari constructs him as an apolitical musician as well as the ideal Brahmin. We are told that Abdul Karim sang *ganpati stavan* (Ganesh prayer) for Gandhi.[24] When accused of being too pro-British, he responded that he was a musician, his work was music, and no matter who asked him to sing, he sang. Music was exempt from politics.[25] As for the matter of his religion, he was a Sunni Pathan who did not need to go the mosque to find Allah. Abdul Karim showed Paluskar how to sing Sanskrit *sloka*s in *laya* and *sur* and even taught him how to sing *Vande Mataram* at the INC sessions. Abdul Karim noted that Bhatkhande, despite his *pratham shreni* (first-rank) and *ucch koti* (high-order) status, was an inauthentic Brahmin if he could not sing the *Gayatri Mantra* with *sur* and *laya*.[26]

These depictions tell us not that Abdul Karim was a good Brahmin but rather that he was engaging strategically with Brahminism as he encountered it in Pune, in the nationalist sphere, and in rival musicians and musicologists. Let us recall here Abdul Wahid's question about his favoritism to Brahmins and Abdul Karim's response. His life at home with his children could be properly Muslim. But in his public persona, as a performer, he was able to negotiate and accommodate a series of Brahminic expectations. Neither a sell-out to Brahminism, as suggested by Abdul Wahid, nor a consummate Brahmin, as suggested by Bhandarkar and others, Abdul Karim was a political musician, making shrewd decisions about where to make accommodations and where to assert his expertise in order to stay ahead in the changing—and increasingly Brahminic—milieu of his time.

Abdul Karim, Bhatkhande, and Musicology

Abdul Karim's most public exchange and disagreement was with Pandit Bhatkhande. Paradoxically, even though the two men were at odds with each other, they had more in common than either recognized. The history of their antagonism had to do with Raosaheb Krishnaji Ballal Deval, who was not only one of Abdul Karim's friends but also his strong supporter.[27]

Raosaheb Deval was a district collector. His interest in music had been sparked by the publication, in 1884, of the article that became known as the Ellis Report. The article itself, written by an English physicist, challenged the Darwinian view advanced by Helmholtz about the Western tempered scale being the natural culmination of all other primitive scales still in existence.[28] In its stead, Ellis advocated a relativistic view. Ellis's article, despite this claim, seemed to suggest that the Indian music scale was neither natural nor scientific, and every writer who referred to it, from Kapileshwari to Sharat Chandra Gokhale, saw it as a damning piece of work. Distressed by what they perceived as the report's lack of scientific and musicological knowledge, Raosaheb Deval had collaborated with Abdul Karim to give musicological lecture demonstrations that showed that the Indian music scale was in fact both natural and scientific. In order to do so, Deval spoke of the mathematics of *shruti*s and Abdul Karim sang all twenty-two *shruti*s that made up the seven pitches. In 1910, Deval published his rebuttal, *The Hindu Musical Scale and the 22 Shrutees*, which came to the attention of a district judge from Satara, Mr. E. Clements. Subsequently, Deval and Clements invented an instrument called the *shruti* organ, which was designed, in theory, to accurately play all twenty-two *shruti*s. Abdul Karim told them it was unsuitable for Indian music, at which point his formal collaboration with Deval came to an end.[29] But their friendship remained strong. Indeed, one reason Abdul Karim moved his school to Pune was because Deval had retired to the city and it allowed the two friends to stay in close touch. It was the friendship with Deval that led Abdul Karim directly into conflict with Bhatkhande.

Bhatkhande, as we have seen in the previous chapter, had a low opinion of both Deval and Clements. He respected Abdul Karim but was suspicious of musicians in general. When Abdul Karim and Bhatkhande first met, the former was the leading exponent of the *kirana gharana* and of *khayal gayaki*, and the latter was fast acquiring recognition as a prominent and influential musicologist. Unbeknownst to each other, Abdul Karim and Bhatkhande shared a secular understanding of music. Without granting pride of place to organized religion, both men could accommodate belief and faith within music. Neither believed music should be linked to politics or proselytizing. Both men eschewed, from their own vantage points, traditionalist arguments about music. Yet, from the moment they met, they disagreed sharply and publicly.

Kapileshwari's account of their first meeting presents Bhatkhande as a pedantic troublemaker given to ignorant argumentation. The two men met in Mysore, where Abdul Karim had been asked to give a special recital by its ruler on the occasion of Sayajirao Gaekwad's visit to the state. Abdul Karim balked when he heard about the visit. His departure from Baroda, some sixteen years earlier, had been surreptitious and he was worried about being remembered as disrespectful by a prominent and early patron. Sayajirao, when they met, bore him no grudge, and was accompanied by Bhatkhande in whose modernizing work he had great confidence. Within minutes of their introduction to each other and for the duration of Abdul Karim's four-day stay in Mysore, Abdul Karim and Bhatkhande argued.

Bhatkhande asked Abdul Karim to sing a raga named *nayaki kanada.* Abdul Karim retorted that he could sing three different kinds of *nayaki kanada,* one from *kirana gharana,* one from *rampur,* and one that lay musicians sang. He then challenged Bhatkhande to hum a few bars of any *nayaki kanada* he wished and told him that one of his children would sing the *sargam* simultaneously. This was clearly meant to bring Bhatkhande down a peg. Bhatkhande, not being a performer, could not comply with this request. Abdul Karim challenged Bhatkhande's credentials and his self-appointment as the examiner of all musicians.[30] In narrating this encounter, Kapileshwari depicts Bhatkhande as a fool, obsessed only with writing down the pitches in a raga when he could not even hum a few bars. Abdul Karim could, of course, sing it in myriad ways.[31]

The two men argued about other matters as well. Could the pitches in raga *bilaval* truly be considered the foundational scale for Hindustani music? What was the basis for Bhatkhande's categorization of all ragas into ten *thaat*s (groups)? In posing the question of foundations, Abdul Karim was using Bhatkhande's own obsessive rhetoric about *adhaar* (backing/foundation). In the course of his tours, Bhatkhande had asked musicians if there was any textual foundation for their performance. In Mysore, Abdul Karim threw his question right back at him by asking if his groupings of ragas had been authenticated by all musicians, and in a move designed to provoke Bhatkhande, Abdul Karim challenged his Sanskrit knowledge, daring him to deduce the raga he was singing (*maru bihag*) by using his textual reading of the *grantha*s. Bhatkhande could not do so. Abdul Karim then explained to the gathered assembly that his teachers used to call it *pat bihag,* he called it *maru bihag,* and in response to Bhatkhande's question about why one raga should have two names, responded by saying Raosaheb Ballal Deval and Raobahadur Deval were the two names of the same person.

This was clearly a hostile encounter. We know that Bhatkhande's aim was to produce orderly and systematic classical music. Abdul Karim's claim about three varieties of *nayaki kanada* and/or *bihag* would not have produced any difficulty per se, but Bhatkhande wanted differences recorded in musicological terms, so that students would know the varieties within any given raga and between different *gharana* styles. Kapileshwari caricatured Bhatkhande's obsession with writing down everything he observed, but it was a characteristic trait of a scholar who went nowhere without his notebook and kept written records of all his encounters. Bhatkhande asked Abdul Karim about the precise kind of *malhar* Tansen used to sing in the emperor Akbar's time. Abdul Karim snapped back that he could answer all of Bhatkhande's questions by singing the answers and that the dominant *malhar* was the one sung by musicians. This may well have been the answer Bhatkhande wanted, since it confirmed his argument about the newness of classical music. In effect, Bhatkhande's historicizing claim was compatible with Abdul Karim's response as a performer. If Abdul Karim was claiming primacy for the *malhar* sung by musicians, he was in effect saying that the *malhar* that would enter the books as the "classical" type was only a few centuries old. This was exactly what Bhatkhande would himself claim some years later, when he wrote that Indian music was just in the process of being "classicized." Nonetheless, when they met, they could find nothing on which to agree.

Kapileshwari closes his account with the signature accusation leveled by many musicians antagonistic to Bhatkhande: He did not even know the basics. Let us grant, even if improbable, that the accusation was accurate. We still need to note that for Bhatkhande, the question of basics spoke to the issue of foundations. In asking Abdul Karim to explain the origins of the foundational scale of seven pitches, he was perhaps trying to maneuver him into a complicated conversation about *shruti*. Perhaps Abdul Karim saw it coming, because he retorted that having spent close to four days explaining the basics of music to Bhatkhande, this question would have to wait for another meeting.

Given this hostility, it is unsurprising that neither man made an effort to meet the other again. Ten years after their first meeting, however, Bhatkhande and Abdul Karim happened to be traveling on the same train. Had Abdul Karim cast his lot with him, Bhatkhande said, the two of them could have changed the face of Indian classical music together (against Deval and Clements). By 1924, Clements's *shruti* organ had been debunked at the first All-India Music Conference (1916). Bhatkhande was even more famous, sought after, and confident. So, too, was Abdul Karim. As an imagined possibility, Abdul Karim and Bhatkhande might well have forged a different history for music.

Kapileshwari's dismissal of Bhatkhande takes up the single largest section of the book. From it, we can deduce not Bhatkhande's irrelevance to musicians but his importance. It may be appealing, given what we know of Bhatkhande's personality, to join the chorus and dismiss him for not knowing the very basics of ragas musicians could sing in numerous ways. However, that might miss the larger historical point. Musicians asked Bhatkhande whether his typology was correct and dismissed it as incorrect. But they were now engaging in a new conversation about correct and incorrect *typologies*. Musicians' dismissals alone could not turn back the clock. They could pillory the man who had inaugurated a new conversation, but they could not change its terms. They could, however, attempt to make it their own.

The difficulties involved in trying to rationalize a music sung and played across the length and breadth of the country, where regional variations added to an already variegated field, could not have come as a surprise to Bhatkhande. He was trying to cast a disciplinary net around the ragas as the first step in writing a classical system for music. Bhatkhande was not arguing against variety or improvisation. He was making a case for greater transparency in pedagogy and for consensus within the group of performers about what constituted the "classical." Questions about the basics of theory, of music, and of raga, tell us what was at stake. Bhatkhande was attempting to rewrite a classical system for music. Musicians might not have liked his musicology, but by his audacity, he had taken the battle right into their turf, into their performance spaces. By imposing his own theory and system on their music, he had in effect forced them into the open. In the combativeness of his encounter with Bhatkhande, musicians like Abdul Karim chose not to ignore the terms of a new conversation but to engage with it. Kapileshwari is only one among a group of biographers who heap vitriol on Bhatkhande with the intention of demonstrating that the *ustad* triumphed in the encounter with the ignorant musicologist. That may indeed have been so, but it certainly suggests that the *ustad* recognized the musicologist as someone to take seriously.

However, to take Bhatkhande seriously was not to collaborate with him. It is interesting to wonder what the future of music might have been if Abdul Karim had joined with Bhatkhande. But such collaboration was extremely unlikely. Abdul Karim's friendship with Clements and Deval had come about in large part because all three were arguing against Bhatkhande, though they were doing so in musicological and mathematical terms. If the Mysore encounter showed both Bhatkhande's importance as a historical catalyst and cemented the fact that musicology was here to stay, it also showed Abdul Karim's willingness to engage with the new discourse. In 1914, Abdul Karim went back to Pune, secure in both his embodied and theoretical knowledge of the various kinds of *nayaki kanada*. By this time, however, change was afoot, and not just in Bhatkhande's musicological terms. Abdul Karim's marriage was coming apart.

The End of the Marriage and the Removal of Scandal

Shortly after the move to Pune in 1912, Abdul Karim's marriage began to show signs of strain. In the biography, Kapileshwari begins his depiction of Tarabai as an excessively indulgent mother and an impossible, unfair, and dismissive employer to the people hired to look after the children. In the narrative, Tarabai is no longer addressed by Kapileshwari with the respectful and honorific term *matoshree*, respected mother. There were, additionally, other changes. Abdul Karim, we may recall, had been chastised by Abdul Wahid on one of his trips for his favoritism to Brahmin students. In response to that encounter, he had laid down new and strict rules for his children. His daughters were no longer allowed to learn music, nor could they travel with him. They were to stay at home, enroll in a school, and take private lessons about Islam from a *qazi*. They also had to dress in the appropriate manner for Muslim girls. Perhaps this is what made Tarabai uncomfortable. But her explicit complaint had to do with her growing sense that he was untrustworthy.

After coming back from Mysore, in 1914, Abdul Karim went on the road again, this time to Ichalkaranji, Meraj, Burhanpur, and Bombay. It was around that time Tarabai voiced her concern about her husband. His new school attracted a large number of students, including many *baiji*s, who made Tarabai suspicious. When she demanded that he stop taking on such women as his students, Abdul Karim conducted private tuitions behind Tarabai's back, treating her suspicions as female hysteria.[32] Infidelity is hinted at here in the rhetorical guise of a gesture to a milieu in which it was common, but Kapileshwari never states it explicitly. In 1918, while Abdul Karim was away on tour, Tarabai simply left, for no apparent reason, taking all his belongings, along with the children. We find out nothing about the reasons for the breakup from the narrative. Kapileshwari remembers only that Abdul Karim, upon receiving the telegram informing him of Tarabai's departure, had responded that she had finally revealed her true colors as a mercenary woman whose only interest was to prostitute her children on the stage.[33] In other words, the only explanation Kapileshwari offers is Tarabai's character deficiency, though the upbringing of the children was clearly an issue. She was a bad woman who tricked Abdul Karim and took his children away from him.

When Tarabai left Abdul Karim, she put music back into the girls' lives, turning their attention to theater and remaking them into Hindu girls, using their Hindu names in place of their Muslim names. In 1918, their oldest son, Abdul Rahman/Sureshbabu, was sixteen years old, and Champakali/Hirabai was thirteen. The other children were eleven (Gulab Bano), eight (Hamid) and three (Sakina). Abdul Karim did not see his children again—nor did he wish to. He held Tarabai responsible for corrupting them.[34] She had gathered around her a group of supporters, stalwarts in the new Marathi music theater world, such as Govindrao Tembe, Savai Gandharva (the Brahmin singer who betrayed Abdul Karim), and Ganpatrao Bodas. These were men Abdul Karim believed had helped turn his children into stage and film performers against their and his will.[35]

Bereft at the loss of his children and distressed at the slander Tarabai was spreading, Abdul Karim traveled again. Within a year, he took two new students, two sisters, Hira and Banno. In 1922, he married Banno, who became his third wife, and the couple moved to Meraj permanently. In the years after Tarabai left him, Abdul Karim traveled from one *jalsa* to the next. He participated in fundraising recitals for Gandhi's satyagraha and sang at music appreciation societies, and performed in music competitions.

Toward the end of his life and around the same time his estranged daughter, Hirabai, began making her own recordings of Marathi *bhajans*, Abdul Karim cut his first record with the Ruby Recording Company. It was a momentous event. The authentic voice that Sharatchandra Gokhale's memory describes met a new generation of audiences through his records. If Kapileshwari's biography is the definitive text in which we meet Abdul Karim, it has been the recording industry that allowed music lovers to hear Abdul Karim's voice range across three octaves for successive generations since his death.

Abdul Karim's last recital was in Madras in October 1937. He was sixty-five years old and had spent most of his life traveling. The journey from Meraj to Madras was difficult for him, but he insisted on going. His recital in Madras was very well received, and while in the city he received a pleading invitation from Sri Aurobindo in Pondicherry. He left by train with his students for Pondicherry but felt so unwell en route that he got off the train at a station soon after the train left Madras, at Singer Perumalcoilam, or Kokila station. He lay down on a *charpai*, a mat made of bamboo stalks, and breathed his last surrounded by his students. None of his immediate family was present.[36] His students took his body back to his home in Meraj. Years before, when he had first arrived in Meraj, Abdul Karim miraculously recovered from a mysterious ailment after singing at the *dargah* of *mirasaheb*. He had made it a point thereafter to sing at the annual *urs* (festival) of the *dargah* every year. Abdul Karim was buried under the shade of a lime tree within the premises of the same *dargah*.

So died a Muslim *ustad*. In the course of his professional life, he had made shrewd decisions and unorthodox compromises that had helped him withstand both Brahmin pressure and the musicological devaluing of musicians. I have told Abdul Karim's story briefly to show that musicians, of whom I have taken Abdul Karim as a signal example, did not simply stand by silently while Paluskar's bhakti nationalism turned music Hindu and Bhatkhande's musicology turned music systematic. But if Abdul Karim's life is an exemplary case of the resistance of *ustad*s to both Bhatkhande and Paluskar, his daughter's life in many ways was the opposite, demonstrating the success of Paluskar's project for women, nationalism, respectability, and music.

Hirabai Barodekar's life traced a rather different path from that of her father. After her mother left Abdul Karim, the key points of her musical journey came together on occasion with her father's career trajectory but, more often than not, parted company with it. Indeed, Hirabai's life can be characterized as a movement from scandal to respectability couched in middle-class, Marathi, upper-caste terms. Her grandmother, Hirabai Govekar, after whom she was named, was a *baiji*. Her mother, Tarabai, had run away with a Muslim musician. In stark contrast, Hirabai's life was marked by an absence of scandal. She became the icon of Marathi, married, middle-class women who pursued a career in music without compromising hearth and home.

In 1937, Hirabai sang in Calcutta at a music conference organized by Bhupendra Ghosh. As reported in the newspaper *Amrit Bazaar Patrika*, "There is no doubt that this year's conference reached its peak in Hirabai's singing on Sunday. There was only one other person in India in recent times who could sing as she did that morning and Abdul Karim Khan, alas is no more. Today Hirabai is peerless. It is difficult to speak of her voice and her art in the language of restraint. Her voice is a marvel. . . . As for her style, it is Abdul

Karim's own, and what higher praise one can conceive?"[37] It was poignant praise. Her father had died earlier that year. She had not seen him for almost two decades and was, reportedly, devastated by the news. However, her devastation was not publicly described as the grief a daughter might feel at the death of her father. It was ascribed instead to the loss for the *kirana gharana* of its exemplary representative.

Ironically, when her father died, Hirabai was shooting a film called *Sant janabai.* Abdul Karim disliked theater, and we may surmise that he would have thought even worse of film. His daughter had tried her hand at both. This was not a simple rebellion against her father; it was the recognition of a new venue that would capture Marathi audiences like no other. As a very young child, she had already been recognized as a prodigy who could, with her older brother, sing the *sargam* of whichever raga a musician was singing. In the years to come, she would be called *gaan hira* (diamond of music) and *gaan kokila* (the nightingale of music).[38]

Sharatchandra Gokhale, who had the good fortune to hear both Abdul Karim and his daughter sing, wrote of Hirabai's talent:

> Everyone praises Hirabai's singing, with good reason. But Hirabai's unique style is not quite as famous. What most people note is that her *sa* [the first pitch of the second septet] is the most *surel* [perfect pitch combined with tunefulness]. Has any singer with a *besur* [off-pitch] *sa* ever become famous? Even little girls place *sa* correctly. But Hirabai's *sa* emerges slowly, it doesn't just get placed. [Her technique is to] go toward *sa*, go close to it, retreat, go close again, retreat again and that *sa* which seems to wait with anticipation to be touched [she makes sure] to not overexcite but to keep it desirous of her touch and then to touch it slowly, delicately, as if with a cat's paw. This only Hirabai does. . . . She is the unquestioned mistress of such numerous delicate, emotive, feeling touches. Behind such delicacy can we even imagine how much labor there must have been? But that labor, those techniques, those are not famous.[39]

This description of her musical abilities is of a piece with the manner in which Abdul Karim's voice was often praised. It fit Abdul Karim's daughter perfectly. When her mother was still married to Abdul Karim, she had not been at all keen for Hirabai to pursue a career in music, wanting her instead to receive an English education and become a doctor. This may have been because she had recognized that chasing after music had led to the destruction of her own life.[40] But after Tarabai left Abdul Karim, things changed. Perhaps Tarabai came to accept what Abdul Karim himself was to remark many years later when he heard about Hirabai's prowess, namely, that it was his blood which ran in Hirabai's veins, making music come naturally to her.

But who would teach her? Hirabai's first teacher had been her own brother, who had studied under Abdul Karim, but now she needed a guru of her own. She tried to study with Mohammed Khan, son of the famous Agra musician, Nathhan Khan, but felt that her *kirana* training interfered. "'Mohammad Khan is teaching me only [different] *cheez*s [compositions]. This is not music . . . these are only words, words, words. . . . but *sur, aalaap, tan, palta* [technicalities of raga] there was no sign of, or any systematic teaching . . . all he was teaching [me] was poetry.' Upon hearing this, Mohammad Khan got so angry he declared that he would not continue to teach her."[41] Hirabai needed a father substitute and, by an odd turn of events, she was soon able to acquire one in the form of Abdul Wahid Khan. Known in musical circles as *behre* Abdul Wahid, because he was a little hard of hearing, he was the same Wahid Khan who years earlier had accused Abdul Karim of favoritism toward Brahmins. One year after her parents separated, Hirabai's *taleem* (training) began in earnest, with Abdul Wahid, a *kirana gharana* musician who had been a close associate of her father's.

Hirabai's course of study lasted four years, from 1918 to 1922. In 1920 her mother founded the Nutan Sangeet Vidyalaya in Girgaum. Close to the end of Hirabai's studies, Paluskar invited her to sing at his fourth GMV conference. Unable to refuse an invitation by such a *thor gayak* (legendary singer), she sang, against Abdul Wahid Khan's wishes.[42] The performance was a great success. A year later, her career was launched.

Professional Debuts

Hirabai began recording music in 1923. She started with *bhajan*s and went on in successive years to record Marathi theater music (*natya sangeet*) and *khayal*.[43] In 1924, Hirabai got married, in a match arranged by her mother. We know little about her married life from the biographies other than that she was happy and gave birth to her first child two years after her marriage. Two years after her debut recording, she gave her first ticketed performance in

Pune's Arya Bhushan theater. Pune's conservative citizenry, who had been a thorn in her father's flesh even though they greatly appreciated his singing, informed her that she was turning music into a market (*bazaar*). No women attended this first performance, but she began to receive increasing recognition. And then, her father's nemesis, Marathi music theater, became the ironic staging point for even greater success.

Marathi Natak *and* Natya Sangeet

In the late nineteenth century and well into the first decade of the twentieth century, the most melodious women's voices in theater were, in fact, men's. All three theaters, Parsi, Marathi, and Gujarati, employed men to play women's roles. Jayshankar Sundari from the Gujarati stage and Bal Gandharva from the Marathi stage were two of the most successful stage actors, and the extent of their success may be seen in their trendsetting roles for middle-class women. Bal Gandharva, through his role in productions such as *Manapmaan,* set fashions for Marathi women's clothing and gestures, popularized the nose ring, carrying handkerchiefs, and wearing flowers in one's hair. Even his manner of speaking was mimicked as the ideal speech for cultivated, refined, and educated women.[44] He was perhaps exactly the kind of musician Abdul Karim recoiled from, but Bal Gandharva had captivated Pune and Bombay's music audiences. Among those spellbound were Hirabai and her brother, Sureshbabu.

Sureshbabu had seen Bal Gandharva perform in the Marathi play *Swayamvar.* Marathi theater drew from Puranic mythology and combined lyric poetry with a diluted classical music that appealed to the new middle classes. Entranced by Bal Gandharva, Sureshbabu took Hirabai to see his performance of *Ekach pyaala* (Just One More Glass) in a play about alcoholism. Hirabai, like her brother, was immediately smitten with theater and its potential. In the same year in which she gave her first ticketed performance, began an active recording career, and acquired titles that stayed with her all her life, Hirabai also launched her stage career.

The first step in this career was the founding of a *natak* company, ironically, by Tarabai and Savai Gandharva (Rambhau Kundgolkar). When married to Abdul Karim, Tarabai had been vociferous in her anger at his departure for the theater. To underscore her contempt of his choice to act on stage and as an insult to his masculinity, she had sent him bangles, a sari blouse, and a sari when he left Abdul Karim's tutelage. However, she must have changed her mind both about theater and Rambhau after leaving Abdul Karim, because Tarabai joined with Rambhau to found the Nutan Natak Company. The school of music founded by Tarabai in 1920, the Nutan Sangeet Vidyalaya, opened a wing dedicated to the training of stage performers, the Nutan Sangeet Vidyalaya Natyashakha.

The new company's first stage production was *Saubhadra*, based on a story from the Mahabharata, with Hirabai and her sister Kamalabai cast as Subhadra and Rukmini and their brother, Sureshbabu, as Arjun. It meant that brother and sister would play husband and wife. When Abdul Karim heard about it he was outraged. Even though it was only make-believe, it violated the incest taboo. But what was scandalous for a *gharana* musician in the early twentieth century was commonplace for Marathi stage audiences, accustomed to seeing men playing women's roles. What was new in this case was that women were playing women's roles, coming out into the public, and acting on stage. The first show, in September 1929, was a landmark in more ways than one. Through her performance and demeanor, Hirabai had taken an effective step in showing that a respectably married Marathi upper-caste woman (and mother) could act and sing on stage.

Saubhadra's success brought Hirabai to the attention of people like M. M. Kunte of the Poona Gayan Samaj, as well as noted music critics and musicians like Baburao Painter, Keshavrao Bhole, and Vasant Desai, all of whom were well known for their musical talents.[45] The family followed *Saubhadra* with another play based on the life of the poet saint Mirabai, which was also successful. After these successes, the Nutan Sangeet Vidyalaya, founded initially as a school for music, virtually became a new music theater company.

The family's euphoria at their early success was tempered by the daunting reality that theater companies cost an enormous amount of money to maintain. There were over seventy employees, all of whom had to be housed and fed. In addition, the family needed to purchase stage props, costumes, furniture, and musical instruments. Still, for a while, the trio of Hirabai, Kamalabai, and Sureshbabu staged successful productions. Hirabai even became famous for singing Bal Gandharva's theatrical songs. In 1927 and 1928, with Bal Gandharva himself in the audience, she sang one of his compositions, and he joined the audience in applauding her performance.

Alongside her theatrical career, Hirabai continued with her *jalsa*, becoming steadily more famous. P. L. Deshpande, comic novelist and de facto ethnographer of middle-class Marathi life, described the Bombay of the 1930s and its musical offerings during the ten days of the Ganesh festival (*Ganeshutsav*). The description speaks to the quality of a new cultural sphere both private and public, in which music was central, as were women performers:

> For music lovers, the ten days of the festival were somewhat difficult. In one little location, Girgaum, numerous singers would sing in different *vada*s (private homes). One Saturday night and so many music performances! In Ambevadi [there was] Mallikarjun Mansur, in another [there was] Kagalkarbua, in Brahman Sabha [there was] Master Krishnarao (Phulambrikar), in Shastri Hall [there was] Rambhau Savai Gandharva, in Tara Temple Lane [there was] Gangubai [known in Maharashtra as *gandhari* Hangal], in Chunam Lane [there was] Hirabai Badodekar—one would get completely torn and anxious! Who should one listen to? . . .
>
> Until about 3:30 in the morning, we ran from place to place and eventually wound up in front of Goodman, Persian-Indian, Mervaan, Viceroy of India, or some other Iranian restaurant and wait for their doors to open to have *brun-maska* [hard-crusted bread with fresh butter]. Staying awake all night listening to music, we needed a night cap, [which had to be] tea from an Iranian restaurant without which the evening was not complete. And at that hotel, an impromptu music round table conference would come together . . . some would say Rambhau's voice had reached new heights that night, some would praise Gangubai's *miyan malhar*.[46]

This was the milieu in which, and the new audience for whom, Hirabai sang. It was an audience familiar with the fine points of music, with more than a fleeting knowledge of ragas and their different renditions by performers, and an appreciation of Marathi *natya sangeet* to boot. The disreputability of women singers was not completely gone but fading fast. Hirabai was not a sexual figure, as *baiji*s were said to be, but was perceived as a sister, a friend, a neighbor's daughter and, most tellingly, a singer whose talent was unquestionable. P. L. Deshpande, when writing about Hirabai, had used her familial name Champutai. In his description of the music performances in Bombay, P. L. Deshpande also remembered that at the impromptu music conference someone would say, "but nothing to beat Champutai's rendition today of *vad jau'* [a theater composition] and a novice would ask, 'who's Champutai?' "

P. L. Deshpande answers the question himself before returning to his narration. "'Champutai' is what Hirabai's mother called her, her sister called her, she was someone who shouldered the weight of an enormous familial responsibility and was known as a lifelong loyal friend." But his description concludes with this account: "'About Hirabai's singing, nothing more needs to be said,' said a veteran music connoisseur, dipping his *brun maska* into his tea, 'Listen carefully to what I say . . . tea from an Irani hotel and Hirabai's singing—even if the heavens rain down on us, their quality remains same-to-same!' "[47] Acting on stage had seemed scandalous for her father, but it was becoming a profession that middle-class women would consider, even at the risk of broaching social disfavor. As P. L. Deshpande's description reveals, both Hirabai's serious classical music and her renditions of well-loved theater compositions were appreciated by a knowledgeable audience, one that also recognized the social position of someone who could be called Champutai. But despite all its successes, theater in the end was the family's financial undoing.

Savai Gandharva left the company in 1932. Hirabai continued to sing and act on stage in other productions—including *Vidyaharan* and *Punyaprabhav*— all based on Sanskrit drama and epic literature, but under the constant pressure to produce newer plays, their eighth production, *Jaagti jyot,* staged in 1933, did not do well. Matters worsened because of internal friction between the actors in the company and the family. By July 1933, the theater crumbled under the weight of its debt, and all its possessions were confiscated. Hirabai and her family were taken to court by people they considered friends and now not only lost their investment but accumulated a large debt that needed to be repaid.

Hirabai, however, had gathered around her a stalwart group of friends and supporters, among them B. R. Deodhar (Paluskar's biographer and student) and Govindrao Tembe (*ustad* Alladiya Khan's student and biographer). Although her theatrical career had come to an end, the same could not be said about her career in classical music. Hirabai sang at numerous *jalsa*s and paid off the family's debt in small installments. She acted in a few films as well, not because of the fame it offered as much as because it paid close to Rs. 1,500 per month. One such film was *Sant janabai,* and it was on the set for that film that she heard that Abdul Karim had died at a railway station in South India.

By that time—1937—Hirabai had been recording for over a decade and her career was well established. It had not always been an easy road. In the early years of her singing career, her arrival in a town or village had been treated like a circus event, and she had been perceived as someone of ill repute. Before she was famous, she had to sing without a loudspeaker for hours on end, well into the small hours of the morning. One incident Hirabai remembered well signaled the manner in which she took on the whole question of disrespectability. She had been invited to sing, but her patron had housed her in a little space away from the main house, and the women of the family would not talk to her. She walked into the kitchen, uninvited, offered to share household chores, peeled garlic cloves, and gradually overcame the resistance to her presence in the house.[48] By dint of such self-effacing efforts, Hirabai earned her reputation as a respectable woman performer. She always dressed in a sari with its *padar* wrapped around her, wore pearl earrings and bangles that were the trademark of upper-caste Marathi women, tied her hair in a sedate bun, and sang calmly, without flamboyance or hand gestures.[49]

Hirabai's mother died in 1946, nine years after her father's death. Since 1918, she had been the only parent to her five children.[50] She had arranged Hirabai's marriage in 1924 and her first son's marriage in 1926. In the early years of her daughter's career, she was her de facto stage manager. Hirabai had a career in music Tarabai never had, nor could have had. In her later years as a national artist, Hirabai toured North India and sang at numerous music conferences and in most cities in which music was loved—Hyderabad, Bangalore, Mysore, Hubli, Dharwad, and Kurundwad. She sang with Kesarbai Kerkar, whom she met the year her father died; she sang for Sayajirao Gaekwad, who remembered that her grandmother was one of the *kalavant*s in the Baroda employ and invited her to join his court. (She refused on the grounds that singing in only one venue would not aid her career.)[51] She sang at *Ganeshutsav*s, *Durga Puja*s, at weddings, in clubs and music circles, colleges and schools. She traveled to China as an ambassador for independent India's cultural heritage. In a career that spanned forty years, she was said to have had wheels under her feet, and P. L. Deshpande wrote that "the Indian Railways should honor her with the award of Star traveler."[52]

Hirabai was a national artist, the exemplary *kulin stree* who was also a performer, and a household name in Maharashtra. In her life, she exemplified one of the most notable transformations in the musical life of Maharashtra in the mid–twentieth century: upper-caste Hindu women increasingly took the place of the *baiji*s of earlier years. Anjanibai Malpekar, Kesarbai Kerkar,

Mogubai Kurdikar, Menakabai Shirodkar, and Gangubai Hangal were all gradually replaced by upper-caste women such as Manik Bhide, Veena Sahasrabuddhe, Padmavati Shaligram, and Ashwini Bhide, among many others. This road to respectability owes much to Hirabai Barodekar, even as it became responsible for the extraordinarily important role Hindu women were to come to play in Hindustani music. But this same history also rests on the erasure from its narrative of some of the key musicians of the earlier century.

Conclusion

Let us return one more time to the period before this erasure, to the time of the father. Abdul Karim Khan had been born on November 11, 1872, to a musician father, Kale Khan, in Delhi. His grandfather, Wajid Ali Khan, had also been a Delhi court musician. Abdul Karim had two brothers, Abdul Latif and Abdul Haq. All three boys were taught enough Urdu to be able to read and write, but the emphasis in their education was on music. The *gharana* to which they belonged was the *kirana gharana*, named after a village some miles from Kurukshetra.[53]

The origin story of this *kirana gharana* has a myth attached to it that concerns two *nayaks*, Dhondu and Bhannu. Dhondunayak, a Krishna devotee, was granted a personal audience with the Almighty in Vrindavan and granted a boon for his devotion. Dhondunayak asked that the sweetness of one *sur* of Krishna's legendary flute be transferred into his throat. It was granted, and as a result, all *kirana* singers thenceforth had voices notable for their sweetness. Some of the best-known *kirana* singers in the late nineteenth century were Sunni Muslims who retold this story, a combination of myth and history, as a way of showing that the original fathers of their *gharana* were Hindu and that their music was linked to the practice of bhakti, not to religious or sectarian divides.[54]

Abdul Karim was one such Sunni, Pathan, *kirana gharana* musician. In previous chapters, he made a guest appearance, as did Hirabai, but in this last chapter, both have played leading roles. This is not to claim that either of them can be seen as representing all musicians, all female musicians, all Hindu and Muslim musicians, or even all *gharana* or *khaandani* musicians. My aim, instead, has been twofold: to show how musicians reacted to the changes around them and to suggest that claims about musicians as a unified group speaking a common language that resisted the onslaught of theoretical musicology or new schools need to be recognized as complicated. At the very least, we have to understand the significance of the transformations I have charted in this book for musicians as well as for audiences and the national emergence of a newly Hinduized public sphere. Indeed, this chapter helps make clear precisely the role of gender, class, caste, and religion in the new world of music that emerged during the middle decades of the twentieth century.

Abdul Karim and Hirabai, both in their own way *kirana gharana* musicians, interacted with the changes in music's pedagogy and performance as father and daughter, as Muslim father and Hindu daughter, and as gendered subjects separated by a generation. Abdul Karim maneuvered his way through the thicket of musicology and Hinduization, rejected theater as immoral, and became the leading light of the *kirana gharana*. Hirabai Barodekar transformed music theater by defining herself as a Hindu, upper-caste and respectable woman. Their connection might have been severed in 1918 when Abdul Karim and Tarabai Mane's marriage came apart, but it could not ever go away completely. Her musical lineage always took her back to the *kirana gharana*, and even more important, her singing voice was clearly related to Abdul Karim's.

In Abdul Karim Khan, we see not the unscathed survival of the *gharana* system but a *gharana* musician willing to risk the ire of his community and making strategic accommodations to a changed sociological milieu. He acknowledged the presence and importance of new middle-class audiences for the future of music without sacrificing his reputation as a singer of great virtuosity. Musicology, Hinduization, and notation, as metaphors for significant changes, were not irrelevant for musicians. Musicians responded with as much corporeal anxiety to these changes as they did to the uncertainties of their professional lives, as manifested in the fears about poison, evil spirits, black magic and malevolent gods and spirits. Musicology called for an active engagement from musicians, and Abdul Karim did so. By his engagement, he can be said to have transformed *gharana*s into something new. He also refashioned himself, his performances, and his pedagogy. Hirabai, his daughter, was a product of that new *gharana* pedagogy. However, even as her life as a musician in India was recognized as genealogically connected not just to her father but the tradition that had molded him, her own emergence as a successful performer required both gendered caste respectability and a total break with her musician Muslim father.

At the start of this book, I remarked that there were dominant assumptions about Hindustani music that only a critical history could undo. One such assumption concerns the romantic conception of the performer who, by virtue of his artistic talent, transcends the irrelevant arguments made by musicologists. This claim, however important these romantic conceptions continue to be, masks the far more important changes in the domain of performance, for performers and audiences alike. In the absence of serious historical attention, an ethnomusicological claim about the performer as a subaltern subject—one who deliberately privileges practice over theory, and the body over the mind—tends to reproduce an uncomplicated assertion of this traditional romance in terms that go back to colonial languages. (James Mill, let us recall, wrote that Indians had no artists, only artisans and craftsmen.) I have used Abdul Karim to show that such claims are unsustainable for the late nineteenth and early twentieth centuries. Hindustani music itself is often held up as the one art form in modern India that survived the colonial period untouched, thereby claiming for itself a unique place in modern Indian history as a cultural artifact that has an innocent past beginning in ancient times and seamlessly blending itself into the modern period. This book has rested on the conviction that historical scrutiny puts this claim in some jeopardy.

Abdul Karim Khan shows us the adaptability of *ustad*s to the changes that were being put in place by musicologists. Indeed, the undeniable particularity—even uniqueness—of Hindustani music lies in the fact that with very few exceptions, and unlike other fields such as painting and art, the leading performers of Indian classical music are not trained in modern schools of music. They are still trained by *ustad*s, within the *gharana* system, albeit one that was refashioned in the late nineteenth and early twentieth centuries. This is undoubtedly the triumph of the *gharana*s and of the *ustad*s, and this last chapter is intended to recognize both. However, it is necessary to qualify the story of triumph and success. The audience for the refashioned *ustad*s was produced by precisely the musicologists they despised. It was an audience that asked questions that could be disparaged, such as the name of the raga, but it was an audience that was increasingly becoming a part of the musical milieu of the future. Additionally, and perhaps more importantly, an exclusive focus on the *ustad* would take away from the vital recognition that inasmuch as *ustad*s and *gharana*s refashioned themselves in response (and resistance) to the juggernaut of musicology and bhakti nationalism in music, they did so in every realm except that of women performers. Women performers in the nineteenth century were *baijis* who were taught music, often reluctantly, by court musicians. In the early years of the twentieth century, early modern *ustads* like Abdul Karim Khan taught similar women students in their schools. From court to school, the status of women performers did indeed change, as we see from Hirabai Barodekar, in that courtesans and *baijis* were replaced by respectable bourgeois performers. In colloquial Marathi terms, the suffix -*bai*, connoting disreputability, was replaced by -*tai*, which means "older sister." However, throughout the period of change, *ustads* qua *ustads* remained male. Women performers were never considered *ustads*, and what was true of the nineteenth century remained true of the twentieth. While there was a theoretical term for female *ustads*, namely *ustani*, it was never used for women performers, who were called, variously, *tai* (older sister), *shreemati* (Mrs.), or occasionally, pandit.

The abovementioned historical fact can perhaps serve to halt an unqualified celebration of the figure of the Ustad as representing the successful struggle against musicology. Women performers in modern India may still receive *taleem* from an *ustad* but are hardly considered legitimate or true heirs to an *ustadi* tradition; they are recognized as having studied with a master but never actually acquiring the same status. Women teach and learn music, but the "true" line of transmission, whether conceptualized in terms of music as the purity of heritage or as inherited property to be handed down generationally, remains male. Women entered the musical domain through and because of the contradictions of Paluskar's bhakti nationalism, because of the flawed egalitarianism of Bhatkhande's project, and because music theater revamped its fare. In this book, I have been critical of the agendas of all three. It is perhaps fitting that I end this chapter with the concomitant criticism that women's entry into the modern, public space of music did not come about because of the *ustads*, who maintain their resistance to thinking of them as musical equals. The contradictions and unintended consequences of modernizing projects, couched in terms of bhakti and religion, made it possible for women performers to be recognized as musicians.

A corollary of the above claim is that Hindustani music is one of the few truly nonreligious spaces in India wherein communal tensions are suspended. As evidence for this, the number of Hindu men and women who were students of Muslim *ustads* was repeatedly cited to me in the course of my research. In response, one might ask how many Muslim students, men and women, were students of Hindu *ustad*s in the late nineteenth century and through the twentieth? If there has been a visible and marked decline in the number of Muslim students of music in contemporary India, is there an easy answer as to why that might be so? Abdul Karim and Hirabai make easy answers difficult to offer, and at the same time, they pose a new series of questions for the mid- to late-twentieth-century history of Hindustani music, questions about *ustad*s, *gharana*s, and *khaandani* musicians, and about new ways of teaching, refashioning strategies, and additional accommodations. They also complicate, without completely abandoning, the possible meanings of the romantic idea that the present space of music in India is either genuinely traditional or, for that matter, an ideal domain of secular harmony.

⊛ CONCLUSION ⊛

A Critical History of Music: Beyond Nostalgia

and Celebration

Hirabai Barodekar, daughter of a Muslim *ustad* and granddaughter of a princely court *baiji*, was the voice of Indian classical music's future. She chose auditoriums and modern recording technology over princely courts. She gave her first public performance at Paluskar's GMV conference against the wishes of her teacher, a *gharana ustad* with whom she completed her music training. *Sangeet natak* and film appealed to her, but she was untouched by any taint of scandal. In music circles, she was known by her familial nickname, Champutai. Hirabai was sister, mother, wife, grandmother, and nationally famous musician by the end of her life. Gendered respectability, devotion, and professional music had come together in Hirabai, but in the course of becoming a performer of national repute, her parents' histories were taken over and sidelined by reformists and nationalists who sought to cleanse them from the public cultural sphere. In choosing Hirabai as the last historical figure discussed in this book, I have picked a woman performer in whose life story culminate all the different histories I have told so far.

Each chapter of this book has told a single history that has moved toward the end goal: the creation of Indian classical music and its history, pedagogy, and institutions. While the individual chapters all follow a single trajectory, the conclusions that can be drawn at the close of the book are neither singular nor straightforward. A key aspect of music's history, as shown in this book, is that unequivocal claims about its transformation do not stand the test of time. Every successful change, or conversely, every resistance to change, has been less than complete and brought with it unintended consequences.

I began this project with the assumption that there was only one story to tell of music's history: the move from "Muslim music" to "Hindu nation," aided by colonialism. Clearly there was more. By paying attention to colonial forms of knowledge about music, we see the constitutive role of colonialism and colonial religiosity in the making of music's modernity and the growing division of early "Hindu" and "Muslim" music. But while colonial forms of knowledge are undoubtedly a central part of the narrative, other histories appear constitutive as well. In particular, the central roles played by Bhatkhande and Paluskar have enabled me to take Hirabai's choices seriously without turning her history into the success story of music.

The princely state of Baroda, where Hirabai's story begins, inaugurates what might be called the "yes, but" line of historical argument of this book. Using the princely state of Baroda as an exemplary case, the first chapter showed that even though a great many *ustad*s, like Hirabai's father, mourned the loss of princely patronage and benevolent rulers, the actual situation was rather different than they remembered. Musicians were seen not as the inheritors of a classical tradition but rather as specialized servants in the employment of an early and thoroughly modernized department of entertainment. The so-called feudal court had been revamped, reconceptualized, and bureaucratized by upper-level officials in the ruler's employ in order to bolster the image of the ruler as simultaneously progressive and traditional. Music was not treated as an ancient art form, nor did it escape the reach of a modern disciplining apparatus. Along with the drive to bring under the control of the state disparate projects such as education and research, dams, wells, and plumbing, music, too, was disciplined and turned systematic. Colonial reforms, curiously, had taken hold in precisely that domain of India that, in theory, was autonomous and untouched by colonial rule.

Hirabai's history could have been easily written as a move from one category to another: from disrespectable to respectable, from feudal to modern, from Muslim to Hindu, from court to center stage, from colonial to national, from unsystematic to disciplined. However, as my discussion in chapter 2, on the cultural public sphere, demonstrates, no single historical trajectory is adequate to the task of telling the robust history of music. Furthermore, while Hirabai's story is clearly that of a talented and persistent performer who secured for herself the respectability rarely afforded to women musicians, it has also revealed the underbelly of both Bhatkhande's and Paluskar's accomplishments. Hirabai would not have been able to imagine a life as a performing musician without their contributions, but the casualties of her successful career were her *baiji* grandmother's and *ustad* father's history and genealogy, both of which had been targets of Bhatkhande's and Paluskar's reformist agendas. Yet even these casualties were not absolute. No matter how powerful the attempt to remove them, Hirabai's parents' histories remained essential for music's future, even as they were shunted to the side of its new historical narrative.

In the course of the various debates about music—its history, pedagogy, and origins—a space was created that women were able to use to enter the public cultural sphere. I recognize that the simple presence of women in large numbers cannot be sufficient to term music's history feminist, but it does call for a recognition of a newly gendered cultural public sphere. This sphere, as evidenced in early Marathi theater, music appreciation societies, and educational reform societies, was conceptualized in reaction to colonial writings on music over the course of the nineteenth century. In response, reformers and nationalists envisioned the new woman as one who was proficient in music, while they simultaneously viewed music as in need of cleansing and sacralizing so that women could perform it. Whatever the motivations of elite reformers and nationalists, once the "woman question" had entered the discourse, women were able to use it to their advantage to enter a new domain of public performance. Music, in other words, played a key role as a modernizer of Indian society at the same time that it was itself modernized.

The complex course of music's modernization was steered by Bhatkhande and Paluskar. Both men have been enormously influential in determining the direction of music's national future. Bhatkhande's influence can be seen in the next generation of scholar musicians such as S. N. Ratanjankar, Acharya Brihaspati, Thakur Jaidev Singh, and M. R. Gautam, who, in turn, were hugely influential in universities and academies, as well as in the formation of perhaps the largest modern patron of all musicians, All-India Radio. Paluskar's devotees have kept his legacy alive through the countrywide syndication of his Gandharva Mahavidyalayas, where teachers are treated (and addressed) as gurus and the sacredness of music's pedagogy is accepted as a matter of routine.

Bhatkhande and Paluskar have typically been seen in most accounts as simple exemplars of the modern and the traditional or the theoretical and the practical in music, but this too fails to hold up in the light of historical evidence. In their lives and works, constitutive contradictions loomed large. The more conservative of the two men, Paluskar, encouraged women's education, spurned elite theory, and championed the grassroots takeover of the public sphere. By contrast, music's modernist champion, Bhatkhande, scorned such easy democratic measures, instituting instead a rigorous and impossible pedagogy, railing against Muslims in his many texts. While both their politics lay squarely within the modal mainstream of Indian cultural politics, the differences between them, particularly as they relate to gender, religion, and nationalism, have been much more significant.

Paluskar's Hindu nationalist agenda was transparent, unabashed, and straightforward. Bhatkhande, on the other hand, was much more complex and contradictory. Paluskar's triumph was to sweep the stage clean of its previous association with the debauchery of the princely court, to sacralize music, and to elevate the role of women as teachers of music. Because of his particular version of populist bhakti nationalism, music became respectable, and many more women than before were able to claim it as a professional performance space. Music's teachers became modern incarnations of ancient gurus. However, the sacralization of the musical milieu had serious consequences. Even though Hindu middle-class women were able to enter the professional field of music, Paluskar's conviction that there was an inextricable link between Hindu religiosity and music has been used directly to attack the authority of *gharana ustads,* and more generally to claim that all that is good in Indian culture is necessarily ancient Hindu rather than recent Muslim.

In contrast to Paluskar, Bhatkhande did not champion women musicians and believed music and religion needed to stay separate. Bhatkhande's musicology, typology, and pedagogical publications gave Indian music its classical history. His interest lay in creating a national academy for music that would be open to all—an academy both transparent and scholarly. His achievement was to create for India a bona fide national classical music, with historical pedigree, theoretical complexity, and a system of notation. These efforts paved the way, as well, for the creation of a knowledgeable audience for future performances of classical music. However, the cost of his success was the erasure of the individual contributions of performers, most of whom were Muslim.

Of the two men, Bhatkhande was a historical figure of greater complexity. While it is fashionable to dismiss the liberal secularism represented by a figure such as Bhatkhande, I have argued that there is much to recuperate in his complicated if sometimes troubling vision. While I have tried to lay bare his liberal conceits along with his considerable problems, I have tried as well to emphasize that the contradictions of his vision allow us to imagine a different kind of cultural modernity for contemporary India.

Bhatkhande's volumes of *Hindustani Sangeet Padhati* reveal his arrogance. They also, however, contain an extraordinarily wide-ranging discussion of music and its history. While scathing about women performers and *gharana* musicians, his criticism was made on the grounds of lack of order and transparency rather than gender and religion per se. Bhatkhande's signal contribution was to force musicians into a new conversation with him even when they might have done so only to scoff at his obsession with notation and typology. If musicians wished to expose Bhatkhande's ignorance about musical matters, or show the discrepancies in his system of ten *thaat*s, they still had to argue in his new musicological terms. Paradoxically, even though Bhatkhande's project altered the terms of music's discourse in unabashedly modern, disciplined, orderly, and systematic ways, it was ultimately less colonially derived and sectarian than Paluskar's bhakti nationalist agenda.

The flip side of the national project represented by Bhatkhande and Paluskar is the resistance to it by the *ustad*s. Once again, this acknowledgment of *ustadi* resilience in withstanding both Paluskar's bhakti nationalism and Bhatkhande's musicology is tempered by the recognition of the limits of their imaginations. The institutional reforms implemented by the two men of music were vastly successful, but when the modernizing dust had settled, *gharana ustad*s were still very much around. Well into the present day, with a few exceptions, most famous musicians are trained not in schools and colleges but within the purview of a differently "modern," somewhat diminished, but by no means extinct *gharana* protocol. Exceptional students easily complete their formal institutional schooling in music only to gravitate to a *gharana ustad* for their upper-level, professional training. However, even as the *gharana* system refashioned itself to accommodate the demands placed on musicians by a lay musical student population that was growing in leaps and bounds, it rarely admitted women into its upper ranks. No women musicians, however talented or virtuoso, were accepted as *ustad*s. The paradoxical triumph for women is that they could aspire to the status of a sacralized Hindu, male, and Brahminic guru, but never to that of an *ustad*.

From princely courts to modern auditoriums, this book has traversed the history of music's transformation in terms that might succinctly be labeled as "*bai* to *tai*"—from Hirabai's *baiji* grandmother to her own nickname within the music world, Champu*tai*. Hirabai's career also marks the beginning of a transition in Maharashtra most noticeable in the decade immediately following Indian independence from British rule, when upper-caste Hindu women increasingly dislodged an earlier generation of *baiji*s. Anjanibai Malpekar, Kesarbai Kerkar, Mogubai Kurdikar, Menakabai Shirodkar, and Gangubai Hangal, to name a few, were gradually replaced by Padmavati Shaligram, Ashwini Bhide, and Veena Sahasrabuddhe. While Hirabai's choices have guided the chapters of this book, a detailed examination of the politics of those choices and those of the later period of transition are beyond the historical scope of this book.

This book has focused neither on performers nor on contemporary performances of classical music. However, this examination of two men and music has nevertheless sought to offer a historical perspective on the quotidian, layered world(s) of contemporary Indian classical music. Classical music performances in modern India can be large spectacles staged in large auditoriums, smaller spectacles in rented halls, or small and informal *baithak*s held in the living rooms of connoisseurs. I began by noting that it was not easy to compare the development of Indian classical music with the history of Western classical music because of the absence of easy separations between the secular and the sacred in the former. In contemporary Indian classical music performances, the milieu is hybrid: it is neither entirely religious nor genuinely secular. The stage, depending on the performer, is often decorated with the accoutrements of Hindu ritualism, such as incense holders, marigold garlands, and oil lamps. Many members of the audience will have learned music somewhere in the course of their lives, using either Bhatkhande's or Paluskar's method. It may not be an audience of connoisseurs, but it will be a knowledgeable one. Conversations take place in both Marathi and English, and the typical dress code for such performances is not suits and ties but *kurta pajama*s (loose drawstring pants worn with a long shirt).

Without the historical perspective provided by this book, the milieu at the performance could lead to the easy conclusion that syncretism and secularism had weathered both colonial influence and the more recent Hindu nationalist storm. I had myself initially assumed that in the space of music, irrespective of the larger politics of Maharashtra, which include the RSS and the Shiv Sena, there was a marked absence of sectarian and religious tension. By putting Bhatkhande and Paluskar at the center of this book, however, a more complicated history has emerged, and it has been impossible to avoid a certain ambivalence when analyzing and evaluating the dichotomous historical categories that govern music's history.

That being said, my primary target of criticism has been the Marathi middle class, which has comfortably incorporated a Brahminic culture of sacrality, piety, and ritual into everyday life. At the same time, even within this culture, an ambivalent fear of and fascination with Muslims continues to exert influence. At the risk of generalization well beyond the scope of this book, I would suggest that this attitude is not unique to Maharashtra, but common to the Indian bourgeoisie from Bengal to Maharashtra, Tamil Nadu to Punjab.

I would further argue that this regional history has, for a variety of reasons, had especially important national implications. There were other modernizers in other parts of India, most notably Rabindranath Tagore in Bengal. But while the history I have told here has for the most part concerned people and institutions from the Deccan region, part of which became Maharashtra in independent India, it is not without significance that I began this history in Baroda, and when treating both Paluskar and Bhatkhande, I found myself writing about Lahore, Lucknow, and other important locales in northern India. It may be all too easy to dismiss the politics of figures such as Bhatkhande and Paluskar as specific to modern Maharashtra, but in fact, I have been able to show that their relationship to Maharashtra predicated their extraordinary influence on vast regions of northern India. This is hardly to celebrate regional exceptionalism; indeed, that is precisely a historical tendency I would decry. But given that discussions of the role of Bhatkhande and Paluskar have sometimes elicited statements such as, "this could never have happened in Calcutta—we don't have communalism like you do in Maharashtra," or "things are totally different in Madras (or Calcutta or Delhi)," I need to end with one final disclaimer. While I unapologetically target Marathi chauvinism, I do so in the hope that it will not simply provide an alibi for other regional exceptionalisms. While some Marathi chauvinists might read this history as about the salience of Maharashtra over other regions, I have tried more simply to show how the accomplishments of this region cannot be separated from the special burden it must shoulder for the prejudicial self-satisfaction it uses to wave aside its own important role in the communalization and politicization of the cultural public sphere. To do so, I believe, ideological critique is as necessary as affirmation. I intend this book to be a first step in that direction.

❈ NOTES ❈

Introduction

1. I have offered here the simplest possible description of *khayal*. It is also an improvisational form. For a detailed musicological description of the genre, see chapter 1 in Bonnie Wade, *Khyal: Creativity within North India's Classical Music Tradition* (Cambridge, 1985).

2. M. V. Dhond disputes such a claim, arguing that it was popular in Maharashtra in less elite circles than princely courts for well over a century before Balkrishnabua Ichalkaranjikar made it popular among the upper castes. Dhond has by far the best historical treatment of the evolution of *khayal*, in which he makes the case that both Hindu and Muslim musicians nourished it as a form of music as early as the thirteenth century against opposition from their respective orthodoxies. Dhond also gives us some interesting arguments about the form flourishing, not because of its origins, but because Muslim musicians who were more secular about their music addressed their singing to the audience, as opposed to Hindu musicians who sought constantly to propitiate the divine through their music. He wrote that "the music of the Muslim musician is free and exuberant, while that of the Hindu is rigid and inhibited. . . . Most of the Hindu classical singers are Brahmins brought up in the traditions of Haridasa and hence their performance smells of camphor and aloe. The Hindu musician usually concludes his performance with a devotional song, while the Muslim does it with a *thumri*

or a *gazal*" (20). Dhond skewers the inaccurate claims about the origins of *khayal* made by a number of authors, arguing instead that even though it is likely that *khayal* is as old a form as *dhrupad* and, thereby, "Hindu" in origin, he makes very little of origins. Indeed, wherever one is posited, he pries it loose in a manner that suggests it is altogether irrelevant when and where *khayal* originated. See M. V. Dhond, *The Evolution of Khyal* (New Delhi, 1982).

3. For an important work that views *gharana*s as artisanal guilds, see Tirthankar Roy, "Music as Artisan Tradition," *Contribution to Indian Sociology* 32.1 (1998): 131–63.

4. I am grateful to Partho Datta for pointing this out to me.

5. As few examples of a very large body of writing in English on music, see Vinay Aggarwal, *Traditions and Trends in Indian Music* (Meerut, 1966); Vamanrao Deshpande, *Maharashtra's Contribution to Music* (New Delhi, 1972); B. V. Keskar, *Indian Music: Problems and Prospects* (Bombay, 1967); Swami Prajnananda's two-volume *Historical Development of Indian Music* (Calcutta, 1960 and 1965); Ravi Shankar, *My Music, My Life* (New Delhi, 1968); and B. C. Deva, *Indian Music* (New Delhi, 1979).

6. See William Jones, *On the Musical Modes of the Hindus* (Calcutta, 1789), 15.

7. Ibid., 17.

8. Ibid., 25.

9. Ibid., 25.

10. See Thomas R. Trautmann's *Aryans and British India* (Berkeley, Calif., 1997), in particular, chapter 2, in which Jones's biblical interests are particularly well described and analyzed in relation to linguistics, chronology, and etymology.

11. Jones, *On the Musical Modes of the Hindus*, 6.

12. See E. P. Thompson's *Making of the English Working Class* (New York, 1966), 12.

13. Of course, there are also several critiques of the assumption of an undifferentiated "West," the easy assumption of an evolution from folk to classical. See note 19 for some of the challenges to the dominant historical narrative.

14. See Talal Asad's *Genealogies of Religion: Discipline and Reasons of Power in Christianity and Islam* (Baltimore, 1993). For works that follow in Asad's footsteps in the context of India, see Peter van der Veer, *Religious Nationalism: Hindus and Muslims in India* (Berkeley, Calif., 1994), and *Imperial Encounters: Religion and Modernity in India and Britain* (Princeton, N.J., 2001). See also Gauri Viswanathan, *Outside the Fold: Conversion, Modernity, and Belief* (Princeton, N.J., 1999).

15. See Stuart Isacoff's *Temperament: The Idea That Solved Music's Greatest Riddle*, (New York, 2001).

16. As just a few examples of ethnomusicological work on South Asia, see Wade,

Khyal; Peter Manuel, *Thumri in Historical and Stylistic Perspective* (New Delhi,1989); James Kippen, *The Tabla of Lucknow: A Cultural Analysis of a Musical Tradition* (Cambridge, 1988); Regula Qureshi, *Sufi Music of India and Pakistan: Sound, Context and Meaning in Qawwali* (Chicago, 1995), and *Music and Marx: Ideas, Practice, Politics* (New York, 2002); Daniel Neuman, *The Life of Music in North India: The Organization of an Artistic Tradition* (Detroit, 1980); Peter Manuel, *Cassette Culture: Popular Music and Technology in North India* (Chicago, 1993). This is by no means a comprehensive list, but this group of writers has greatly aided the study of contemporary music in India, and I wish here to acknowledge the contributions of these prominent ethnomusicological scholars since I build on their work.

17. I am grateful to Peter Manuel for pointing this out to me and for tempering my overly critical tone in general.

18. See Sharatchandra Gokhale's historical essay on music in Maharashtra in *Vishrabdha Sharada*, vol. 2 (in Marathi; Bombay, 1975), 144–70; and Ashok Ranade, *Hindustani Music* (New Delhi, 1997).

19. In particular, see Lakshmi Subramanian's superb articles, "The Reinvention of a Tradition: Nationalism, Carnatic Music, and the Madras Music Academy, 1900–1947," *IESHR* 36.2 (1999): 131–63, and "The Master, Muse, and the Nation: The New Cultural Project and the Reification of Colonial Modernity in India," *South Asia* 23.2 (2000): 1–32. Also see her forthcoming book, *From the Tanjore Court to the Madras Academy: Essays in the Making of a Classical Tradition*. On a similar subject with rather a different theoretical take, see Amanda Weidman, *Questions of Voice: On the Subject of "Classical" Music in South India*, forthcoming from Duke University Press.

20. Gerry Farrell, *Indian Music and the West* (Oxford, 1997).

21. See Rajeev Bhargava, *Secularism and Its Critics* (New Delhi, 1998), for reprints of articles that outline the debate. In particular, see Ashis Nandy, "The Politics of Secularism and the Recovery of Religious Tolerance," and T. N. Madan, "Secularism in Its Place." For a look at constitutionalist debates about secularism, see Upendra Baxi and Bhikhu Parekh, eds., *Crisis and Change in Contemporary India* (New Delhi, 1995). See Partha Chatterjee, "Secularism and Toleration," *Economic and Political Weekly* 29, 28 (1994): 1768–77, for a historicist view of secularism in the context of the nation-state.

22. Unpublished keynote address at the Conference on South Asian Studies, Madison, Wisconsin, 2001, soon to be published in revised form as the first of three Schoff Lectures by Columbia University Press.

23. I have drawn here from Gyan Prakash, *Another Reason: Science and the Imagination of Modern India* (Princeton, N.J., 1999).

1. See *Huzur Hukumaanchi Nond, HHNh/7/1896–97*, Indumati Palace Library and Archive, Baroda. These were confidential published compilations of Sayajirao Gaekwad's royal orders, compiled by year, although the actual orders are not recorded in a consistent manner. All orders were signed and presented to the ruler by the Khaangi Karbhaari, and in most cases, countersigned by the ruler to signify his acceptance of the order. All translations from the Marathi are mine.

2. Fatesinghrao Gaekwad, *Sayajirao of Baroda: The Prince and the Man* (Bombay, 1989, x).

3. Ibid., 291.

4. My short history of the Gaekwad family is taken from Rao Bahadur Govindbhai H. Desai and A. B. Clarke, *Gazetteer of the Baroda State*, vol. 1, *General Information*, 421–621 (Bombay, 1923), and Gaekwad, *Sayajirao of Baroda*, 1–45.

5. The colonial government appointed Khanderrao's brother, Malharrao, to the throne. Jamnabai moved to Poona where she plotted to kill Malharrao, and in 1874, after four stormy years, the British deposed him and invited her to return to Baroda.

6. Desai and Clarke, *Gazetteer of the Baroda State*, 610.

7. For a detailed critical examination of the relationship between the colonial government, the native ruler, and the Brahmins at court, see Nicholas Dirks, *The Hollow Crown: An Ethnohistory of a Princely Kingdom* (Cambridge, 1987).

8. See Desai and Clarke, *Gazetteer of the Baroda State*, 597.

9. Because of his commitment to such endeavors, he was a favorite of the British government. He began his career in the princely state of Travancore, where he stayed for fourteen years. In 1873, he became *dewan* of Indore and moved to Baroda in 1875.

10. See Gaekwad, *Sayajirao of Baroda*, 66.

11. *Kalavant Khatyache Niyam* (in Marathi; Baroda, 1899), hereafter *KKN*, Indumati Mahal Library and Archive, Baroda. All translations are mine.

12. The author of the *Niyam* is unnamed. I am assuming one or more *khaangi karbhaari*s collaborated to write the rules and the history.

13. *KKN*, 3. This rule was first stated in the *Niyam* of 1899 and reiterated in 1925.

14. See Gaekwad, *Sayajirao of Baroda*, 133, 333.

15. Ibid., 133.

16. See the preface (*prastaavana*) in the *Kalavant Khatyachya Antar vyavasthe sambandhi Niyam* (in Marathi; Baroda, 1925), hereafter *KKASN*, 1–11. Raosaheb Parab, the *khangi karbhaari* in 1924, and author of the subsequent *Niyam* published in 1925, identified this act as the founding of the khaata. All translations are mine.

17. In Marathi, the term *khaata* can be used interchangeably to mean "accounts" or "department." The term *karkhaana* can mean "warehouse" or "workshop."

18. Women entertainers were paid around Rs. 200 per month, while male singers earned a little less, Rs. 185.

19. In 1824, a *dakshini* troupe was permanently retained at the court, and in 1825, two singing girls, two *pakhawaj* players, three male singers, and four instrumentalists (*holaar*) were added to the roster. A *ghaadigavai* in the Gaekwad court was also known as *Hindubhaat*. The latter term *bhaat* was used as a caste marker of those singers who primarily sang couplets in praise of royalty. *Ghaadi gavai*s were Hindu, and Muslim singers who performed similar music were called *kadkatvale*. See the preface to *KKASN*, 3.

20. *Lalitacha tamasha* is literally the performance on the last day of an auspicious festival called *Shivaratri*. The mimes were called *bhaand*s, and they specialized in mimicking animal sounds.

21. The *khaata* added a *sarod*, sitar, *sarangi*, *pyaala*, and *tasha* player, two more mimes, and a *Carnataki dashavataari natak*.

22. Khanderrao Gaekwad (1857–1870), the ruler noted earlier for his financial extravagance and support of the British during the Rebellion of 1857, reduced the numbers of entertainers significantly. Not being a patron of music any more than his predecessor, he cut down the number of singers, added a dance instructor, and retained only one permanent mime troupe on a monthly salary of Rs. 250. However, five years after the Rebellion, in 1862, the *khaata* swelled again in size. Once again southern troupes and mime troupes earned as much as Rs. 600 and 400, respectively; 23 *gavai*s (male singers) were recorded as permanent employees, and salaries for both male and female singers and dancers jumped to Rs. 200 individually.

23. Mimes received Rs. 700, and the troupes received Rs. 475, while female singers earned Rs. 225 and male singers earned Rs. 150.

24. In the *Niyam* published in 1925 (3), this depriviileging is explained as a result of the newness of the *khaata*. The author goes on to write that Ganpatrao was particularly fond of southern troupes and that Malharrao liked *tamasha*s.

25. Salaries for male singers ranged from Rs. 20 to 185 in Sayajirao I's reign, Rs. 10 to 150 in Ganpatrao's reign, Rs. 5 to 200 in Khanderrao's reign, Rs. 5 to 100 in Malharrao's reign, and by 1925, from Rs. 50 to 150 in Sayajirao Gaekwad III's reign. I have taken these figures from the table related to salaries in the preface to the *KKASN*, 4.

26. Female singers (*gaanarni*) and dancers (*kalavantini*) earned between Rs. 250 and 430. See note 57.

27. *KKN*, 3.

28. In 1843, the total expense was Rs. 38,913. They had risen to Rs. 58,599 in

1873, during the heyday period, and skyrocketed in Khanderrao's period to Rs. 93,026.

29. The allotted budget by 1924 was Rs. 32,956, less than what it was in 1843. All figures taken from the table of salaries in the *KKASN*, 1–11.

30. *HHN*/29/1882–83.

31. See *HHN*/60/1888–89, 69. In this order, Sayajirao ruled that the older of the two girls who danced at the court be paid Rs. 30 per month, and the younger receive Rs. 15. Of these two girls, one of them, Chandra, was deemed suitable to be hired in the *kalavant khaata*. See *HHN*/64/64, 1892–93, for a continuation of the earlier order. .

32. In *HHN*/51/1888–89, a dancing girl named Shardamba was brought to Baroda by one of Sayajirao's employees, Atmaram Jadhav. The description of her performance at the court reads: "Even though she is not as trained as she should be there is talent, and so she is kept on at the monthly salary of Rs. 50, which will be increased if her performance improves." The date of the approved order was July 15, 1888.

33. "When the *khaangi karbhaari* or any other officer has to ascertain my inclination only, he cannot interpret it as a distinct order given; but may on his responsibility decide the case and not count upon the bare wish expressed as a distinct order. In matters which are purely those of *khushi*, where the question is one of retaining or not retaining a person in service and not of reducing him because of a fault he has committed, this ascertaining of a wish may do; but where one's interests are likely to be affected the matter must be formally submitted for orders" (*HHN*/238/492, 1889–90, 225). The request was made in Marathi, but Sayajirao in this case responded in English. For the original order about retaining Shardamba, see note 52.

34. These troupes received between Rs. 250–300 as *bakshees*. See *HHN* 55/56, 1888–89, 65–66.

35. See *HHN*/153/141, 1892–93, 251–53. I have substituted "I" in place of the royal "We" used by Sayajirao in the Marathi original. See also *HHN*/41/226, 89–90, in which such grading was used but the remuneration was deemed inadequate for the performance of the Bharat Natak Company in 1895.

36. See *HHN*/31/189, 62–64, 1895–96. A seven-member troupe from Tanjavur, for instance, was employed at the court on a six-month probationary period, and each member of the troupe earned Rs. 30, bringing the overall expenses for the entire troupe to no more than Rs. 210. *HHN*/18/271, 1889–90, 13. Two other *natak* companies, a Gujarati company and one from Kolhapur, earned Rs. 325 each, and a magic show received Rs. 200. *HHN*/120/375, 1889–90, 95, and *HHN*/122/377, 1889–90, 97. Such shows were fairly routinely performed, and the payments ranged between Rs. 200 and 500. A *natak* company from Umrath per-

formed three shows, for which the details of their expenditure was reported as Rs. 100 for the actors, Rs. 150 for the "goods," Rs. 60 to rent a bullock cart, Rs. 100 for meals, Rs. 125 miscellaneous. Sayajirao authorized Pestonjee Dorabjee to pay Rs. 500 for each of the performances, and an additional Rs. 500 as *bakshees*, bringing the total remuneration to Rs. 2,000 (*HHN*/228/482, 1889–90, 169–70). Pestonji Dorabjee was also ordered to write his requests using Marathi and not transliterated English.

37. Ghulam Rasool valde Mohammed, a singer from the *khaata* in the first category, earning a monthly salary of Rs. 100, died in May 1884. Since then his slot had been empty, and because Ghulam Rasool had been a servant of the court for many years, Sayajirao ordered that his slot be given to his son, but in order not to let him believe that the slot was his by right of succession, he was paid only Rs. 50 per month and a condition was attached to his employment. *HHN*/3/1884–85.

38. *HHN*/91/606, 1887–88,127–30.

39. *HHN*/94/620, 1887–88, 132–34.

40. *HHN*/94/620, 1887–88, 132–34.

41. See, for instance, *HHN*/263/517, 1890–91, 254, in which Sayajirao orders that vacant slots should often be maintained as such, so as to save money to perhaps hire more theater troupes!

42. In 1891, on November 17, a theater troupe, the Kanakeshwar Prasadik Hindu Stree Natak Mandali, performed *Othello* for the court. They waited for around three weeks without performing again or receiving payment before leaving; their due payment of Rs. 300 was sent to them many months later. See *HHN*/78/82, 1891–92. Theater troupes and singers often left without receiving their due, preferring to move on to another court where perhaps another ruler might pay them sooner. Some years later, three singers from Meraj, Jaipur, and Delhi were owed between Rs. 130 and 150 each but were not paid immediately following their performance at Makarpura palace; Sayajirao sharply reprimanded his staff to ensure that such laxity in matters of money not be repeated. See *HHN*/30/163, 1896–97, 50.

43. Sayajirao Gaekwad authorized the publication and filing of each one of his orders (*huzurhukumnamah*). Requests were made to him either directly or through a senior official, the *khaangi karbhaari*, or his secretary, and he ruled on each request. The requests were made most often in Marathi, occasionally in Gujarati, and very rarely in English. The rulings on each petition were classified by department—personal, military, financial—and compiled by the year in which the decisions were handed down and published in several confidential volumes. The compilation was entitled *Khangi Khatya Sambandhi Huzurche Hukumanchi Nond* (Compilation of Orders relating to the Personal Department).

44. This happened with a singer from the *khaata* in the second category, Kadam Husein valde Ghulam Husein, whose monthly salary was Rs. 100. In September 1882 he went on leave, ostensibly for a year. Two years later he had not returned. He was therefore considered dismissed and in his place, Imadan Husaid valde Mehboob Khan was to be employed, whose singing Sayajirao found acceptable. His salary at appointment on September 1, 1884, was Rs. 75, with a supplement of Rs. 25 to maintain a horse for his transportation. *HHN*/2, 1884–85.

45. See *HHN*/291/545(a), 1890–91.

46. See *HHN*/52/297,1895–96, 101–2.

47. See report of the second Gandharva Mahavidyalaya Sangeet Parishad (in Marathi), 21, located at Akhil Bharatiya Gandharva Mahavidyalaya Mandal, Vashi, Bombay. My translation.

48. Sayajirao's wife, Maharani Chimnabai, had six vehicles at her disposal and had authorized the use of one of them to Mangmabai, but Sayajirao viewed the singer as having abused her privilege and ordered that she be fined. Her travel allowance for the year was Rs. 20. She was fined Rs. 20 for one instance of use of the *sarkaari gaadi*, which would have meant that for the rest of the year she would have to use her salary for travel. See *HHN*/31/169, 1896–97.

49. Balkrishnabua Kapileshwari, *Abdul Karim Khan yaanche jeevan charitra* (in Marathi; Bombay, 1972). See section on Baroda, 155–91, for a description of his life while at Baroda.

50. See, for instance, Dipali Nag's *Faiyaz Khan* (New Delhi, 1985), 15–25. See also report of the second Gandharva Mahavidyalaya Sangeet Parishad, 21, in which Balkrishnabua Ichalkaranjikar, court musician at Meraj, is reported as having remembered when musicians were brought to the court on the backs of elephants.

51. See *KKN*, 29, 30, 31. The form required the singer to sign off on a list of conditions promising to not repeat what he or she had sung before, to sing for the number of hours agreed upon at a time, not sing anything the ruler did not wish him or her to sing, and to declare that his or her services were completely at the disposal of the ruler and that all rules would be abided by, including compliance with being sent elsewhere. The singer also had to agree that noncompliance would elicit immediate dismissal, or at the very least a cut in pay.

52. See *KKN*, sec. 3, "Examinations and Procedures," 24–26.

53. Male dancers (called *nachya porya*) who performed in the *tamasha*s had to be between twelve and twenty years of age, and the dancing girls between fifteen and thirty. There is an entire section of the *KKN* devoted to the rules and regulations for performers during the Holi season and for those belonging to one of the theater troupes; see page 28. In order to perform in the court, particularly on festive occasions such as the *Navratri Garba*, yearly auditions/examinations were held, with the numbers of performers to be hired and the salary scale determined in

advance. See *HHN*/169, 1907–8, for the actual order, and *KKN*, 33, for the salary specifications, which ranged from Rs. 100 for female singers to Rs. 40 for the *tamasha* troupe.

54. See *HHN*/15/14/1899.

55. Balkrishnabua Kapileshwari noted that Abdul Karim Khan, while at Baroda, objected to the rule that he had to report to duty every day. Abdul Karim apparently told the superintendent that he felt disrespected as a singer by having to behave like a menial servant (72–73). Singers disliked this rule, believing it demeaned them.

56. See *KKN*, section on the composition of the *khaata,* called *khatyachi rachana,* that provides job descriptions for each of the four categories of entertainers, 6–10.

57. Entertainers were required to sign next to their names on a form that documented for official purposes that they had picked up the uniforms to be worn at a particular performance on a given day and that they were willing to perform their jobs without complaint (*KKN*, 12).

58. See *KKN*, 13–18, in particular rule 8, tip #1: "If it is so ordered by the ruler that these people have to go perform somewhere, they must do so without complaint."

59. I have summarized and translated section II of the *KKN*, "The Duties of the Superintendent," 11–14.

60. See *HHN*/112/209, 1902. Appasaheb Mohite, *khaangi karbhaari,* wrote that "in order that singers and singing girls who are desirous of improving their skills by associating with others should receive the opportunity to do so, Shrimant Sarkar Maharaj Saheb has magnanimously declared that when he is out of town they too, if they desire, engage in travel."

61. See *KKASN*, 6.

62. "1) While the ruler was taking his *mangal snaana* [auspicious bath] the various instrumentalists were to wait in readiness. 2) If the royal heir, Pratap Singh Raje, who was also to take a *mangal snaan,* asked for the musicians, they were to be sent as soon as it was convenient for the maharaja. 3) While the *pujas* [worship rituals] were in progress the instrumentalists were to wait in readiness at the Indumati Mahal." To facilitate the correct conducting of these rites the *kalavant*s were ordered to remain in waiting at some specified location, ready to perform at a minute's notice. As the rule book specified: "For the ceremonial lunch, either an Indian Orchestra or a collection of instrumentalists was to be prepared to play . . . and after the ceremonial lunch, during the distribution of betel leaves and betel nuts, one female singer would have a *baithak* (seated performance.)" *Puravani Aine Rajmajal, Prakaran 2, Varshapratipada Gudhicha Padva,* 1919–20 (in Marathi), the Indumati Mahal Palace Library and Archive, 104–5. My transla-

tion. The last stipulation calls attention to the fact that at the culmination of an auspicious event a woman singer was asked to perform, not a man. Gender in this royal court was being linked to religion through the regulation of ritual.

63. In 1922, a booklet of rules for the proper conducting of the *Chaitragouri Halad kunku*—a ritual worship (*puja*) performed by women—proposed similar rules for the *kalavants*. Musicians and other entertainers were present for one main reason: to augment the royal family's participation in a religious ritual. "On the day of the *halad kunku* before the *darbar* fills up with people, the dancing girls should be ready to perform for one half hour with all accompaniments next to the *darbari diwankhaana* and 2) As soon as the *darbar* starts to fill, the performance should begin and should cease as soon as the darbar is full. 3) Everyone is to obey orders without any complaint." *Puravani Aine Rajmahal, Prakaran 5, Chaitragouri Haladkunku*, 1922–23, the Indumati Mahal Palace Library and Archive, Baroda, 351. In 1924, in the rule book for a *puja* called *Vatsavitri Pujan*, also performed only by women, members of the *kalavant karkhaana* were so instructed: "During the *puja*, one singer and one tabla player should be on attendance at the west veranda of the *devghar* (temple). At closer proximity the assigned instrumentalists should wait in preparation to accompany the *aarti* [singing/chanting]." *Puravani Aine Rajmahal, Prakaran 8, Vatsavitripujan*, 1924–25, Indumati Palace Library and Archive, Baroda, 412–13.

64. See *HHN*/64/63, 1890–91.

65. See *HHN*/172/1969, 1912–13. Faiyaz Khan's brother, Tassaduq Hussain Khan, who was also appointed at the court, received a monthly salary of much less—Rs. 45—and no travel allowance.

66. See *HHN*/120, 1913–14.

67. Very few orders were written in English, but from this one, Sayajirao's tone and sentiment toward his collection of artists can be discerned. "(1) His Highness the Maharaja Saheb heard singers and players upon musical instruments this afternoon and has been pleased to order that Inayet Husen Fazle Husen [*sic*] be promoted by Rs. 6 (six) and Alamgir Alladin Khan be given an extension for one year and Sakharam Pralhad be degraded by Rs. 5 (five) if he does not show improvement in a month. (2) Gulam Mahamad Gulam Rasul, whose pay is Rs. 40, should be told that he did not sing as well as he should. If he does not improve, his pay may be reduced." The order goes on to state that musicians should purchase their own instruments and cover their minor contingent expenses, and "the object of making this alteration is to reduce unnecessary accounts and to prevent senseless distribution of work and responsibility." See *HHN*/224, 1909–10, 44–45.

68. Dipali Nag has a chapter in her book on Faiyaz Khan about his life in Baroda. I have taken her anecdotes as exemplary of a certain style of writing about music and musicians. See in particular 30–34.

69. Ibid., 32.

70. Ibid., 30–32.

71. See the 1925 *KKN*, 7. In 1907, when the rules were reconsidered, Sayajirao had made this recommendation. There was, interestingly, a debate in Bengal in the mid-1850s when the popular singers were condemned for singing while standing. The "proper" classical form, imputed from northern India, was to sit. I am grateful to Partha Chatterjee for giving me this information.

72. Gaekwad, *Sayajirao of Baroda*, 291.

73. Every now and then Sayajirao, too, could be capricious and unpredictable. A Professor Michle was found wanting in his performance, and even though it had been agreed that he would receive Rs. 250, Sayajirao ordered that since his performance was not satisfactory it deserved no remuneration. See *HHN*/13/17, 1898–99 and 1899–1900.

74. Kapileshwari, *Abdul Karim Kham*, 135–37.

75. See *Biography of Pir-o-Murshid Inayat Khan*, (East/West Publications, 1979), 26.

76. See Inayatkhan Rahimat Khan Pathan, *Inayat Geet Ratnavali* (in Marathi/Gujarati, Baroda, 1903). There is little information about Maula Baksh in primary sources. However, there are a few biographical articles about him in Gujarati and the odd one in Marathi, while a biography of his grandson gives us some information about Maula Baksh. There is a biography of Maula Baksh written by his student Ganpati Gopal Barwe, but I was unable to locate it in either Bombay or Baroda.

77. I have compiled biographical information about Maula Baksh from the following sources: *Biography of Pir-o-Murshid Inayat Khan*, 19–26; Sharatchandra Gokhale's "Payache dagad," *Shabdashri*, 82, Diwali issue: 56–63; Shaila Datar's biography of Bhaskarbua Bakhle, *Devagandharva* (Pune, 1995); and Shri Madhusudan Manilal Thakkar, "Sangeet Kshetrama Pro. Maulabakshni Sadhna ane Pradhan," (in Gujarati), from the Souvenir of the Seventieth Anniversary College of Indian Music, Dance and Dramatics, Baroda 1886–1956, Gujarati Section, Baroda, 107–113. I have also crosschecked dates and events, as far as possible, against the official princely court documents such as the *huzurhukumnamah*s and the *kalavant khatyache niyam*.

78. Kapileshwari, *Abdul Karim Khan*, 101.

79. *Biography of Pir-o-Murshid Inayat Khan*, 22. The author, Maula Baksh's grandfather, narrated incidents where Maula Baksh had to cope with Brahmin prejudice against teaching "classical" art to a non-Brahmin, which he coped with by being persistent and diligent, eventually winning over his teacher's affections.

80. No biographer offers dates for these arrivals and departures, so the early history is difficult to pin down.

81. Sharatchandra Gokhale claimed that Maula Baksh was examined in music by

Faiz Mohammed Khan, but Shaila Datar writes that Faiz Mohammed Khan was appointed in 1875, five years *after* Maula Baksh's appointment (*Devagandharva*, 30). Since Datar's work is a fictionalized account based on some primary source research, it is relatively reliable, except that in order to augment the narrative the author has attempted to turn it into a readable story rather than a historical account, and in places the dates are completely inaccurate. What sets Datar's book apart from almost all other Marathi accounts is the detailed list of sources, replete with complete bibliographical details.

82. Both Datar and Gokhale are in agreement about the date of publication of the magazine, which is further corroborated in the preface to Maula Baksh's first pedagogical publication in Gujarati, *Sangitanubhav* (Baroda, 1888). This publication is written in Gujarati but the script is Devanagari.

83. See Thakkar, "Sangeet Kshetrama Pro." In the four years of Malharrao's reign there were two successive residents, Colonel J. T. Barr (1866–73) and Colonel Robert Phayre (1873–74), followed by two specially appointed commissioners and agents to the governor general, Colonel Sir Lewis Pelly (November 1874–April 1875) and Sir Richard Meade (appointed in May 1875). See Gaekwad, *Sayajirao of Baroda*, 31–41. Maula Baksh probably learned what he did from either Barr or Phayre, since Pelly and Meade had been appointed to look into the matter of deposing Malharrao.

84. See Thakkar, "Sangeet Kshetrama Pro."

85. See Annual Report on the Administration of the Baroda State for 1885 and 1886, Indumati Palace Library, Baroda, 118.

86. See, for instance, Chinnaswamy Mudaliar's *Indian Music along the Lines of European Notation* (Madras, 1881); Pramod Kumar Tagore, *First Thoughts on Indian Music, or Twenty Indian Melodies Composed for the Pianoforte* (Calcutta, 1883); Sourindro Mohun Tagore, *The Musical Scales of the Hindus with Remarks on the Applicability of Harmony to Hindu Music* (Calcutta, 1884); and Purshottam Ganesh (Anna) Gharpure and V. M. Herlekar, *Studies in Indian Music* (Bombay, 1889). See also H. Krishna Rao, *First Steps in Hindu Music in English Notation* (London, 1906).

87. See Annual Report of the Vernacular Educational Department, Baroda State (Sayajirao Gaekwad University Library, Baroda), for the Year 1896–1897, in which a brief history of Maula Baksh's school is given.

88. See Kapileshwari, *Abdul Karim Khan*, 72–76.

89. Annual Report of the Baroda State, 1885–1886, 119.

90. Forty-two of these students took exams in the music. Thirty-seven of the students passed giving the school a hefty 88.1 percent passing record, which secured for it another year of funding. Annual Report on the Administration of the Baroda State, 1886–87, 116.

91. Pandit Brijlal to M. V. Dhamankar, unpublished letter, March 18, 19??, property of Shaila Datar and the Bhaskarbua Bakhle Foundation, Pune, 2001. Marathi, my translation.

92. See Annual Report of the Vernacular Educational Department, Baroda State, for the Year 1895–1896, 30.

93. G. S. Sardesai remained in Baroda's employ for thirty-five years before leaving to write his monumental work of Marathi history, *Marathi Riyasat*.

94. M. V. Dhamankar was a student of Bhaskarbua Bakhle, who was a student of Faiz Mohammed Khan in Baroda. Dhamankar intended to write a biography of his guru, Bhaskarbua Bakhle, and solicited letters from a number of people who knew him. Sardesai's letter made clear that he did not remember Bakhle so much as he remembered his teacher, Faiz Mohammed Khan, and his competitor at Baroda, Maula Baksh.

95. G. S. Sardesai, unpublished letter to Mr. Dhamankar, January 13, 1944. Marathi (my translation), property of Shaila Datar and Bhaskarbua Bakhle Foundation, Pune, 2001.

96. Annual Report on the Administration of the Baroda State, 1887–88, 550–52, and Annual Report on the Administration of the Baroda State, 1888–89, 101.

97. Annual Report on the Administration of the Baroda State, 1891–92, 97, 98. The cost of maintaining two schools and two classes for the Gujarati and Marathi Girls school rose to approximately Rs. 2,516 and grew steadily, to Rs. 3,343 in 1889 and Rs. 3,602 in 1890.

98. Annual Report on the Administration of the Baroda State, 1893–94, 123–24.

99. See Maula Baksh, *Sangitanubhav*.

100. These were *Sangitanubhav* (providing general knowledge about music); *Sitarshikshak* (information on how to play the sitar giving different compositions); *Taal Padhati* (information about the table and notated taals), *Sangitanusaar Chhandomanjari* (fifty-eight melodic and lyrical compositions in different ragas and different taals); *Narsingh Mehtanu Sangeet Mameru* (notated poems of Narsingh Mehta); *Balasangitmala* in Marathi (songs in Marathi for students from the Deccan) and *Balasangitmala* in Gujarati (for Gujarati students), both published in 1890 (Annual Report, 1890–90, 88); *Gayan Shalaon me Chalte Gayanon ka Pratham Pustak* (the first book of instruction for the music school), published for each year of the six-year program; *Bhagwant Garbavali* (garba songs); *Gujarati vachan malaki kavitaon ka notation book* (poems set to notated music for students in the music school); *Inayat harmonium shikshak* (information about how to play the harmonium), *Inayat fiddle shikshak*, and *Inayat ratnavali*, compilations of compositions along with information on how to play the fiddle. This compilation includes a variety of musical forms, such as *thumri* and *ghazal*, and English songs including "Home Sweet Home," "Gaily the Trouba-

dour," and "God Save the Maharajah." See Pathan, *Inayat Geet Ratnavali*, 40, 110, and 127 for these songs. It should be noted that pedagogical texts such as these were often reissued, and dates of publications should be seen as approximations. There is also an *Inayat Geet Ratnavali* that was written by Maula Baksh, published in 1894. For this book, the Hindi edition published in 1903 was consulted.

101. In the statement of accounts for the financial year 1896–97, we see evidence of Sayajirao's investment in furthering education. There were Urdu schools, girls' schools, music schools, Sanskrit schools, and even some boarding schools. In addition, there were funds allocated for and spent by the Sanskrit Library; far and above the most significant expenditure was on the furthering of Sanskrit literature, on which close to one-and-a-half dakhs (Rs. 150,000) was spent. See Annual Report on the Administration of the Baroda State, 1896–97, 152.

102. See Annual Report of the Vernacular Education Department, Baroda State, for the Year 1895–1896, 60, 30.

103. Bhaskarbua Bakhle, Faiz Mohammed Khan's most famous student, taught in his school in 1887 for a monthly salary of Rs. 10. See M. V. Dhamankar's notes for the book, property of Shaila Datar, Bhaskarbua Bakhle Foundation, Pune. Marathi, my translation. Bhaskarbua Bakhle was Maharashtra's most famous musician. About him, retired industrial court judge R. S. Date wrote, "Rajab Ali Khan used to constantly say to me the Hindus have produced only one singer who all of us Musalmans respect and that is our brother, Bhaskarbua." Marathi, my translation. Unpublished letter to Mr. M. V. Dhamankar, property of Bhaskarbua Bakhle foundation and Shaila Datar, Pune. For a biographical account of Bhaskarbua Bakhle based on fairly extensive research, see Datar, *Devgandharva*.

104. See Annual Report of the Vernacular Education Department, Baroda State, for the Year 1895–1896, nos. 61, 30.

105. See *HHN*/174/428, 1889–90.

106. See Report of the Administration of Baroda State for 1897–98, 79.

107. He received a monthly salary of Rs. 50 and a transportation allowance of Rs. 15. See *HHN*/37/218, 1895–96, 5.

108. See Annual Report of the Vernacular Educational Department, Baroda State, for the Year 1896–1997, 57.

109. See *HHN*/3/14, 1895–96, 4–5. He received Rs. 5 in scholarship for his performance, but Maula Baksh was rewarded with a hefty Rs. 500 *bakshees* that he was told to spend on jewelry.

110. See Annual Report of the Vernacular Education Department, Baroda State, for the Year 1895–1896, 64, 65, 31. Many years later, in 1916, the girls' chorus sang at the opening of the All-India Music Conference in Baroda.

111. See Annual Report on the Administration of the Baroda State, 1904–1905, 228, and 1905–6, 164.

112. See Shivram Sadashiv Manohar, *Sangitshikshak* (in Marathi; Bombay, 1905).

113. See Shivram Sadashiv Manohar, *Swaraprastaar* (in Marathi; Bombay, 1903).

114. See *Kesari*, August 23, 1904. All translations from *Kesari*, published in Marathi, are mine.

115. See Report on Public Instruction in the Baroda State for the Year 1907–1908, 63.

116. See Report on Public Instruction in the Baroda State for the Year 1911–1912, 49.

117. See Report on Public Instruction in the Baroda State for the Year 1907–1908, 63.

118. See Sharatchandra Gokhale, "Payache dagad," *Shabdashri* 82, Diwali issue: 56–63. Gokhale's article has a few chronological errors; for instance, he claims that Maula Baksh died in 1893, but there are Baroda state records that state the correct date as 1896. Moreover, this article is intended to take issue with Barwe's biography, which Gokhale found full of mistakes.

119. See *Sangeet Samrat Khansaheb Alladiya Khan: My Life,* as told to his grandson Azizuddin Khan (Calcutta, 2000), 18. Maula Baksh may indeed have prevented Alladiya Khan Saheb from securing a post at Baroda, but the larger point is that there was a modern regime of regulation in place to which all musicians were subject.

120. Report of the Second Gandharva Mahavidyalaya Sangeet Parishad, 21.

121. See Kapileshwari, *Abdul Karim Khan*; Govindrao Tembe, *Gayanmaharshi Alladiya Khan yanche charitra* (Bombay, 1956), and Datar, *Devagandharva*, as just three examples of writing in Marathi in which maharajas are presented as *kadardaar* even as later in the narrative we are told that the maharajas of Kolhapur and Baroda knew nothing about music.

122. See Norbert Peabody, *Hindu Kingship and Polity in Precolonial India* (New York, 2003); Adrian Mayer, *Caste and Kinship in Central India: A Village and Its Region* (Berkeley, Calif., 1970); Joan Erdman, *Patrons and Performers in Rajasthan: The Subtle Tradition* (New Delhi, 1985); and Philip Zarili, *The Kathakali Complex: Actor, Structure and Performance* (New Delhi, 1984). These authors provide cultural details without history. Michael Fisher and Nick Dirks are rare exceptions to this trend. Fisher has provided the most detailed and massively documented account of indirect rule in Princely India in *Indirect Rule in India: Residents and the Residency System, 1764–1858* (New York, 1991), while Dirks (*The Hollow Crown*) has examined the complex relationship between colonialism, Brahminism, and kingship in the progressive hollowing of the princely crown.

123. See Manu Bhagavan, "Demystifying the 'Ideal Progressive': Resistance through Mimicked Modernity in Princely Baroda, 1900–1913," *Modern Asian Studies* 35 (2001): 385–409.

Chapter 2

1. See Kathryn Hansen, "Making Women Visible: Gender and Race Cross-Dressing in the Parsi Theater," *Theater Journal* 51.2 (1999): 127–47.

2. As other examples of this kind of writing, see Sir W. Ouseley, "An Essay on the Music of Hindustan," in *Oriental Collections illustrating the History, Antiquities, and Literature &c., of Asia* (London, 1797–1800), vol. 1.

3. In princely India, too, rulers used bands to honor and respect visiting dignitaries, traveled with their bands to other princely states, and used them to highlight their power and status through pomp, military parades, and the playing of a state anthem by the military band.

4. See N. Augustus Willard, *A Treatise on the Music of India* (1793; Calcutta, 1962), 77.

5. Ibid., 78.

6. See letter from Thacker Spink and Co. to Lieutenant Day, June 12, 1886, Records of the Educational Department of Bombay Presidency, vol. 34, 1886, compilation 565.

7. See letter from C. R. Day to C. S. Bayly, undersecretary to the government of India in Records of the Educational Department, June 30, 1886, compilation 565.

8. See compilation 565 of letters in Records of the Educational Department, vol. 34, 1886, "Opinion of this Government as to Lt. Day's qualifications to produce a work on Indian Music."

9. Ibid.

10. See compilation 284 of letters in Records of the Educational Department, vol. 63, 1892, "The Music and Musical Instruments of Southern India by Captain C. R. Day."

11. See C. R. Day, *The Music and Musical Instruments of Southern India and the Deccan* (Bombay, 1891), 1. One copy of the book had been deposited in the Royal Asiatic Library of Bombay, where it remains in the rare book collection.

12. Ibid., 2.

13. Ibid., 4.

14. Ibid., 12.

15. See chapter 5, section on the AIMCs where similar opinions were voiced even in the early twentieth century.

16. For a detailed examination of the development of vernacular education and its relationship to elite forms, as well as the formation of the literary public sphere in Maharashtra, see the insightful book by Veena Naregal, *Language Politics, Elites, and the Public Sphere: Western India under Colonialism* (New Delhi, 2001).

17. See Christine E. Dobbin, *Urban Leadership in Western India: Politics and Communities in Bombay City, 1840–1885* (Oxford, 1972), 55.

18. See Proceedings of the Students Literary and Scientific Society (hereafter SLSS),

Fourth Report, 16–17, Bombay University Library and Archives. The vernacular branch societies were the Marathi Dnyan Prasarak Sabha, The Gujarati Dnyan Prasarak Mandali, and the Buddhi-Vardhak Hindu Sabha. Dobbins identifies these vernacular branch societies as having emerged out of communal tensions, but there is no evidence to suggest that they were anything other than particularistic as opposed to antagonistic.

19. Naregal, *Language Politics, Elites, and the Public Sphere*, 134.

20. See Proceedings of the SLSS Bombay for the years 1854–55 and 1855–56, introduction.

21. See Proceedings of the SLSS Bombay for the years 1854–55 and 1855–56, 2, address.

22. See Report of the SLSS for the Session of 1862–63, 7.

23. See Appendix C, 43–44, Report of the SLSS 1863–64.

24. See Appendix C, Report of the SLSS 1863–64, 46.

25. See Govardhan Vinayak Chatre, *Geetlipi*, preface by Viswanath Narayan Mandlik (Bombay, 1864). Translations from the Marathi are mine.

26. Ibid., 11.

27. See appendix B to Report of the SLSS, 1863–64, letter to Raosaheb Vishwanath Narayan Mandlik reporting on the three Marathi girls' schools of the society, December 10, 1863.

28. *Times of India*, October 25, 1876.

29. For a very useful and enlightening treatment of the relationship between the development of native science tied to antiquity and colonial forms of knowledge, see Gyan Prakash, *Another Reason* (Princeton, N.J., 1999).

30. See Poona Gayan Samaj, *Svarashastra: The Science of Sound: A Treatise in Music* (in Marathi; Poona, 1878), 3.

31. Ibid., 21.

32. See preface to second edition of Purshottam Ganesh Gharpure, *Sataareeche Pahile Pustak* (in Marathi; Poona, 1883). An earlier book on the sitar was Suryaji Sadashiv Mahatme and Vishwanath Ramchandra Vakil, *Tantuvadya: Sataar Shikanyache Pahile Pustak* (in Marathi; n.p., 1872).

33. See 8, Balwunt Trimbuk Sahasrabuddhe, "Hindu Music," in *Hindu Music and the Gayan Samaj* (Poona, 1887).

34. See Purshottam Ganesh Gharpure and V. M. Herlekar, *Studies in Indian Music* (Poona, 1889).

35. Pandit Paluskar, *Sangit Balbodha* (in Marathi; Bombay, 1901).

36. Priya Nath Roy, *Indian Music in European Notation*, part 1 (Darjeeling, 1889).

37. Sourindro Mohun Tagore, *English Verses Set to Hindu Music in Honor of His Royal Highness, the Prince of Wales* (Calcutta, 1875).

38. I am grateful to Partha Chatterjee for pointing this out to me.

39. For a history of Parsis in Bombay, see H. D. Darukhanawala, *Parsi Lustre on In-dian Soil*, vols. 1 and 2 (Bombay, 1939).

40. Seventy-five years later, Pestonjee Firozeshah Kapadia published a report of the GUM that is one of the rare and few sources we have for the society's activities and, in particular, the personality and drive of its founder.

41. See Pestonjee Firozeshah Kapadia, *Gayan Uttejak Mandali: Teni Poni Sadani Tawarikhno Ahewal* (Bombay, 1946), 10, my translation from the Gujarati.

42. Ibid., 10.

43. Ibid., 12.

44. Ibid., 13.

45. Ibid., 14. While the word used in Gujarati is *randi* or *veshya*, I have used "whores" as a translation rather than "prostitutes" to convey a sense of the invective embedded in words like *randi*.

46. Ibid., 14.

47. See Sharatchandra Gokhale's introduction to *Maharashtrateel Sangeet*, in *Vishrabdha Sharada* (in Marathi; Bombay, 1975), 2:152–53, my translation.

48. Kapadia, *Gayan Uttejak Mandali*.

49. Ibid., 24.

50. See *Rast Goftar*, June 21, 1874, 416. My translation.

51. Kapadia, *Gayan Uttejak Mandali*, 29. See also Gokhale, *Vishrabdha Sharada*, 142–43.

52. See Kapadia, *Gayan Uttejak Mandali*, 34–36.

53. Ibid., 36–40.

54. Ibid., 42.

55. Ibid.

56. Ibid., 43. My translation.

57. See *Times of India*, October 25, 1876.

58. The term *goon* is a poor English transliteration of *gun*, which means virtue.

59. See Annual Report of the Poona Gayan Samaj, 1906–7. Property of Abasaheb Muzumdar Foundation, Pune, Shaniwar Wada.

60. *Dnyan Prakash*, January 18, 1877, 37–40, in Sahasrabuddhe, *Hindu Music and the Gayan Samaj*.

61. Ibid., 43.

62. General Department Records of the Bombay Presidency, no. 736, 1882, "Application from the Committee of the Gayan Samaj of Poona soliciting patronage of their Royal Highness the Prince of Wales and the Duke of Connaught"; located in the Maharashtra State Archives, Elphinstone College, Bombay.

63. Ibid., 86.

64. Ibid., 87.

65. Ibid., 98.

66. See *Kesari*, January 2, 1883.

67. See *Kesari*, June 17, 1883.

68. See *Kesari*, September 25, 1883.

69. M. M. Kunte was the first Indian headmaster of the Poona High School and author of a number of works in Marathi on Shivaji, and several in English as well, the most famous of which was *The Vicissitudes of Aryan Civilization in India: An Essay Which Treats of the History of the Vedic and Buddhistic Polities, Explaining Their Origin, Prosperity and Decline* (Bombay, 1880).

70. General Department Records of the Bombay Presidency, 1883, no. 1835.

71. Sahasrabuddhe, *Hindu Music and the Gayan Samaj*, 44.

72. See C. V. Kelkar, *Bharat Gayan Samaj, Pune: San 1911 te 1940 ya kaalkhandateel sansthecha itihaas* (in Marathi; Pune, 1940), 13–14.

73. See *Kesari*, September 17, 1895.

74. See Report of the Poona Gayan Samaj, 1906–7, 4–6. Abbasaheb Muzumdar, Private Collection.

75. A list of music teachers is given in Kelkar, *Bharat Gayan Samaj, Pune*, 13–14. The names are as follows: Annasaheb Gharpure, Murarbuwa Govekar, Balkoba Natekar, Balkrishnabua Ichalkaranjikar, Balwantrao Ketkar, Shankarbua Ashtekar, Ganpatibuwa Bhilawdikar, Vinayakbua Thakurdas, Eknath Pandit, Gangarambua Achrekar, Shankarbhaiya Ghorpadkar, Chintubua Gandhe. One of the patrons of the *samaj* was Abbasaheb Muzumdar, and important functionaries of the PGS were Dattatreya Joshi, Nilakanth Chatre, Mahadev Vishnu Sane, Pandit Tambe, Pandit Shastri, Nanasaheb Natu, and so on. Most of these are Brahmin names. In this sense in Maharashtra too there was a "Bhadralok" similar to that in Bengal, but it would be a mistake here (and I believe in Bengal as well) to assume that because Brahmins and non-Brahmin Hindus came together in the founding of the PGS that it was anything other than Brahminic.

76. Annual Report of the PGS, 1919–1920, 7.

77. Eknath wrote three hundred *bharud*s designed to be used in theatrical productions such as *gondhali*s, *garudi*s, and *wasudev*s. I am immensely grateful to Indira Peterson for sharing with me her vast research on performative traditions and forms, which she analyzes in her forthcoming book, *Imagining the World in 18th Century India: The Kuravanci Fortune-Teller dramas of Tamilnad*. For descriptions and definitions of *bharud* and *gondhal* see Eleanor Zelliott and Maxine Bernstsen, eds., *The Experience of Hinduism: Essays on Religion in Maharashtra* (New York, 1988). See especially the essays "On the Road: A Maharashtrian Pilgrimmage," by Iravati Karve, and "The Gondhali: Singers for the Devi," by Chintaman Dhere. On Eknath's *bharud*s see Eleanor Zelliott, "Eknath's Bharude: The Sant as Link between Cultures" in *The Sants: Studies in a Devotional Tradition of India*, ed. Karine Schomer and W. H. McLeod (Berkeley, 1987).

78. See Kusumawati Deshpande and M. V. Rajadhyaksha, *A History of Marathi Literature* (New Delhi, 1988), 18.
79. See Gokhale, *Vishrabdha Sharada.*
80. See *A History of Marathi Literature*, by Kusumawati Deshpande and M. V. Rajadhyaksha, 55–56. Sahitya Akademi, New Delhi: 1988.
81. See contract signed by Sitaram Balambhatt Purohit, in Gokhale, *Vishrabdha Sharada*, 2:10.
82. Ibid., 12. Letter to Ruler of Sangli, August 7, 1855. Marathi, my translation.
83. Ibid. Bhave lists the names of the fourteen offenders, stressing that they are violating a contract and urging the ruler to prohibit them from taking their show on the road.
84. See Ashok Ranade, *Stage Music of Maharashtra* (New Delhi, 1986), 24.
85. See Christine E. Dobbin, *Urban Leadership in Western India: Politics and Communities in Bombay City, 1840–1885* (London, 1972), chapter 1.
86. See Hansen, "Making Women Visible." Hansen not only documents the polyglot theater culture in the city of Bombay, she also narrates a fascinating history of cross-dressing in the theater of the late nineteenth century.
87. Records of the Bombay Theater Company, Maharashtra State Archives, Bombay.
88. Sir D. E. Wacha, *Shells from the Sands of Bombay: My Recollections and Reminiscences, 1860–1875* (Bombay, 1920), 347.
89. See Ranade, *Stage Music of Maharashtra*, 7.
90. Wacha, *Shells from the Sands of Bombay*, 349.
91. See Gokhale, *Vishrabdha Sharada*, 2:9. The price of the tickets ranged from one rupee to four for the upper level seats.
92. Letter to the Ichalkaranjikar Natak Mandali, signed by forty-two patrons from the princely state of Baroda including the *dewan*, in ibid.
93. See Ranade, *Stage Music of Maharashtra*, 27.
94. Letter from H. S. Hewett, M. General to Mr. Balwant Pandurang, September 5, 1881, in *Vishrabhdha Sharada*, 19–20.
95. See *Stage Music of Maharashtra* for Ashok Ranade's description of Shripad Krishna Kolhatkar's plays as one such exception, 29–30.
96. See Hansen, "Making Women Visible."
97. See Gokhale, *Vishrabdha Sharada*, 2:5–8.
98. Chiplunkar taught theater to the members of the Ichalkaranjikar Natak Mandali, for instance, and in the twentieth century, Lalitkaladarsha and the Gandharva Natak Company staged a production of the Marathi play, *Maanaapmaan* for the Tilak Swarajya Fund in 1921.
99. See Gokhale, *Vishrabdha Sharada*, 2:50–54, for a summary history of the founding of various *natak mandalis*.
100. Vijay Tendulkar's searing social critiques made their way onto the stage only in

the 1960s, with his most famous stage adaptations of Brecht's Three Penny Opera called *Teen Paishyacha Tamasha,* and his most radical critique of Peshwai Brahminism in *Ghashiram Kotwal* in 1976.

101. Ranade, *Stage Music in Maharashtra,* 24.
102. Ibid., 10.
103. Ibid., 29, 40, 54, 56.
104. See Kapileshwari, *Abdul Karim Khan,* and chapter 1.
105. Abdul Karim Khan recorded *"Chandrika hi janu"; Dev Gandhar,* 78 rpm.

Chapter 3

1. Letter to Rai Umanath Bali, May 26, 1922. Property of Rai Swareshwar Bali, Lucknow. Published in *Bhatkhande Smruti Grantha* (Hindi and English), Indira Kala Sangeet Vishwavidyalaya, Khairagarh, 1966.
2. Bhatkhande's musicological contributions were as follows: (1) he established ten *thaat*s, or groups, into which he placed all of the 150 ragas most commonly sung or played. These were *kalyan, kafi, khamaj, bhairav, bhairavi, bilaval, todi, marwa, purvi,* and *asavari.* Each of the ragas belonging to a group followed a set of rules about the combination and order of pitches that both distinguished it from other ragas within the same *thaat* but also from other *thaat*s themselves. (2) Bhatkhande also explained the "theory of time," which was fundamentally important for the performance of ragas. Every raga according to this classically derived system has a stipulated time for its performance, so designated as to maximize the force of its affective qualities. Ragas typically convey a mood, an affect or emotion, and there are suggested rules for the appropriate time of day or night when they should be performed. There are early morning ragas, afternoon ragas, early evening ragas, night ragas, and late-night ragas. (3) In addition to formulating a notation system, partly borrowed from a Western high art music, he wrote down the basic definition of a raga: five pitches are minimally necessary in both the ascension and descension of the raga, without which its character can not be gauged; *sa* (the fixed first pitch of any scale) can never be discarded and both *ma* (the fourth pitch) and *pa* (the fifth) cannot be discarded, so all ragas have either *sa* and *ma* (the interval of a fourth) or *sa* and *pa* (the interval of a fifth); ragas can be broadly classified under three categories, *audava,* five pitches; *shadava,* six pitches; and *sampurna,* which means complete, and thus seven pitches.

In other words, for a raga to be classified as such, it must minimally contain five pitches and an interval of either a fourth or a fifth; Bhatkhande's most esoteric contribution related to microtones and pitches. In Bharata's *Natyashastra* (from the second century B.C. to the second century A.D.), a Sanskrit treatise on the performing arts, the author gives us the gamut of twenty-two *shruti*s (microtones) that we can hear. In order to arrive at a fixed scale, the seven principal notes, or pitches, were placed along this spectrum. The pitches are *shadja* (*sa*), *rishabh* (*re*), *gandhara* (*ga*), *madhyama* (*ma*), *pancham* (*pa*), *dhaivata* (*dha*), and *nishad* (*ni*). According to the couplet in the *Natyashastra*, the formula for the number of microtones contained within each successive pitch is as follows: 4-3-2-4-4-3-2. In effect, the number of microtones denoted the range within which the pitch could be located. We are told that in ancient times the fixed scale was derived by fixing the pitches on the *last* microtone in the range of microtones contained within each pitch. By this definition, the first pitch, *shadja*, would be located on the fourth *shruti*, *rishabh* on the seventh *shruti*, *gandhar* on the ninth *shruti*, *madhyam* on the thirteenth *shruti*, *pancham* on the seventeenth *shruti*, *dhaivat* on the twentieth *shruti,* and *nishad* on the twenty-second *shruti*. To determine the actual measurement of a microtone, the text tells us that two *veena*s (an ancient instrument that predates the sitar) were used. The first one was tuned according to the microtonal formula; the second one was lowered by one microtone on one pitch. *Pancham* (the fifth scale degree) was lowered by one microtone, and the difference between the *pancham* of the first and second *veena* was considered the sound gap between two *shruti*s. Bhatkhande found this scale inadequate as the basis for contemporary music performances and arrived at a slightly different formula, which had one difference: he located the pitches on the first *shruti*s, as opposed to the last. The new ascription was *shadja*—first *shruti*, *rishabh*—fifth *shruti*, *gandhara*—eighth *shruti*, *madhyama*—tenth *shruti*, *pancham*—fourteenth *shruti*, *dhaivata*—eighteenth *shruti*, and *Nishadh*—twenty-first *Shruti*. This new configuration coincided with the pitches belonging to what is known as the *bilaval saptak* (*saptak* means seven notes, as opposed to an octave; in Hindustani music the high *sa* is the first note of the next *saptak*). This scale is widely used as the foundational scale of modern Hindustani music by Bhatkhande's students.

3. See Sobhana Nayar, *Bhatkhande's Contribution to Music* (Bombay, 1989), 66–67.

4. Ibid., 350. Nayar defines *dhrupad* as "a type of classical song set in a raga having intricate rhythmic patterns which flourished in the 15th and 16th centuries" and *khayal* as "the highest form of classical art in North India. It allows melodic variation and improvisation within the framework of a raga and is more free and flowery compared to Dhrupad."

5. All biographical information is taken from the preface to *Hindusthani Sangeet Padhdhati* (*HSP*), vol. 1 (in Marathi; Bombay, 1992); Nayar, *Bhatkhande's Contribution to Music*; Shrikrishna Ratanjankar, *Sangeet Acharya Pandit V. N. Bhatkhande* (Bombay, 1973); Gokhale, *Vishrabdha Sharada*, vols. 1–3; and articles from the Marathi journal *Sangeet Kala Vihar*. All translations are mine.

6. See Nayar, *Bhatkhande's Contribution to Music*, 69. Also see prefatory remarks to all volumes of his diaries.

7. The five volumes of diaries are the property of Ramdas Bhatkal, Popular Prakashan, Bombay. I shall refer to the diaries hereafter as BD, vols. 1–4. Volume and page numbers are here cited as they are given in the unpublished manuscripts. All translations mine.

8. BD, 4:110.

9. See, for example, his conversation with Mr. Tirumallya Naidu, November 17, BD, 1:21, and November 21, 1904, 1:44.

10. The *Sangit Ratnakara* is a thirteenth-century text that was partially reprinted in Calcutta in 1879. In 1896, the first complete edition in two volumes was published in Poona, edited by Mangesh Ramakrishna Telang, with some critical notes in Marathi. The best-known critical edition was published by the Adyar Library and Research Center, Madras, in 1943. It included the entire text in Sanskrit, with two commentaries by Kallinatha and Simhabhupala. For my purposes, I am using an English translation of the Adyar edition of the Sanskrit text, by R. K. Shringy and Prem Lata Sharma (Delhi, 1991).

11. BD, 1:21, and November 21, 1904, 1:44.

12. Ibid., 46.

13. See B. R. Deodhar, "Pandit Vishnu Narayan Bhatkhande: Vyaktitva tatha Karya" (Hindi), *Sangeet Kala Vihar* 10 (1947): 24–34.

14. In the diaries, Bhatkhande spells Dikshitar's name incorrectly, and throughout the chapter I have chosen to use the correct spelling. In her review of the Hindi translation of his Southern Tour Diary, Sakuntala Narasinhan notes that "like most lay north Indians, Bhatkhande too mis-spells south Indian names. Subbarama Dikshitar is given as Subram Dikshit. . . . Most long and short vowels are messed up." Narasinhan goes on to ask a most pertinent question: "One wonders how he missed the correct names of those he sought meetings with" (book reviews, *Journal of the Indian Musicological Society* 18.1 [1987]: 54–59).

15. BD, 2:186.

16. BD, 2:273–306.

17. BD, 2:184.

18. BD, 1:52.

19. "I had heard that Southern music was systematic. In one sense, this is absolutely true. . . . they even have some knowledge of Swaras . . . However, it would be wrong to claim that there is knowledge of Sanskrit *grantha*s here or that Sanskritic music is performed here" (BD, 1:37).

20. BD, 2:219.

21. BD, 2:220.

22. In Ranade's *Hindustani Music*, n. 123, S. M. Tagore is listed as having written the

following books: *Jatiya Sangeetvishayak Prastav* (1870), *Yantra Kshetra Deepika: Sitar Shiksha Vishayak Grantha* (1872), *Mridangmanjari* (1873), *Harmonium Sootra* (1874), *English Verses Set to Hindu Music* (1875), *Yantrakosha* (1875), *Six Principal Raga-s-with a Brief View of the Hindu Music* (1876), *A Few Lyrics of Owen Meredith Set to Hindu Music* (1877), *Hindu Music from Various Authors* (1882), *Sangeetsara Sangraha* (1884), and *Nrityankura* (1885). Complete citations for these titles are absent. A few pages after giving the list of Tagore's publications, Dr. Ranade gives a chronological list of publications on music, in which the date of publication of one of Tagore's works is different than that given earlier. Balkrishnabua Ichalkaranjikar is listed as having authored a book in 1881, yet his biographers claim he could not read or write. Yet Dr. Ranade's work is a beacon of light and I am deeply grateful to him for his help.

23. BD, *My Eastern Travels*, 4:115. Conversation with Gaurihar Tagore.

24. BD, 4:76.

25. BD, 2:226.

26. In Ashok Ranade's *Hindustani Music* (26), Tohfat-ul-Hind is given as a text written in the early eighteenth century for the son of the last powerful Mughal emperor, Aurangzeb (1666–1707).

27. BD, 3:44–45.

28. BD, 3:160.

29. BD, 3:170.

30. Benedict Anderson, *Imagined Communities: Reflections on the Origin and Spread of Nationalism* (London, 1983).

31. See Anupa Pande, *A Historical and Cultural Study of the Natyasastra of Bharata* (Jodhpur, 1996), chapter 1.

32. This assertion is made even more forcefully in contemporary India, where musicians will claim that there is no need for proof since it is all given in the *shastra*s. Personal communications with musicians, February 2000.

33. *HSP,* 1:161.

34. *HSP,* 1:181. In the most recent translation of the *Natyashastra*, the most precise dating of its origination remains unclear and the most that scholars can claim is that it was probably published between 200 B.C. and 200 A.D. Not merely is the dating of the text a problem, it remains a thorny and contested issue whether there was actually someone named Bharata who wrote the text or whether it was a pseudonym. See Pande, *A Historical and Cultural Study of the Natyasastra of Bharata.*

35. *HSP,* 2:8.

36. *HSP,* 1:129.

37. BD, 5:96.

38. BD, 5: 51, 103.

39. See *HSP*, 3: 1–2, in which Bhatkhande wrote, "Remember that because a few Muslim musicians have succeeded in capturing our music, it doesn't stand to reason that there is a Yavanick text that can do the same." He went on to cite as necessary milestones the same authors he had earlier mentioned, Bharat, Sharangdeva, Lochan, and Ahobal. Also see 48 and 49, in which he narrated an encounter with a "Khansaheb" that sounds very much like his meeting with Karamatullah Khan in Allahabad.

40. See Jones, *On the Musical Modes of the Hindoos*.

41. For a literary history of the debate between Anglicists and Orientalists, see Gauri Viswanathan, *Masks of Conquest: Literary Study and British Rule in India* (New York, 1989), and Bernard Cohn, *Colonialism and Its Forms of Knowledge* (Princeton, N.J., 1998).

42. B. R. Deodhar, *Pillars of Hindustani Music*, trans. Ram Deshmukh (Bombay, 1993), 45.

43. The first volume did not have a table of contents, unlike the other three. *HSP* was translated into Hindi and Gujarati, but the second Marathi edition of these texts was published only in 1999. In the new edition, a few changes were made, but the attempt was to keep the text in the original as untouched as possible. In a few places the Marathi has been copyedited, but most of it has been left unchanged. Editorial changes to the original text are in the form of introductory prefaces, lists of texts referred to in the original, an annotated chronology of Bhatkhande's life, select quotations from his diaries and explicatory glosses of his theory, all written by his student Prabhakar Chinchore. The actual text of the original *HSP* has been left basically unchanged. Finally, a new table of contents, in conformity with the style of the original volumes 2, 3, and 4, was also composed for the new edition of volume 1, and volume 4 was divided into two.

44. Letter to Rai Umanath Bali, May 30, 1929. Property of Rai Swareshwar Bali, Lucknow.

45. Nayar, *Bhatkhande's Contribution to Music*, 100.

46. *HSP* 2:9.

47. These were *Raga Tarangini, Hridaya Kautuk, Hridaya Prakash, Sangeet Parijat, Raga Tattva Vibodha, Sadraga Chandrodaya, Raga Manjari, Raga Mala, Anupa Sangeet Ratnakar, Anupa Sangeet Vilas, Anupankush, Rasa Kaumudi, Swaramelakalanidhi, Raga Vibodha, Chaturdandi Prakashika, Sangeet Saramrit*, and *Raga Lakshana*. For more on these books, see Nayar, *Bhatkhande's Contribution to Music*, 101–109.

48. *HSP*, 1:14.

49. *HSP*, 1:23.

50. *HSP*, 1:58.

51. *HSP*, 1:163.

52. *HSP*, 2:190.

53. *HSP*, 1:192–93.

54. These are all names of ragas that clearly bespeak their Muslim origin, or as Bhatkhande might say, derivation.

55. *Shastra* is one of those words, common now to a few modern Indo-Aryan languages derived from Sanskrit, which is impossible to translate accurately. The acceptable translation would be "science" but also "classicism" and "rules."

56. *HSP*, 1:59; emphasis mine.

57. *HSP*, 1:80.

58. The *Panchatantra* was a collection of Puranic fables that had hortatory morals at the conclusion of each tale.

59. *HSP*, 3:160–65.

60. See, for example, *HSP*, 2:139.

61. It was a common myth that in Akbar's time, the singer Tansen was able to light fires by singing the raga *Deepak*—which means light—and needed to immerse himself in water before doing so in order to avoid being burned to death by the power of the raga.

62. *HSP*, 2:146.

63. *HSP*, 1:141.

64. *HSP*, 1:160.

65. *HSP*, 3:1.

66. By 1932, when Bhatkhande published his fourth and final volume, he had left much of his anger behind. By now, he had countrywide fame and had less to prove than in the earlier volumes, written soon after his tours. In the last volume, he concentrated on the explication of the differences between the various Sanskrit and Persian texts, on more esoteric matters such as the theory of affect related to music (*rasa*), and on the mathematics of microtones (*shruti*). There are fewer polemical utterances in this last volume than in the first three. He even provided a genealogical list of Muslim musicians going as far back as the early twelfth century. The tone is not angry, sarcastic, or denigrating, as in the other volumes. His most expansive anecdote in this volume points to the ignorance of princely state rulers about music. The moral of this story for his students was simple and even gracious, advising his students against demanding the performance of rare ragas by musicians in public forums so as not to needlessly humiliate them. From a man who spent a great deal of his life finding ways to provoke and dismiss musicians, this is a rare change. Bhatkhande expresses genuine sympathy for the plight of a musician subjected to the whimsical and ignorant demands of rich princes (*HSP* 5:177). It is not that there are no dismissive paragraphs on musicians at all to be found in this volume, but there is a marked difference in both the number and quality of his comments compared to those in earlier volumes. In this one, they are still ignorant

but not arrogant and willing to concede their lack of knowledge in Bhatkhande's presence. When confronted with a question they could not answer, they deferred to Bhatkhande's superior knowledge of the subject and freely confessed that their education was not bookish or systematic. Of course, Bhatkhande does here what he did in his tours, which is to show off his excellence. But in 1932, he was seventy-two years old, and perhaps he had mellowed a little.

67. In addition to these publications, his speech at the first All-India Music Conference in 1916, "A Short Historical Survey of Hindustani Music and The Means to Place it on a Scientific Foundation with a View to Make its Study as Easy as Possible," was published as a short book. In it, he summarized what he had observed in his tours, written in his Marathi volumes, and believed about music's history. In his grandiosely titled *Music Systems in India: A Comparative Study of Some of the Music Systems of the 15th, 16th, 17th, and 18th Centuries*, he evaluated a number of Sanskrit texts for their musicological contributions to the study of music. Both booklets are condensed and shortened versions of his writings in Marathi, so I will not dwell on them here. He also collected "popular" songs in Gujarati and Marathi and wrote some journal articles. At the time of his death, he had published sixteen music-related works, and two additional ones were released posthumously.

68. See Gokhale, *Vishrabdh Sharada*, 2:177–79, in particular, Gokhale's comment about Bhatkhande's constant willingness to clear up a misunderstanding about music.

69. Letter to Rai Umanath Bali, May 15, 1931. Property of Rai Swareshwar Bali, Lucknow.

70. Popley was the author of *Music of India* (Calcutta, 1910) and a key member of the music conferences.

71. Nayar, *Bhatkhande's Contribution to Music*.

72. As cited in ibid., 343, from *Bhatkhande Smriti Grantha*, ed. N. Chinchore (Khairagarh, 1967).

73. Unpublished letter to Rai Umanath Bali, February 4, 1928.

74. Letter to Rai Umanath Bali, July 28, 1928. Published in *Bhatkhande Smruti Grantha* (in Hindi and English; Khairagarh, 1966).

75. V. N. Bhatkhande, "Propoganda for the betterment of the present condition of Hindusthani Music" (Delhi, 1922).

76. Unpublished letter to Rai Umanath Bali, May 26, 1922. Property of Rai Swareshwar Bali, Kaisar Bagh, Lucknow.

77. Unpublished letter to Rai Umanath Bali, May 15, 1931. Property of Rai Swareshwar Bali, Kaisar Bagh, Lucknow.

78. See Prabhakar Chinchore, "Ullekhaneeya Ghatnakram," preface to new edition of *Hindusthani Sangeet Paddhati*, vol. 1 (in Marathi; Bombay, 1999).

79. Letter to Rai Umanath Bali, May 30, 1929. "I may have to go to Benares to see what they are doing in the H. University. Pandit Madan Mohan Malaviya came to me yesterday and requested me to spend a week in Benares." Property of Rai Swareshwar Bali, Lucknow.

80. See B. R. Deodhar, *Thor Sangeetkar*, trans. Ram Deshmukh (in Marathi; Bombay, 1993), 38–50.

81. See K. B. Deval, *Music East and West Compared* (Poona, 1908), *The Hindu Musical Scale and the 22 Shrutis* (Poona, 1910); and *Theory of Indian Music as Expounded by Somnatha* (Poona, 1916); E. Clements, *A Note on the Use of European Musical Instruments in India* (Bombay, 1916). Deval and Clements founded the Philharmonic Society of Western India at Satara in 1911. Clements was a retired district judge and Deval was a retired deputy collector. Both came from the district of Satara, in western India. Deval had published the first "scientific" work on microtones and constructed a harmonium in accordance with his findings. He had presented it at the first All-India Music Conference, where it was soundly rejected by Bhatkhande and others.

82. See Vinayak Purohit, *The Arts in Transitional India*, vols. 1 and 2 (Bombay, 1997).

83. See Deodhar, *Thor Sangeetkar*, 43–44.

84. *Kesari*, June 3, 1924. The article reported a talk given by Professor Krishnarao Mule at the house of one of Poona's most respected music patrons, Abbasaheb Muzumdar, on the subject of music and musicology.

85. Unpublished letter to Rai Umanath Bali, May 30, 1929. "D. K. from Poona wrote to me asking if it was true that you are trying to hand over the college to the University on the ground that you were unable to go on with it. . . . The only difficulty with me is that I have never asked anybody to give me money for any of my activities and find it awkward to begin to do it now." Property of Rai Swareshwar Bali, Lucknow.

86. See *Acharya Shrikrishna Ratanjankar "Sujaan": Jeevani tatha Smritisanchay* (in Hindi, Bombay, 1993), 372.

87. *Sangeet Kala Vihar* 9 (1949): 9–13.

Chapter 4

1. For a festschrift on Paluskar, see Akhil Bharatiya Gandharva Mahavidyalaya Mandal, *Vishnu Digambar Paluskar Smriti Granth* (Miraj, 1974).

2. See Gurandittamal Khanna, *Gayanacharya Shriman Pandit Vishnu Digambarji Paluskar ka Sankshipt Jeevan-Vritaant* (Lahore, 1930). All translations from the Hindi are mine.

3. In 1891, the colonial government passed a bill raising the age of consent from ten to twelve. This caused a furor among the conservative Hindu Brahmin community, which argued that such a change violated the rules set down in the *Manusmriti* and that the colonial state was tampering in cultural matters. Liberal support for the bill was widespread. On the Ilbert Bill Controversy, see Edwin Hirschmann, *White Mutiny: The Ilbert Bill Crisis and Genesis of the Indian National Congress* (New Delhi, 1960), and Mrinalini Sinha, *Colonial Masculinity: The "Manly Englishman" and the "Effeminate Bengali" in the Late Nineteenth Century* (Manchester, U.K., 1995).

4. All biographical information comes from the following books: Khanna, *Gayanacharya Shriman Pandit Vishnu Digambarji Paluskar*; Vinayak Narayan Patwardhan, *Mazhe Gurucharitra* (in Marathi; Poona, 1956); B. R. Deodhar, *Gayanacharya Pandit Vishnu Digambar* (in Marathi; Bombay, 1971); V. R. Athavale, *Vishnu Digambar Paluskar* (New Delhi, 1967); Gokhale, *Vishrabdha Sharada*, vol. 2; G. H. Ranade, *Maharashtra's Contribution to Music* (Bombay, 1965), and *Art Music in Maharashtra*, 80–86; Purohit, *The Arts in Transitional India*.

5. The smaller states in south Maharashtra were mostly ruled by the Patwardhans, a clan of chieftains who had risen to power during the Brahmin-controlled Peshwa Period (1682–1818). At the end of the nineteenth century, they functioned more in the nature of *zamindars* than rulers, since these were not all states that were independent of colonial rule.

6. M. V. Dhond disputes such a claim, arguing that it was popular in Maharashtra in less elite circles than princely courts for well over a century before Balkrishnabua Ichalkaranjikar made it popular among the upper castes. See *The Evolution of Khyal*.

7. See Deodhar, *Gayanacharya Pandit Vishnu Digambar*, 4–9.

8. For Paluskar's frustration with old ways of learning music, see the entry "Music Schools" in *Encyclopaedia of Indian Cinema*, ed. Ashish Rajadhyaksha and Paul Willeman (New Delhi, 1974).

9. Ibid., 7–9.

10. For good summaries of kinship rituals and familial practices, see Daniel Neuman, *The Life of Music in North India: The Organization of an artistic tradition* (Detroit, 1980).

11. See Deodhar, *Gayanacharya Pandit Vishnu Digambar*, 4–9. The other two students were Shri Balwant Kane and Krishna Hari Herlekar (Khanna, *Gayanacharya Shriman Pandit Vishnu Digambarji Paluskar*, 7). Kane stayed with Paluskar until 1904, Herlekar until 1902, after which, at Annie Besant's encouragement, he went to Benaras, where he taught music at the Central School.

12. N. R. Pathak studied music with Paluskar in Lahore between 1905 and 1907. Ap-

parently, Paluskar was particularly fond of him and treated him not only as a confidante but also sought his advice from time to time. See "Gayanacharya K. Vishnu Digambar va Unke Karya," *Sangeet Kala Vihar* 10 (1947): 2–12.

13. A *jagrut* temple or deity is reputed to have immense power, both negative (if one's faith is shaky) and positive (if it is firm), and it is a relatively common belief that if one is not fully persuaded of one's faith, one should give *jagrut* temples and deities a wide berth.

14. For a summary of reform movements countrywide, see Kenneth W. Jones, *Socio-Religious Reform Movements in British India*, New Cambridge History of India (Cambridge, U.K., 1989).

15. See Pande, *A Historical and Cultural Study of the Natyashastra of Bharata*.

16. Patwardhan, *Mazhe Gurucharitra*. In Maharashtra, four musicians were called *gandharva*. They were Rahimat Khan, ?–1922, called *Bhugandharva*, Rambhau Kundgolkar (1886–1952), called *Savaigandharva*, Narayanrao Rajhans (1888–1967), called *Balgandharva*, and most recently, Shivaputra Komkali (1925–97), called *Kumar Gandharva*. See Dhond, *Evolution of Khyal* (Marathi).

17. For a summary of Tilak and Agarkar's early writings and controversies regarding the *Kesari*, see Stanley Wolpert, *Tilak and Gokhale: Revolution and Reform in the Making of Modern India* (Berkeley, Calif., 1961), esp. 20–27.

18. For details on the split between Tilak and Agarkar, see Wolpert, *Tilak and Gokhale*. See also R. I. Cashman, *The Myth of the Lokmanya: Tilak and Mass Politics in Maharashtra* (Berkeley, Calif., 1975). For a general summary of Hindu reform and revival, see Charles Heimsath's *Indian Nationalism and Hindu Social Reform*, and Jones, *Socio-Religious Reform Movements in British India*. See also Richard Tucker, *Ranade and the Roots of Indian Nationalism* (Bombay, 1977), for a look at the ideals and ideologies of a liberal nationalist opposed to Tilak. For an all-India look at nationalist politics and the best source book on modern Indian history, see Sumit Sarkar, *Modern India: 1885–1947* (New Delhi, 1983). For anti-Brahmin movements, see Gail Omvedt, *Cultural Revolt in a Colonial Society: The Non-Brahman Movement in Western India* (Bombay, 1976). See also Rosalind O'Hanlon, *Caste, Conflict, and Ideology*, Jim Masselos, *Toward Nationalism: Public Institutions and Urban Politics in the Nineteenth Century* (Bombay, 1974); B. R. Nanda, *Gokhale* (New Delhi, 1977); V. V. Thakur, ed., *Miscellaneous Writings of M. G. Ranade* (Bombay, 1915). For overall historical context, see Ravinder Kumar, *Western India in the Nineteenth Century* (London, 1968), and Christine E. Dobbin, *Urban Leadership in Western India: Politics and Communities in Bombay City, 1840–1885* (London, 1972); however, it should be pointed out that Dobbin's work does not so much as acknowledge the existence of colonialism in India and, as such, is an examination conducted in a political vacuum.

19. See Khanna, *Gayanacharya Shriman Pandit Vishnu Digambarji Paluskar*, 17.

20. *Kesari*, letter from Lahore correspondent, August 3, 1901.

21. See Narhar Pathak, "Gayanacharya K. Vishnu Digambar va Unke Karya," *Sangeet Kala Vihar* 10 (1947): 2–12. Hindi, my translation.

22. *Kesari* (Marathi), letter from Lahore Correspondent, August 3, 1901.

23. See *Journal of the Music Academy* 2.3 (1919).

24. See Pathak, "Gayanacharya K. Vishnu Digambar va Unke Karya."

25. Admission rules for entrance into the *Upadeshak* class, Gandharva Mahavidyalaya, 1919. Archives of the Gandharva Mahavidyala Mandal, Meraj.

26. Khanna, *Gayanacharya Shriman Pandit Vishnu Digambarji Paluskar*, 27.

27. The bond was signed by a Balkrishna Gaurishankar and dated January 28, 1911. Part of the text of this eight-anna bond is in Modi. The *Upadeshak* class was designed for teacher training.

28. *Sangit Amrit Pravaha* (Hindi) 3.2 (1907): 30–32, GMV Archives, Meraj.

29. *Journal of the Music Academy* 2.3 (1919).

30. Annual Report of the Lahore Gandharva Mahavidyalaya, 1904–5, 6. GMV Mandal Archives, Meraj.

31. The thread ceremony is a ritual initiation of a young Brahmin boy into the first phase of his life, commemorated by the giving to him, by a Brahmin priest, of the Gayatri Mantra and a sacred thread that he is expected to wear all his life. The accompanying Brahminic belief that buttresses the ceremony is that the sun will not rise unless a Brahmin, somewhere, chants the *Gayatri Mantra.* It is a ritual signifying the seriousness with which boys must take the charge of Brahminhood. In modern India, under the rubric of stripping Brahminic authority from Brahmins, this mantra (which is typically whispered into the boy's ear at the ceremony) is now available in pendants, mock scrolls, and in audio recordings in which it is set to music and sung by women. As with the Arya Samaj and the Sanatan Dharm, what this signifies is that while on the one hand Brahminic authority is decentralized, Brahminic "culture" pervades the public sphere. Brahmin women, no doubt, see the widespread use of the Gayatri Mantra as having broken the rigid control over chants held by Brahmin men, but the popularization of a Brahminic chant cannot be seen as liberatory if viewed through the optic of anti-Brahmin movements.

32. "Assorted News Items," *Sangit Amrit Pravaha* 3.2 (1907): 31. My translation.

33. *Sangit Amrit Pravaha* 3.2 (1907): 32 reported that on February 2, 1907, a musical party was sent to Rai Bahadur Gangaramji on the occasion of his son's wedding. *Sangit Amrit Pravaha* (4.2 [1908]: 28) reported that Pandit Paluskar himself sang at the wedding of Rai Saheb Jyotiprasad's daughter and received, in addition to his usual fee, Rs. 150, from Lala Ramanujdayal, Hon. Magistrate of Meerut. Students traveled out of Lahore, to Farakkabad, as in the case of the wedding of a Mr. Ganesh Prasad, where they received Rs. 50.

34. The *tanpura* is commonly called a drone. It is the instrument used by a vocalist to ensure he or she does not sing off pitch. Four pitches are strummed in succession.

35. The funds of the school fell from Rs. 578 to Rs. 470. Annual Report, 1904–5.

36. See Pathak, "Gayanacharya K. Vishnu Digambar va unke Karya," 8–9. Hindi, my translation.

37. For the best work so far on the Swadeshi movement, which lasted from 1905–8, see Sumit Sarkar, *Swadeshi Movement in Bengal, 1903–1908* (New Delhi, 1973).

38. *Sangit Amrit Pravaha* 3.2 (1908).

39. See *Sangit Amrit Pravaha* 5.1 (1909): 9–10.

40. See *Sangit Amrit Pravaha* 7.12 (1911): 182–84.

41. Ibid. The categories are religious, so students are identified as Hindu or Parsi. From the list of Hindu students, I was able to identify all but six students as Maharashtrian.

42. Ibid. Twelve of the sixteen women were unmarried.

43. See *Gandharva Mahavidyalaya*, August 1915, 24–25.

44. See *Sangit Amrit Pravaha* 7.12 (1911): 186–87. It seems unlikely that 27,000 children could have gathered at the GMV, but it is so reported.

45. *Sangit Amrit Pravaha* 9.6 (1913): 82–83 reports that a meeting was held in the Bombay GMV on June 20 at which two hundred people gathered to celebrate the birthday of the viceroy of India. The GMV's honorary secretary, Mr. Kalyanrai Gulabrai Ghoda, made a speech in English. "The object for which we all have met here this evening is well known to you all. It is to express our felicitations, on account of the most narrow escape of Their Excellencies from the bomb thrown on them at Delhi on the 23rd December, 1912, at the time of the State entry . . . We have today sent in most suitable terms a short telegram conveying our hearty congratulations and good wishes to Their Excellencies . . . Ladies &gentlemen. I must thank you one and all for taking the truble [*sic*] to come here & join with us in celebrating this most joyous occasion which as you know will be an unique one of its kind in the annals of the History of India."

46. *Kesari,* January 10, 1911.

47. Sarkar, *Modern India: 1885–1947*, 132.

48. *Kesari,* January 10, 1911.

49. Ibid.

50. *Times of India*, January 4, 1911. It was also reprinted in the *Gandharva Mahavidyalaya* and reported in the *Kesari*, January 10, 1911.

51. Deodhar, *Gayanacharya Pandit Vishnu Digambar*, 49.

52. There is a discrepancy in the reportage about the number of students at the Gandharva Mahavidyalaya. In the reprint of the *Times of India* article about the awards ceremony in the *Gandharva Mahavidyalaya,* the number is given as 704.

In this article, we are told that fifty-one of the women students were Parsi, the rest Hindu.

53. See *Gandharva Mahavidyalaya* 3.2 (1912): 19–20.

54. Ibid., 22.

55. Ibid., 18–19. See also *Gandharva Mahavidyalaya* 6.9 (1915):139, for more on Pandit Paluskar's growing religiosity and insistence on singing parts of the *Ramayana* at all gatherings. In subsequent issues, there are news items in which Paluskar's emphasis on the *Ramayana* is noted. See *Gandharva Mahavidyalaya* 6.10 (1915–16): 11–12.

56. Christine Dobbin has written about the fortunes of industrialists in the Bombay of the period in *Urban Leadership in Western India*.

57. See *Gandharva Mahavidyalaya* 3.5 (1912): 80.

58. See Deodhar, *Gayanacharya Pandit Vishnu Digambar*, 60–61.

59. See G*andharva Mahavidyalaya* 5.4 (1914): 52.

60. In every new publication, a list of previous publications with their availability and price was printed. In the 1933 edition of *Mahila Sangeet* (*Women's Music*), the full list included *Bharatiya Sangeet Lekhan Padhdhati* (Hindi, *Indian Music Notation System*), a three-book series on *balodaya sangeet* (children's music) in Hindi, one in Marathi, a two-book series on *mahila sangeet* (women's music), fifteen small books used as textbooks in Paluskar's schools (in Hindi), eighteen small books on the ragas: *bhairavi, bhoopali, khamaj, bhairav, badahans, sarang, hameer, bhimpalas, kedar, asavari, puriya, barwa, bageshri bahar, malhar, deshi khamaj, multani, lalit, and desh,* two books on music to accompany exercise, two books on Sitar instruction, eight small books notating devotional music, one on patriotic music, and one each on Bengali and Carnatic music. In addition to all this, there were nine small prayer books, with notated music, all based on his *Ramayana Pravachan*. He also published his conference reports, of which only a very few copies have survived. All told, his music books numbered over fifty.

61. The New English School had been founded by Tilak's mentor, Vishnu Krishna Chiplunkar (1850–82), who founded and published a literary magazine called *Nibandhamala*, in which he wrote rousing prose in literary Marathi on the evils of foreign occupation and the need to revive a vanquished Hindu spirit. Tilak was much influenced by Chiplunkar, with whom he ventured forth on the founding of a private school, the New English School in 1880.

62. See *Kesari*, May 14, 1918.

63. See *Kesari* , September 4, 1917.

64. The cofounder of *Kesari*, Gopal Ganesh Agarkar, died in 1895. His politics were far more radical than Tilak's. There are many books and articles about Lokmanya Tilak, and I cannot here give an adequate bibliography. For a quick look at

Tilak's role in nationalist politics, see Sarkar, *Modern India: 1885–1947*; and Wolpert, *Tilak and Gokhale*.

65. Deodhar, *Gayanacharya Pandit Vishnu Digambar*, 60–61.

66. According to Deodhar, he held two memorable performances, one in 1921, and one in 1928. There were rumors afloat that he had lost his voice, and apparently his students were so distressed by such slanderous accusations that they persuaded Paluskar to host a *jalsa* and demonstrate to his detractors that this was not the case. In 1921, he sang a composition in *raga yaman* that he had learnt from his guru, and in 1928, he sang a composition in *raga miyan-ki-malhar*. Ibid., 52–53; see 89–92 for details of the performances.

67. See *Kesari*, January 8, 1924. The actual line is "nokarshahi cheech areravi zhaali," which translated literally means "the arrogance of a servants' government." By extrapolation it suggests an affront to legitimate government or rule. Paluskar demonstrated his ability in using the political rhetoric of his time at the same time he highlighted his devotion to a specific national cause.

68. This issue was reported in many articles of the *Kesari*. See for instance, the September 29, 1925, issue, in which the article states that there is no justice to be had for Hindus from the district magistrate on this subject and that Hindus should expect relentless trouble from the Muslims. The only recourse proposed by the writer is that a committee composed solely of Hindus be allotted the task of inquiring into the matter. See *Kesari*, June 27, 1926; January 25, 1927; June 14, 1927; and October 18, 1927. In the October 18, 1927, issue, an interview with a Dr. Munje purports to put forth to its readers the truth of the matter. Among the claims made in this article is that Muslims have no authority or right to demand that music not be played outside their mosques, since "Musalman history is replete with the horrors of their destruction of Hindu temples, and Hindus, being of superior religious sentiments are not merely responding reactively to such a history. Hindus, characteristically, respect mosques as they do temples. But they do not see the necessity to impose a ban on music. Indeed, it is not accepted by all Muslims either. But if this new way of showing respect is being instituted through force then Hindus have to unite and protect their own religion." The issue remained thorny through the next year as well. See *Kesari*, April 17, 1928; July 10, 1928; Sept 11, 1928; and August 24, 1929.

69. See Khanna, *Gayanacharya Shriman Pandit Vishnu Digambarji Paluskar*, 41.

70. In Patwardhan, *Mazhe Guru Charitra* (82), this is the account given of their subsequent meeting. "Later on, Maulana Mohammad Ali met Panditji in Deccan Hyderabad [*sic*], where Mohammad Ali said to Panditji, "you really let me have it in Kokinad," upon which Panditji responded [in Marathi] "I didn't perceive you as insulting me personally, but music itself, and because I could not bear such an insult I had to speak up."

71. Deodhar, *Gayanacharya Pandit Vishnu Digambar,* 98.

72. According to B. R. Deodhar (ibid., 82–83), he owed Seth Vithaldas Thackersay Rs. 2 Lakhs. But Paluskar was so bent on not registering the school as a public school, he preferred to go bankrupt. This view is challenged by Balwantrao Joshi, the current registrar of the GMV, who points to Paluskar's meticulous financial accounting as proof that he was not in over his head. Until Vithaldas Thackersay's death in 1923, Paluskar could rest easy in the confidence that Thackersay would not hound him to repay the debt. After Thackersay's death in 1923, his heirs were less inclined to give Paluskar quite so much leeway and insisted that he pay off the debt.

73. Deodhar would go on to train one of India's most famous vocal musicians, Kumar Gandharva, who, the story goes, refused to sing ragas such as *Miyan ki Malhar* because they were considered Muslim ragas.

74. For a tremendously touching narration of Paluskar's last years, see Deodhar, 120–29.

75. See ibid., 104. The Mandal, in 1971, had over five hundred members and over two hundred affiliated institutions of music. The number of students who took their examinations exceeded 10,000.

76. B. R. Deodhar included in *Gayanacharya Pandit Vishnu Digambar,* 104–5, a list of the institutions founded during and after Paluskar's death. I translate the list here in its entirety to demonstrate the sweep of Paluskar's program. "1. Saraswati Sangeet Vidyalaya, Karachi. Shri Kalyanabharati who had studied music using Panditji's books and held him to be his guru founded this school in 1916. 2. Gopal Gayan Samaj, Pune, founded 1918. Founder: Pandit Govind Gopal Desai. 3. Gandharva Mahavidyalaya, Kolhapur, founded in 1920 by Waman Hanmant Padhye. 4. School of Indian Music, Mumbai, founded in 1925 by Professor B. R. Deodhar. 5. Shriram Sangeet Vidyalaya, Sitabardi, Nagpur, founded in 1926 by Shri Shankarrao Sapre, who held Panditji in high esteem as his guru. 6. Maharashtra Sangeet Vidyalaya, Mumbai, founded in 1926 by Baburao (Ganesh) Ramchandra Gokhale. 7. Shriram Sangeet Vidyalaya, Solapur, founded in 1926 by Ramchandra Bhikhaji Soman. 8. Prayag Sangeet Samiti, Allahabad, founded in 1926. [Prayag, as it would come to be called, would be the rival institution to Bhatkhande's Marris College.] Pandit Vishnu Annaji Kashalkar's efforts combined the forming of both the Sangeet Samiti (society) and the Sangeet Vidyalaya. 9. Deodhar then lists two other schools that were founded in Old Delhi by Pandit Brahmanand Vyas and Umadatta Sharma in Jammu, but doesn't give us the dates."

   The list goes on to include schools that were founded after Paluskar's death. I begin my translation again with that list. "11. Gandharva Mahavidyalaya, Nasik, founded in 1931 by Paluskar's widow, Shrimati Gangabai Paluskar. 12. The Gandharva Mahavidyalaya Mandal. 13. Vishnu Sangeet Vidyalaya, Nasik, founded in 1932 by Pandit Bhagwati Prasad Trivedi. 14. Gandharva Mahavidyalaya, Pune, founded in 1932 by Pandit V. N. Patwardhan. 15. Gandharva Mahavidyalaya, Ahmedabad, founded in 1935, by Pandits Narayanrao Khare, Shankarrao Vyas and Gopalrao Joshi. 16. Vyas Sangeet Vidyalaya, Dadar, Mumbai, founded in 1937 by Pandits Shankarrao Vyas and Narayanrao Vyas. 17. Gandharva Mahavidyalaya, Karachi, founded in 1937, by Laxmanrao Bodas. This school functioned well until the country's partition. 18. Gandharva Mahavidyalaya, Amritsar, founded in 1938, by Raghunath Rao Kulkarni. 19. Gandhi Sangeet Vidyalaya, Kanpur, founded in 1948 by Pandit Shankar Shripad Bodas and Pandit Lalmani Mishra. 20. College of Music and Fine Arts, founded in 1952 was incorporated as a permanent part of Benares Hindu University, through the tremendous efforts made in this direction by Pandit Omkarnath Thakur."

77. See appendix for copies of forms used by the Mandal to proctor examinations.

78. Pandit V. R. Athavale is also one of Pandir Paluskar's biographers. See his *Vishnu Digamba Paluskar* (New Delhi, 1967).

79. Personal communication with Pandit V. R. Athavale, Nana Bodas, and Balwantrao Joshi, June 2000, at Pandit Athavale's apartment in Vashi. All three men gave generously of their time when they found out I was working on a chapter on Pandit Paluskar. The conversations were all in Marathi, and all translations are mine.

80. See Fourth Annual Report, Gandharva Mahavidyalaya, Bombay, October 1911–September 1912, in *Gandharva Mahavidyalaya* 3.10 (1912): 156–60.

81. See *Kesari*, September 4, 1917.

82. See Deodhar, *Gayanacharya Pandit Vishnu Digambar*, 50–51.

83. *Gandharva Mahavidyalaya*, January 10, 1911; *Times of India*, January 4, 1911.

84. See Shriram Nam Adhaar Ashram, *Mahila Sangeet* (in Hindi), part 1 (Nasik, 1933).

85. In the fourth Annual Report of the Gandharva Maha Vidyalaya, the Sanatan Dharm Sabha Jagadri and Lala Lajpat Rai of the Arya Samaj are listed as donors. There are additionally a number of donors whose names all begin with "Lala," which was the typical address for someone belonging to the Arya Samaj. I do not state that because their names all began with "Lala" they were definitely members of the *samaj*, but it is a likely possibility. If it is true, then the *samaj* was a large donor to the Gandharva Mahavidyalaya. See also Deodhar, "K. Vishnu Digambar tatha Unke Karya," *Sangeet Kala Vihar* 9 (1949): 9–13.

86. Personal communication with Pandit Shruti Sadolikar, a contemporary musician who claims Alladiya Khan as her guru, in her home in Hindu Colony, Bombay, October 1999. The implication was that Alladiya Khan was not a "real" Muslim but came from a Brahmin family that had been coerced into conversion.

87. See Deodhar, *Gayanacharya Pandit Vishnu Digambar,* 52–53.

88. See *Gandharva Mahavidyalaya* 610–12 (1915–16): 147–60, 177–90.

89. See Patwardhan, *Mazhe Gurucharitra,* 61–63.

90. Ibid. See also the *Report of the All-India Music Conference, Baroda, March 20–25* (Baroda, 1917), 25.

91. See Sharatchandra Gokhale, *Vishrabdha Sharada,* vol. 2, *Marathi Rangbhumi, Maharashtrateel Sangeet.*

92. As told to me in Marathi by Dr. Sharatchandra Gokhale in Bombay, November 1999. Dr. Gokhale has since passed away.

Chapter 5

1. For an examination of the role of modern Indian science in the discourse of nationalism, see Gyan Prakash, *Another Reason: Science and the Imagination of Modern India* (Princeton, N.J., 2000).

2. *Report of the All-India Music Conference; Report of the Second All-India Music Conference Held at Delhi, December 14–17, 1918* (New Delhi, 1919); *Report of the Third All-India Music Conference Held at Benares, December 19–22, 1919* (Kashi, 1919); *The Report of the Fourth and Fifth All-India Music Conference, Lucknow,* vol. 1 (Lucknow, 1925). Henceforth referred to as AIMC 1, 2, 3, 4, and 5.

3. See Letter to Rai Umanath Bali, printed in *Bhatkhande Smriti Grantha* (Hindi and English), Indira Kala Sangeet Vishwavidyalaya, Khairagarh, 1966, 383–384.

4. I use the following sources in this chapter: Bhatkhande's music conference reports (in English); Paluskar's music conference reports, articles from the *Kesari* and Paluskar's biographies (in Marathi); selected newspaper reports from *Jayaji Pratap* (the publication of the princely state of Gwalior, where Bhatkhande established his first school of music) published in a collection of primary source material related to Bhatkhande called *Bhatkhande Smriti Grantha* (in Marathi and Hindi); papers presented at Bhatkhande's conferences (in English); Bhatkhande's published and unpublished letters (in English and Marathi).

5. *AIMC* 1, 52.

6. Ibid., 50.

7. Selected Letters of His Highness, the Maharaja Sayaji Rao Gaekwar, Letter 1256, vol 2, 829, Baroda University Library.

8. See Deodhar, *Gayanacharya Pandit Vishnu Digambar Paluskar,* 117–18.

9. Ibid., in which a conversation between Bhatkhande and Deodhar is reported.

10. The book in question was written by Hermann von Helmholtz, titled *On the Sensations of Tone As a Physiological Basis for the Theory of Music,* and initially published in 1884 (reprint, New York, 1954).

11. See Alexander J. Ellis, "On the Musical Scales of Various Nations," *Journal of the Society of Arts*, March 27, 1885, 485–527. It is also addressed directly in K. B. Deval, *The Hindi Musical Scale and the 22 Shrutees*.

12. See Deval, *The Hindu Musical Scale and the 22 Shrutees*.

13. Unpublished letter from V. N. Bhatkhande to Nawab Ali, undated, from Malabar Hill, Thursday, sometime in 1910 or 1911.

14. Ibid.

15. Ibid.

16. From the announcement sent to Professor Bhaskarbua Bakhle, Bharat Gayan Samaj, by K. B. Deval, Esq., Hon. Secretary Phil-Harmonic Society of Western India, Satara. Bhaskarbua Bakhle Foundation, Pune.

17. *AIMC* I, 11.

18. Ibid., 10–11.

19. Ibid., 15.

20. See K. B. Deval's *Theory of Indian Music as Expounded by Somanatha*.

21. D. K. Joshi and his brother, M. K. Joshi, were enlisted by Bhatkhande ten years after the conference to be music teachers at his school. They were friends of his from Pune and presented papers at the conference on *shruti*.

22. *AIMC* I, 23.

23. Ibid., 25.

24. Ibid., 25.

25. Ibid., I, 31.

26. Ibid., 33.

27. Maulvi Abdul Halim Sharar was the famous author of a fictional historical account of life in old Lucknow, titled *Guzishtah Lucknow: Mashriqi Tamaddun ka akhiri Namunah* (*Lucknow of Old: The Last Example of Eastern Civilization*) (Lucknow, 1965).

28. Part of the text of Maulvi Abdul Halim Sharar's speech was published in a journal edited by Bhatkhande's student, Shrikrishna Ratanjankar, called *Sangita: A Quarterly Journal of Hindustani Music* 2.1 (1932): 38–66.

29. *AIMC* I, 19.

30. Tassaduq Hussain Khan was the brother of the famous Faiyaz Khan, also in the employ of the ruler of Baroda. Faiyaz Khan was appointed to the court as per an order dated March 27, 1913, and was paid Rs. 100 per month with a transportation allowance of Rs. 15. His brother, Tassaduq Hussain Khan, was paid Rs. 45 per month and given no transportation allowance. See *HHN* 1914–15, 70–71, book number 123, related to 1912–13, 540. See also book number 123, 533, Baroda State Records, Indumati Mahal, Baroda.

31. *AIMC* I, 57.

32. Ibid., 58.

33. *AIMC* 2, 10.

34. See Ritu Birla, "Hedging Bets: The Politics of Commercial Ethics in Late Colonial India" (unpublished dissertation, Columbia University, 1999).

35. *AIMC* 2, 7.

36. Ibid., 13.

37. Ibid., iii.

38. See, for instance, *AIMC* 2, 51, in which Rai Saheb Pundit Sriniwas Pandeya of Ahrura delivered a paper on "Todi Varieties," in which he claimed that "the antiquity of Indian music is simply patent and does not require much of arguments to prove the fact. . . . One of the Vedas which is called Sama Veda is composed of songs alone and those songs are sung even now, although sparingly. It is thus clear that the Indian music claims the remotest antiquity in the land." He goes on to claim, on the subject of music's corruption that "what words were used in Alap have now come to be corrupted. The words used now-a-days are *anantari* which are meaningless from the point of Sanskrit glossary. I believe this corruption came to be in vogue since the art fell entirely into the hands of Mohammedan musicians. Most of them were not and are even generally not students of Sanskrit literature and thus in their attempt to grapple at a Sanskrit sentence thoroughly mispronounced it."

39. Ibid., 10.

40. Ibid., 26.

41. There were no major differences between Bhatkhande's notation system and those used by Fredilis and Clements, except that Bhatkhande's was by far the simplest of the three.

42. See appendix D, National Academy of Music, Foreword, *AIMC* 2.

43. See *AIMC* 3, appendix, paper read by Begum F. Rahamin, 90–100.

44. See Patwardhan, *Mazhe Gurucharitra*, for a recapitulation of the polemics between Bhatkhande and Paluskar, although in this narration, Bhatkhande comes across as irrational and arrogant, while Paluskar is viewed as calm, serene and indifferent.

45. *AIMC* 3, 70.

46. Ibid., 71.

47. The objectives of the Bharat Kala Parishad were to found a "first grade school and studio for teaching Indian music, painting, sculpture and other Indian arts and crafts," and to establish galleries, museums, provide scholarships for students of the arts and generally promote public interest by preserving the individuality of Indian art. See draft rules of the Bharat Kala Parishad.

48. Unpublished letter from Nawab Ali to Rai Umanath Bali, Nabha, August 25, 1920. Property of Rai Swareshwar Bali, Lucknow.

49. Unpublished letter from Rai Umanath Bali to Bhatkhande, from Daryabad Estate, Barabanki, Oudh. Property of Rai Swareshwar Bali. Undated; possibly written on August 23, 1920.

50. Letter from Bhatkhande to Rai Umanath Bali, Rampur, September 1. The year is not given, but since Bhatkhande refers to an upcoming *AIMC* in Indore, which came to nothing by 1922, I surmise this letter would have been written in 1920.

51. Chinchore, *Bhatkhande Smriti Grantha*, letter from Bhatkhande to Rai Umanath Bali, May 1922, 376–78.

52. "Uttar Pradesh ka Param Saubhagya," in ibid., 273–76.

53. Unpublished letter from Nawab Ali Khan, Akbarpuri, PO Laharpura, District Sitapura, June 13, 1924, to Rai Umanath Bali. Property of Rai Swareshwar Bali, Lucknow.

54. *AIMC* 4, 9.

55. *AIMC* 4, 80, 81.

56. See Chinchore, *Bhatkhande Smriti Grantha*, letter to Rai Umanath Bali, 385: "Rajas and Maharajas remain so in name only. Approach them with an appeal for money and they will turn their faces away from you."

57. See *AIMC* 3, financial statement, 3–6.

58. See *AIMC* 4, 102.

59. Speech delivered by Hon'ble Rai Rajeshwar Bali, O.B.E., Minister of Education, at the opening ceremony of the Marris College of Hindustani Music, held at the Kaisarbagh Baradari, Lucknow, on September 16, 1926. From the library archives of the Bhatkhande Hindustani Sangeet Mahavidyalaya. The Bali family still owns the Kaisarbagh Baradari, which is run by Rai Umanath Bali's son, Rai Swareshwar Bali.

60. See "Marris College of Music, Lucknow," *Sangeeta* 1.1 (1930): 47–52.

61. At the college, exams were held twice a year, and after a five-year course a degree of music was granted. First-year students paid Rs. 2 per year, and the amount increased in small increments, with fifth-year students paying Rs. 4 per year.

62. See "Marris College of Music, Lucknow."

63. Letter to Rai Umanath Bali, February 28, 1927. Property of Rai Swareshwar Bali.

64. See Gyanendra Pandey, *The Ascendancy of Congress in Uttar Pradesh: Class, Community and Nation in Modern India*, 2nd ed. (London, 2002).

65. Bhatkhande, letter to Rai Umanath Bali, March 8, 1928. Property of Rai Swareshwar Bali, Lucknow.

66. Bhatkhande, letter to Rai Umanath Bali, February 28, 1927. Property of Rai Swareshwar Bali, Lucknow.

67. Bhatkhande, letter to Rai Umanath Bali, May 16, 1928. Property of Rai Swareshwar Bali, Lucknow.

68. Bhatkhande, letter to Rai Umanath Bali, February 24, 1928. Property of Rai Swareshwar Bali, Lucknow.

69. Bhatkhande, letter to Rai Umanath Bali, February 24, 1928. Property of Rai Swareshwar Bali, Lucknow.

70. Bhatkhande, letter to Rai Umanath Bali, May 30, 1928. Property of Rai Swareshwar Bali, Lucknow.

71. See Chinchore, *Bhatkhande Smriti Grantha*, 384, published letter from Bhatkhande to Rai Umanath Bali, September 3, 1932. Property of Rai Swareshwar Bali, Lucknow.

72. See Bali's remembrances in *Acharya Shrikrishna Ratanjankar, "Sujan": Jeevani tatha Smrutisanchay* (Bombay, 1993), 336. The Vidyapeeth is an administrative body that oversees the workings of the college.

73. Gandharva Mahavidyalaya, *Pahili Sangeet Parishad*, 1. ABGMV Archives, Meraj.

74. Ibid., 3.

75. See *Story of My Life*, M. R. Jayakar. Jayakar was a liberal barrister who opposed Gandhi's noncooperation movement.

76. Gandharva Mahavidyalaya, *Pahili Sangeet Parishad*, 3.

77. Ibid., 13.

78. See *Kesari,* January 6, 1925.

79. See *Kesari,* March 20, 1928.

80. See *Kesari,* December 7, 1929.

81. I was able to get a copy only because of family connections to numerous musicians, but it was still extraordinarily difficult because the musicians I talked with were suspicious about my motives and what I might write about Bhatkhande.

Chapter 6

1. I am grateful to Milind Wakankar for this insight.

2. Kapileshwari, *Abdul Karim Khan*, 52, 55.

3. Ibid., 57.

4. See note 37 to chap. 1.

5. Kapileshwari, *Abdul Karim Khan*, 61.

6. The day I wrote these words, Edward Said passed away. He was one of my most influential teachers, even though I took only one course with him in graduate school. He was not only a teacher, but also a supportive senior colleague. His influence permeates this book, in my attempt to write a secular, critical history of music and my critique of regional exceptionalism and insularity, both of which he detested.

7. Kapileshwari, *Abdul Karim Khan*, 455, 464.

8. See Rajaram Humne, *Dhanya Janma Jaahla: Shrimati Hirabai Barodekar yaanche jeevan gane* (Poona, 1980), 3.

9. Kapileshwari, *Abdul Karim Khan*, 236.

10. Humne, *Dhanya Janma Jaahla*, 73.

11. Ibid.

12. Kapileshwari, *Abdul Karim Khan*, 425–38.

13. Ibid., 599–600.

14. Ibid., 459. Emphasis mine.

15. Ibid., 454, 460.

16. Ibid., 452.

17. Ibid., 453.

18. Ibid., 468.

19. Ibid., 496.

20. Ibid., 488.

21. Ibid., 489–504.

22. Ibid.

23. Ibid., 616, my translation.

24. Ibid., 790.

25. Ibid., 785.

26. Ibid., 811.

27. See Chapter 5 for an extensive discussion of the disagreement between Bhatkhande and Deval, Clements and Abdul Karim.

28. See footnote 11 to chapter 5. I am grateful to James Kippen for the exact citation as well as for clarifying my misperception of this article.

29. Kapileshwari, *Abdul Karim Khan*, 444–48. See also chapter 5 of this book.

30. Ibid., 643.

31. The entire argument is presented over twenty pages. See Kapileshwari, *Abdul Karim Khan*, 641–66.

32. Kapileshwari addresses the difficulties in the marriage over several pages in *Abdul Karim Khan*. See especially 670–75.

33. Ibid., 715.

34. Ibid., 764–65.

35. Ibid., 799.

36. Ibid., 895–97.

37. See Humne, *Dhanya Janma Jaahla*, 50–51.

38. See ibid., 22. I have also consulted Shailja Pandit and Arun Halwe, *Gaanhira* (in Marathi; Bombay, 1985).

39. Humne, *Dhanya Janma Jaahla*, 60.

40. Ibid., 6.

41. Ibid., deeksha, 7.
42. Ibid., jadan ghadan, 14.
43. For a complete list of Hirabai's recordings, see Humne, *Dhanya Janma Jaahla*, 111–13.
44. I have drawn extensively from Kathryn Hansen's work on Parsi theater, "Making Women Visible."
45. See Humne, *Dhanya Janma Jaahla*, Ek natyanubhav, 31–33.
46. See ibid., 28.
47. Ibid., 28–29.
48. See ibid., ashya mehfili, ase shrotey, 99.
49. See ibid., jadan ghadan, 20.
50. See Humne, *Dhanya Janma Jaahla*, 117.
51. See ibid., 94.
52. Ibid., 60.
53. The origins of *gharana*s themselves go back, we are told, to the Mughal Period (1526–1858). A few professional singers and dancers, known as *ghaadi-mirasi*, secured positions at the court and were known as *nayak*. From this group of professional singers and dancers derive the four major *gharana*s—Gwalior, Jaipur, Agra, and Kirana. Over the years, they evolved into semiprofessional guilds with elaborate rules about commensality, known as *roti-beti vyavhaar*. Prescriptive protocols turned into proscriptive rules because of evolving competitiveness and rivalry.
54. Kapileshwari, *Abdul Karim Khan*, 11–14; see also Humne, *Dhanya Janma Jaahla*, 69.

❀ GLOSSARY ❀

The definitions provided here are meant to indicate my use and understanding of the Marathi, Hindi, and Gujarati words included. The definitions do not by any means include all possible uses and meanings of the words in question but are meant to indicate how they have been used in the text. Where the language is not indicated in parentheses, the word in question is common to two languages, Hindi and Marathi. I have glossed a selection of musicological terms, paying attention to their colloquial usage. So, for instance, the word *aalaap* is more accurately glossed by Raghava Menon in *Indian Classical Music* as "improvised melody figures that gradually reveal the raga," but I have chosen to gloss it, more simply, as the beginning, or introductory, section of a performance. In producing this glossary I have crosschecked my terms with glossaries in published ethnomusicological and musicological texts. I am grateful to my colleague, Susham Bedi, who has looked over the glossary and offered suggestions and corrections. That being said, all errors are mine and mine alone.

Aalaap. Introductory section of a performance
Aarti. Devotional prayer
Aavartan. Metric time cycle

Abhang. Devotional song (Marathi)

Adhaar. Backing/foundation/authority (Marathi)

Aftab-e-Mausiki. Radiance of music (Urdu)

Agarbatti. Incense

Akhil Bharatiya Gandharva Mahavidyalaya Mandal (ABGMV). All India Gandharva Mahavidyalaya Organization

Akhil Bharatiya. All-India

Akhyans. Stories (Marathi)

Akkal-hushaari. With the full knowledge and use of intellect (Marathi)

Amar Chitra Katha. Series of comic books for children

Amchyaat. Within our community (Marathi)

Antara. Second part of a vocal composition

Anuvadi swar. Succeeding note (second in importance after the predominant note)

Ardhaswar. Half a note

Arya Samaj. Hindu reform association founded in 1875

Arya Sangeet. Ancient music

Ashaadi ekadashi. Day of prayer in the month of Ashaad, in praise of Shiva

Ashram. Sanctuary/free boarding house

Asthayi. First part of a composition, usually focused on the lower range of the raga scale

Bahuroopi. Impersonations/impersonators, a form of courtly entertainment

Baijis. Women courtesan performers

Bairaagi. Mendicant who has renounced worldly pleasures

Baithak. Performance

Bakshees. Payments/reward

Bamman. Non-Brahmin Marathi pejorative term for Brahmin

Been. North Indian stick zither, also known as *vina* in South India

Beenkar. One who plays the been

Besur. Off-tune

Bhaand. Performing artist focusing mainly on mime

Bhajan. Devotional song

Bhajani haridas. One who sings only *bhajan*s

Bhakti. Devotion

Bhandkhor. Someone who picks fights easily (Marathi)

Bin bobhat. Without demur (Marathi)

Bin takraar. Without complaint (Marathi)

Chaitragouri puja. Worship of Gouri (consort of Shiva) in the first month of the
Marathi calendar, Chaitra

Chandrika hi janu. Title of a Marathi theater composition

Charpai. Bed/bamboo mat

Chaturpandit. Clever pandit

Dadra. Rhythmic cycle of six beats, also a vocal compositional form, light in style

Darbari gavai. Court singer

Darbar. Court

Dargah. Shrine

Deepak. Lamp, light, name of a raga

Deshi. Native

Desh-seva. Patriotic service to the nation

Dewan. Prime minister

Dhamar. Rhythmic cycle

Dharmashastras. Code books

Dhrupad. Compositional music form in four sections, *sthayi, antara, sanchari,*
and *abhog*

Dhruvapad. Sanskrit word for *dhrupad*

Dilruba. Stringed instrument played with a bow

Doha. A rhyming couplet, in which each line consists of half-lines made up of
feet of 6+4+3 and 6+4+1 *maatras*

Dokyaat nahi. Not in one's head (Marathi)

Dwija. Twice born

Faujdar Khaata. Military department

Galyaachi taiyaari. Voice preparation (Marathi)

Galyaat ahe. In one's throat (Marathi)

Gandharva Mahavidyalaya. Name of Pandit Paluskar's school

Gandharva Veda. Name of an eponymous fifth Veda

Ganpati stavan. Prayer sung to the god Ganpati

Garba. Gujarati dance and music form

Gayan Prakash. Bhaushastri Ashtaputre's hand-illustrated history of ragas and
raginis

Gayan shastra. Classical science of music

Gayatri Mantra. A Vedic meter, the name of a particularly sacred verse of the Rig
Veda typically recited by Brahmin and Dwija boys

Gharana ustad. Maestro from a gharana

Gharana. Literally, "of a house," semiprofessional guilds

Gharanedar. From a gharana

Gondhal. Form of courtly entertainment (Marathi)

Grama. Ancient scale

Granthas. Authoritative texts

Gudhicha padava. Marathi new year, also the first day of the month Chaitra (Marathi)

Gurav vajantri. Instrumentalist to accompany a priest at prayer (Marathi)

Guru. Preceptor/teacher

Gurukul. School in which guru-shishya parampara is maintained

Guru-shishya parampara. Tradition/lineage of preceptors, traditional pedagogical exchange between student and preceptor

Haathpeti. Musical instrument also known as harmonium (Marathi)

Halad kunku. Turmeric and vermillion, distributed to women on auspicious days (Marathi)

Haveli. Traditional homes (mansions) of rich elites

Hindi sanskriti. Hindi culture/civilization

Holaar. Instrument

Hori. Light-hearted musical composition

Ilm. Knowledge (Urdu)

Itihaas. History

Jaati. Community/fold/race

Jadu tona. Black magic

Jagrut. Term used to suggest that a particular temple deity is powerful (Marathi)

Jalsa. A musical event or music recital, performance

Jaltarang. Musical instrument

Kagad dene. Giving of paper (Marathi)

Kalavant khatyache niyam. Rules for the *kalavant karkhaana*

Kalavants. Artists of the *kalavant karkhaana*

Kalsutri. Cunning

Kansen. Play on Tansen, the name of the famous singer in the Mughal Emperor Akbar's court, in which instead of *tan* the word *kan*, meaning "ear," is substituted. The neologism refers to musically trained listeners who may or may not themselves be performers.

Karmanuk. Distraction/entertainment (Marathi)

Kavita. Poem

Kesari. Title of Marathi newspaper

Khaangi karbhaari. Official in charge of the department's finances (Marathi)

Khaata. Financial term, also used for financial balance

Khandaani ustad. Hereditary musician

Khayal. Dominant vocal compositional form of North Indian music, in two parts, *sthayi* and *antara*, built through a variety of improvisations

Khel. Literally, play, but used interchangeably with performance or show

Kirtankar. Devotional singer

Kirtans. Devotional songs (Marathi)

Kramik Pustak Malika. Textbook by Bhatkhande

Krishna jayanti. A night that religious people spend in prayer

Kulaswaminichi shapath. Oath sworn in the name of the family deity (Marathi)

Kulin. Upper-caste, Brahmin, respectable, from a good family

Lalitacha tamaasha. Show performed on auspicious occasions (Marathi)

Lavani. Entertainment form, combining music, dance, and singing; can be ribald and raucous (Marathi)

Laya. Rhythm, tempo

Maatra. One beat

Madhukari. Alms given to a Brahmin student (Marathi)

Mahapaap. Great sin

Manajirao. Shivram Mahadev Paranjpe's transation of *Macbeth*

Mandra saptak. Lower septet

Mehfil. A small and intimate gathering in which a musician performs

Mridang. Two-faced percussive drum

Nalayak. Slacker (Marathi)

Natak. Drama

Nirupyogi panditya. Useless pedantry/knowledge (Marathi)

Paan supari. Betel nut

Pakhawaj. Double-headed barrel drum

Panchatantra katha. Stories from the *Panchatantra*

Pandals. Tents set up for festive occasions

Pati. Husband (Hindi)

Payacha dagad. Foundational stone (Marathi)

Pehelvaan. Wrestler

Pheta. Turban

Prachaarit sangit. Current music (Marathi)

Prachaar. Spread (Marathi)

Pramukh. Head musician

Pratham shreni. First rank

Pravachan. Speech similar to a sermon, based on a text (Marathi)

Prayog. Literally, experiment; in the musical sense it means performance (Marathi)

Purna upyog. Full use (Marathi)

Raga. Scale of notes that has a minimum of five notes, with an ascent and descent (*aaroha* and *avroha*)

Rajashraya. Princely patronage/protection (Marathi)

Rajikhushi. Uncoerced choice (Marathi)

Rajmaata. Mother of the king

Rajputra. Son of the king

Rakshas. Demons

Riaz. Practice

Rishi. Sage

Sadhu. One who has renounced the world and spends time in meditation and prayer

Sam. First beat of a rhythmic cycle

Samvadi. Note in the upper tetrachord of a raga, separated from the *vadi* by at least four notes and equal in importance to the *vadi* note

Sangeet Vidya. The science/wisdom/knowledge of music

Sangeetache niyam. The rules of music (Marathi)

Sangit parijat. Seventeenth-century treatise on music theory

Sangit Ratnakara. Thirteenth-century treatise on music

Sansaari sadhu. Worldly monk

Sant manus. Saintly person (Marathi)

Sarangi. Twenty-seven-string, fretless bowed instrument

Saraswati. Goddess of knowledge

Sardar. Nobleman

Sarkaari gaadi. State vehicle

Sarkaari nokar. Court servants or employees

Senapati. Warrior

Shloka. Couplet

Shruti. Microtone

Siddha purusha. Enlightened man

Sthayi. See *asthayi*

Surel. Tuneful

Sutradhar. Storyteller

Swadeshi. Self-reliance

Swarajya. Self-rule

Tabla. Set of two drums, the other being the *dagga*

Tai. Older sister (Marathi)

Tala. Rhythmic cycle

Taleem. Training (Urdu)

Tamasha. Light-hearted staged theatrical production

Tan. Musical phrase in which the notes have patterns that grow in speed

Tanpura. Four-stringed drone (can also be five- or six-stringed)

Tansen. Legendary musician in the court of the Mughal emperor Akbar

Tappa. Light classical song

Thaat. Grouping of ragas

Thor gayak. Famous singer/artist (Marathi)

Thumri. Romantic vocal composition, sometimes melancholy

Tondaal. Someone who shoots his or her mouth off (Marathi)

Traatika. Vasudevrao Kelkar's version of *The Taming of the Shrew*

Ucch koti. First rank, top echelon

Upa Veda. Ancillary Veda

Upadeshak. Teacher

Urs. Death anniversary of a saint (Urdu)

Ustad. Teacher/master, used as an honorific term

Vachak. Reader (Marathi)

Vadi swar. Dominant note in the scale of a raga, usually positioned in the lower tetrachord, the note responsible for conveying along with the *samvadi* note the emotive feeling of a given raga

Vidushak. Comedian

Vidya. Knowledge

Vikarvilasit. Bal Gangadhar Tilak's translation of *Hamlet*

Vivadi swar. Discordant note

Wada. Ancestral home (Marathi)

Zamindar. Landlord

Zunzarrao. G. B. Deval's Marathi adaptation of *Othello*

BIBLIOGRAPHY

Abbate, Carolyn. *Unsung Voices: Opera and Musical Narrative in the Nineteenth Century*. Princeton, N.J.: Princeton University Press, 1991.

———. *In Search of Opera*. Princeton, N.J.: Princeton University Press, 2001.

Adorno, Theodor W. *Philosophy of Modern Music*. Translated by Anne G. Mitchell and Wesley V. Blomster. New York, 1948.

———. *In Search of Wagner*. Translated by Rodney Livingstone. London, 1981.

Adorno, Theodor W. *Sound Figures*. Translated by Rodney Livingstone. Stanford, Calif.: Stanford University Press, 1999.

Agarwala, V. K. *Traditions and Trends in Indian Music*. Meerut: Rastogi Publications, 1975.

Ahmad, Najma Perveen. *Hindustani Music: A Study of Its Development in Seventeenth and Eighteenth Centuries*. New Delhi: Manohar Publications, 1984.

Alam, Muzaffar. *The Crisis of Empire in Mughal North India: Awadh and the Punjab, 1707–1748*. New Delhi: Oxford University Press, 1986.

Ali, Irshad. *Muslim Lokgeetonka Vivechanatmak Adhyayan* (in Hindi). Anubhav Publications, 1985.

Ali, M. Athar. *The Mughal Nobility under Aurangzeb*. Bombay: Asia Publications, 1968.

"Annual Report." *Gandharva Mahavidyalaya*, Lahore, 1904–5.

Asad, Talal. *Genealogies of Religion: Discipline and Reasons of Power in Christianity and Islam.* Baltimore: Johns Hopkins Press, 1993.

Ashtaputre, Bhaushastri. *Gayan Prakash* (in Marathi). Bombay, 1850.

Athavale, V. R. "A Historical Account of Marathi Stage Music." *NCPA Periodical* 7.2 (1978): 16–29.

Athavale, V. R. *Vishnu Digambar Paluskar.* New Delhi: National Book Trust, 1967.

Awasthi, S. S. *A Critique of Hindusthani Music and Music Education.* Jullunder: Dhanpat Rai and Sons.

Baksh, Maula. *Sangitanubhav* (in Gujarati/Marathi). Baroda, 1888.

Bal, Samant. *Marathi Natya Sangeet* (in Marathi). Bombay: Brihanmumbai Mahanagar Palika, 1975.

Bangre, Arun. *Gwalior ki Sangeet Parampara* (in Hindi). Hubli: Yashoyash Prakashan, 1995.

Banhatti, Balkoba Natekar, and Narayan Daso. *Sangit Balbodha* (in Marathi). Poona, 1901.

Banhatti, Narayan Daso. *Gayan Samaj Pustakmala* (in Marathi). Poona: Poona Gayan Samaj, 1906.

Barnett, Richard. *North India between Empires: Awadh, the Mughals, and the British, 1720–1801.* Berkeley: University of California Press, 1980.

Bayly, C. A. *Indian Society and the Making of the British Empire.* Cambridge: Cambridge University Press, 1988.

———. *Empire and Information: Intelligence Gathering and Social Communication in India, 1780–1870.* Cambridge: Cambridge University Press, 1996.

———. *Origins of Nationality in South Asia: Patriotism and Ethical Government in the Making of Modern India.* New Delhi: Oxford University Press, 1998.

Benjamin, Walter. *Illuminations: Essays and Reflections.* Translated by Harry Zohn. New York, 1968.

Bhagavan, Manu. "Demystifying the Ideal 'Progressive': Resistance through Mimicked Modernity in Princely Baroda, 1900–1913." *Modern Asian Studies* 35.2 (2000): 385–409.

Bhagwat, Neela. *Krishnarao Shankar Pandit: A Doyen of Khayal.* Bombay, 1992.

Bhandari, Prem. *Hindustani Sangeet me Gazal Gayaki* (in Hindi). New Delhi: Radha Publications, 1992.

Bhargava, Rajeev, ed. *Secularism and Its Critics.* New Delhi: Oxford University Press, 1998.

Bhate, G. C. *History of Modern Marathi Literature, 1800–1938.* Pune, 1939.

Bhatkhande, V. N. *A Comparative Study of Some of the Leading Music Systems of the 15th, 16th, 17th, 18th Centuries.* Lucknow, 1916.

———. *A Short Historical Survey of the Music of Upper India.* Baroda: Indian Musicological Society, 1916.

———. "Propoganda for the Betterment of the Present Condition of Hindustani Music." Laxmi Press: Delhi, 1922.

———. "A Stray Thought." *Sangeeta* 2.1 (1933).

———. *A Short Historical Survey of the Music of Upper India.* Bombay: B. S. Sukthankar, 1934.

———. *Hindusthani Sangeet Padhdhati*, vols. 1–5 (in Marathi). 2nd ed. Bombay: Popular Prakashan, 1999.

Bhole, Keshavrao. *Majhe Sangeet Rachana ani Digdarshana* (in Marathi). Bombay: Marg Prakashan, 1964.

———. *Je Athavate te* (in Marathi). Pune: Prestige Prakashan, 1974.

Blaukopf, Kurf. "National Identity and Universalism in Music." *NCPA Periodical* 9.3–4 (1982): 15–17.

Bourdieu, Pierre. *Distinction: A Social Critique of the Judgement of Taste.* Translated by Richard Nice. Cambridge: Harvard University Press, 1984.

Brihaspati, Acharya. *Musalman aur Bharatiya Sangit* (in Hindi). Delhi: Rajkamal Publications, 1974.

———. "Mussalman, Gazal, Qawwali aur Khayal (in Hindi)." *Sangeet* 1–2 (1976): 57–63.

———. *Sangeet Chintaman* (in Hindi): Hathras, 1976.

Cannadine, David. *Ornamentalism: How the British Saw Their Empire.* Oxford: Oxford University Press, 2001.

Cashman, R. I. *The Myth of the Lokmanya: Tilak and Mass Politics in Maharashtra.* Berkeley: University of California Press, 1975.

Chakrabarty, Dipesh. *Rethinking Working-Class History: Bengal, 1890–1940.* Princeton, N.J.: Princeton University Press, 1989.

———. *Provincializing Europe.* Princeton, N.J.: Princeton University Press, 2000.

Chakraborty, Shekhar Mriganka. *Indian Musicology.* Calcutta: KLM Private Ltd., 1992.

Chandra, Satish. *Parties and Politics at the Mughal Court, 1707–1740.* 3rd ed. New Delhi: Oxford University Press, 1982.

Chatterjee, Partha. *Nationalist Thought and the Colonial World: A Derivative Discourse?* London: Zed Books, 1986.

———. "Two Poets and Death: On Civil and Political Society in the Non-Christian World." In *Questions of Modernity*, edited by Timothy Mitchell. Minneapolis: University of Minnesota Press, 2000.

———. *The Nation and Its Fragments: Colonial and Postcolonial Histories.* Princeton, N.J.: Princeton University Press, 1994.

———. "Secularism and Toleration." *Economic and Political Weekly* 29, 28 (1994): 1768–77.

Chhatre, Nilakanth Vinayak. *Geetlipi* (in Marathi). Bombay, 1864.

Chinchore, Prabhakar, ed. *Bhatkhande Smriti Grantha* (in Hindi). Khairagarh: Indira Kala Sangit Vishwavidyalaya, 1966.

———. "Pandit Bhatkhande's Thoughts on Thumri." *Journal of Indian Musicological Society* 19 (1988): 22–23.

Clarke, A. B., and Rao Bahadur Govindbhai Desai, *Gazetteer of Baroda State: Volume I, General Information.* Bombay, 1923.

Clements, Ernest. *Introduction to the Study of Indian Music.* London, 1913.

———. *A Note on the Use of European Musical Instruments in India.* Pune, 1916.

———. *The Ragas of Hindustan*, vols. 1–2. Sanghi, 1918, 1919.

Cohn, Bernard. "Representing Authority in Victorian England." In *The Invention of Tradition*, edited by Terrence Ranger and Eric Hobsbawm. Cambridge: Cambridge University Press, 1983.

———. *Colonialism and Its Forms of Knowledge: The British in India.* Princeton, N.J.: Princeton University Press, 1994.

Dahlhaus, Carl. *Between Romanticism and Modernism.* Translated by Mary Whittall. Berkeley: University of California Press, 1980.

———. *Esthetics of Music.* Translated by William Austin. Cambridge: Cambridge University Press, 1982.

Daniel, E. Valentine. *Charred Lullabies: An Anthropography of Violence.* Princeton, N.J.: Princeton University Press, 1998.

Danielou, Alain. "Ethnomusicology." *Journal of Music Academy, Madras* 27 (1956): 47–60.

Datar, Shaila. *Devagandharva* (in Marathi). Pune: Rajhansa Prakashan, 1995.

Day, C. R. *The Music and Musical Instruments of Southern India and the Deccan.* Bombay, 1891.

Deodhar, B. R. "Pandit Vishnu Narayan Bhatkhande: Vyaktitva tatha Karya" (in Hindi). *Sangeet Kala Vihar* 10 (1947): 24–34.

———. *Gayanacharya Pandit V. D. Paluskar* (in Marathi). Bombay: Akhil Bharatiya Gandharva Mahavidyalaya Mandal, 1971.

———. "K. P. Vishnu Digambar va unke Karya (in Hindi)." *Sangeet Kala Vihar* 9 (1949).

———. *NCPA Periodical* 10.1 (1981): 27–32.

———. *Thor Sangeetkar* (in Marathi). Bombay: Popular Prakashan, 1993.

Desai, Chaitanya. "Indian Music: Ancient, Medieval and Modern." *Journal of the Indian Musicological Society* 4.3 (1973): 31–40.

Deshpande, A. N. *Adhunik Marathi Vangmayacha Itihaas* (in Marathi). 2nd ed. Pune, 1970.

Deshpande, Vamanrao. *Maharashtra's Contribution to Music.* Bombay: Popular Prakashan, 1972.

———.*Indian Musical Traditions: An Aesthetic Study of the Gharanas in Hindustani Music.* Bombay: Popular Prakashan, 1973.

———. *Between Two Tanpuras.* Bombay: Popular Prakashan, 1989.

Deva, B. C. *Indian Music.* New Delhi: Indian Council on Cultural Affairs, 1979.

———. *The Music of India.* New Delhi: Munshiram Manoharlal, 1980.

Deval, K. B. *Music East and West Compared.* Pune: Aryabhushan Press, 1908.

———. *The Hindu Musical Scale and the 22 Shrutis.* Pune: Aryabhushan Press, 1910.

———. *Theory of Indian Music as Expounded by Somanatha.* Poona: Aryabhushan Press, 1916.

———. *The Ragas of Hindustan.* Poona: Philharmonic Society of Western India, 1921.

Dharmavrat, Swami. *Mala Umajlele Alladiya Khan* (in Marathi). Bombay: Marg Prakashan, 1988.

Dhond, M. V. *The Evolution of Khayal.* New Delhi: Sangeet Natak Akademi, 1982.

Dikshitar, Venkateshwar. *Chaturdandi Prakashika.* Bombay: b.c. Sukthankar, 1918.

Dirks, Nicholas B. *The Hollow Crown: Ethnohistory of an Indian Kingdom.* Cambridge: Cambridge University Press, 1987.

———. *Castes of Mind: Colonialism and the Making of Modern India.* Princeton, N.J.: Princeton University Press, 2001.

———, ed. *Colonialism and Culture.* Ann Arbor: University of Michigan Press, 1992.

Dixit, K. D. "Abdul Karim Khan and the Kirana Gharana of Hindusthani Music." *NCPA Periodical* 2.1 (1973): 37–43.

Dobbin, Christine E. *Urban Leadership in Western India: Politics and Communities in Bombay City, 1840–1885.* Oxford: Oxford University Press, 1972.

Ekalavya. *Aajache Prasiddha Gayak va tyanchi Gayankala* (in Marathi). Girgaum: Sahitya Manvantari, 1933.

———. *Sangeetache Maankari* (in Marathi). Girgaum: G. P. Parchure Prakashan, 1949.

Ellis, Alexander J. "On the Musical Scales of Various Nations." *Journal of the Society of Arts* (March 1885): 485–527.

Erdman, Joan. "The Maharaja's Musicians: The Organization of Cultural Performances at Jaipur in the Nineteenth Century." *American Studies in the Anthropology of India*, edited by Sylvia Vatuk. New Delhi: Manohar, 1978.

———. *Patrons and Performers in Rajasthan: The Subtle Tradition.* New Delhi: Chanakya, 1985.

———. "Petitions to the Patrons: Changing Culture's Substance in Twentieth Century Jaipur." In *Arts Patronage in India: Methods, Motives, and Markets,* edited by Joan Erdman. New Delhi: Manohar, 1992.

———, ed. *Arts Patronage in India: Methods, Motives and Markets.* New Delhi: Manohar, 1992.

Fergusson, James. *The History of Indian and Eastern Architecture.* London, 1876.

Fisher, Michael. *A Clash of Cultures: Awadh, the British, and the Mughals.* New Delhi: Oxford University Press, 1987.

———. *Indirect Rule in India: Residents and the Residency System, 1764–1858.* Oxford: Oxford, 1991.

Freitag, Sandria B. *Collective Action and Community: Public Arenas and the Emergence of Communalism in North India.* Berkeley: University of California Press, 1989.

———, ed. *Culture and Power in Banaras: Community, Performance, and Environment, 1800–1980.* Berkeley: University of California Press, 1989.

Fyzee-Rahamin, Atiya Begum. *The Music of India.* New Delhi: Oriental Reprint, 1970.

G. N. Joshi. *Swargangecha Kaathi* (in Marathi). Bombay: Orient Longman, 1984.

Gaekwad, Fatehsinghrao. *Sayajirao of Baroda: The Prince and the Man.* Baroda: Popular Prakashan, 1989.

Gandharva, Kumar. *Anoop Ragvilas* (in Marathi). Bombay: Marg Prakashan, 1965.

Gandharva Mahavidyalaya. "Vividha Samachar" (in Hindi). *Sangit Amrit Pravaha* 3.2 (1907): 30–32.

———. "Vividha Samachar" (in Hindi). *Sangit Amrit Pravaha* 4.2 (1908): 27–28.

———. "Vividha Samachar" (in Hindi). *Sangit Amrit Pravaha* 5.1 (1909): 11–13.

———. "Vividha Samachar" (in Hindi). *Sangit Amrit Pravaha* 7.12 (1911): 177–82.

———. *Annual Report* (in Marathi). Bombay: Gandharva Mahavidyalaya, 1912.

———. "Vividha Samachar" (in Hindi). *Sangit Amrit Pravaha* 9.6 (1913): 81–85.

———. "Fifteenth Anniversary Commemorative Issue" (in Marathi). Bombay: Gandharva Mahavidyalaya, 1915.

———. *Report* (in Marathi). Bombay: Gandharva Mahavidyalaya, 1918.

———. *Admission Rules for Entrance into the Upadeshak Class* (in Marathi). Bombay: Gandharva Mahavidyalaya, 1919.

———. *Report* (in Marathi). Bombay: Gandharva Mahavidyalaya, 1919.

———. *Balodaya Sangeet* (in Marathi and Hindi). Bombay: Gandharva Mahavidyalaya.

———. *Bharatiya Sangeet Lekhan Padhdhati* (in Hindi). Bombay: Gandharva Mahavidyalaya, n.d.

Garg, Lakshminarayan. *Hamare Sangit Ratna* (in Hindi). Hathras: Sangeet Karyalaya, 1957.

Gharpure, Purshottam Ganesh. *Sataareeche pahile Pustak* (in Marathi). Poona, 1883.

Gilmartin, David. *Empire and Islam: Punjab and the Making of Pakistan.* Berkeley: University of California Press, 1988.

Gokhale, Sharatchandra. "Payache Dagad" (in Marathi). *Shabdashri* 82: 56–63.

Guha, Ranajit. "Dominance without Hegemony and Its Historiography." *Subaltern Studies* 6 (1989): 210-309.

———. *Dominance without Hegemony: History and Power in Colonial India.* Cambridge: Harvard University Press, 1997.

Guha-Thakurta, Tapati. *The Making of a New "Indian" Art: Artists, Aesthetics, and Nationalism in Bengal, c. 1850–1920.* Cambridge: Cambridge University Press, 1994.

Hardiman, David. "Baroda: The Structure of a Progressive State." In *People, Princes and Paramount Power*, edited by Robin Jeffrey. New Delhi: Oxford University Press, 1978.

Hariharan, M., and Gouri Kuppuswamy, eds. *Oriental Music in European Notation by Mudaliyar.* New Delhi: Cosmo Publications, 1982.

Havell, E. B. *The Ideals of Indian Art.* London, 1911.

Haynes, Douglas E. *Rhetoric and Ritual in Colonial India: The Shaping of a Public Culture in Surat City, 1852–1928.* Berkeley: University of California Press, 1991.

Heimsath, Charles H. *Indian Nationalism and Hindu Social Reform.* Princeton, N.J.: Princeton University Press, 1964.

Herlekar, V. M., and Purshottam Ganesh Gharpure. *Studies in Indian Music.* Bombay, 1889.

Hermand, Jost, and Michael Gilbert, eds. *German Essays on Music.* New York: Continuum, 1994.

Hesmondhalgh, David, and Georgina Born, eds. *Western Music and Its Others: Difference, Representation, and Appropriation in Music.* Berkeley: University of California Press, 2000.

Hobsbawm, Eric, and Terrence Ranger, eds. *The Invention of Tradition.* Cambridge: Cambridge University Press, 1983.

Holsinger, Bruce W. *Music, Body, and Desire in Medieval Culture: Hildegard of Bingen to Chaucer.* Stanford, Calif.: Stanford University Press, 2001.

Houle, George. *Meter in Music, 1600–1800.* Bloomington: Indiana University Press, 1987.

Humne, Rajaram. *Dhanya Janma Jaahla: Shrimati Hirabai Barodekar yaanche jeevan gane.* (in Marathi). Poona: 1980.

Ingle, K. G. *Pandit Gayanacharya K. Balkrishnabua Ichalkaranjikar yanche Charitra* (in Marathi). Poona: Aryabhushan Press, 1936.

Isacoff, Stuart. *Temperament: The Idea That Solved Music's Greatest Riddle.* New York: Knopf, 2001.

Jairazbhoy, Nazir Ali. "Ethnomusicology in the Indian Context." *NCPA Periodical* 13.3 (1984): 31–39.

Jalal, Ayesha. *The Sole Spokesman: Jinnah, the Muslim League, and the Demand for Partition.* Cambridge: Cambridge University Press, 1985.

———. *Self and Sovereignty: Individual and Community in South Asian Islam Since 1850.* London. Routledge, 2001.

Jariwalla, Jayantilal. *Abdul Karim: The Man of the Times, Life and Art of a Great Musician*. Bombay: Balkrishnabua Kapileshwari, 1973.

Jones, Kenneth. *Arya Dharma: Hindu Nationalism and Hindu Social Reform*. Princeton, N.J.: Princeton University Press, 1976.

———. *Socio-Religious Reform Movements in British India*. New Cambridge History of India. Cambridge: Cambridge University Press, 1989.

Jones, Sir William. "On the Musical Modes of the Hindoos." *Asiatick Researches* 3 (1789).

Joshi, G. N. "Music in Maharashtra." *Journal of the Indian Musicological Society* 1.3 (1972): 5–12.

Kapadia, Pestonjee Firozeshah. "Gayan Uttejak Mandali: Teni Poni Sadani Tawari-khno Ahewal" (in Gujarati). Bombay, 1946.

Kapileshwari, Balkrishnabua. *Abdul Karim Khan yaanche jeevan charitra* (in Marathi). Bombay, 1972.

Kejariwal, O. P. *The Asiatic Society of Bengal and the Discovery of India's Past, 1784–1838*. New Delhi: Oxford University Pres, 1988.

Kelkar, C. V. *Bharat Gayan Samaj Pune: San 1911 te 1940 ya kaalkhandateel sansthecha itihaas* (in Marathi). Pune, 1940.

Keskar, B. V. *Indian Music: Problems and Prospects*. Bombay: Popular Prakashan, 1967.

Khan, Abdul Karim. *Sangeet Swara Prakash* (in Hindi). Belgaum: Shriram Tatva Prakash, 1911.

Khan, Azizuddin. *Sangeet Samrat Khansaheb Alladiya Khan: My Life*. Translated by Amlan Das Gupta and Urmila Bhirdikar. Calcutta, 2000.

Khan, Inayat. *Bhagwant Garbavali* (in Gujarati). Baroda, 1903.

———. *Biography of Pir-o-Murshid Inayat Khan:* East/West Publications, 1979.

Khan, Maula Baksh Ghisse. *Sangitanubhav* (in Gujarati). 1st ed. Baroda, 1888.

———. *Sangitanusaar Chandomanjari* (in Gujarati). Baroda, 1888.

———. *Sitarshikshak* (in Gujarati/Marathi). Baroda, 1888.

———. *Taal Padhati* (in Gujarati/Marathi). Baroda, 1888.

———. *Gujarati Vachan malaki kavitaon ka notation book* (in Hindi/Gujarati). Baroda, 1889.

———. *Balasangitmala* (in Marathi). Baroda, 1890.

———. *Gayan Shalaon me Chalte Gayanon ka Pratham Pustak* (in Hindi/Gujarati). Baroda, 1890.

———. *Narsingh Mehtanu Sangeet Mameru* (in Gujarati). Baroda, 1890.

Khan, Mobarak Hossain. *Music and Its Study*. New Delhi: Sterling Publications, 1988.

———. *Islamic Contribution to South Asia's Classical Music*. New Delhi: Sterling Publishers, 1992.

Khanna, Lala Gurandittamal. *Gayanacharya Shriman Pandit Vishnu Digambarji*

Paluskar ka Sankshipt Jeevan-Vritaant (in Hindi). Lahore: Bombay Machine Press, 1930.

Kinnear, Michael. *The Gramophone Company's First Indian Recordings, 1899–1908.* Bombay: Popular Prakashan, 1994.

Kippen, James. *The Tabla of Lucknow: A Cultural Analysis of a Musical Tradition.* Cambridge Studies in Ethnomusicology. Chicago: University of Chicago Press, 1988.

Kittel, Reverend F. "Review of Nijaguna Sivayogi's Notes on Indian Music." *Indian Antiquary* 3 (1874): 244.

Koselleck, Reinhart. *Futures Past: On the Semantics of Historical Time.* Cambridge, Mass.: MIT Press, 1985.

Kramer, Lawrence. *Music as Cultural Practice: 1800–1900.* Berkeley: University of California Press, 1990.

Krims, Adam, ed. *Music/Ideology: Resisting the Aesthetic:* G&B Arts International, 1998.

Kshirsagar, D. B. *Jodhpur Riyasat Ke Darbari Sangeetagyonka Itihaas* (in Hindi). Jodhpur: Maharaja Mansingh Pustak Prakash, 1942.

Kumar, Ravindra. *Western India in the Nineteenth Century: A Study in the Social History of Maharashtra.* London, 1968.

Leppert, Richard. *The Sight of Sound: Music, Representation, and the History of the Body.* Berkeley: University of California, 1993.

Lobo, Antsher. *Three Monographs on Music.* Bombay: Indian Musicological Society, 1980.

Mahajani, H. R. *Natyasangeet* (in Marathi). Bombay: Makarand Sahitya, 1958.

Mani, Lata. *Contentious Traditions: The Debate on Sati in Colonial India.* Berkeley: University of California Press, 2000.

Manohar, Shivram Sadashiv. *Swaraprastar* (in Marathi). Bombay: Induprakash Press, 1903.

———. *Sangitshikshak* (in Marathi). Bombay: Induprakash Press, 1904.

Manuel, Peter. *Cassette Culture: Popular Music and Technology in North India.* Chicago: University of Chicago Press, 1993.

"Marris College of Music, Lucknow." *Sangeeta: A Quarterly Journal of Hindustani Music* 1.1 (1930): 47–53.

Masselos, Jim. *Towards Nationalism: Group Affiliations and the Politics of Public Associations in Nineteenth-Century Western India.* Bombay: Popular Prakashan, 1974.

Mayer, Adrian C. *Caste and Kinship in Central India: A Village and Its Region.* Berkeley: University of California, 1970.

Mayer, Geeta. "Homage to Bhatkhande." *NCPA Periodical* 9.3 (1980): 31–40.

McClary, Susan, and Richard Leppert, eds. *Music and Society: The Politics of Composition, Performance and Reception.* Cambridge: Cambridge University Press, 1987.

McClary, Susan. *Feminine Endings: Music, Gender and Sexuality.* Minneapolis: University of Minnesota Press, 1991.

Meer, Wim van der. "Cultural Evolution: A Case Study of Indian Music." *Sangeet Natak* 35 (1975): 49–65.

Meer, Wim van der. "The Influence of Social Change in Indian Music." *World of Music* 20.2 (1978): 123–34.

Melton, James Van Horn. *The Rise of the Public in Enlightenment Europe.* Cambridge: Cambridge University Press, 2001.

Metcalf, Thomas. *An Imperial Vision: Indian Architecture and Britain's Raj.* Berkeley: University of California Press, 1989.

Mill, James. *The History of British India.* Abridged reprint. Chicago, 1975.

Misra, Susheela. *Music Profiles.* Lucknow: Bhatkhande Music College, 1960.

———. *Great Masters of Hindusthani Music.* New Delhi: HEM, 1981.

———. *Music Makers of the Bhatkhande College of Hindusthani Music.* Calcutta: Sangeet Research Academy, 1985.

———. *Some Immortals of Hindustani Music.* New Delhi: Harman Publications, 1990.

Mitter, Partha. *Much Maligned Monsters: History of European Reactions to Indian Art.* Cambridge: Cambridge University Press, 1978.

———. *Art and Nationalism in Colonial India, 1850–1922: Occidental Orientations.* Cambridge: Cambridge University Press, 1994.

Mongredien, Jean. *French Music from the Enlightenment to Romanticism, 1789–1830.* Translated by Sylvain Fremaux. Portland, Ore.: Amadeus Press, 1986.

Mote, H. V., ed. *Vishrabdha Sharada,* vols. 1– 3 (in Marathi). Bombay: Mote Prakashan, 1997.

Mudaliar, Chinnaswamy. *Indian Music along the Lines of European Notation.* Madras, 1881.

Mutatkar, Sumati. "Alladiya Khan Gharana and Kesarbai Kerkar." *NCPA Periodical* 1.1 (1972): 2–7.

———. "Pt. Shrikrishan Narayan Ratanjankar." *Sangeet Natak* 31 (1974): 13–19.

Nag, Dipali. *Ustad Faiyaz Khan.* New Delhi: Sangeet Natak Akademi, 1985.

Nandy, Ashis. "An Anti-Secularist Manifesto." *Seminar*, no. 314 (1985): 14–24.

———. "The Politics of Secularism and the Recovery of Religious Tolerance." In *Mirrors of Violence: Communities, Riots, and Survivors in South Asia*, edited by Veena Das. New Delhi: Oxford University Press, 1990.

———. "Hinduism versus Hindutva: The Inevitability of a Confrontation." *Times of India*, Feb. 18, 1991.

———. "Secularism." *Seminar*, no. 394 (1992): 29–30.

Narasinhan, Sakuntala. "Book Reviews." *Journal of the Indian Musicological Society* 18.1 (1987): 54–59.

Narayan, Prakash. *Hamare Sangeetadnya* (in Hindi). Allahabad: Kala Prakashan, 1961.

Nayar, Sobhana. *Bhatkhande's Contribution to Music.* Bombay: Popular Prakashan, 1989.

Naregal, Veena. *Language Politics, Elites, and the Public Sphere: Western India under Colonialism.* New Delhi: Permanent Black, 2001.

Neuman, Daniel. *The Life of Music in North India: The Organization of an Artistic Tradition.* Detroit: Wayne State Press, 1980.

Norris, Christopher, ed. *Music and the Politics of Culture.* New York, 1989.

O'Hanlon, Rosalind. *Caste, Conflict and Ideology: Mahatma Jotirao Phule and Low Caste Protest in Nineteenth Century Western India.* Cambridge: Cambridge University Press, 1985.

Omvedt, Gail. *Cultural Revolt in a Colonial Society: The Non-Brahman Movement in Western India, 1873–1970.* Bombay, 1976.

Paluskar, Vishnu Digambar. "Report (in Marathi)." *Gandharva Mahavidyalaya* 3.2 (1912).

———. "Sphut lekh (in Marathi)." *Gandharva Mahavidyalaya* 9 (1915).

———. *Mahila Sangeet* (in Hindi). Panchvati, Nasik: Shri Ram Nam Adhaar Ashram, 1933.

Pande, Anupa. *A Historical and Cultural Study of the Natyashastra of Bharata.* Jodhpur, 1996.

Pandey, Gyanendra. *The Construction of Communalism in Colonial North India.* New Delhi: Oxford University Press, 1992.

Pandit, Damodar. *Sangeet Darpan.* Bombay: Ratansi Leeladhir Thakkar, 1910.

Pandit, Shailja, and Arun Halwe. *Gaanhira* (in Marathi). Bombay: 1985.

Parekh, Bhikhu, and Upendra Baxi, eds. *Crisis and Change in Contemporary India.* New Delhi: Oxford University Press, 1995.

Pathak, Narharpant. "Gayanacharya K. P. Vishnu Digambar va Unke karya (in Hindi)." *Sangeet Kala Vihar* 10 (1947): 2–12.

Pathan, Inayat Khan Rahimat Khan. *Inayat Fiddle Shikshak* (in Hindi/Gujarati). Baroda: 1903.

———. *Inayat Geet Ratnavali* (in Marathi/Gujarati). Baroda: 1903.

———. *Inayat Harmonium Shikshak* (in Hindi/Gujarati). Baroda: 1903.

Patwardhan, Vinayak Narayan. *Mazhe Gurucharitra* (in Marathi). Poona: Vishnu Digambar Smarak Samiti, 1956.

Peabody, Norbert Worthington. *Hindu Kingship and Polity in Precolonial India.* New York: 2003.

Perera, E. S. *The Origin and Development of Dhrupad and Its Bearing on Instrumental Music.* Calcutta: K. P. Bagchi, 1994.

Phadke, Visnu Vasudeo. "The Old Hindu Scale of Twenty Two Srutis." *Sangeeta: A Quarterly Journal of Hindustani Music* 2.1 (1933): 11–18.

Phaldesai, Amrita. *Surashri Kesarbai Kerkar* (in Marathi). Panjim: Panjim Rajahansa Vitman, 1980.

Poochwale, Rajabhaiyya. *Dhrupad Dhamar Gayan* (in Hindi). Gwalior: Ramchandra Sangit Pustak Bhandar, 1954.

———. *Taan Malika: Gwalior ki Khas Gayaki* (in Hindi). Gwalior: Ramchandra Sangeet Pustak Bhandar, 1971.

Popley, Reverend H. *Music of India.* Calcutta, 1910.

Prakash, Gyan. *Bonded Histories: Genealogies of Labor Servitude in Colonial India.* Cambridge: Cambridge University Press, 1990.

———. *Another Reason: Science and the Imagination of Modern India.* Princeton, N.J.: Princeton University Press, 1999.

Purohit, Vinayak. *Arts of Transitional India*, vols. 1–2. Bombay: Popular Prakashan, 1988.

Qureshi, Regula Burckhardt. *Sufi Music of India and Pakistan: Sound, Context, and Meaning in Qawwali.* Cambridge: Cambridge University Press, 1986.

Raghavan, V. *The Great Integrators: The Saint Singers of India.* New Delhi: Publications Division, 1969.

Rahamin, Begum F. *Darool-ooloome Sangit Hind.* Benares: Commercial Printing Press, 1919.

Rai, Amrit. *A House Divided: The Formation of Hindi/Hindavi.* New Delhi: Oxford University Press, 1988.

Rajadhyaksha, Kusumawati Deshpande and M. V. *A History of Marathi Literature.* New Delhi: Sahitya Akademi, 1988.

Ranade, Ashok. "Ustad Bade Ghulam Ali Khan, 1901–1968." *NCPA Periodical* 10.2 (1981): 17–21.

———. "Categories of Music." *NCPA Periodical* 14.4 (1985): 6–19.

———. *Stage Music of Maharashtra.* New Delhi: Sangeet Natak Akademi, 1986.

———. *Maharashtra's Art Music.* New Delhi: Maharashtra Information Centre, 1989.

———. *Music and Drama.* New Delhi: Shri Ram Centre, 1992.

———. *Hindustani Music.* New Delhi: National Book Trust, 1997.

Ranade, G. H. *Maharashtra's Contribution to Music.* Bombay, 1965.

Rao, H. P. Krishna. *First Steps in Hindu Music in English Notation.* London, 1906.

Rao, Subba. *Studies in Indian Music.* Bombay: Asia Publishing House, 1962.

Rastall, Richard. *The Notation of Western Music: An Introduction.* London: J. M. Dent and Sons, Ltd., 1983.

Ratanjankar, S. N. *Sangeet Paribhasha* (in Marathi). Pune: Ideal Book Service, 1973.

———. *Sangeetacharya Pandit V. N. Bhatkhande* (in Marathi). Bombay: Maharashtra Rajya Sahitya Samskriti Mandal, 1973.

Report. First All-India Music Conference. Baroda: Baroda Printing Works, 1916.

Report. 2 vols. Second All-India Music Conference. Delhi, 1918.

Report. 2 vols. Third All-India Music Conference. Banaras, 1919.

Report. Fourth All-India Music Conference. Lucknow: Taluqdar Press, 1925.

Report. Fifth All-India Music Conference. Lucknow: Taluqdar Press, 1926.

"Report" (in Marathi). *Gandharva Mahavidyalaya* 3.5 (1912).

"Review of Mr. J. Grosset's essay on the 28th Adhyaya of Bharata's Natyashastra." *Indian Antiquary* 19 (1890): 72.

Rice, Stanley. *Life of Sayaji Rao III, Maharaja of Baroda.* London: Oxford University Press, 1931.

Richards, J. F., ed. *Kingship and Authority in South Asia.* Madison: University of Wisconsin Press, 1978.

Rieger, Bernhard, and Martin Daunton, eds. *Meanings of Modernity: Britain from the Late-Victorian Era to World War II.* New York: Berg, 2001.

Rowell, Lewis. *Music and Musical Thought in Early India.* Chicago: University of Chicago Press, 1992.

Roy, Hemendralal. "Hindustani Music and the Modern World." *Sangeeta* 2.1 (1933): 57–61.

Roy, Priya Nath. *Indian Music in European Notation.* Darjeeling, 1889.

Sadie, Stanley, ed. *The New Grove Dictionary of Music and Musicians.* Vol. 13. London: Macmillan, 1980.

Sahasrabuddhe, Balwant Trimbuck. *Swarashastra: The Science of Sound.* Poona, 1878.

———. *Hindu Music and the Gayan Samaj.* Poona, 1887.

Said, Edward W. *Musical Elaborations.* New York: Columbia University Press, 1991.

"Samachar" (in Marathi). *Gandharva Mahavidyalaya* 6 (1916): 10–12.

Sambamoorthy, P. *History of Indian Music.* Madras: The Indian Music Publishing House, 1982.

Sangoram, Shrirang. *Sangeet Natak ani Natya Sangeet* (in Marathi). Pune: Progressive Dramatic Association, 1993.

———, ed. *Acharya Shrikrishna Ratanjankar 'Sujaan': Jeevani tatha Smrutisanchay.* (in Hindi). Bombay: Acharya Shrikrishna Ratanjankar Foundation, 1993.

Sardesai, G. S., ed. *Selected Letters of His Highness the Maharaja Sayaji Rao Gaekwad.* Vol 1, *1866–1901.* Baroda, 1979.

Sarkar, Sumit. *Modern India: 1885–1947.* New Delhi: Macmillan, 1986.

Sengupta, Shankar. "Cultural Instincts of Ethnomusicology." *Folklore* 16.6 (1974): 213–230.

Sergeant, Philip. *The Ruler of Baroda.* London, 1928.

Shankar, Ravi. *My Music, My Life.* New Delhi, 1968.

Sharangdeva. *Sangeet Ratnakara.* Translated by R. K. Shringy and Premlata Sharma. New Delhi: Munshiram Manoharlal, 1991.

Sharar, Maulvi Abdul Halim. "Hindustani Music." *Sangeeta* 2.1 (1933): 38–66.

Sharma, Amal Das. *Musicians of India: Past and Present.* Calcutta: Naya Prakash, 1993.

Sharma, Satyavati. *Khayal Gayan Shaili* (in Hindi). Jaipur: Panchsheel Prakashan, 1994.

Shirgaonkar, A. B. *Nadabrahma* (in Marathi). Girgaum: Ramkrishna Depot, 1969.

Singh, Raja Raghavendra Pratap. "Report by President, Marris College Managing Committee." In *Silver Jubilee Souvenir English Section*. Lucknow: Bhatkhande Sangeet Vidyalaya, 1976.

Solie, Ruth, ed. *Musicology and Difference: Gender and Sexuality in Music Scholarship.* Berkeley: University of California Press, 1993.

Srivastava, Indurama. *Dhrupada: A Study of Its Origins, Historical Development, Structure and Present State.* New Delhi: Motilal Banarsidas, 1980.

Stoler-Miller, Barbara, ed. *The Powers of Art: Patronage in Indian Culture.* New Delhi: Oxford University Press, 1992.

Strangways, A. H. Fox. *The Music of Hindostan.* Oxford: Clarendon, 1914.

Subotnik, Rose. *Developing Variations: Style and Ideology in Western Music.* Minneapolis: University of Minnesota Press, 1991.

Subramanian, Lakshmi. "The Reinvention of a Tradition: Nationalism, Carnatic Music, and the Madras Music Academy, 1900–1947," *IESHR* 36.2 (1999): 131–63.

———. "The Master, Muse, and the Nation: The New Cultural Project and the Reification of Colonial Modernity in India," *South Asia* 23.2 (2000): 1–32.

Sundar, Pushpa. *Patrons and Philistines: Arts and the State in British India.* New Delhi, 1995.

Tagore, Pramod Kumar. *First Thoughts on Indian Music, or Twenty Indian Melodies Composed for the Pianoforte.* Calcutta, 1883.

Tagore, Sourindro Mohun. *The Musical Scales of the Hindus with Remarks on the Applicability of Harmony to Hindu Music.* Calcutta, 1884.

———. *Universal History of Music From Divers Sources Together With Various Original Notes On Hindu Music.* Calcutta, 1896.

Tagore, Sourindro Mohun. *English Verses Set to Hindu Music in Honor of His Royal Highness, The Prince of Wales.* Calcutta, 1875.

———. *Six Principal Ragas with a Brief View of Hindu Music.* New Delhi: Neeraj Publishing House, 1877.

———. *The Eight Principal Rasas of the Hindus.* Calcutta, 1880.

———. *Victoria-Samrajyan: Sanskrit Stanzas On Various Dependencies of Her Most Gracious Majesty the Empress of India.* Calcutta, 1887.

———. *The Seven Principal Musical Notes of the Hindus, with Their Presiding Deities.* Calcutta, 1892.

———, ed. *Hindu Music from Various Authors.* Calcutta, 1882.

Taruskin, Richard, and Piero Weiss, eds. *Music in the Western World: A History in Documents.* New York: Schirmer Books, 1984.

Tembe, Govindrao. *Majha Jeevan Vihar* (in Marathi). Kolhapur: Bharat Book Stall, 1948.

———. *Gayanmaharshi Alladiya Khan Yanche Charitra* (in Marathi). Bombay: Maharashtra Rajya Sahitya Samskriti Mandal, 1954.

———. *Majha Sangeet Vyaasang* (in Marathi). Bombay, 1954.

Thakkar, Madhusudan Manilal. "Sangeet Kshetrama Professor Maullabakshni Sadhna ani Pradhan" (in Gujarati). *Souvenir of the Seventieth Anniversary of the College of Indian Music, Dance, and Dramatics* (1957): 107–13.

Thakurdas, Manikbua. *Khayal Darshan* (in Hindi). Ajmer: Krishna Brothers, 1990.

Thapar, Romilla, ed. *Communalism and the Writing of Indian History*. New Delhi: Oxford University Press, 1969.

Thielemann, Selina. *The Music of South Asia*. New Delhi: APH Publishing Corporation, 1999.

Tomlinson, Gary. *Music in Renaissance Magic: Toward a Historiography of Others*. Chicago: University of Chicago Press, 1993.

Trautmann, Thomas R. *Aryans and British India*. Berkeley: University of California Press, 1997.

Tucker, Richard. *Ranade and the Roots of Indian Nationalism*. Bombay, 1977.

Tulpule, S. G. *Classical Marathi Literature*. Wiesbaden, 1979.

Vaid, Kumkum Sangari and Urvashi, ed. *Recasting Women: Essays in Indian Colonial History*. New Delhi: Kali for Women, 1996.

Vakil, Suryaji Sadashiv Mahatme, and Vishwanath Ramchandra. *Tantuvadya: Sataar Shikanyache Pahile Pustak* (in Marathi). Poona, 1872.

Veer, Peter van der. *The Torchbearer of Indian Music: Maharishi V. D. Paluskar*. New Delhi: Pankaj Publications, 1978.

———. *The Music of India: 1,001 A.D. to 1986 A.D.* New Delhi: Pankaj Publications, 1986.

———. *The Music of India: 6,000 B.C. to 1,000 A.D.* New Delhi: Pankaj Publications, 1986.

———. *Religious Nationalism: Hindus and Muslims in India*. Berkeley: University of California Press, 1994.

———. *Imperial Encounters: Religion and Modernity in India and Britain*. Princeton, N.J.: Princeton University Press, 2001.

Velankar, A. D. *Marathi Natyapad: Swarup va Sameeksha* (in Marathi). Nagpur: Sudha Arun Velankar, 1986.

Viswanathan, Gauri. *Masks of Conquest: Literary Study and British Rule in India*. New York: Columbia University Press, 1989.

———. *Outside the Fold: Conversion, Modernity, and Belief*. Princeton, N.J.: Princeton University Press, 1998.

Wacha, D. E. *Shells from the Sands of Bombay: My Recollections and Reminiscences, 1860–1875*. Bombay, 1920.

Wade, Bonnie. *Music in India: The Classical Traditions*. Cambridge: Cambridge University Press, 1979.

———. *Khyal: Creativity within North India's Classical Music Tradition*. Cambridge: Cambridge University Press, 1984.

Waghorne, Joanne P. *The Raja's Magic Clothes: Re-Visioning Kingship and Divinity in England's India*. State College: Pennsylvania State University Press, 1994.

Weber, Max. *The Rational and Social Foundations of Music*. Translated by Don Martindale, Johannes Riedel, and Gertrude Neuwirth. Carbondale: Southern Illinois University Press, 1958.

Weidman, Amy. *Questions of Voice: On the Subject of "Classical" Music in South India*. Duke University Press, forthcoming.

Widdess, Richard. *The Ragas of Early Indian Music: Modes, Melodies, and Musical Notations from the Gupta Period to c. 1250*. Oxford: Clarendon, 1995.

Willard, N. Augustus. *A Treatise on the Music of India*. Calcutta, 1793.

Wolpert, Stanley. *Tilak and Gokhale: Revolution and Reform in the Making of Modern India*. Berkeley: University of California Press, 1968.

Zarrilli, Philip. *The Kathakali Complex: Actor, Performance, and Structure*. New Delhi: Abhinav Publications, 1984.

INDEX

Kapileshwari, Balkrishnabua, 217, 224–25, 270
  biography of Abdul Karim Khan, 35
karmanuk, 24. *See* Baroda, *kalavant khaata*
Karnad, Shankarrao, 189
Kashalkar, V. A., 157, 168
Kelkar, Vasudevrao, 89
Kelkar, Vithabai (Paluskar's wife), 141
Kerkar, Kesarbai, 227, 250, 261
Kerr, Lord Mark, 65, 77
Kesari, 79–80, 89, 147–49, 155, 159, 164–66, 170, 209
khaandani, 251, 253
khaangi karbhaari, 23–24, 28–29, 269
Khan, Abdul Karim, 12, 30, 34–35, 50, 53, 91–93, 112, 179, 185–86, 188, 217, 224–25, 271
  biography by Balkrishnabua Kapileshwari, 35
  disagreements with Bhatkhande, 236–241
  encounter with Brahminism, 236, 243, 252
  participation in Gandhi's *satyagraha,* 242
  as *gharana ustad,* 23
  and Khadeem Husein Khan, 35
  Baroda and Maula Baksh, 222
  modernized *gharana,* 253
  musicology, 238, 240–41, 252
  notation, 222
  challenged by Paluskar, 234
  Ruby Recording, Company, 242
  separation from Tarabai, 242
Khan, Abdul Wahid (*Behre* Wahid Khan), 228–29, 236
  and Abdul Karim Khan, 241
Khan, Ahmed, 202
Khan, Alauddin, 44–45
and Maula Baksh, 43
Khan, Aliya, 221
Khan, Alladiya, 35, 92, 173–74, 249, 298
Khan, Bismillah, 173
Khan, Faiz Mohammed, 29, 31, 38, 185, 224
  rivalry with Maula Baksh, 41–43
Khan, Fattu, 221
Khan, Faiyaz (*Aftab-e-Mausiki),* 32–33, 185, 300
Khan, Ghasit (and Maula Baksh), 38
Khan, Ghulam Husein, 32
Khan, Karamatullah, 104, 119–20, 213–14
  and Bhatkhande, 109–113
Khan, Kareem Husein, 32
Khan, Khadeem Husein, 35
Khan, Khan Saheb Imadad, 73
Khan, Maula Baksh Ghisse. *See* Maula Baksh
Khan, Natthan, 35
Khan, Ramzan Ali, 32
Khan, Tassaduq Hussain, 192–93
Khan, Wajid Ali, 251
Khangi Khatya Sambandhi Huzurche Hukumanchi Nond (Compilation of

Orders relating to the Personnel [?] Department), 269
Khanna, Lala Gurandittamal, 139, 290
Khare, Narayan Rao, 168, 208–209
khayal, 3, 5–6, 26, 47, 70, 73, 91, 101, 141, 202, 227, 245
  manner of performance, 5
khayal gayaki, 214
khel, 83–84, 90
khelapad, 5
Khilafat Movement, 165–66
kirana gharana, 91, 187, 214, 235, 251–52
Kippen, James, 265, 304
Kirloskar, Balwant Pandurang, 88
Kirloskar Natak Mandali 90, 94
kirtan, 139–43, 153, 163, 167
kirtankar, 140
Kirtane, Vinayak Janardhan, 87
Kolhapurkar Natak Mandali, 85, 88
Kolhatkar, Shripad, 91
Kotwaleen, Amba, 26
Koul, Mr., 198
Kramik Pustak Malika, 126
Krishna jayanti, 162
kulaswaminichi shapath, 84
kulin, 170
Kumar, Ravinder, 292
Kundgolkar, Rambhau. *See* Savai Gandharva
Kunte, Mahadev Moreshwar, 79, 247, 281
Kurdikar, Mogubai 251, 261
Kyd, Robert, 54–55, 65

Lala Hansraj, 148
Lad, Bhau Daji, 62, 86
lalit, 83
lalitacha tamaasha, 25
lavani, 4, 47, 89–91
Lord Northbrook (Viceroy of India), 39

maatra, 106
Madan, Trilokinath (T. N.), 18, 265
Maharani Chimnabai, 47, 270
Maharani Jamnabai, 22
Mahratta, 147
Makarpura (Palace), 30
Malaviya, Pandit Madan Mohan, 133, 204
  AIMC, 209
Malpekar, Anjanibai, 250, 261
Manajirao, 89
Manapmaan, 246
Major General Hewett, 88
Mandlik, Raosaheb Vishwanath, 63–64, 71
Mane, Marutirao (Sardar Mane), 91, 216, 224
Mane, Suresh Babu, 92
Mane, Tarabai (aka Tahirabibi), 215, 219, 224–25
Mangeshkar, Dinanath, 93
Mangeshkar, Lata, 93

.